CONTRIBUTIONS OF THE UNIVERSITY OF CALIFORNIA

ARCHAEOLOGICAL RESEARCH FACILITY

Number 49   *December 1991*

THE ARCHAEOLOGY AND ETHNOHISTORY

OF FORT ROSS, CALIFORNIA

VOLUME 1 INTRODUCTION

KENT G. LIGHTFOOT, THOMAS A. WAKE,

AND ANN M. SCHIFF

ARCHAEOLOGICAL RESEARCH FACILITY

UNIVERSITY OF CALIFORNIA AT BERKELEY

Publication of this volume is made possible by generous donations from Vernon Lightfoot, M.D., Dan Lightfoot, M. D., David Lightfoot, M. D., and the American Home Shield Company of Santa Rosa, California.

Available open access at
https://escholarship.org/uc/item/1476895n

1st edition 1991
2nd edition 2019
Ebook: ISBN 978-0-9982460-1-7
POD: ISBN 978-0-9982460-2-4

Library of Congress Catalog Card Number 91-77906

© 1991 by the Regents of the University of California
Archaeological Research Facility
University of California at Berkeley

Printed in the United States of America

CONTENTS

PREFACE

This volume inaugurates a new series on the archaeology and ethnohistory of the Ross Colony, an early nineteenth century Russian trade outpost established in northern California. Founded by the Russian-American Company in 1812, and operated as a commercial enterprise until 1841, the Ross Colony comprised an early multi-ethnic community composed of Europeans, Creoles (people of Russian/Native American ancestry), native Alaskans, and local Kashaya Pomo, Southern Pomo, and Coast Miwok peoples. Located 110 km north of San Francisco on the scenic Sonoma County coastline, the Ross Colony is now a state historic park administered by the California Department of Parks and Recreation.

The intent of the *Archaeology and Ethnohistory of Fort Ross, California* series is to publish the results of archaeological investigations, as well as related archival research, currently being undertaken by a collaborative team of scholars from the California Department of Parks and Recreation, the Kodiak Area Native Association (Kodiak Island, Alaska), the Sakhalin Regional Museum (USSR), Santa Rosa Junior College, Sonoma State University, and the University of California, Berkeley. In the first volume of the series, we outline the long-term research objectives of the Fort Ross Archaeological Project,

sketch the historical context and natural history of the Ross region, and synthesize archaeological research to date, including the results of a recent survey of the Fort Ross State Historic Park.

ACKNOWLEGDEMENTS

The archaeological research described in this volume was supported by funds from the National Science Foundation (Grant #BNS-8918960), the California Department of Parks and Recreation, and the American Home Shield Company of Santa Rosa, California. A generous donation from the Lightfoot, Lightfoot and Lightfoot Group of Ophthalmologists in Santa Rosa, California and the American Home Shield Company covered the costs of publishing the volume.

We owe a tremendous debt of gratitude to the many people who have supported or participated in the Fort Ross Archaeological Project since its inception in 1988. Field investigations in the summers of 1988 and 1989 were undertaken by U.C. Berkeley students enrolled in the summer field school course (Anthropology 133) taught by Kent Lightfoot. The 1988 field crew included Eugenia Andruchowicz, Marie Binneweg, Traci Carlson, Alan Carpenter, Bruce Dahlstrom, Christine Denezza, Brian Drope, Elizabeth Fassett, Paul Hays, Vickie Ives, Dean

Matsuno, Mary Robbins, Okashi Robles, Susan Schalit, Ann Schiff, Virginia Staubach, Loyda Tubis, and Lauren Wang. The staff consisted of Marcia-Anne Dobres, Mark Hall, and Roberta Jewett. The 1989 field crew consisted of Sara Atchley, Adele Baldwin, Shannon Bonilla, Denise Boyce, Patrick Clifford, Jordi Davis, Patricia Dolan, Christine Franco, Susan Goddard, Michele Harrell, Allegra Kim, Richard Kwak, Katherine MacKinnon, Anthony Marais, Leslie Nelson, Kelly Park, Lloyd Pena, Stacy Richardson, Patricia Rowley, Silvia Sierra, and Helen Wu. The staff included Paul Hays, Richard Hitchcock, Heather Price, Ann Schiff, and Thomas Wake. Michael Love served as field chef, photographer, and general archaeological consultant to the project during both field seasons. We greatly appreciate Robert Schiff who volunteered his efforts in setting up and closing down the field camps.

Archaeological materials from the 1988 and 1989 field seasons were sorted, processed, and initially analyzed in the Archaeological Research Facility's laboratories at U.C. Berkeley. Much of the preliminary work was undertaken by students in the Analysis of the Archaeological Record course (Anthropology 134) taught by Kent Lightfoot. Students enrolled in the fall semester of 1988 included Eugenia Andruchowicz, Bradford Bentz, David Brittin, Alan Carpenter, Bruce Dahlstrom, Christine Denezza, Emmanuel Gabet, Kristen Hauge, Paul Hays, Renee Hendricks, Vickie Ives, Alison Kopf, Cynthia Mc Clellan, Chinyere Madawaki, Laurie Nielson, Mary Robbins, Okashi Robles, Mark Shepard, Robert Smith, and Yvette Wojciechowski. Mark Hall and Michael Love served as Graduate Student Instructors. Students enrolled in the fall semester of 1989 were Sara Atchley, Shannon Bonilla, Denise Boyce, Jodi Davis, Patricia Dolan, Christine Franco, Linn Gassaway, Susan Goddard, Carol Halden, Michele Harrell, James Hoelter, Dennis Hurlbut, Kelli Kelley, Richard Kwak, Cynthia Lawlor, Anthony Marais, Leslie Nelson, Stacy Richardson, Matthew Riggsby, Patricia Rowley, Julie Ruiz-Sierra, Ranbir Sidhu, Alexei Vranich, Helen Wu, and John Yelding-Sloan. Heather Price and Thomas Wake served as Graduate Student Instructors. Ann Schiff has served as the Laboratory Director of the Fort Ross Archaeological Project since 1989.

The Fort Ross Archaeological Project would not be possible without the support and assistance of many people in the California Department of Parks and Recreation (DPR) who administer the Fort Ross State Historic Park. We are especially indebted to Carl Chavez (Regional Director, Northern Region Headquarters), Donald Ito (Manager, Visitors' Services), Glenn Burch (Regional Historian), Ronald Hanshew (former District Superintendent), and Ronald Brean (Acting District Superintendent). The DPR provided camping facilities at Fort Ross, logistical support during the field seasons, and funds for laboratory analyses. The park staff at Fort Ross is one of the finest that we have had the pleasure to work with. Special thanks are due to Denise Abbott (Interpreter), Doreen Mennell (Administration), William Mennell (Chief of Maintenance), Daniel Murley (Ranger), Michael Stephenson (Supervising Ranger), and Bill Walton (Ranger).

Two scholars of the California Department of Parks and Recreation have made critical contributions to our field program at Fort Ross. Breck Parkman (Regional Archaeologist) and Glenn Farris (State Archaeologist) have been instrumental in providing background information on the Ross Colony, assisting in both field and archival research, and evaluating various interpretations outlined in this volume.

The Fort Ross Interpretive Association (FRIA), a nonprofit citizens group dedicated to the interpretation of the Fort Ross State Historic Park, has been extremely helpful in facilitating our fieldwork. We are especially grateful to Lyn Kalani for her assistance over the last three years, as well as Jay Harris (past president), John Middleton (president), and the Board of Directors of FRIA. Kaye Tomlin has been particularly helpful in providing historical information of the ranching period at Fort Ross.

A number of scholars from Sonoma State University and Santa Rosa Junior College have contributed greatly to the Fort Ross Archaeological Project. David Fredrickson and Thomas Origer imparted to us important insights on the prehistory of the North Coast Ranges, and advice on archaeological methods that have proved effective in this region. The Obsidian Hydration Laboratory at Sonoma State University undertook the analysis of all obsidian hydration data reported in this volume. Margaret Purser analyzed the historical materials from survey sites, including ceramic, glass and metal artifacts. The amiable staff at the Northwest Information Center, Sonoma State University, went out of their way to assist us in finding and duplicating site records and reports from the Fort Ross region. June Matsuko of the Cultural Resources Center, Sonoma State University, worked many long hours processing paperwork for members of the Fort Ross Archaeological Project.

Daniel G. Foster has been extremely helpful in providing information on sites on file with the California Department of Forestry and Fire Protection. We also appreciate the advice and consultation of other archaeologists who have worked along the north coast of California—Susan Alvarez, Alan

Bramlette, Lynne Goldstein, Thomas Layton, Sannie Osborn, Rene Peron, William Pritchard, Jim Quinn, Dwight Simons, and Greg White. We would also like to thank the following publishers for permission to use material from their books: the Oregon Historical Society Press, the University Press of Hawaii and the Hawaiian Historical Society, and the University of California Press.

The administrative staff of the Department of Anthropology and Summer Sessions at the University of California at Berkeley deserve our special thanks. We are especially obliged to M., J. Tyler, Julie Martinson, Darlene Wright, and Catherine Calderon who administered the summer field school program in the Anthropology Department for the 1988 and 1989 sessions. William Simmons provided valuable support to the field school program while serving as Vice-Chair for Personnel in the Anthropology Department. Sally Senior and John Wheeler of Summer Sessions greatly facilitated the summer field program at Fort Ross.

We are most grateful for the excellent support that the Archaeological Research Facility at U.C. Berkeley has provided the Fort Ross Archaeological Project. Tanya Smith, editor of the monograph series published by the Archaeological Research Facility, designed this volume's format, copy edited the text, and produced the camera-ready copy. Anne Sauter is the administrator who oversees the distribution and promotion of our publications. Karyn Klinger drafted all the illustrations included in the present volume. The publications program of the Archaeological Research Facility has been greatly enhanced by the Office for Research. We deeply appreciate the support and assistance of Joseph Cerny, Provost for Research, Linda Fabbris, Executive Assistant, and Jeanne Segale, Administrative Analyst.

We are grateful for the continued support of the Pedotti family of Fort Ross. The weekly poker games with the Pedotti clan during the summer field seasons netted us ample funds to eat very well at the "archy camp." We anticipate working with Alex, David, Renie, Lucas, and Tyral for many years to come.

We are also most grateful for the continued interest of coast Pomo and Miwok peoples in our project. We appreciate their taking the time to talk with us about the Fort Ross region, and look forward to continued and closer collaboration in the future. We are especially thankful to Violet Chappell, George Frank, Vana Lawson, Ben Lucas, Jackie Marufo, Warren Parrish, Delbert Pinola, Lanny and Esther Pinola, Alice Poe, Lynn Poe, and Lorin Smith.

Finally, we would like to acknowledge the years of work that John and Alice McKenzie have dedicated to the study and public interpretation of Fort Ross. John McKenzie served as the curator/historian/ranger at the Fort Ross State Historic Park beginning in 1948. The senior author was fortunate, as a budding archaeologist growing up in Santa Rosa, to meet John and Alice during his formative years. They were patients of the distinguished ophthalmologist, Dr. Vernon F. Lightfoot, who used to make house calls to Fort Ross with his son and Peg Ligthfoot in the 1960s and 1970s. The McKenzies contributed greatly to the education of the young scholar by emphasizing the need for basic research on the multi-ethnic community of Fort Ross. We are very grateful for their continued support and friendship as we attempt to follow their pioneering footsteps in the study and interpretation of the Ross Colony.

CHAPTER ONE

RESEARCH OBJECTIVES OF THE

FORT ROSS ARCHAEOLOGICAL PROJECT

THE FORTHCOMING quincentenary of Columbus's voyage to the Americas is sparking renewed interest among anthropologists in native responses to European and American colonialism. The consequences of European expansion into North America have been perceived in many different ways over the years. In the early decades of this century, native cultures were viewed as timeless and static entities. This concept of the "ethnographic present" was widely employed by anthropologists to trace native traits back into early contact and even late prehistoric times by interviewing elders in contemporary contexts (e.g., Barrett 1908; Kroeber 1925). By the late 1930s and 1940s, acculturation studies became an integral component of American anthropology, involving the investigation of how native societies changed with the encroachment of the dominant Euro-American culture (e.g., Redfield et al. 1936; Herskovits 1938). Some acculturation studies tended, however, to assume that the expansion of a monolithic European colonial system produced similar effects among native peoples across all of North America, leading to the eventual destruction and breakdown of native societies in general (see Fitzhugh 1985:6,9). Other anthropologists found the study of native acculturation baffling, a "hodgepodge of accident rather than a clue to a social process" (Mead 1932:4).

It is now evident that native responses to European colonial practices varied greatly across both space and time in North America. Some native groups became completely engulfed in Euro-American culture. Other groups maintained strong social identities while outwardly adopting many traits of Euro-American culture. Still other groups steadfastly refused to accept nontraditional innovations and they exhibited little outward sign of European acculturation (see Fitzhugh 1985:7; Simmons 1988:8-9). While understanding how and why native societies varied in their responses to European encounters will require more than assuming it was a "hodgepodge of accident," it is nonetheless an extremely complex process that is rapidly becoming a focus of culture theory and studies of cultural change in anthropology today (e.g., Deetz 1989:434; Simmons 1988; Sahlins 1985; Wolf 1982; Thomas 1989).

In studying native responses to European colonial practices, we advocate examining three critical factors that contributed to the specific historical contexts in which early interactions took place.

1) *Late Prehistoric Societies.* The native cultures that confronted early Europeans varied greatly in their population densities, economic organizations, religious practices, and sociopolitical structures. It is not unexpected that native responses to Europeans may

have varied among nomadic bands, larger tribal groups, and complex chiefdoms (Fitzhugh 1985:8). Trigger (1981:11) stresses that studies of culture contact should begin with an understanding of the specific developments of native societies in prehistoric times. Native sociopolitical structures, economic organizations, and ideology, especially in late prehistoric times, would "set the stage" for how native peoples would react to European expansion into their territories.

2) *European Introduced Diseases.* Specific native populations may have been influenced by "virgin soil epidemics" prior to their first face-to-face contact with Europeans. Dobyns (1983:8-25) provocatively argues that the demographic structure of some native populations may have collapsed prior to any direct meetings with European populations. He hypothesizes that widespread depopulation took place across North America with the rapid transmission of the first smallpox pandemic in A.D. 1520-1524. As Dobyns (1983:25-26) notes, the demographic devastation of native societies would have affected their traditional lifeways and, in turn, greatly influenced their responses to Europeans. Dobyns's (1983) hypothesis is hotly debated among North American specialists. Studies to date suggest that the timing, magnitude, and virulence of particular lethal pathogens varied greatly across North America (see Ramenofsky 1987; Snow 1980; Snow and Lanphear 1988). It is clear that the impact of European diseases must be considered in their specific historical contexts.

3) *European and American Colonial Policies.* Native peoples of North America did not encounter a monolithic European culture, but rather a "many-headed" world-system that was the product of English, French, Spanish, Swedish, Italian, German, Portuguese, and Russian spheres of interest (Simmons 1988:6). Native populations in California also had to contend with a variety of American and Mexican colonial practices. Not only were many countries involved in the colonial process, but the individual participants varied greatly in their reasons for transgressing into native territory. Some came as businessmen representing mercantile companies, others as Christians to convert the pagans, while still others came as permanent colonists. Each colonizing party developed its own Indian policies that were motivated by varied economic, political, and religious considerations. Consequently, native peoples were subjected to a wide range of colonial practices that elicited different kinds of responses from them.

The study of native responses to European and American colonialism should be undertaken on a case-by-case basis that examines the above three factors in their specific historical contexts. By implementing such case studies, we may better understand how different native societies responded to colonial policies of agrarian expansion, mercantilism, proselytization, and slavery. In this way, we may begin to compare how various kinds of native societies reacted to particular colonial practices.

The Fort Ross
Archaeological Project

The Fort Ross Archaeological Project serves as a case study for evaluating how Pacific Coast hunter-gatherers responded to the mercantile policies of a fur trade company. The Russian-American Company at Colony Ross enlisted large numbers of native peoples from Siberia, Alaska, and northern California to work as sea mammal hunters and agricultural laborers. The purpose of the Fort Ross project is to evaluate how mercantile colonialism impacted the traditional lifeways of these diverse native populations. We will evaluate the degree to which native participation in the broader Ross community resulted in significant changes in their material culture, subsistence activities, religious practices, sociopolitical organization, and gender relations.

This chapter outlines the research objectives of the Fort Ross Archaeological Project in detail. We begin by considering the diverse ethnic populations of the Ross Colony. We then argue that research on mercantile colonies, such as this one, is critical for understanding the character of early contacts between European and American colonial institutions and hunter-gatherer societies along the Pacific Rim of North America. Here, beyond the Spanish missions, presidios, and pueblos of central and southern California, representatives of British, Russian, and American merchant houses competed with each other over access to natural resources and the exploitation of native labor. The final section of the chapter outlines our research design for evaluating native acculturation in a mercantile colonial environment. We will employ the direct historical approach in a long-term diachronic study that examines different lines of evidence of cultural change before, during, and after the Russian colonization of Fort Ross.

The Native Population of Ross:
The Silent Majority

In March 1812, the schooner *Chirikov* from the Russian-American Company's commercial capital of New Archangel (Sitka, Alaska) dropped anchor off the northern California coast. On board was Commerce Councillor Ivan Kuskov, who had been making reconnaissance voyages to California since 1808 to locate a suitable site for a southern colony. The new colony was to serve as a staging area for hunting sea mammals along the California coast, and as an agricultural base for raising crops and livestock primarily to supply the North Pacific colonies. In close collaboration with Aleksandr Baranov, Chief Manager of the Russian-American Company, he chose a windswept cliff overlooking a small cove about 29 km north of Port Rumiantsev (Bodega Bay) (Tikhmenev 1978:134). After disembarking the *Chirikov*, Kuskov directed a work force of twenty-five Russian men and eighty native Alaskans (primarily from Kodiak Island, Alaska) in felling nearby redwood timber for the construction of a stout, square-shaped, palisade wall. The "fort" would soon enclose administrative offices and dwellings, barracks, warehouses, a kitchen, and other service buildings (Khlebnikov 1976:107-108). On August 30, 1812, in an official dedication ceremony, the colony was named Ross or Fort Ross as it is known today.

Today we view the Ross Colony primarily from the vantage of the elite Europeans who resided in and visited the stockade complex founded by Kuskov and his men. Eyewitness accounts were written either by 1) upper class Russians who functioned as Russian-American Company administrators, military officers, and natural scientists or 2) erudite visitors from other countries, especially ship captains, who kept detailed journals of their travels. Accounts of the Russian-American Company dwell upon the economic operation of Fort Ross, including the costs of maintaining the colony and the proceeds accumulated from such economic ventures as sea otter hunting and agriculture (e.g., Tikhmenev 1978:133-42; 224-33 [1861-1863]). Foreign visitors, who perceived the Russian colony as competition in the broader arena of early nineteenth century geopolitics, tend to depict the fortifications of the colony in detail and to describe the Russian managers and officers who entertained them (e.g., Duhaut-Cilly 1946:4-15 [1828]; Duflot de Mofras 1937:5-13 [1841]; Vallejo 1979:5-6 [1833]; Payeras 1979:2-3 [1822]).

The European view of the Ross Colony is further accentuated today at the Fort Ross State Historic Park by the impressively restored stockade complex. The stockade walls and blockhouses have been carefully and faithfully reconstructed along with several Russian period buildings that were enclosed in the "fort." By touring the palisade compound today, park visitors can behold firsthand the architecture and material culture of the Russian elite who managed the Ross Colony.

Yet the prevailing focus on the Russians in historical texts and museum displays tells only part of the story. Little is said about the sizeable non-European work force who labored outside the palisade walls in a variety of critical jobs. Native laborers were the economic lifeblood of the Ross Colony, and the Russians depended upon them to build, maintain, and support the settlement during its three decades of operation. Native workers, in fact, greatly outnumbered ethnic Russians in the local community. While fluctuations took place from 1812 to 1841, ethnic Russians made up only about 8-12% of the total population (see Farris 1989a:489). The remainder consisted of Creoles (mixed Russian/native ancestry); native Alaskans from the Aleutian Islands (Aleuts), Kodiak Island (Alutiiqs or Koniag Eskimos), and Cook Inlet (Athabascans); and local Kashaya Pomo, Southern Pomo, and Coast or Bodega Miwok peoples.

Unfortunately, little is known about this pluralistic population, and few exhibits in the Fort Ross State Historic Park document their daily lifeways. At least two factors account for the paucity of information. One concerns the uneven ethnographic observations of the native populations at the colony. The other is that past archaeological projects have focused almost entirely on the excavation of Russian structures.

Eyewitness accounts of native peoples at Fort Ross tend to be spotty, abbreviated, and potentially biased, often highlighting unusual native customs (i.e., gambling games) and the physical appearance of people, especially women (Cyrill LaPlace 1986 [1839]; P. Kostromitinov 1974 [1830-1838]; F. P. Von Wrangell 1974 [1833]; A. B. Duhaut-Cilly 1946 [1828]). Of the few early "ethnographic" accounts of Ross natives, most describe the Kashaya Pomo and Bodega Miwok whose first sustained contact with Europeans took place with the colonization of Fort Ross. We have found very few primary archival sources that provide any substance on the daily lifeways, residences, religious activities, material culture, and social organization of the native Alaskan population stationed there. European observers apparently perceived little that was noteworthy about the native Alaskans in California. Certainly, the Aleut and Koniag workers were well known to the Russians, since most of them had grown up under Russian domination in North Pacific colonies prior to the founding of the Ross Colony.

Since the early 1950s, when archaeological fieldwork began in earnest at Fort Ross, the great majority of research has focused on Russian architecture inside the "fort." Most of this work was conducted to assist in the restoration of the stockade complex (see Farris 1989a:490-92; O'Connor 1984:11-13 for summaries of Ross archaeology). This research has generated an excellent data base on the material culture of the Russian administrators and officers who lived and worked in the palisade compound. In contrast, very few excavations have been undertaken on archaeological remains in the hinterland of the stockade.

NATIVE ACCULTURATION IN A MERCANTILE COLONY

The primary goal of our project is to study the greater Fort Ross community by investigating archaeological remains in the hinterland of the stockade complex. Specifically, we will evaluate how Russian mercantile policies influenced the acculturation processes of Pacific Coast hunter-gatherers who participated in the broader colonial community. Furthermore, we are interested in assessing how native populations, in turn, influenced the lifeways of Europeans stationed there. We propose to examine the material remains of native Californians and native Alaskans, as well as Creoles and lower class Russians, who lived and worked outside the palisade walls, and to compare and contrast this information with that already known about the elite Russian managers.

The ultimate purpose of this project is to continue the development of a public interpretative program in the Fort Ross State Historic Park. The archaeological study of hinterland sites will provide the background research to develop a "culture" trail as proposed in the 1975 General Development Plan for the park. The trail will consist of trailside displays and on-site interpretations that will take the public beyond the Visitor's Center and reconstructed stockade compound to view the archaeological remains of the multi-ethnic Fort Ross community.

Fort Ross as a Mercantile Colony

In examining native responses to the Ross Colony, we recognize from the outset the unique historical context of this settlement in early nineteenth century California. In contrast to the agrarian missions of the Franciscan fathers in central and southern California, which were the cornerstone of Spanish colonial expansion into North America, Fort Ross was founded as a mercantile colony with the primary purpose of making a profit in the North Pacific fur trade. The Russian-American Company, a mercantile monopoly that represented Russia's interests in the lucrative fur trade, harvested sea otters in Pacific waters, then shipped the pelts to China to meet the market demands of Manchu elites who trimmed their clothing with the fine fur (Gibson 1986:5). The high prices paid for sea otter pelts provided capital to acquire tea, silk, linen, porcelain, candy, rhubarb, and other Asian goods. The Chinese merchandise was then transported back to Europe and sold at great profit. The Russian entrepreneurs established a chain of colonies across the North Pacific, from the Kurile Islands and Kamchatka, across the Aleutian Islands and the Ko-

diak Island archipelago, and throughout coastal southern Alaska. Fort Ross was the company's southern-most outpost in the Pacific. These colonies served as bases not only for hunting sea otters, but for acquiring other fur products, such as fur seal pelts, that were earmarked primarily for Southeast Asian, American, and European markets (Gibson 1976:34-35, Fedorova 1973:187, Ogden 1933:42).

Mercantile Companies in the North Pacific Rim

Studies of mercantile colonies, such as Fort Ross, are important for understanding the character of early encounters between Europeans and hunter-gatherer societies along the Pacific Rim of North America. Here, beyond Spanish held territory to the south, the natives' first sustained contact was not with missionaries carrying the holy cross or settlers arriving in Conestoga wagons, but rather with European and American businessmen. The colonization of this region was initiated by large, international mercantile companies whose common agenda was to exploit local resources at great profits (see Jacobs 1988; Horsman 1988; Pierce 1988; Ray 1988; Swagerty 1988; Farris 1989a). While some companies, such as the Russian-American Company and some Boston trading houses, specialized in the procurement of marine mammal pelts from the North Pacific in the late eighteenth and early nineteenth centuries, other companies focused on trapping terrestrial game, especially beaver, from interior freshwater wetlands. These latter British (Hudson Bay's Company, Northwest Company) and American (American Fur Company, Pacific Fur Company) companies maintained strings of trade outposts deep in the heart of what was then referred to as "Indian territory."

The colonization of the North Pacific Rim took place with amazing rapidity. Fur companies were continually searching for pristine rivers and creeks or suitable coastal habitats where new outposts could be established near untapped beaver dens or sea mammal rookeries. As local regions became hunted out, the incentive to push into new territory grew. In relatively short order, trade outposts and rendezvous sites were founded across western United States and along the entire coastline of the North Pacific Rim. The Lewis and Clark expedition in 1806 passed no fewer than eleven separate parties on the Missouri River who were trading for furs with Arikara, Sioux, and Pawnee people (Swagerty 1988:361). By the mid-1830s most tribes in North America had access to a trade outpost and company store, and in many regions stores were placed no farther than 320 km from any native family (Swagerty 1988:369-70; Ray 1988:343).

Mercantile Companies as Agents of Cultural Change

Eric Wolf (1982) in his seminal book on European and native encounters worldwide, recently raised the question about the overall impact that mercantile operations had on North American Indians. He notes that the blitzkrieg expansion of companies into native territories had far-reaching implications for the perpetuity of traditional native lifeways. He suggests (see also Trigger 1981:12-13) that significant cultural changes took place long before ethnographers of the late nineteenth and twentieth centuries began to study native people in earnest. In fact, Wolf argues that ethnographers, far from observing "pristine" native societies, were making observations of tribal entities that were largely shaped by the spread of the fur trade (1982:194).

In considering native responses to mercantile policies, we will focus our investigation on two important developments that characterized many fur companies by the early nineteenth century. These include: 1) the integration of native laborers into a market economy and 2) the rise of multi-ethnic communities. We believe these two developments may be important factors that stimulated a feedback cycle of cultural change among native populations who lived and worked around trade outposts.

1) *Native Laborers.* Native people were incorporated as laborers in fur companies in many different ways. Some served as independent middlemen who sold or exchanged fur products to traders (Ray 1988:342). Others served as day laborers who paddled canoes, carried supplies, or provided necessities to outposts. Some native laborers became wage-earning employees of the company (Swagerty 1988:365). Still other natives served as specialized hunters who worked on company-financed hunting expeditions. These hunters often received a share of the hunt or were paid an annual salary (Gibson 1988:377).

Native workers participated in a market economy by either exchanging their labor directly for trade commodities and/or food, or selling their labor for wages which were used to purchase goods in company stores. As Swagerty (1988:351) argues, native participation in the fur trade of western North America stimulated cultural change not only in material culture, but also in subsistence patterns, gender roles, and sociopolitical organizations. The scheduling of fur hunting trips often conflicted with the timing of traditional harvests of plant and animal resources, a problem that increased native laborers' dependence on foodstuffs from company stores (Wolf 1982:175). Swagerty (1988:367-68) notes that the fur trade differentially affected the role of women in native societies of western North America, in some cases enhancing their status and prestige, in other cases advancing the dominant relations of male hunters. Where women served as the primary laborers who cured thousands of hides for the market, polygyny among

successful hunters increased, as well as intertribal raiding for women. Access to European goods also stimulated changes in native political hierarchies, especially in those societies where the accumulation of wealth provided the basis for political power. This change was especially evident in the Northwest Coast, where a proliferation of potlatches and chiefs took place, and among neighboring interior groups who adopted some characteristics of coastal political ceremonies (Gibson 1988:389; Goldman 1940).

2) *Multi-Ethnic Communities.* It was common practice for mercantile companies to transfer native workers from over-hunted regions to newly-established outposts. By the early nineteenth century, fur companies were recruiting native labor from former outposts across the continent to work at new colonies. These pluralistic communities were established in the territories of other native people who became integrated into the regional economic system as day laborers. For example, British trade outposts in the Northwest were managed primarily by British, Orkney Islanders, and Metis (mixed French/Indian) personnel, while Eastern Woodland Indians, primarily the Iroquois, as well as other native peoples (Cree, Nipissing, and Abenaki) served as trappers, hunters, and camp tenders. In fact, by 1821 Iroquois made up one-third of the hired hands in the Columbia River region (Swagerty 1988:365). In addition, about 300 Hawaiians who had been hired to serve as deck hands, freighters, and general laborers worked in many British outposts throughout the Northwest Territory (Swagerty 1988:365).

The pluralistic trade outposts of the larger fur companies (i.e., Hudson's Bay Company, Northwest Company, etc.) were organized into tightly-stratified, ethnic hierarchies. A worker's job, social status, and wage were largely determined by ethnicity. At the apex of the stratified pyramid were a few ethnic Europeans who managed the company's affairs at home and in the field. The second tier, divided into various ranks, consisted of a larger number of "other" ethnic Europeans and people of mixed European and native blood who served as clerks, traders, artisans, and skilled or semi-skilled tradesmen. The lowest tier contained the contract and day laborers who performed the bulk of the work in the field, most of whom were native peoples from many different North American tribes. This tier composed the majority of the population of most trade outposts (for specific examples, see Shay 1985; Hamilton 1985; Monks 1985; Burley 1985; Ray 1988).

The rise of pluralistic communities containing stratified work forces of Europeans, mixed bloods, and natives from many different homelands represents another potential agent of cultural change. Yet scholars have paid little attention to the consequences of ethnic pluralism on the acculturation process of native peoples in colonial social environments. Considerable interaction took place between ethnic groups in early nineteenth century mercantile colonies, and inter-ethnic marriages or cohabitations were common (Swagerty 1988:371; Prager 1985:388; Farris 1989a:489; Jackson 1983). The close interaction of ethnic groups from many different homelands represents a fertile ground for stimulating cultural exchange of architectural styles, material goods, methods of craft production, subsistence practices, diet, dress, and ceremonial practices.

In sum, the specific research issues we will address in this project concern the effects that mercantile labor and inter-ethnic relationships had on the acculturation process of native workers in the Ross Colony. When native workers received commodities or wages for their labor, did this serve as a source of cultural change, influencing the acculturation process of native Alaskans and native Californians? How did the multi-ethnic environment of mercantile outposts, such as Fort Ross, modify traditional native lifeways? Did inter-ethnic interactions and marriages in company outposts serve as important sources of cultural change, ultimately affecting the architectural styles, subsistence practices, diet, and material culture of native workers? Did many traditional native lifeways remain intact during the process of mercantile colonialism?

Direct Historic Analogy in California Archaeology

The question of whether mercantile companies served as agents of cultural change is not moot for North American archaeologists. Since the beginning of the discipline, archaeologists working in this region have relied on late nineteenth and early twentieth century ethnographies as sources for interpreting the prehistoric past. Known as direct historic analogy (Charlton 1981:133, 136), this method is still commonly used today to generate models that can be tested with prehistoric data. The method is predicated on the assumption that significant cultural change has not taken place between ethnographically described peoples and their late prehistoric ancestors.

Direct historic analogy remains a cornerstone in the practice of California archaeology. Here anthropologists have long emphasized cultural continuity during late prehistoric, protohistoric, and historic times. Support for this assumption is based on the late entry of Europeans into this region, and continuity over time in some aspects of native material culture, including house construction, hunting and gathering practices, and the use of tools such as mortars and

pestles (Heizer and Elsasser 1980:28-56). While it is generally recognized that the central and south coasts of California were impacted relatively early by Spanish missionaries, and that the Gold Rush of 1848 had devastating ramifications for some native peoples, isolated pockets of Indians reportedly lingered on uncontaminated by Euro-American influences into the twentieth century (Heizer and Elsasser 1980:2-3). The assumption of cultural continuity was so strong that Alfred Kroeber and other ethnographers attempted to reconstruct traditional native societies by interviewing elders into the late 1930s and early 1940s (Heizer 1978:8-10). The childhood memories of these elders provided ethnographers with a view of mid-nineteenth century native lifeways that supposedly reflected traditional aboriginal culture. This "golden age" of ethnography still provides the interpretative foundation from which many California archaeologists reconstruct past lifeways and prehistoric linguistic/tribelet boundaries (see, for example, Moratto 1984:530-74).

There are, however, ample reasons to be cautious about using California ethnographies to reconstruct prehistoric societies, even in the most remote areas of the state. First, it is not yet clear whether lethal epidemics of pathogens swept across California in the 1500s and 1600s when European explorers first began to probe the coastline, but before permanent colonies were established. Second, the founding of early colonies possibly had substantial repercussions far beyond the local area of settlement. The founding of Fort Ross in the heart of Kashaya Pomo territory may have had reverberations across a broad region, possibly extending throughout the linguistic region defined by ethnographers as "Pomo and Coast Miwok." The Russians explored many kilometers of interior Sonoma County, following the Russian River in pursuit of beavers and other game and making firsthand observations about the agricultural potential of the land (Wrangell 1974 [1833]; Golovnin 1979:170 [1818]). They also "recruited" native laborers from as far as 70 km away (Wrangell 1969:211 [1833]).

At the same time that the Russians were exploring the Russian River watershed, fur trappers from small American companies, including the renowned Jedediah Smith, and the giant Hudson's Bay Company were hunting beaver and other terrestrial game along interior drainages throughout northern and central California (Farris 1989b; Batman 1985:193-214). By 1840, the Hudson's Bay Company opened a factory in San Francisco from which it administered its commercial operation in California during the last years of viable fur trapping in the state (Batman 1985:315, 320, 335-36).

One must also consider the broader consequences of Hispanic colonization in California. Heizer

(1941:105-112), Castillo (1978:103-107), and Phillips (1981:33-40) describe how Spanish/Mexican occupation along the central and south coasts had a rippling effect among native communities throughout California. As a result of historic epidemics and Spanish raids in the interior to "recruit" natives into the missions, native villages were often relocated to defensible, inaccessible places far from Hispanic settlements. Here, escaped neophytes and landless Indians from the missions often found refuge. Heizer (1941:112) describes how refugees from many different homelands who spoke diverse languages aggregated into these large villages for mutual protection. Phillips (1981:33-41) notes that some of these villages were established by influential native leaders who actively recruited Indian refugees to their settlements.

In their exploration beyond the Ross Colony, the Russians observed at least one native village composed primarily of runaway neophytes from Spanish missions (Wrangell 1969:212 [1833]). Furthermore, the Russians reported that many Indians were terrified of Spanish/Mexican raids (Wrangell 1974:2 [1833]; Golovnin 1979:160 [1818]; Lutke 1989:267 [1818]) and continually relocated their villages beyond the frontier to escape them. This practice became increasingly difficult by the 1830s, however, as Mexican ranchos were established in strategic areas to isolate the Russians from the rest of California and to contain northern California tribes (Duflot de Mofras 1937:5 [1841]; Batman 1985:282-85).

By at least the 1820s and 1830s, the combination of mercantile operations and Spanish colonization may have had far-reaching repercussions for native peoples across California. One must seriously question—in light of reported refugee populations, the shifting location of villages, deadly epidemics, and the fur trade—how accurately ethnographic accounts reflect "traditional" or pre-contact native lifeways. Caution should be exercised in employing ethnographic accounts to model prehistoric settlement patterns, subsistence practices, sociopolitical organizations, tribelet units, and linguistic boundaries. In fact, one can not help but wonder what the linguistic and tribelet boundaries, which ethnographers have so neatly traced out for different California native groups (e.g., Kroeber 1925), are really depicting—especially in light of the significant population movements that were underway at least one hundred years before most of the seminal ethnographic studies were completed.

THE DIRECT HISTORICAL APPROACH

We recognize the potential problems of employing post-colonial ethnographies to reconstruct pre-colonial or even colonial period native societies in California. However, we also recognize the tremendous wealth of information that California Indian ethnographies can provide archaeologists. These studies describe in great detail the material culture associated with subsistence practices, residential architecture, political activities, and religious ceremonies. Should archaeologists dismiss this information out-of-hand simply because some descriptions may not reflect pre-contact lifeways? Should archaeologists, as suggested by Dunnell (1990), treat ethnographically described native peoples and ancestral prehistoric groups as two separate and distinct populations?

We argue that ethnographic data should continue to play an important role in California archaeology, but that the emphasis should shift away from analogy. Rather than employing ethnographic observations to flesh out the prehistoric past, we advocate their use as part of the "direct historical approach" to develop a diachronic framework for comparing and contrasting native societies before, during, and after contact with European and American colonial institutions. It is important not to confuse the direct historical approach with direct historic analogy, as do most current textbooks (e.g., Sharer and Ashmore 1987:387; Knudson 1985:337; Bower 1986:381). The former is a straightforward study of cultural change, while the latter evokes analogy based upon the assumption of cultural continuity.

In its classic usage (see Strong 1935; Wedel 1938; Heizer 1941; Steward 1942, 1944), the direct historical approach traces the ancestors of contemporary native peoples back through historic, protohistoric, and prehistoric contexts using ethnographic, ethnohistoric, and archaeological data to study the dynamics of cultural change. This approach developed, in large part, as an offshoot of "acculturation" research that was popular in American anthropology in the 1930s and 1940s (e.g., Redfield et al. 1936). The early advocates of the direct historical approach recognized that European contact and settlement produced tremendous upheavals in some North American native cultures (see especially, Heizer 1941; Strong 1935). As Julian Steward (1942:340) stated succinctly, its great strength is that it provides the temporal framework to evaluate systematically "revolutionary changes in economy, village types, village distributions, migrations and tribal contacts" brought about by European contact. He argued that such an approach would tend "to correct ethnography's attempts to reconstruct pre-contact cultures" (Steward 1942:341).

We will employ pertinent ethnographic information in this project to help measure the rate and magnitude of cultural change. Rather than employing ethnographic data as models to reconstruct the past, we view historic observations as revealing of the time when they were recorded, and as the end sequences of long-term developments in native societies (see, for example, Kirch and Green 1987). The Historic period represents an additional sequence of time for evaluating cultural change in a long-term diachronic framework, and not a mirror of the prehistoric past.

In using the direct historical approach, we will minimize the boundary between "prehistoric" and "historical" archaeology. Unfortunately, there is a growing trend in North American archaeology for students to specialize in either the prehistoric or historical periods. Prehistoric archaeologists tend to work on Native American sites that are still pristine, having not yet been "tainted" by European contact. Post-contact times are the domain of historical archaeologists who still tend to focus on the archaeology of Europeans, such as the analysis of colonial America and the reconstruction of nineteenth century forts, battlegrounds, and plantations (Fitzhugh 1985:3-4; Ramenofsky 1987:32). Yet by continuing this dichotomous study of archaeology, the transition from prehistory to history, which represents one of the most interesting times of cultural change, tends to fall between the cracks. As Deetz (1989:434) succinctly notes, "it seems to have been relatively neglected by prehistorians because it was just too late to be of much interest, and by historical archaeologists since it is prehistoric from their point of view. Yet this is the time when some of the most radical changes were worked on the peoples of the world as a result of wholesale colonization, and its study, which by necessity must be archaeological, will shed light on many current world problems."

The study of cultural change, by its very definition, requires a broad-scale, diachronic approach. To evaluate the consequences of the European world-system on native peoples demands that *both* prehistoric and historical archaeology be undertaken. Prehistoric archaeology is needed to establish a baseline from which to measure changes taking place after European contact. As Trigger (1981:12-13) notes, without this prehistoric baseline it is impossible to determine the magnitude of change involved, since any written records may be describing native societies already affected by colonial processes.

In a nutshell, the research design for the Fort Ross Archaeological Project requires a holistic and diachronic approach that involves the study of pertinent ethnohistorical documents, ethnographic sources, native texts, native oral traditions, and the implementation of archaeological fieldwork (see Simmons 1988:10; Deetz 1988: 362-63). We have initiated field research in the hinterland of the Ross stockade that is identifying prehistoric, protohistoric, and historic sites. In this study we follow Trigger's (1981)

lead in distinguishing the early contact or Protohistoric period from the Historic period. The Protohistoric period is defined as the "interval between the first evidence of European contact influencing a native culture, however indirectly, and the beginning of the intimate well-documented contact that characterizes the beginning of the Historic period" (Trigger 1981:11).

At the Ross Colony, the Protohistoric period is defined as beginning about A.D. 1500 for two reasons. First, at this time Dobyns (1983) hypothesizes that possible lethal epidemics of pathogens may have spread across North America. Second, this is roughly the time that early contacts with native peoples were made by Spanish and English explorers along the coast of nearby Marin County. These brief visits included Juan Rodriguez Cabrillo in 1542, Sir Francis Drake in 1579, Sebastian Rodriquez Cermeno in 1595, and Sebastian Viscaino in 1603 (Beardsley 1954:15; Barrett 1908:27-37). Barrett (1908:36-37, note 7) suggests that representatives of the Kashaya Pomo or Southern Pomo visited Sir Francis Drake and his men when the *Golden Hinde* made an extended landfall somewhere along the Marin County coast. Barrett's interpretation is based on Drake's descriptions of native words, baskets, and ornaments.

The Historic period, when Europeans first settled in the region and sustained contact took place with native peoples, begins with the construction of the Ross Colony in 1812.

The Advantages of the Fort Ross Region

We feel that Fort Ross represents an ideal study area to examine the effects of a mercantile colony on native peoples using the direct historical approach. The reasons are threefold.

1) This region is characterized by less commercial and residential development today than during the Russian occupation. Consequently, archaeological sites have not been destroyed by creeping urban sprawl, as has happened at many other trade outposts, providing ideal conditions for undertaking archaeological survey work. Most of the coastal strip, even beyond the Fort Ross State Historic Park, is now owned by the state of California and administered by the California Department of Parks and Recreation as public park land. The Northern Regional Office of the Department is committed to the development of public interpretative programs that examine the local histories of different ethnic groups who once resided or still reside in northern California.

2) The direct historical approach is greatly facilitated by the rich ethnographic literature on coastal Pomo peoples that describes their culture subsequent to the Russian occupation. The Pomo remain one of the best-documented native groups by California

ethnographers (Kunkel 1974:11; Stewart 1943:29), a legacy of Alfred Kroeber and the many U.C. Berkeley graduate students who worked in Sonoma and Mendocino counties. Beginning in the early years of the twentieth century with Samuel Barrett (who received the first Ph.D. from the Anthropology Department at U.C. Berkeley for his work on the Pomo), and continuing through the 1950s, a long line of anthropologists, geographers, and linguists from the University of California recorded the subsistence practices, social organization, and religious ceremonies of the Kashaya and other nearby Pomo groups. More recent research beginning in the 1950s has involved the transcription of Kashaya Pomo oral traditions as native texts (Oswalt 1964).

Today several hundred coastal Pomo people live in rancherias at Stewart's Point and at Point Arena/ Manchester not far from Fort Ross. Several Pomo "tribal" scholars are currently documenting the lifeways of their people, reconstructing the movements of their families across Pomo territory over time, and recording their oral traditions (e.g., Lawson and Lawson 1976; Goodrich, Lawson and Lawson 1980). We are working with Pomo scholars in constructing a substantive, long-term diachronic framework for examining different dimensions of local native culture throughout prehistoric and historic times to the present.

3) The greater Fort Ross region presents the opportunity to examine the effects of other kinds of colonial practices on similar hunter-gatherer societies. In nearby Sonoma and San Rafael, Spanish/ Mexican missions were established several years after the founding of Fort Ross. By comparing the acculturation processes at the Ross Colony with those at the nearby missions, one can begin to evaluate critically how similar hunter-gatherer populations responded to very different colonial policies. Studies of neophytes in Spanish missions in California (see Costello and Hornbeck 1989; Deetz 1963; Johnson 1989; Hoover 1989; Farnsworth 1987) highlight important differences in the imperial colonial policies of Spain and the economic policies of mercantile companies, such as the Russian-American Company. While both missions and mercantile companies depended on native people as cheap sources of labor, the Spanish system is characterized as one of "directed historical change" in which one of their primary policies was to enculturate neophytes in European ways (Hoover 1989:395; Hornbeck 1989:425). This active enculturation process involved widespread proselytizing to Catholicism, teaching European crafts and trades to Indian men and women, and changing their traditional work habits, subsistence practices, dress, and menu. In contrast, as will be described in more detail in chapter 2, at Fort Ross no concerted

effort was made to enculturate local natives in Russian ways. Rather, the Russians were perfectly happy to let the local Indians continue their traditional ways, as long as they remained an economical and reliable source of labor. While Spanish priests frowned on inter-ethnic marriages, the Russian-American Company actually supported it as a way of increasing their labor pool in Russian-America (Fedorova 1973:206). Thus, one of the long-term goals of the Fort Ross project is to compare the nature, extent, and direction of cultural change of coastal hunter-gatherer peoples in a pluralistic mercantile colony with similar hunter-gatherer groups who were subjected to the tightly controlled, directed enculturation practices of nearby Spanish missions.

CONCLUSION

The study of the native laborers who toiled in the Ross Colony is long overdue. Fort Ross will serve as a case study in which we will examine how the Russian-American Company's mercantile practices affected native Californian and native Alaskan laborers. We suggest that studies of mercantile colonies are important for providing the historical context of early contacts between native peoples and European and American businessmen. The direct historical approach will be employed to examine long-term cultural change among native populations before, during, and after the Russian occupation. We will address whether the integration of native laborers in a market economy and the development of a pluralistic community with inter-ethnic social relations and marriage stimulated fundamental changes in native lifeways. We are especially interested in evaluating whether some components of native societies, such as diet, technology, material culture, architectural styles, sociopolitical organizations, religious practices, and gender relations are more receptive to change than others in mercantile communities. We are also interested in identifying those cultural components that are more conservative and resistant to change under these colonial conditions.

In the remainder of the volume we synthesize current information on the region, including its history, physical environment, and past archaeological and ethnographic fieldwork, from which we will construct a diachronic framework for implementing the direct historical approach. In chapter 2, we sketch a brief history of the Ross Colony, the purpose of which is to tease out the specific policies of the Russian-American Company influencing its treatment of native workers. Chapter 3 describes the study area of the project, including the plant communities, geology, topography, and zoology of the area. In chapter 4 we summarize previous archaeological investigations in the greater Fort Ross region. The results of recent archaeological fieldwork in the Fort Ross Study Area, a 5 by 10 km area in the vicinity of the original Russian colony, are discussed in chapter 5. Here we outline diachronic changes in subsistence-settlement patterns over time. In chapter 6 we synthesize past ethnohistorical observations, ethnographic studies, and native texts of the Kashaya Pomo. The seventh and final chapter provides a summary of our current understanding of cultural change in the Fort Ross region employing the direct historical approach.

CHAPTER TWO

NATIVE LABORERS IN A

MULTI-ETHNIC COMMUNITY

THIS CHAPTER WILL PROVIDE the historical context for examining how the colonial policies of the Russian-American Company may have influenced the acculturation processes of Pacific Coast hunter-gatherers at Fort Ross. We begin with a brief discussion of the Russian-American Company, particularly its administrative organization and how the company established policies for treating native workers. A description of the commercial activities that employed native workers and how these workers were compensated for their labor follows. Next we consider how the Russian-American Company integrated European and native peoples into a multi-ethnic community. The stratified hierarchy that structured inter-ethnic relations at Fort Ross is delineated. Also, population estimates of the four ethnic neighborhoods and their spatial layout are provided. Finally, we examine specific effects that the tightly stratified, multi-ethnic community may have had on native Alaskan and native Californian workers.

THE RUSSIAN-AMERICAN COMPANY

The Russian-American Company was chartered in 1799 by Tsar Paul I and granted exclusive monopoly to the Russian exploitation of Pacific marine mammals, as well as other natural resources, in North America. The imperial charter eliminated the competition of a number of smaller Russian fur companies which had participated in the maritime trade since the early 1700s. The newly-chartered company was modelled after other commercial monopolies of the day, including the Hudson's Bay Company and the East India Company, which played significant roles in the mercantile colonization of North America and Southern Asia (Gibson 1976:10; Fedorova 1973:132). The Russian monopoly was run as a private commercial company, financed primarily by private capital from joint stockholders, and was closely monitored by the tsar and the Russian Imperial government.

Although the bureaucratic structure of the company changed during its years of operation from 1799 to 1867, the basic administrative organization of the Russian-American Company consisted of four tiers.

1) *The Imperial Russian Government.* At the apex was the tsar and the Imperial Russian government. The tsar had the final say on any matter concerning the company, and a number of government departments dealt with company matters concerning foreign powers, religious jurisdictions, defense, and criminal actions (Dmytryshyn et al. 1989a:xxxvi). The tsar's family owned stock in the company, with the majority of the dividends earmarked for various charities and educational institutions (Tikhmenev 1978:56).

Dmytryshyn, Crownhart-Vaughan, and Vaughan (1989a:li) argue that the Russian-American Company served as a "de facto agency of the Imperial Russian Government." Especially in its later years (1840-1867) the company's administration became increasingly bureaucratic and bloated, employing a greater number of naval officers and government officials (Gibson 1976:23). However, the company was none-theless a commercial operation that had to answer to stockholders and produce dividends. Profits had to be generated to operate its fur trade enterprise, and it appears the commercial end of the business was subsidized very little by the government. Although the Russian government sent naval ships and troops to North America to protect and supply the Russian-American colonies, the company was responsible for covering the costs of sending ships around the world (from the Baltic Sea), as well as paying at least some of the salaries and expenses of navy and army personnel stationed in the colonies (Gibson 1976:87; Fedorova 1973:157-8).

2) *The Board of Directors*. The general commer-cial policies of the company were established by the board of the directors of the company. The stockhold-ers elected four directors who administered the com-pany from the "Main Administration" offices in St. Petersburg. They were responsible for maintaining capital assets, for increasing profit margins, and for developing economic strategies of fur hunting and world trade (Dmytryshyn et al. 1989a:xxxvii). The board of directors reported directly to the tsar on critical issues of the company. During the early years of the company (the first twenty-year charter), the majority of the board were pragmatic merchants who had worked in the North Pacific fur trade (Tikhmenev 1978:55). However, in latter years an increasingly greater number of government officials and naval officers served on the board (Gibson 1976:23).

3) *Chief Manager*. The company's commercial operations in Russian America were directed by the "Chief Manager" or "Chief Administrator." Essen-tially, the chief manager served as a governor for the Russia-American colonies, supervising branch of-fices, entertaining foreign visitors, enforcing Russian laws, and hiring much of the work force (Dmytryshyn et al. 1989a:xxxviii-xl). The chief manager reported directly to the board of directors. Beginning in 1804 the commercial and administrative capital of the chief manager shifted from Kodiak Island to New Archan-gel on Sitka Island, Alaska.

During the first twenty-year charter of the com-pany, the Chief Manager—Aleksandr Baranov—was selected by the board of directors. However, in accordance with the next two government charters of the company (1821 and 1841), the tsar appointed the chief manager from among senior Russian Imperial Navy officers (Dmytryshyn et al. 1989a:xxxix).

4) *Administrative Counters*. The Russian-Ameri-can colonies were divided into primary administra-tive units, known as counters (Gibson 1976:10). The chief manager appointed the manager for each admin-

istrative unit, as well as other key personnel, and they reported directly to his office in New Archangel. Seven major administrative units were defined in Russian-America: 1) Sitka (Northwest Coast of America); 2) Kodiak (Kodiak archipelago and Alas-kan Peninsula); 3) Mikhailovsk Redoubt (Norton Sound area); 4) Unalaska (the eastern Aleutian and Pribilof islands); 5) Atkhinsk (the western Aleutian, Near, and Komandorskie islands); 6) Kurile (Kurile archipelago); and 7) Fort Ross (Dmytryshyn et al. 1989a:xl).

The administrative structure of the company is reflected in the settlement pattern of the Russian-American colonies. The settlement system is highly primate, with nearly half of the company's ethnic Russian population and capital assets in North America aggregated in New Archangel (Gibson 1986:6). New Archangel dwarfed all the other administrative units in the size of the Russian population, the construction of elite architecture, including "Baranov's Castle," and the availability of European goods.

The settlements, farms, and outposts of the Fort Ross Counter extended along a 90 km stretch from the fort to the Farallon Islands, due west of San Francisco in northern California (figure 2.1). The settlement of Fort Ross, consisting of the original stockade compound and three ethnic neighborhoods that sprang up alongside it, served as the administra-tive headquarters of the counter. The main port of the counter, where most supplies were shipped and stored for delivery to and from Fort Ross, was Port Rumiantsev, situated 29 km south in what is now known as Bodega Bay. A permanent artel or hunting camp was established on the Farallon Islands, 90 km south of Fort Ross and 45 km west of San Francisco, where sea lions and fur seals were slaughtered. At least three farms were established between Port Rumiantsev and Fort Ross: Kostromitinov's ranch near the confluence of the Russian River and Willow Creek; Khlebnikov's ranch about 8 km inland of Port Ruminastev in the upper Salmon Creek valley; and the Chernykh ranch situated about 16 km inland between the contemporary towns of Occidental and Graton on Purrington Creek (Tomlin and Watrous 1990:16-17; figure 2.1).

COMPANY POLICIES

REGARDING NATIVE LABORERS

Official policies and practices regarding the treat-ment of native laborers emanated from the tsar and the company's board of directors. In the three twenty-year charters of the company (1799, 1821, 1841), the Russian imperial family decreed that native workers were to be treated equitably as Russian subjects,

Big River

Albion River

Navarro River

Eel River

Lake
Pillsbury

Lake
Mendocino

Clear
Lake

Russian River

Garcia River

North Fork Gualala River

Lake
Sonoma

ROSS

River

KOSTROMITINOV RANCH   Russian

CHERNYKH RANCH

KHLEBNIKOV RANCH

PORT RUMIANTSEV

Drakes Bay

San

FARALLON ISLANDS

Francisco Bay

N

Scale 1:500,000

0   15km

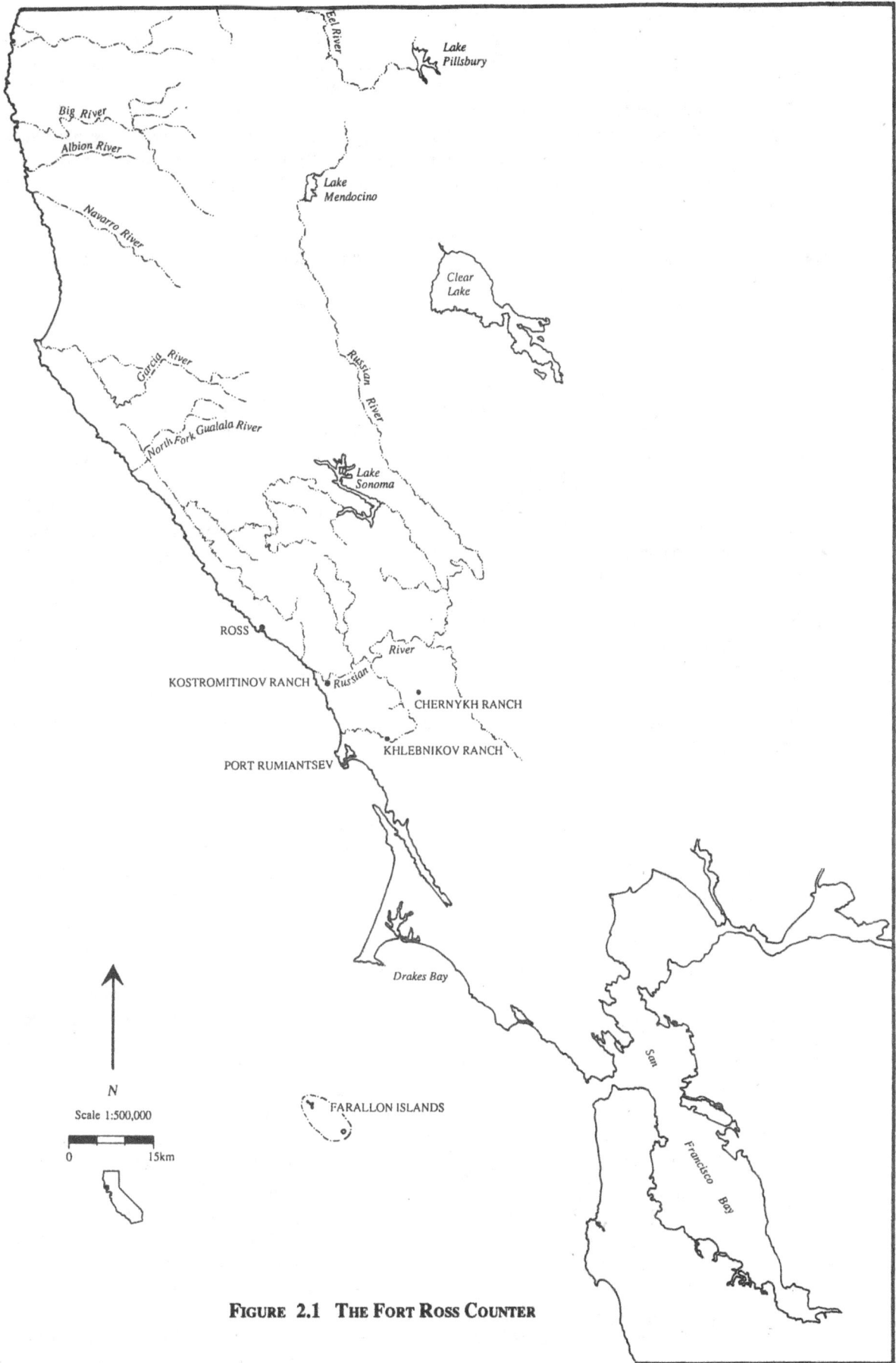

FIGURE 2.1 THE FORT ROSS COUNTER

compensated fairly for their work, and provided educational opportunities at the expense of the company (Dmytryshyn et al. 1989a:xxxvi). In the second charter of 1821, the government specified rates the Russian-American Company would pay its native employees, and the degree to which natives would be compensated with food, tobacco, and hunting equipment while participating in company hunting trips (Fedorova 1975:16; Khlebnikov 1976:50-53).

However, the actual implementation of these policies was left to the chief manager and the managers of the seven counters. In reality, the chief manager and counter managers enjoyed considerable liberty in their treatment of native workers. Abuse of the tsar's policies was not uncommon, with native workers being overexploited, mistreated, and underpaid (Dmytryshyn et al. 1989a:xliii, Wrangell 1969:211[1833]). The relative autonomy of the company's managers in North America resulted from their isolation and distance from the Main Administration offices in St. Petersburg. New Archangel was more than 19,000 km from St. Petersburg, via Siberia and the Arctic Ocean, and nearly twice that distance for Russian ships sailing from Baltic ports (Gibson 1976:44). It commonly took two years for managers in Russian-America to get a reply back from the Main Administration about company policies (Gibson 1976:45). Consequently, most decisions concerning field operations in North America were probably made on the spot, and if the Main Administration office was informed at all, it was long after the fact.

NATIVE LABORERS IN THE
RUSSIAN-AMERICAN COMPANY

The Russian-American Company depended upon native labor for its survival. Throughout its six decades of operation, the company could never recruit enough ethnic Russians to work in its North American colonies. The sparse recruitment and low retention rate of Russian workers were a product of several factors. Company employees were paid a low wage to work hundreds or thousands of kilometers from home in often dangerous or even life threatening operations. Housing conditions in the colonies were bad, food shortages common, and epidemics among the counters' populations rampant (Gibson 1987:23-24). While the men worked long hours enduring cold and wet conditions, the company charged them expensive prices for food, clothing, and other necessities at company-run stores (Dmytryshyn et al. 1989a: xlv). Fedorova (1973:237) estimates that up to 75% of their salaries was spent on food at company stores, and most of the employees were greatly in debt to the company (Gibson 1976:48-50; Wrangell 1969:211 [1833]).

Census figures highlight the fact that relatively few Russians worked in the Russian-American colonies. While Russian fur traders founded more than sixty settlements across the North Pacific Rim from the Kurile Islands (due north of Japan) to California, only about 550 Russian men, on the average (range = 225 to 823) were stationed across this vast region (Fedorova 1973:151, 1975:8). This is an extremely low population density when one considers that about half of them resided in the New Archangel. Few Russian women lived or worked in the colonies, especially in the early years. In 1819 the ratio of Russian men to women was about 29 to 1, while by 1836 an increasing influx of women lowered it to 8 to 1 (Gibson 1987:27).

The reliance on native laborers may also have been a pragmatic commercial strategy of the Russian-American Company based on four lines of reason.

1) By employing native laborers rather than ethnic Russians the company realized considerable salary savings. In general, native men were paid on a much lower salary scale than ethnic Russians undertaking comparable tasks. For example, in 1821 the company agreed to *raise* the salaries of native hunters to one-fifth the rates paid to Russian hunters (Fedorova 1975:16-18). Native women were even more of a bargain to the company since they made only about half as much as native men (Tikhmenev 1978:157; Khlebnikov 1976:51). It was not uncommon to pay native workers in kind. That is, they received clothes, tobacco, and food in compensation for their work.

2) The upkeep of native workers cost far less in comparison to ethnic Russian workers. While the Russian workers had to be provided with housing, many native laborers, such as at Fort Ross, were "commuters" who often returned home to their villages after work. Russian workers also demanded that they be supplied with ethnic Russian foods, and they became rebellious over food shortages which were quite common in the colonies (Gibson 1976:47; Fedorova 1973:233). Consequently, the company went to considerable effort and expense to provide its colonists with ethnic "European" foods such as grain, beef, sugar, and fruits (see Gibson 1976 for an excellent description). In contrast, native workers ate "colonial supplies" that consisted of locally available fish, sea mammal meat, terrestrial game, roots, and berries (Gibson 1976:48).

The problems of supplying "European" foods to the colonies highlight the difficulties of maintaining European workers thousands of kilometers from their homelands. Since the northern latitudes are poorly suited for growing grains or raising cattle, almost all ethnic European foods had to be imported into the North Pacific colonies. The Russians relied on a mixed strategy for supplying the colonies. Some foodstuffs were shipped from Russia, either over the unpredictable Siberian land route to the port of Okhotsk and then across the North Pacific Ocean, or they were transported by ship around the world from the Baltic port of Cronstadt. In either case it proved to be very costly, and spoilage rates were very high (Gibson 1976:57-87). Other options included sending ships to Spanish California and Chile to purchase foodstuffs, or relying on American traders to transport food and goods to the colonies (Gibson 1976:153-98). However, these options were fraught with uncertainty given the volatile nature of international trade, with ports being closed to Russian ships with no prior notice and prices skyrocketing overnight. No matter which option was used, importing European foods to the colonies cut into the profits of the Russian-American Company. To mollify its Russian work force, the company allocated monthly flour rations to each worker and sold the remainder at a loss in company stores (Fedorova 1973:237; Gibson 1976:48). Other imported foodstuffs, however, were marked up as high as seventy-seven percent in company stores (Fedorova 1973:237; Gibson 1976:87).

3) Native people were employed as hunters. The commercial success of the Russian-American Company in the North Pacific fur trade was based on a very different economic strategy than that of competing British and American fur companies. The latter relied on commodity exchange to obtain sea mammal pelts from independent native hunters and trappers in the Northwest Coast region (Gibson 1988:380-85; Batman 1985:101-34). In the late 1700s and early 1800s, American skippers, sailing primarily from Boston, made 127 voyages to the Northwest Coast. They brought firearms, blankets, liquor, tobacco, trade beads, iron, and copper goods to trade with Tlingit, Haida, and other coastal peoples in exchange for sea otter, fur seal, beaver, and other pelts (see Gibson 1988:386-88; Tikhmenev 1978:61-62). The furs were then transported to Canton where they were sold for teas, silks, nankeens, and porcelains. The Chinese goods, in turn, were shipped back to New England where they were sold at a handsome profit.

The Russian-American Company could not compete with American and British traders in the exchange of European goods for pelts harvested by independent native hunters. Not only were Russian trade goods generally of lower quality, less plentiful, and higher priced (Gibson 1988:377-78; Khlebnikov 1990:119-21), but it cost the Russian-American Company much more to transport these goods to North America than the more efficient American and British maritime trade houses. In 1842, the Russian-American Company's costs of shipping goods to New Arch-

angel were between 1.6 to 7 times higher than that of the Hudson's Bay Company (see Gibson 1976: 60, 87).

The Russians avoided direct competition for native trade by conscripting native peoples to hunt exclusively for them. In fact, the most effective sea otter hunters in the world were Aleuts and Koniag Eskimos. Trained from childhood to become skilled hunters, they employed lightweight, maneuverable *baidarkas* (skin kayaks) to pursue sea otters in kelp beds and shallow, rocky intertidal waters. Using teams of *baidarkas*, the northern hunters paddled quietly into position to surround unsuspecting otters sunning on the surface. Once in range, they accurately cast short darts tipped with detachable, barbed-bone points using throwing sticks or shot arrows tipped with barbed bone points with bows (see Ogden 1941).

Aleut and Koniag hunters were the backbone of the Russian-American Company's fur trade. Without these specialized sea mammal hunters, the Russians could never have competed with Anglo and American companies for access to North Pacific furs. The Russians enlisted the natives to hunt across the entire habitat range of the sea otter, including much of the North Pacific Rim from the Kurile Islands to Baja California. Teams of native Alaskan hunters were dispatched to almost every Russian outpost in North America, and in many settlements they comprised the majority of the population.

4) Native peoples also provided indispensable foodstuffs to the Russian-American Company. Given the tremendous logistical problems of importing food to the North Pacific colonies, the Russians relied extensively on native peoples to provide fresh supplies of locally available foods (see especially Gibson 1987:13-21). While it irked the Russian workers, especially during those frequent times when flour and salted beef were in short supply, the major component of just about everyone's diet, except possibly the top managers, was fish (Fedorova 1973:234: Gibson 1987:17). The Russians employed Aleut and Koniag men, women, and children to harvest and clean tons of salmon, halibut, and cod on the Aleutian Islands and Kodiak Island. Most were salted for export to other Russian colonies or counters. For example, more than a half million fish were dried and salted each year on Kodiak Island alone (Gibson 1987:18-20). In addition to the fish, Aleut and Koniag peoples also provided blueberries, cranberries, mushrooms, and roots to the Russian colonies (Gibson 1987:21).

On the Northwest Coast, a substantial portion of the food consumed by the Sitka counter was provided by local Tlingits. As Gibson (1987:13-18) documents, the Tlingit provided mountain sheep, venison, fish (halibut, herring, salmon, cod), shellfish, wildfowl, bird's eggs, berries, and roots to the Russians.

The local natives provided one of the few sources of fresh vegetables, and often the only source of fresh meat in the winter. Interestingly, the local natives learned how to grow potatoes from the Europeans, and, in turn, began to intensify production to meet the market demand of the local Russian population. By the mid-1840s, 100 to 200 canoe loads full of potatoes arrived each year at New Archangel for sale from as far away as the Queen Charlotte Islands (Gibson 1987:15). A marketplace flourished for many years outside the palisade walls at New Archangel where Russians bartered with tough Tlingit saleswomen over the exchange rates of potatoes, mountain sheep, and halibut (Gibson 1987:13).

NATIVE LABORERS IN THE ROSS COLONY

Native workers were also the linchpin of the Fort Ross Counter. Native labor was especially critical because the company had a difficult time attracting decent Russian workers to this counter. In general, Russian-American Company employees, other than those in management positions, endured a reputation of being drunken, incompetent, and lazy (see quotes in Gibson 1987:24-25). Fort Ross was considered to be the end of the world, isolated almost completely from Russia or even Siberia, and only the "worst of the worst" Russian workers were stationed here (Gibson 1976:129). Bancroft (1886:632) claims that many of the common Russian workers there were from the "criminal class," and that company officials had to maintain strict discipline in the counter.

We suggest that native labor was also critical in attempting to keep down the operational expenses of the counter. Company records indicate that Fort Ross was never a profitable counter, as the costs of maintaining and supporting the settlement greatly outweighed the combined revenues from all its economic ventures. Tikhmenev (1978:141, 228) describes the first ten years of operation as a major loss, then shows that by the late 1830s the deficit went from bad to worse, with annual losses of more than 44,000 rubles per year. It was largely for this reason that the colony was sold to John Sutter in 1841.

Native laborers participated in all three major economic activities at the Ross Colony—sea mammal hunting, shipbuilding, and agriculture—as well as other miscellaneous tasks.

Sea Mammal Hunting

Fort Ross served as a staging point for hunting sea otters, fur seals, and sea lions along the Californian coast from Trinidad Bay in the north down to San Francisco Bay in the south (Farris 1989a:484). The Fort Ross counter was also a supply center and storage center for Russian and American ships (under con-

tract to the Russian-American Company) on hunting expeditions to southern California and Baja California waters (Ogden 1933:41-49; Khlebnikov 1990: 130-63; 198-99). Sea otter and fur seal pelts were sent to New Archangel for trade in the Chinese and European markets, or sold directly to American and British captains whose merchant vessels frequently visited the Russian colony (Ogden 1933:41-42; Khlebnikov 1990: 148). Sea lions were hunted primarily for use at Fort Ross. Their skins were used in the production and repair of *baidarkas* and waterproof clothing, and their meat, blubber, and oil were consumed by native Alaskan workers (Ogden 1933:42). Khlebnikov (1990:59) reported in 1820 that the primary food source for *both* Russian and native Alaskan workers at Fort Ross was sea lion meat.

The hunting of sea mammals was done almost exclusively by native Alaskans. The work was both demanding and dangerous. Teams of *baidarkas* paddled up the shore to Trinidad Bay, and south along the Sonoma and Marin county coasts, where the lightweight kayaks were portaged over to the San Francisco and San Pablo bays (Farris 1989a:484). However, to the north hostile Indians living on the shore ambushed the sea mammal hunters (Khlebnikov 1976:108-109), while in the San Francisco Bay presidio soldiers guarded freshwater springs, hoping to capture Aleut/Koniag hunters (Khlebnikov 1976:108). Between 1814 and 1823, Russian ships with *baidarkas* lashed on deck carried native Alaskans into Spanish territorial waters, where they secretly poached sea otters from San Francisco Bay down to the Baja coast (Ogden 1933:42-45). Some native Alaskan men and a few Russians were captured by the Spanish (Tikhmenev 1978:138-39; Khlebnikov 1990:91). By 1823, the Russian-American Company had signed an agreement with the Mexican government to legally hunt sea mammals in southern California. The harvest was to be split evenly between the Mexicans and Russians, but the Russians would often under-report the actual number of sea otters taken (Khlebnikov 1976:110-11; 1990:159). American and Mexican merchants also contracted with the Russian-American Company to hire native Alaskans to hunt sea otters in southern California in the 1820s and 1830s (Ogden 1933:49-50; Khlebnikov 1990:198-99).

The Russians established an artel on the Farallon Islands in 1812 as a base for hunting fur seals and sea lions, and for harvesting sea gull feathers, meat, and eggs. In the first six years, 1200 to 1500 fur seals were garnered each year, after which the harvest decreased to about 200 to 300 a year (Bancroft 1886:633). About 200 sea lions per year were harvested for use at the Fort Ross Counter and about 5,000 to 50,000 gulls were hunted for meat, which was dried and shipped to

Fort Ross. A staff of one Russian overseer and from six to thirty natives were stationed at the artel. They lived on the windswept rocky islands in earthen dugouts or stone houses and received supplies from Fort Ross about six times a year (Khlebnikov 1976:122-3; Corney 1896:74A-75A). It is not clear how long a worker was stationed there before being rotated back to the Ross community. Riddell (1955:1,7,13) believes native Californian women, probably wives of the native Alaskan workers, were also stationed at the artel. His conclusion is based on both archival research and archaeological fieldwork he undertook on the Farallons in the late 1940s (see also Corney 1896:74A).

Sea otter hunting was only profitable at the Fort Ross Counter for a relatively few years. In comparison to northern sea otters, pelts from California were typically smaller, brown-colored, and of poorer texture, yielding only one-half to two-thirds the price in China (Khlebnikov 1976:35; Gibson 1976:32-34). Also fewer sea otters were found in California waters. Since sea otters are prone to overexploitation—most mothers only produce one pup per year (Gibson 1987:2)—yields quickly declined in California.

In their initial trip to Bodega Bay in 1808, Ivan Kuskov and his men harvested more than 1400 prime sea otters. When they returned in 1811, few sea otters were found, and they shifted their hunting operation to San Francisco Bay. Here they collected more than 1100 prime sea otter pelts (Khlebnikov 1976:107). By the time Fort Ross was founded, sea otters had become relatively scarce in local waters. Yields plummeted from only 714 prime pelts harvested in the years 1812-1815 to only ten to fifty-eight pelts each year after 1817 (Khlebnikov 1976:108). Tikhmenev (1978:135) suggests that sea otters were extirpated from Trinidad Bay to the entrance of San Francisco Bay by 1817, and that few fur seals remained on the Farallon Islands. The situation was bleak enough by 1818 that Leontii Hagemeister, the new chief manager of the company, issued a memo stating that the Fort Ross Counter contained no sea otters and little fur trade (Gibson 1976:16). While hunting shifted to more distant southern California locales in the 1820s, it was never very profitable given the considerable costs of maintaining the Ross Colony. By the 1830s sea mammal hunts in southern California had to be undertaken under Mexican licenses that provided little economic incentive for the company (Ogden 1933:49-50).

Shipbuilding

The Russian-American Company experimented briefly, from 1818 to 1824, with shipbuilding at Fort Ross. The reasons are twofold. One is that company ships, always in short supply, were needed in increasing numbers to service the developing maritime trade network. The other concerns the commercial health of the Ross Colony. Once sea otter yields began to plummet in the late 1810s, company officials began searching for new mercantile ventures that could turn a profit, or at least justify the continued drain of rubles necessary to subsidize the southernmost counter. The nearby forests of redwood, Douglas fir, tan oak, and laurel trees made Fort Ross an ideal choice for a shipyard. The first 160-ton brig, the *Rumiantsev*, was launched in 1818, followed shortly by the *Buldakov* (200 tons) in 1819, the *Volga* (160 tons) in 1821, and finally the *Kiakhta* (200 tons) in 1823. Unfortunately, none of the ships lasted for more than six years before extensive repairs had to be made due to wood rot (Khlebnikov 1976:116). Given what the Russians considered to be inferior wood (Khlebnikov 1976:116-17), and the fact that it was less expensive to buy American ships than to build ships at the Fort Ross Counter (Tikhmenev 1978:228), the company terminated its production of large brigs after the launching of the *Kiakhta*.

Little is known about the specific details of shipbuilding at Fort Ross. The shipmaster was the *promyshlennik* (Russian worker) Vasilii Grudinin, a carpenter who had worked with the American shipbuilder Lincoln in New Archangel (Khlebnikov 1976:116; 1990:100). We also know that a large number of men were needed to cut and transport the timber from the forests to Fort Ross Cove where the shipyard was located (Tikhmenev 1978:228; Khlebnikov 1990:97), one reason why shipbuilding was so labor intensive. We suggest that some of those laborers were probably native Californians, supervised by Russian foremen (see also Kennedy 1955:63). Below we will detail other labor intensive tasks performed by this work force at Fort Ross. This organization of labor probably carried over to cutting and hauling timber for shipbuilding.

Agriculture

A significant commercial activity at Fort Ross was the production of grain, beef, and fruit to meet local needs and for export to the company's counters in the North Pacific. Company officials optimistically believed that the Fort Ross Counter would serve as the "granary to the colonies" (Tikhmenev 1978:228). They maintained that if this colony could produce a steady food supply, then that would reduce the expensive import of ethnic European foodstuffs from Russia, and decrease the company's dependence on trade with Spanish Californian, Chilean, and American merchants.

Agricultural production began slowly at Fort Ross. During the early years (1812-1817), Ivan Kuskov was primarily concerned with sea mammal hunting, which occupied most of his men from spring through fall (Gibson 1976:110). Since the scheduling of sea otter hunts conflicted with the growing season, there was little time for farming. Beginning in 1817, as sea otter yields began to decline, more emphasis was placed on agricultural pursuits. Subsequent counter managers continued to intensify agricultural production in the 1820s and 1830s, until "every patch" of arable land around the garrison was in cultivation, and at least three outlying farms were in operation (see Gibson 1976:116-18). By the 1830s farming was the primary economic operation in the Fort Ross Counter.

Chernykh (1967 [1841]; 1968 [1836]), Gibson (1976:116-22) and Khlebnikov (1976:117-19) provide considerable detail on the agricultural practices at Fort Ross. The primary crops were fall wheat and fall barley: fields were plowed during the first rains in November and December, sown in December and January, and harvested in July and August. A wide assortment of vegetables was double cropped in small garden plots, including lettuce, cabbage, beans, peas, potatoes, melons, pumpkins, beets, radishes, and watermelons. Orchards containing apple, pear, cherry, and peach trees grew not far from the Ross stockade, in what is now called the Old Russian Orchard and on some of the outlying farms. Finally, livestock production was begun at the Ross Colony with the gift of twenty cattle and three horses from the Spanish in 1813. Eventually a large number of cattle, pigs, sheep, and horses ranged freely in the hinterland of Fort Ross.

The agricultural practices at this counter were very labor intensive, a consequence of local environmental conditions and antiquated agrarian methods. They are outlined below.

1) Fields tended to be small and widely dispersed in the immediate hinterland of Fort Ross. About 33 ha of land were eventually cultivated in the vicinity of the Ross stockade (Gibson 1976:118). A narrow strip of flat, arable land extends along the coastal terrace. Beyond this strip is a ridge system in which pockets of tillable land are scattered. Early attempts at growing wheat and barley along the coastal strip met with mediocre success, as high winds and prevalent summer fogs reduced yields (Chernykh 1968:52-53 [1836]). Fields were then established on the ridge slopes and ridge tops above the fog belt of the coastal terrace. Eventually a number of small fields were dispersed along the coastal terrace and ridge system within three versts (about 3 km) of the stockade (Khlebnikov 1976:117). The ridgetop fields were only accessible by foot or horseback, and the plowing, sowing, and cultivation of crops involved considerable work climbing up and down the rough terrain. Just about all tillable land within walking distance of the Ross community was under cultivation by the

1830s (Chernykh 1968:52 [1836]). When harvested, the grain had to be carried on the backs of laborers a considerable distance to be threshed near the palisade compound (Wrangell 1969:208 [1833]).

2) Outlying farms had to be staffed. One strategy for increasing crop yields in the 1830s was to place farms in outlying, interior valleys out of the summer fog belt. The holdings of these farms greatly expanded the overall agricultural production of the Fort Ross Counter. The Khlebnikov Rancho, the Kostromitinov Rancho, and the Chernykh Rancho encompassed holdings of 28 ha, 40 1/2 ha, and 83 ha respectively, of fields, orchards, and pasture land. Another farm also operated at Bodega Bay, but the size of this operation is unknown (see Gibson 1976:117-118; Tomlin and Watrous 1990:16-17). An overseer and a small group of farmhands stayed in barracks at each of these farms (Duflot de Mofras 1937:7 [1841]). Additional labor was needed during the harvesting season.

3) Agrarian methods were labor intensive. A common observation of the agricultural operation at Fort Ross is that few workers knew much about farming. The Russian "riffraff" stationed there showed little interest in farming, and innovative agrarian methods were not part of their repertoire (Tikhmenev 1978:135; Wrangell 1969:208 [1833]). Not until 1836, with the arrival of Yegor Chernykh, did a professionally-trained agronomist work in the Fort Ross Counter. He and others noted in amazement the crude tools and agrarian methods that were employed. Fields along level ground were tilled using simple plows drawn behind oxen (Chernykh 1967:16 [1841]), while rocky ridgetop fields were prepared manually using spades and digging sticks (Khlebnikov 1976:119). Weeds were so pervasive that fields had to be plowed two or three times (Chernykh 1968:53 [1836]). A rotation system was employed so that every three years plots of land were left fallow as pasture land for livestock. This practice kept weeds down and allowed some relief to exhausted soils (Chernykh 1968:60 [1836]). Reaping was done by hand using sickles. Before Chernykh made improvements, wheat was threshed on an open floor about 11 to 17 meters in diameter or larger by running 70 to 150 horses across the grain, which dislodged the kernels from the straw (Chernykh 1968:56 [1836]). At least twenty-five men were needed to drive the horses and collect the kernels (Chernykh 1968:55 [1836]).

4) Free-ranging livestock had to be tended. During the dry season, livestock searched for fodder as far as 21 km from the stockade (Wrangell 1969:209 [1833]). All cultivated plots within this area had to be fenced to keep out the several thousand head of cattle and several hundred sheep that grazed in the hinter-

land of Fort Ross by the late 1830s and 1840. The tending of the livestock required a permanent group of laborers, especially when meat was butchered for local use or for export to New Archangel (Khlebnikov 1976:119-21).

In general, the Russians at Fort Ross were characterized as unmotivated and inferior agricultural workers, at least in the labor they devoted to the Russian-American Company fields as opposed to their own garden plots (Tikhmenev 1978:135; Wrangell 1969:208[1833]; Gibson 1976:128-29; Khlebnikov 1990:97-98). Some Russian men did serve in supervisory positions on outlying farms. Native Alaskans were employed in agricultural tasks and as herdsmen, when they were available (Khlebnikov 1990:98). However, they were frequently absent from Fort Ross while on extended hunting expeditions, so they could not be depended on to perform the bulk of the agricultural labor (see Khlebnikov 1990:210-11). Much of the agricultural labor—tilling the soils, cultivating the plants, hand harvesting and transporting the wheat and barley crops, and threshing grain—was done by native Californians (see Gibson 1976:119; Khlebnikov 1976:119; Wrangell 1969:210-11 [1833]). The local Pomo and Miwok workers also tended livestock, especially when other Russian or native Alaskan herdsmen were unavailable for this duty (Khlebnikov 1976:119; 1990:141; Bancroft 1886:639). Khlebnikov (1990:141 reported in 1824 that he did not trust the Indian workers to tend the herds, believing that they were probably driving "the animals off into the countryside," thereby contributing to the heavy loss of cattle and sheep in the Fort Ross Counter.

Kashaya Pomo oral tradition, as transcribed by Oswalt (1964), provides some insights into the farm work of the native laborers. In Text 60, as told by Herman James, the Kashaya people remember that the undersea people (Russians) raised wheat that "blanketed the land" around Fort Ross. When the wheat was ripe, the Indian workers cut it down by hand and then tied it together. The wheat was then placed in sea lion skins and dragged to the Russian settlement. Here it was threshed in a "big place" where the earth was packed down by running horses around in circles. The threshed grain was then put in sacks and transported to a storehouse. Herman James also related that some grain was threshed at a "flour grinder" that spun in the wind. The Kashaya people remember that at least one woman who tended the flour grinder was caught in the grinding stone and killed. She was cremated in the traditional manner of the Kashaya people (see Oswalt 1964:267-69).

The agricultural endeavor in the Fort Ross Counter was never very successful, and the counter never realized its potential as the "granary of the colonies."

Poor yields resulted from inadequate agrarian methods, and from the combined effects of coastal fog, wind, and rodents (Tikhmenev 1978:135; Khlebnikov 1976:121; Gibson 1976:138). Spanish missions continually produced much better yields than those reported for Fort Ross (Fedorova 1973:241; Gibson 1976:121). In some years the barley and wheat crops at the Ross colony were complete failures. Even in the best years, such as in 1832 when the highest wheat yields were reported, the counter still produced a deficit of more than 7000 rubles (Wrangell 1969:212 [1833]).

In the early 1830s, Ferdinand Wrangell, then chief manager of the company, attempted to expand the size of the Fort Ross Counter to include fertile land along the Russian River watershed some distance from the coast. While he reached an agreement with Mexican officials, Tsar Nicholas I refused to recognize the "revolutionary" Mexican government. Consequently, the agreement between Mexico and the company became null and void (Gibson 1969:214). The company decided to shut down its unprofitable operation at Fort Ross when access to good arable land in the interior was denied, and when an agreement was reached in 1839 with the Hudson's Bay Company to provide wheat and beef to the North Pacific counters at a fair price.

Miscellaneous Endeavors

During the early years of the Fort Ross Counter (1812-1821), a lively trade existed between Fort Ross and nearby Spanish missions. While the trade was officially banned by the Spanish government, a considerable exchange of goods took place between the padres and the Russian businessmen. The padres were in desperate need of manufactured goods, especially items of iron or copper. Craftsmen at Ross manufactured redwood barrels, rowboats, wheels, and cooking implements, and repaired rifles, locks, and instruments in their blacksmith, carpenter, and cooperage shops (Khlebnikov 1976:122; Tikhmenev 1978:227; Bancroft 1886:639). In return, Spanish padres exchanged wheat, barley, beef, tallow, lard, and soap with the Fort Ross Counter. This contraband trade ended with Mexico's independence in 1821, and shortly thereafter California ports were thrown open to foreigners. American and British merchants, who could supply better manufactured goods at cheaper prices, quickly outmuscled the Russians in their competition for Californian products (Gibson 1976:190; Khlebnikov 1990:119-121). High duty taxes and anchoring fees levied by the Mexican government also cut into the profits of the Russian-American Company (Khlebnikov 1990:119).

Other goods were produced at Fort Ross for both local consumption and export, often to the company's colonies in the North Pacific. Fired bricks of fine clay were produced there until 1832, when the brickyard was moved to Bodega Bay (Wrangell 1969:207 [1833]). In 1824 the Russian-American Company requested that 3000 to 5000 bricks be shipped to New Archangel (Khlebnikov 1990:135). Tallow and tanned hides were also produced, the latter providing the raw material for making boots (Khlebnikov 1976:122; 1990:159). The Ross Colony also shipped laurel timber and pine pitch to the Sitka counter and to other settlements in California (Bancroft 1886:639; Duhaut-Cilly 1946:13 [1828]; Khlebnikov 1990:135).

The production of manufactured goods at Fort Ross was undertaken by peoples of diverse ethnic backgrounds. While Russian artisans were represented at Fort Ross, recent translations of Russian-American Company records indicate that many of the skilled craft occupations were filled by Creole and native Alaskan employees (Spencer Pritchard 1991; Khlebnikov 1990). For example, during the period of 1820 to 1824, Khlebnikov (1990:59, 64, 100, 186) recorded that "Aleut" employees served in the following occupations: coopersmith, tanner, blacksmith, mason, and coal miner, as well as hunter and *baidarshchik* (*baidara* crew overseer). Native Californians were also involved in some of the mercantile activities. Wrangell (1969:211 [1833]) noted that the Indians were used to haul clay for the production of bricks.

Another economic role that native peoples probably played at Fort Ross was providing the community with wild foodstuffs. We already noted that native workers on the Farallon Islands artel produced considerable quantities of dried gull meat, gull eggs, and sea lion meat and blubber for local consumption in the Fort Ross Counter. Native Alaskans, using their *baidarkas* and deep-sea fishing lines, also may have provided large, open water fish to the colony. In addition, native Californians may have exploited local game, fish, and plant foods in the hinterland of Fort Ross for barter with the colonists. Fresh venison and elk meat probably were welcome dietary supplements (see Khlebnikov 1990: 59, 192), as were steelhead and salmon from the nearby Gualala and Russian rivers. However, some hunting of deer and elk was undertaken by Russian employees using guns (Khlebnikov 1990:51, 56), and the extent to which local wild foods were provided by Indian hunters and gatherers remains unknown.

COMPENSATION FOR NATIVE LABORERS

The Aleut and Koniag peoples had worked for Russian employers for more than three decades prior to the founding of Fort Ross. In the early, stormy years of that relationship, Russian merchants held members of elite families hostage in the Aleutian Islands and Kodiak archipelago in return for tribute (*yasak*) paid in sea otter pelts (Knecht and Jordan 1985:19). For example, at Three Saints Bay on Kodiak Island, the Russians held 300 natives hostage, of which 200 were daughters of local chiefs (Gibson 1976:3). When tribute extortion was banned by the Imperial Russian government in 1788 (Pierce 1988:121), it was replaced by compulsory service in which native Alaskan males between the ages of fifteen to fifty could be drafted to hunt for the company. Gibson (1987:5-6) describes the native hunters as "corvée serfs" who were paid in kind with clothing, tobacco, and food, much of it produced under company supervision by native women and children (Knecht and Jordan 1985:32).

By the time Fort Ross was founded in 1812, the company had become more enlightened in its treatment of native Alaskans. The native Alaskans were either paid on commission or received daily or yearly salaries in scrip, a parchment token that could be exchanged for goods in the company store (Tikhmenev 1978:144). The timing and amount of payment depended upon the job and overall performance.

Unskilled Labor. In the early 1820s, daily compensation for unskilled labor appears to have been 50 kopeks per person (Khlebnikov 1990:99, 186). Interestingly, the native Alaskans at Fort Ross were paid less than their counterparts in the Sitka Counter (who made one ruble per day), a discrepancy that did not go unnoticed. Khlebnikov (1990:186) justified the difference in salary by noting that at Fort Ross the laborers can "work all day in their shirt-sleeves and without shoes, whereas in Sitkha, owing to the bad weather, clothing and shoes wear out faster."

Sea Mammal Hunters. The native Alaskan hunters appear to have been paid by the pelt. In 1815, some company hunters were credited 30 to 50 rubles per sea otter, depending upon the size, color, and texture of the pelt (Tikhmenev 1978:144). In the second charter of 1821, the company decreed that "Aleut" hunters be "paid for their pelts not less than one-fifth of the amount that earlier Russian *promyshlenniks* received," and that hides, tobacco, clothing, fishhooks, firearms, ammunition, and even rum be provisioned for the hunts (Khlebnikov 1976:50-51). Native Alaskan hunters who participated in joint Mexican and Russian-American Company hunts in the 1820s were credited two piasters per sea otter adult, one piaster per yearling, and four reals per pup (Khlebnikov 1990:182).

Skilled Craftsman. Native Alaskans who served in craft occupations at Fort Ross were paid yearly salaries. In the early 1820s, "Aleut" men working as coopers, blacksmiths, and tanners were paid an annual wage of between 120 and 200 rubles (Khlebnikov 1990:64, 100).

The native Californian workers were paid primarily in kind for their services. They received food, tobacco, beads, and clothing (Kostromitinov 1976:9 [1830-38]; Wrangell 1969:211 [1833]).

The Integration of Native Laborers
in the Ross Colony

At the Ross Counter, as in other Russian-American colonies, a socio-economic hierarchy was employed to define the status, wage, and job classification of its employees. Several factors appear to have been important in assigning a person's position in this economic system, including ethnicity, level of education, job skills, and overall motivation. The Russian administrators classified the multi-ethnic work force of Ross into four major classes (or "estates," after Fedorova 1975): "Russians," "Creoles," "Aleuts," and "Indians" (see Wrangell 1969:210-211 [1833], Khlebnikov 1990:188-94). While these ethnic classes provided the basic foundation of the socio-economic hierarchy, some upward mobility existed for individuals who proved to be good workers or who acquired special skills. Lydia Black's (personal communication) archival research indicates that the Russian-American Company would reward loyal and conscientious workers regardless of their ethnic background, sometimes promoting them above workers from higher status ethnic classes (i.e., Russian).

Russian workers were divided into three groups (Fedorova 1975:15). At the apex of the hierarchy were the "honorable ones" who served as company administrators and/or military officers. "Semi-honorable ones" (men of lower rank) comprised the next step as clerks, soldiers, navigators, and laborers. The third group, "colonial citizens," was made up of Russian laborers who remained in Russian America after they retired from service in the company.

Creoles, children produced from Russian men and native women, were classified as members of a separate "estate." They were often not accepted by either the Russian or Native American communities (see Fedorova 1975:13-14). The Russian-American Company educated them, and some served in important positions as officers on company ships, and as middle-level managers, clerks, and skilled craftsmen (Spencer Pritchard 1991:43). While some of the Creole workers at Fort Ross made a modest wage, they tended to be paid less than ethnic Russians for performing the same jobs. Khlebnikov (1990:63-64) justified this discrepancy by noting that the Creoles were raised and trained at the company's expense.

Native Alaskans from the Aleutian Islands, Kodiak Island, and coastal Alaska were classified collectively as "Aleuts." As outlined above, they were paid different wages depending upon the job. While some of the skilled craftsmen at Fort Ross made the same salaries as those paid to Creole artisans (Khlebnikov 1990:64), the majority of the unskilled laborers were compensated on a lower scale than the Creole workers.

Native Californians filled the lowest rank in the socio-economic hierarchy at Fort Ross, and they were not paid a standard wage. There is little evidence that Indian men were ever promoted into better paying occupations in the Russian-American Company. Khlebnikov (1990:193-94) did not trust the local Indians, and he urged considerable caution in dealing with them.

Social interaction took place between the four major ethnic groups at Fort Ross, and inter-ethnic marriages and cohabitation were common (see, for example, Jackson 1983). However, current evidence suggest that most of the inter-ethnic associations tended to take place between adjacent ethnic classes.

In the best documented census data, taken on June 1, 1820 by Ivan Kuskov (Fedorova 1975:12), the numbers of women either married or cohabiting with Russian, Creole, and Alaskan men were twelve, six, and fifty, respectively. Of the women living with Russian men, four were identified as Creoles, two as native Alaskans, and five as Californian Indians. Four native Alaskan, one Creole, and one native Californian woman lived with Creole men. Finally, of the fifty women living with native Alaskan men, one was Creole, eight were native Alaskans, and thirty-six were native Californians from the Fort Ross, Bodega Bay, Point Arena and the Russian River areas. Thus, of the forty-two native Californian women involved in inter-ethnic relationships, thirty-six were living with men of the next higher adjacent ethnic class. Of the fourteen native Alaskan women, twelve were living with men of their own rank or the next higher adjacent one (Creole). Of the six Creole women identified, one was living with a man of her ethnic class, while four were living with men of the next higher adjacent rank (Russian). Only one woman, a Creole, was associated with a man below her class.

The census data on the nature of inter-ethnic relationships appear to be corroborated by linguistic information. A study of loanwords in the Kashaya Pomo language suggests that they commonly borrowed native Alaskan origin words (Kari 1983:1-3; Oswalt 1988:21). In Oswalt's (1957:245-47; 1988:20-21) study of Russian loanwords still employed in the Kashaya Pomo language, there is evidence that some Russian words they learned originated from Aleutian or Eskimo (Alutiiq) speakers (e.g., see the word *kalikak* for book or letter and *putilka* for broken glass).

In sum, a socio-economic hierarchy existed at the

Ross Colony that was based on both ethnicity and individual achievement. The Russian administrators recognized four primary ethnic classes or estates. While social relationships crosscut the multi-ethnic community, we believe that the closest interactions took place primarily between people of the same or adjacent ethnic classes. In reality, the Kashaya Pomo and Coast Miwok workers probably had very little interaction with the "honorable" Russian managers of the colony. Rather their social relations extended primarily to the native Alaskans, and to a lesser degree with Creoles and lower class Russians.

THE SPATIAL ORGANIZATION OF THE

MULTI-ETHNIC COMMUNITY

We suggest, based on archival research and archaeological fieldwork, that the spatial structure of the Ross Colony was organized into four ethnic residential areas or neighborhoods (figure 2.2). Below we describe each ethnic neighborhood, presenting population estimates when possible, and briefly discuss the nature of the archaeological research completed to date.

1) The Stockade Compound. The nucleus of the Ross community consisted of the stockade and associated administrative and residential buildings that Ivan Kuskov and his men began erecting in 1812. It

was behind the stockade walls that the "honorable" Russian administrators and military officers lived and worked, along with some unmarried Russian men. The structures reflected the elite status of the residents, containing accouterments such as window glass, and other exotic goods not found in the rest of California (Bancroft 1886:630; Duhaut-Cilly 1946:10 [1828]). Census figures (see table 2.1) suggest that the number of Russian men stationed at Fort Ross ranged from about twenty to forty. Of this number, probably only a handful of men, including the counter's manager and close subordinates, resided in the garrison (see Duhaut-Cilly 1946:10 [1828]). No Russian women are reported there until 1833, when four were counted.

As noted in chapter 1, the stockade complex has received considerable archaeological attention since the early 1950s (see Farris 1989a:490-92; O'Connor 1984:11-13). The perimeter of the palisade walls was first investigated in 1953 (Treganza 1954), and later excavations took place in 1984 (Porter 1985) and 1989 (Purser et al. 1990). The foundation of the Kuskov House or Old Commandant's House was excavated in 1971, 1972, 1975, and 1976 (Thomas 1976a). The Officials' Quarters or Officers' Barracks was exposed in 1970, 1971, 1972, 1975, 1976, and 1979 (Thomas 1976b). The foundation of the chapel was tested and mapped in the early 1970s (Spencer-Hancock and Pritchard 1982). During this time exca-

Table 2.1
POPULATION ESTIMATES OF THE ROSS COLONY

		1812	1818	1818-1819	1820	1833
Russian						
	males	23	26	21-27	23	41
	females	0	0	0	0	4
	children	0	0	0	0	5
Creole						
	males	-	-	0	5	10
	females	-	-	0	6	15
	children	-	-	0	-	63
Native Alaskan						
	males	80	102	75-78	116	42
	females	-	-	-	7	15
	children	-	-	-	-	26
Californian Indian						
	males	-	-	-	-	35
	females	-	-	-	41	37
	children	-	-	-	-	?

Sources:	1812 (Fedorova 1973:135)	1820 (Fedorova 1975:12)
	1818 (Golovnin 1979:162)	1833 (Wrangell 1969:210)
	1818-1819 (Gibson 1976:12)	

vations also took place directly outside the north palisade wall, designated the "Mad-Shui-Nui" locus, and along the new right-of-way of Highway 1 (Ritter 1972; O'Connor 1984:12). In 1975 limited testing was done near the southern blockhouse (the "South-East Area") and in the foundations of the eastern barracks (also known as the "Barns Area") (O'Connor 1984:12). Limited testing of the "Old Warehouse" or "Fur Warehouse" took place in the early 1970s (Edwards 1975), and a full scale areal excavation commenced in 1981 (Farris 1981, 1990).

Archaeological fieldwork is also underway at the historic Russian Orthodox cemetery, located 170 m northwest of the stockade complex. The project, undertaken by Lynne Goldstein and Sannie Osborn of the University of Wisconsin, Milwaukee, is providing demographic and ethnic information on the individuals buried in the cemetery. Initiated in the summer of 1990, the project will involve the restoration of the cemetery including the marking of the graves with Russian-Orthodox crosses.

2) The Russian Village. Situated primarily to the south and southwest of the stockade compound, this neighborhood consisted of numerous residential structures, gardens, and orchards as illustrated in several period paintings. In his 1828 visit to Fort Ross, Duhaut-Cilly (1946:4) recorded that the stockade compound and Russian village displayed a "European air" in their architectural style. He (1946:10-11) described the Russian village "as the pretty little houses of sixty Russian colonists." In 1833, Wrangell (1969:207) observed "two rows of small company and private houses" with associated gardens and orchards. The neighborhood probably consisted of a mixed bag of lower class ethnic Russians, ethnic Siberians [three were identified in Kuskov's 1820 census (Fedorova 1975:12)], and Creoles, who served in the capacity as sentries, artisans, cooks, etc. (see Wrangell 1969:211 [1833]). Interethnic households were probably common. Census figures on the Creole population (table 2.1) suggest they were a minor component of the Fort Ross community until the 1830s. By this time the growing number of inter-ethnic households had produced many "Creole" offspring, which by 1833 included sixty-three children. Clearly, had the Russian colony persisted for another decade or two, the Creole rank would have swelled the population of the Fort Ross Counter.

Minimal archaeological research has been undertaken in the Russian village. Glenn Farris (1986a:20) directed an excavation to mitigate the impact of a leach line for the state park's Visitors Center here. The material remains recovered, however, appear to relate to a later Indian village that dates to the 1840s or 1850s when local natives worked for William Benitz who managed a ranch at Fort Ross

from 1843-1867 (see chapter 6). As described in greater detail in chapter 5, the finds of the Leach Line excavation are probably associated with the nearby recorded archaeological site, CA-SON-174.

3) Native Alaskan Neighborhood. The Aleut and Koniag hunters resided in a village directly south of the southern portal of the garrison (see figure 2.2). The village is identified on the 1817 map of Ross, the only known cartographic rendition of the colony undertaken by the Russian-American Company. Reproduced in Fedorova's book (1973:353, 358-60), the map caption describes the village as "14 Aleut Yurts made of planks." In 1816, the Spanish official, Gervasio Arguello, counted thirty-seven huts for the "Aleuts" and forty-seven *baidarkas* (Bancroft 1886:631, footnote 3). Duhaut-Cilly (1946:10) in his visit of 1828 described "the flattened cabins of eighty Kodiaks." Ilia G. Voznesenskii (Blomkvist 1972:107) observed twenty-four "Aleut" buildings in his visit to Fort Ross in 1840-41.

The Russians evidently allowed the native Alaskans great freedom in the style and specific location in which they built their houses (Blomkvist 1972:107; Tikhmenev 1978:134). Some accounts suggest that Russian style plank houses were constructed out of redwood (Blomkvist 1972:107; Khlebnikov 1976:106b), although other observations suggest that a few traditional semi-subterranean *barabaras* (sod houses) or "flattened cabins" were also constructed (Tikhmenev 1978:134; Duhaut-Cilly 1946:10 [1828]). We suspect that various types of households resided in these structures, including single native Alaskan males, native Alaskan couples, and inter-ethnic couples comprised of native Alaskan men and native Californian women. It is also possible that other kin relations of the native Californian women resided here. In 1820, Khlebnikov (1990:102) observed that many Indians lived under the same roof with native Alaskan men in very crowded conditions. A barrack was built near the "Aleuts' huts" that could accommodate fifty Indians during the winter months.

The population estimates for the native Alaskan men, women, and children range from a low of about seventy-five in 1818-19 to one hundred and sixteen in 1820 (see table 2.1). Most accounts indicate that the majority of them were Koniag Eskimos from Kodiak Island (Fedorova 1973:203; Blomkvist 1972:107; Knecht and Jordan 1985:19-20), as well as a few Aleuts from the Aleutian Islands, and Dena'ina Athabascans from the Cook Inlet of Alaska (Kari 1983:1). The dependence on Koniag workers appears to have resulted from a shortage of Aleut hunters. In the early years of colonizing the North Pacific, Russian abuse and epidemics decimated the population of the Aleutian Islands. Two-thirds of the population had perished by 1790 (Gibson 1987:5-6). By the late

1700s and early 1800s, when the Ross Colony was founded, the Russians were increasingly using Koniag peoples to hunt sea mammals as a replacement for Aleuts. Their population, however, soon felt the repercussions of Russian colonization; Gibson (1976:6) estimates the Koniag population decreased by seventy-five percent between 1792 and 1834.

Native Alaskan hunters were frequently gone from Fort Ross on hunting trips from spring to fall (see Khlebnikov 1976:108,131; Golovnin 1979:162 [1818]). In addition, they were frequently rotated to other outposts, including the Farallon Islands artel and other North Pacific colonies, depending upon the regional labor needs of the company, and the general health of workers in other counters. By 1838 most of the native Alaskan workers were permanently transferred to other North Pacific counters (Gibson 1976:127).

In the summers of 1988 and 1989 we undertook a preliminary archaeological investigation of the Native Alaskan neighborhood. We mapped and surface collected the Native Alaskan Village, designated as CA-SON-1897/H in the California state trinomial site numbering system. We also initiated excavations in the nearby Fort Ross Beach Site (CA-SON-1898/H), situated directly below the Native Alaskan Village on the west side of Fort Ross Creek. This area appears to contain native Alaskan material transported down the cliff face from the village above, as well as some materials and architectural features found in situ.

4) The Native Californian Neighborhood. The place where the native Californian Indians resided near Fort Ross is called "Metini" by the Kashaya people (see Oswalt 1964, native texts 60, 61, 64; Barrett 1908:230-31). Based on our archival and archaeological research, we believe that "Metini" does not refer to one large village, but instead to a number of smaller hamlets scattered in the vicinity of Fort Ross. The "cone shaped huts" of these residences were in marked contrast to the "pretty little houses" of the Russian village, or the "flattened cabins" of the native Alaskans (Duhaut-Cilly 1946:10-11[1828]). There are several eyewitness accounts of residential dwellings, including domestic furnishings, and people conducting various household chores. The most useful observations were made by Cyrille LaPlace in 1839 (translated by Farris 1986b, 1988), Ferdinand Wrangell in 1833 (translated by Stross and Heizer 1976), and Peter Kostromitinov who served as counter manager from 1830-38 (translated by Stross and Heizer 1976). In addition, V. M. Golovnin, a Russian naval captain, and Fedor P. Lutke visited the native community at Port Rumiantsev in 1818 (translated by Wiswell 1979; Dmytryshyn et al. 1989b, respectively). We will examine these ethnographic observations in detail in chapter 6. Over time the size and nature of the

native Californian community associated with the Ross Colony changed greatly.

The Early Years. During the first decade of Fort Ross (1812-22), relations between the local natives and colonizers appear to have been relatively good. A friendship pact was signed between the Russian-American Company and local Indian chiefs on September 22, 1817, which acknowledged the right of the Russians to establish their colony in Kashaya territory (Dmythryshyn et al. 1989c:296-98). The local native chiefs received medals from the company, as well as some trade goods (see Bancroft 1886:297). There was some concern among the local natives about the expanding Spanish empire to the south, and the Kashaya appear to have initially welcomed the Russians because of the protection they would provide from Spanish raids (see Golovnin 1979:165 [1818]).

To cement the formal alliance with the Russian-American Company, the Indian chiefs "willingly" offered their daughters as mates to company employees, an action calculated to extend kinship relations among the foreign colonists (see Golovnin 1979:163 [1818]; Kotzebue 1830:124). Native Alaskan men who cohabited with Pomo and Miwok women found they not only gained a wife, but a complete network of kin relations. The Pomos extended full family ties to their foreign in-laws, and reciprocal obligations due to kin relations were observed (Golovnin 1979:163 [1818]). For example, the Indian men helped the Aleuts build houses for their new brides.

Few estimates of the native Californian population exist for the first decade of Fort Ross. We know only of Kuskov's census of 1820, in which he reported forty-two native Californian women cohabiting with Russian, Creole, and native Alaskan men (Fedorova 1975:12). Most of these women probably resided at the colony with their mates. It is possible that native women made up the majority of the native Californian population at Fort Ross at this time, and that other kin relations lived elsewhere.

The Later Years. While relations between the natives and colonists were friendly at first, visits to the Ross settlement, especially by men, became rarer and rarer over time (see Bancroft 1886:209, footnote 11). By the late 1820s and 1830s relations between the company employees and the local native population had begun to sour. The enmity was a direct consequence of the decision to intensify agricultural production in the Fort Ross Counter, which required tremendous investments of labor to till, sow, cultivate, harvest, and thresh wheat and barley crops. The increased labor demands fell squarely on the shoulders of the local natives. Thus, by the 1820s, a subtle change had taken place in the nature of the relationship between Russian administrators and na-

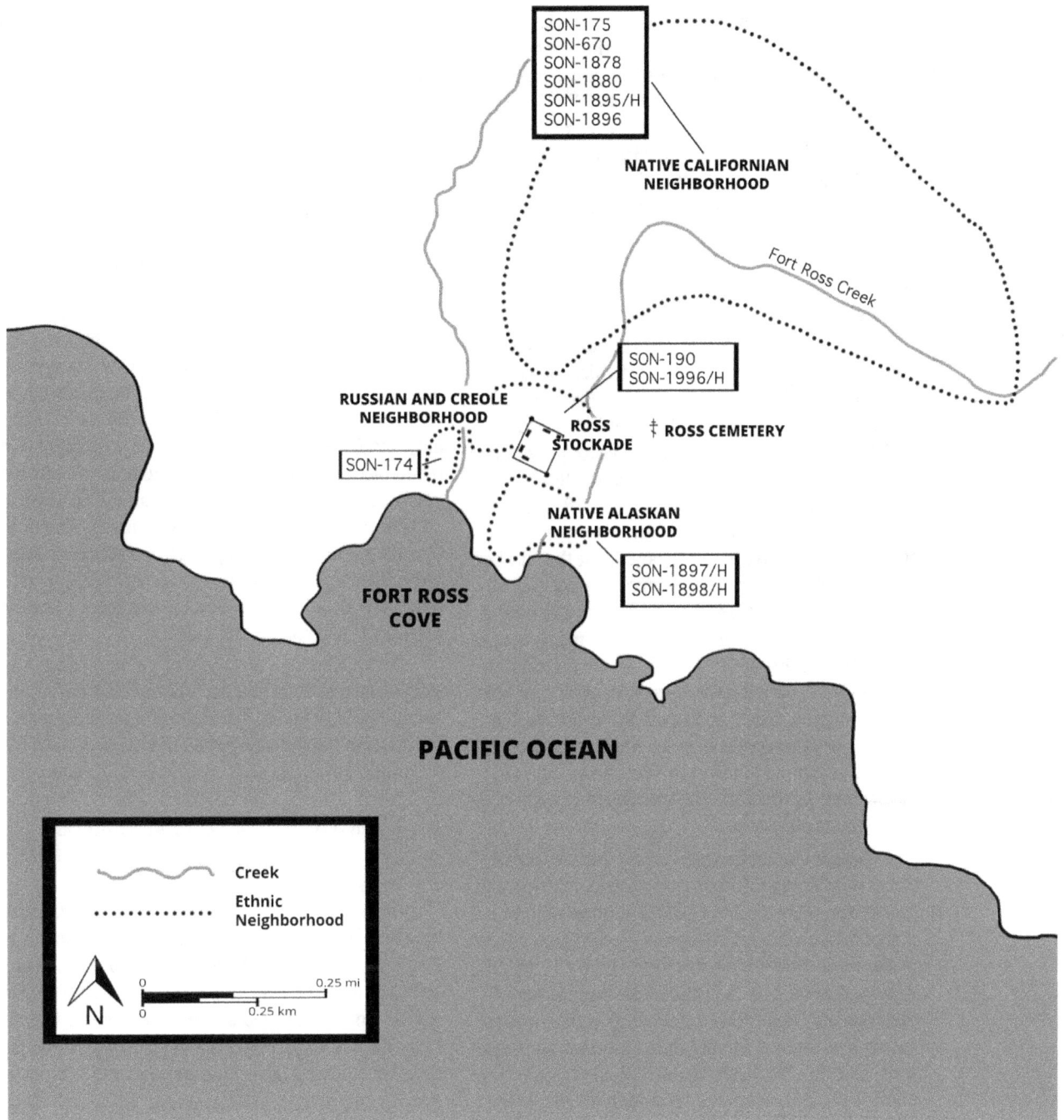

SON-175
SON-670
SON-1878
SON-1880
SON-1895/H
SON-1896

**NATIVE CALIFORNIAN
NEIGHBORHOOD**

Fort Ross Creek

SON-190
SON-1996/H

**RUSSIAN AND CREOLE
NEIGHBORHOOD**

**ROSS
STOCKADE**

‡ **ROSS CEMETERY**

SON-174

**NATIVE ALASKAN
NEIGHBORHOOD**

SON-1897/H
SON-1898/H

**FORT ROSS
COVE**

PACIFIC OCEAN

Creek

Ethnic
Neighborhood

0   0.25 mi

N   0   0.25 km

FIGURE 2.2   THE SPATIAL LAYOUT OF THE FORT ROSS SETTLEMENT

tive Californians, as the former began to view the latter as a cheap and necessary source of agricultural labor.

Not surprisingly, the Russians experienced problems in recruiting an adequate labor force. The native workers were often mistreated, working long hours for very little compensation that often consisted of "bad" food (Wrangell 1969:210-11 [1833]). To make matters worse, the Russians mounted armed raids against distant Pomo communities to capture agricultural workers. Wrangell (1969:210-11 [1833]) describes one such raid in which the Russians drove Indian men, women, and children almost seventy km to Fort Ross "like cattle" with their hands tied. Here they were forced to work without their household possessions for about a month and a half.

Labor shortages during the agricultural season were probably exacerbated by epidemics that swept through the native community at Fort Ross from the 1810s through the 1830s. Kostromitinov (1974:7 [1830-38]) notes that many native Californians north of San Francisco Bay "were exterminated by the pestilences which raged during the years 1815-1822." In 1828, a measles epidemic killed twenty-nine Creoles and Aleuts at the Ross Colony, while the number of native Californian casualties is not reported (Gibson 1976:128). In 1833, another measles epidemic disabled most of the payroll, and killed many native Californians (Gibson 1976:128). In the period from 1836 to 1839, varied epidemics of measles, chickenpox, whooping cough, and small pox struck the Russian-American colonies from the Aleutian Islands and Kodiak Island to California (Fedorova 1973:161; Tikhmenev 1978:198). The number of casualties at Fort Ross is unknown.

Historical sources suggest that the native population at this colony fluctuated greatly on a seasonal and yearly basis. By the late 1820s, a permanent population of natives appears to have been living somewhere in the hinterland of the stockade (Farris 1986a:68; Wrangell 1969:210-11 [1833]). During the agricultural season, from spring to fall, the population of the native Californian neighborhood swelled with seasonal laborers "recruited" from outlying Indian communities. For example, Wrangell (1969:210-11 [1833]) records seventy-two adult native Californians, probably the year-round population, in his 1833 census (table 2.1), and notes that an additional seventy-five people were mobilized from the surrounding region during the agricultural season. The growing labor demands of intensified agricultural production are exhibited in population estimates during the harvest season. The number of farm workers increased from 100 in 1825, to about 150 in 1833, to 200 in 1835 (Gibson 1976:119). In August 1839,

during the height of the harvest, LaPlace reports that "several hundred" native Californians resided in the vicinity of the garrison (see LaPlace 1986:65 [1839]).

The above descriptions point out a paradox in how the Russian-American Company treated native Californians. On one hand, the Russians took great pride in the freedom they gave native Californian workers in practicing traditional lifeways, including religious ceremonies, in contrast to the "despotism of tyrannical monks" in the Spanish missions (Kotzebue 1830:79-80, 123-24). There was little concerted effort by the Russian-American Company at Ross to convert native Californians to the Russian Orthodox faith or to get them to adopt Russian customs, foods, or material culture. What the native Californians did on their own time was their concern. Yet, on the other hand, the Russians could be very brutal about forcing local natives to work against their will. When agricultural production increased the labor demands of the Fort Ross Counter in the late 1820s and early 1830s, the Fort Ross administrators chose to exploit and manipulate the local native population. Ferdinand von Wrangell (1969:211), who toured Fort Ross in 1833 as the Chief Manager of the Russian-American Company, viewed these exploitative practices as counterproductive and attempted to correct them by initiating new policies for the better treatment of native workers in the Fort Ross Counter.

An archaeological survey of the immediate hinterland of the Ross stockade completed during the summers of 1988 and 1989 identified several sites that may date to the Russian period of occupation. A full description of these sites is presented in chapter 5.

The Study of Cultural Change:

Historical Evidence

In the final section of this chapter we examine how the economic practices of the Russian-American Company may have influenced the acculturation processes of the native Alaskans and native Californians at Fort Ross. From the outset we recognize that the two ethnic groups represent very different populations for studying the effects of mercantile colonization.

1) *Length of Time with Russians*. The Aleut, Koniag, and Athabascan workers brought to the Fort Ross Counter had already been exposed to Russian mercantile policies for three to four decades. In fact, some of the Koniags stationed there probably represent second generation hunters who had grown up in Russian colonies in the North Pacific. In contrast, the Kashaya Pomo, Southern Pomo, and Bodega Miwok had little sustained contact with non-Indian peoples until the founding of the Ross Colony, when they were

exposed to the commercial operations of a fur trade company for the first time.

2) *The Fort Ross Region.* The native Alaskans were thrust into a strange environment thousands of kilometers from their North Pacific homelands. The sea mammal hunters had to quickly adapt to alien coastal conditions. In contrast, the local Californians were permanent residents of the Fort Ross region who had developed an efficient regional subsistence-settlement system for exploiting local resources and maintaining local communities, a point taken up in more detail in chapter 5.

3) *Status Ranking.* The native Alaskans enjoyed a higher status in the Ross Colony than the local natives. This translated into better wages that could be used to purchase nonlocal goods and foodstuffs in the company store. As the lowest ranking group in the colony, the native Californians were treated as unskilled seasonal laborers who received little compensation for their work.

A Preliminary Consideration of Native Alaskan Responses to the Ross Colony

As wage earners, the specialized sea mammal hunters and skilled craftsmen participated in a market economy that paid them scrip redeemable at the company store. Beginning in the nineteenth century, the Russian-American Company's administrators established a trade network with American skippers who shipped manufactured goods and luxury foods to the Russian-American colonies. Most of the manufactured commodities appear to have been destined for native consumption (Gibson 1976:172). Did wage earning provide the material basis for altering the lifeways of native hunters brought up under an earlier mercantile system of corvée serfdom and hostage taking? Is there evidence of manufactured goods from around the world in native Alaskan houses or refuse from ethnic European foods? Or, as Wrangell (1969:211 [1833]) observed in 1833, were the salaries so low in relation to the company's high prices that many workers were actually in debt to the company store and unable to afford many luxury or manufactured goods?

The inter-ethnic relationships between the native Alaskans and Californians presents another potential source of cultural change. Pomo and Miwok kin ties may have served as important cultural sources for adapting to an alien environment. Is there evidence for Pomo/Miwok architectural innovations in native Alaskan residences or the adoption of Pomo/Miwok culture material, craft manufacture, and foods? How did the inter-ethnic households established in the native Alaskan village influence the lifeways of native Alaskan males?

It is impossible at this time to evaluate the above questions using archival information alone. The very limited observations that are currently known for the native Alaskan neighborhood preclude this. Rather the evaluation of these questions will depend primarily upon archaeological research. We will undertake the direct historical approach for generating a diachronic framework for studying cultural change among the native Alaskan population. In this case, the direct historical approach will involve the synthesis of late prehistoric and early historical cultural developments on Kodiak Island, Alaska. Fortunately, archaeological and ethnohistorical research has been ongoing on the Kodiak Island archipelago for several years, the purpose of which is to examine how early Russian colonial practices (hostage-taking, corvée labor) impacted the traditional lifeways of Kodiak and Aleut peoples (e.g., Black 1977; 1989; Clark 1974; 1985; Crowell 1990; Knecht 1985; Knecht and Jordan 1985; Jordan and Knecht 1988). By comparing the late prehistoric and early historical sites on Kodiak Island with the native Alaskan neighborhood at Fort Ross, we can begin to measure the degree of cultural change in material culture, architectural styles, diet, craft production, and settlement layout.

The historical context for employing the direct historical approach will be developed in Volume 2 of the Archaeology and Ethnohistory of Fort Ross, California series. In Volume 2, we will summarize late prehistoric and early historical developments on Kodiak Island, and describe the results to date of our ongoing archaeological investigations of the Native Alaskan Village Site and the Fort Ross Beach Site. A preliminary analysis will be undertaken to evaluate similarities and differences between the late prehistoric and early historic Alaskan populations on Kodiak Island and the native Alaskan neighborhood at Fort Ross in order to address the above questions.

A Preliminary Consideration of Native Californian Responses to the Ross Colony

We expect from the outset that the acculturation process of the native Californians may have differed from that of the native Alaskans. Historical texts suggest that the native Californians did not participate as extensively in a market economy as the native Alaskans. Since the former were paid in kind, access to luxury or manufactured goods was probably much more limited. We suspect that the primary agent of cultural change may have been through kin ties that linked Pomo/Miwok families with native Alaskan men, and to a lesser extent, Creole and Russian men. The effects of mercantile colonization were probably felt unequally among various segments of the local native population. We expect that the greatest cultural change would have taken place among the women who cohabited with non-Indian men, and next among families that resided year-round at Fort Ross. The least impact was probably felt among the seasonal farm workers who resided elsewhere but were coerced into working at Fort Ross for a few months a year.

In the remainder of this volume we will develop the direct historical approach in order to begin evaluating the magnitude of cultural change among local Pomo/Miwok people. We will describe the late prehistoric subsistence-settlement system of this region. We will then delineate the historic settlement system of Pomo/Miwok people in the hinterland of the Ross Colony. Finally, we will compare and contrast the findings of the archaeological investiga-

tion with early ethnohistoric observations, later ethnographies, and the oral traditions of the Kashaya Pomo. Employing these different data, we will evaluate those aspects of Kashaya Pomo culture that appear to have been receptive to change in a mercantile environment, and those that were resistant to change. We will attempt to examine changes in subsistence practices, technology, material culture, architectural styles, sociopolitical organization, religious institutions, and gender relations. A significant consideration is to determine whether the direction of cultural change stemmed from Russian influences, from native Alaskan inspirations, or from other sources.

CHAPTER THREE

THE NATURAL ENVIRONMENT OF

THE FORT ROSS REGION

THE FORT ROSS REGION encompasses roughly a 750 sq km area in the southern North Coast Ranges of Sonoma County in northern California (see figure 3.1). The size and boundaries of the region were carefully chosen so that they include much of the ethnographically described territory of the Kashaya Pomo (see chapter 6). This area is part of the Russian River Subregion as defined by Fredrickson (1984a:475-77) in his overview of north coastal archaeology in California. The western boundary of the Fort Ross region is a 50 km stretch of rocky coastline that extends from the contemporary towns of Gualala in the north to Jenner in the south. The North Fork of the Gualala River and the Russian River are the northern and southern boundaries of the region, respectively. The eastern boundary parallels the coast about ten to fifteen km ($\bar{x}$=12 km) into the rugged terrain of the North Coast Ranges, depending upon the shape of the coastline.

In this chapter we describe the overall physical environment of the Fort Ross region, including the topography, hydrology, geology, botany, and zoology. We divide the flora of the region into twelve basic plant communities that extend from the coastline to the interior mountainous habitats. The diverse range of plant and animal resources found in this region is detailed below.

TOPOGRAPHY

The Fort Ross region lies almost entirely within the southern portion of the North Coastal Ranges in a physiographic region known as the Mendocino Pla-

teau (Howard 1951; Kniffen 1939). The dominant topographic features of the area include: the coastline, the coastal terraces, the San Andreas Fault, the mountain/ridge systems, and the major river drainages.

The Coastline

The Sonoma County coast is quite rough, dominated by steep, jagged cliffs and rugged headlands that drop precipitously to a rocky, wave-swept shore. True sandy beaches are few and far between; typically they are found in relatively protected areas where streams and rivers empty into the sea. Some of these drainages, such as the Russian River and the Gualala River, have estuarine environments at their mouths. The majority of the coastline consists of either "open coast" or "protected outer coast" environments. Both of these coastal types support a wide variety of plant and animal species, representing a rich resource base. "Open coast," defined by Ricketts et al. (1985:6) as areas of "entirely unprotected, surf swept shores . . . ," extends along most of the Sonoma County coast. Much of this area is exposed, and at times dangerous, due to high surf and "sleeper waves." "Protected outer coast" is more limited in extent, consisting of relatively protected areas "where the force of the surf is somewhat dissipated . . . by headlands or offshore rocks" (Ricketts et al. 1985:5). This kind of protection is also afforded "by the refraction of waves as they reach headlands or rocks" (Ricketts et al. 1985:6). A number of locations in the Fort Ross region, such as Fort Ross Cove, Timber Cove, Fisk Mill Cove, and Horseshoe Cove can be defined as protected outer coast.

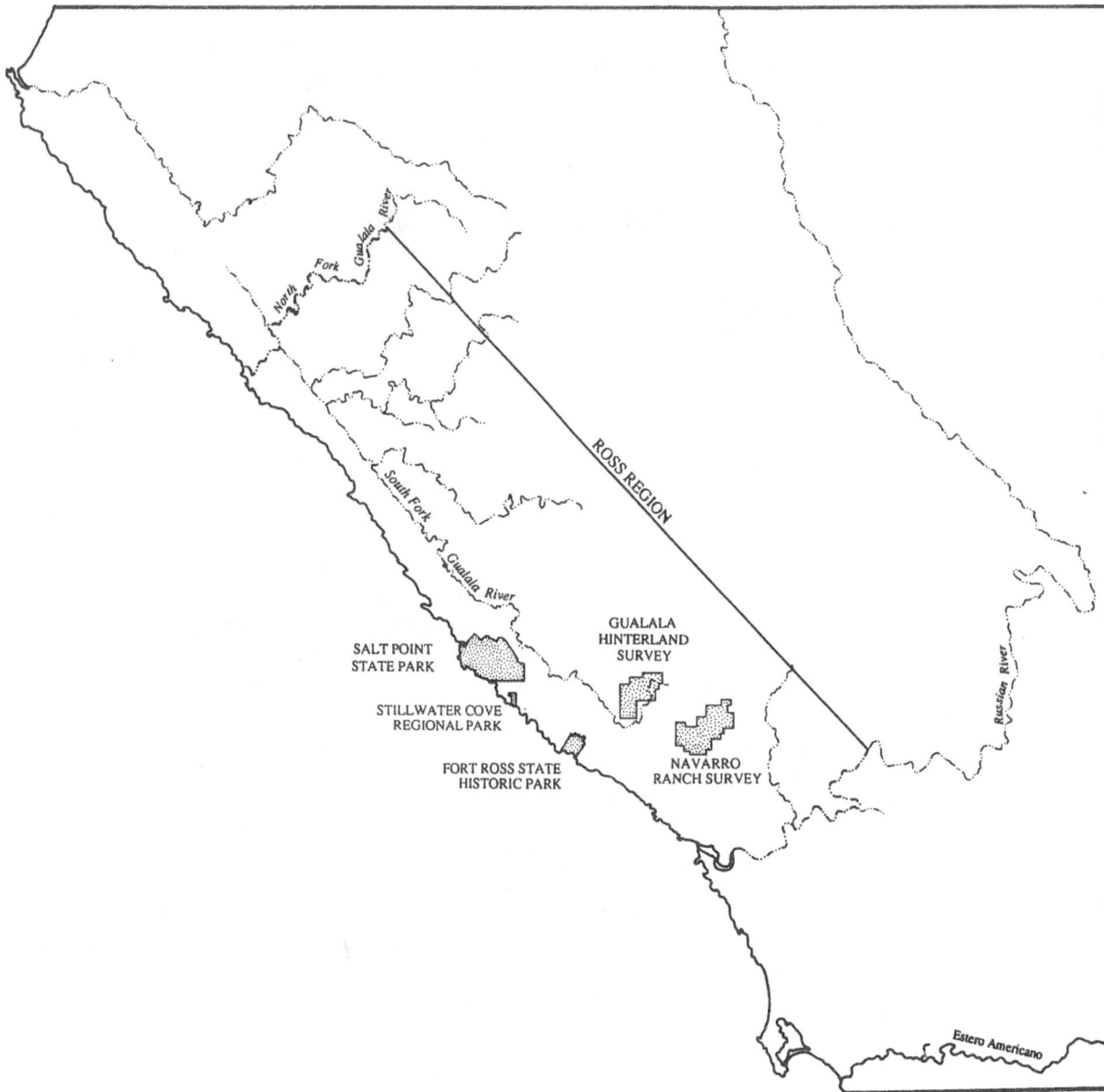

FIGURE 3.1   THE FORT ROSS REGION

Sea Level Change

The California coastline has undergone substantial reshaping over the past 15,000 years, primarily due to sea level change and coastal erosion. According to Milliman and Emery (1968) the average sea level was approximately 128 m lower at 15,000 B.P., 56 m lower at 10,000 B.P., and 18 m lower at 7,000 B.P. This suggests that 7,000 years ago almost 95% of the water locked in the continental glaciers had been released (Bloom 1971). Sea level rise has occurred much more slowly since then (Bloom 1983). The shoreline has been retreating over the last 6,000 years primarily because of coastal erosion. The rate of erosion varies, depending on the composition of the land, exposure to waves, and water depth (Williams and Bedrossian 1977:31). Sedimentary rocks near Santa Cruz, California (Griggs and Johnson 1979:76) erode at a rate of approximately 30 cm per year, on average, as do the formations on the San Mateo County coast (Sullivan 1975:31). Sedimentary rocks found around Fort Ross tend to erode at a rate of 0 to 9 m per 100 years (Ritter 1978:536). Consequently, the shoreline at Fort Ross 6000 years ago could have been as much as 540 m farther west than its present location.

The sea level changes have had a profound effect on the configuration of the coastline in central California. According to Bickel (1978), 20,000 square kilometers of land have been submerged over the past 15,000 years. Bickel (1978) states that these shoreline changes were greatest in areas where the continental shelf is broad and sloping, such as north of Cape Mendocino to the Oregon border and offshore of San Francisco Bay. The latter shoreline was approximately 35 km farther west, past what are now the Farallon Islands. The effects of eustatic change were more limited in areas where the continental shelf is steeper and narrower. In the Fort Ross region, the shoreline was only 15 km west of the modern Sonoma County coast 15,000 years ago (Bickel 1978; Moratto 1984). By about 10,000 years ago, the shoreline had retreated to approximately 5 km off the present day coastline in the study area. The implications of post-Pleistocene eustatic change are clear—the overall terrestrial area in the study area has been reduced considerably. The changing spatial distribution of coastal and terrestrial resources over time may have influenced prehistoric subsistence/settlement practices in the region.

Coastal Terraces

Just inland from the coast and extending up the seaward slope of the outermost Coast Range are a series of raised, wave-cut, marine terraces. These terraces are, in essence, fossil shorelines. Their presence indicates progressive tilting, caused in part by isostatic rebound of land areas no longer weighed down by glaciers (Bickel 1978:7). This uplift is greatest and most noticeable along the coast (Howard 1951:96). Prentice (1989:133) gives an uplift rate of approximately 0.49 mm per year for the southern Mendocino County coast. The highest and oldest terraces are over 300 m in elevation and approximately 420,000 years old. The lower terraces in the Ross region are the most prominent and best preserved since they are youngest. The terraces range in age from 83,000 to 103,000, 133,000, 214,000, and 320,000 years old (Prentice 1989:135). Also Prentice (1989:133) notes at least five submerged terraces offshore younger than 83,000 years old. While most of the lower terraces are only a few hundred meters wide, in certain places they can be as wide as one to three kilometers (Howard 1951).

The San Andreas Fault

Slightly inland from the coast and the terrace system lies the San Andreas rift zone. The San Andreas Fault itself comes ashore for the last time approximately 5.8 km south of Fort Ross (Bowen 1951). Fort Ross State Historic Park contains numerous classic faulting features such as sag ponds, scarps, hummocks, and offset creeks. The rift zone cuts across the younger marine terraces behind the historic stockade, right through the Old Russian Orchard. The 1906 earthquake severely damaged Fort Ross itself. The Russian Orthodox church was knocked down, other buildings flattened, and a number of picket sheep fences were displaced. One of these fences, displaced almost three meters, can still be seen near the state park's water treatment facility. Many Douglas fir and redwood trees were snapped off, bent, and knocked down during the earthquake. They can be seen standing in the forests along Fort Ross Creek and near the sag ponds just north of the Old Russian Orchard. One large redwood even had its trunk split by fault movement (Bowen 1951:323; LaMarche and Wallace 1972). The fault gradually angles farther inland, through Lower Lake and Lake Oliver (West 1988) near Plantation and on north to Manchester State Beach, where it disappears into the Pacific Ocean.

Mountains

The majority of the land in the region is mountainous and, in places, quite rugged. Near the coast, two ridge systems run generally north-south, on either side of the San Andreas Fault. Both of these ridges contain ancient marine terraces and owe much of their altitude to uplifting and tilting due predominantly to isostatic rebound and faulting. The longitudinal orientation of these steeply-sloping, parallel ridges is primarily caused by the slow northward creep of the land to the west of the fault.

The mountainous area to the east of the fault lies within the physiographic region known as the Mendocino Plateau (Kniffen 1939). Howard (1951:95) describes the Mendocino Plateau as a "sprawling dissected upland" which is actually a convergence of the Yolo, Napa, and Marin ranges, three of the four major parallel Coast Ranges just north of San Francisco Bay. The fourth of these ranges, the Sonoma Range, diminishes as it heads north from the bay and essentially disappears before it can converge with the others at the Mendocino Plateau. The plateau proper extends fifteen to thirty kilometers inland from the Marin Range north to Cape Mendocino. The plateau is submaturely dissected (Kniffen 1939), and therefore, quite rugged with steep slopes and deep, V-shaped canyons. Howard (1951:95) suggests that this area is actually an ancient, uplifted peneplain, due to the uniform altitude of the ridge crests and the scattered level summits found throughout the plateau. These summits rise gradually from 600 m in elevation in the west to 1,200 m in the eastern portions of the plateau.

Rivers and Streams

The highly dissected nature of this region is a reflection of its hydrology. Numerous small annual and perennial streams flow through the steep-sided, geologically-young canyons of the Mendocino Plateau. The majority of the creeks in the study area eventually flow into the South Fork or the Wheatfield Fork of the Gualala River, which empties into the Pacific Ocean near the town of Gualala at the Sonoma-Mendocino County line. Movement of the San Andreas Fault has greatly effected the morphology of the Gualala River drainage (Prentice 1989:173-82).

The other major drainage in the study area is Austin Creek. This creek drains the southeastern portion of the study area and empties into the Russian River, the largest river in Sonoma County and the southern limit of the Fort Ross region. A number of small creeks, including Russian Gulch, Fort Ross Creek, and Kolmer Gulch, flow off of the seaward slope of the Mendocino Plateau directly into the Pacific Ocean.

CLIMATE

The climate of the region is locally variable. Nevertheless, the area can be roughly divided into two climatic zones; coastal and interior. The coastal zones typically have cool average temperatures (13°c), much fog in the summer, and approximately 1006 mm of precipitation per year (Carlson et al. 1976). The interior zones are generally warmer and receive less precipitation. June through September are the dry months (less than 10 mm of precipitation) and temperatures can range as high as 40°c in the interior. The prevailing winds are from the northwest in the summer and become southerly in the winter. These winds are commonly 16 to 40 kph, with gusts up to 95 kph.

A study of tree rings from throughout western North America by Fritts (1965) reveals considerable climatic variation in the region over the past 400 years. According to Fritts (1965:439), Fort Ross would have been colonized during a relatively cool, wet period beginning in A.D. 1801, and lasting until 1820. Fritts (1965:439-40) also shows evidence, supported by the historical record, of a relatively hot, dry period (drought) beginning in 1836 and ending in 1865. Interestingly, this dry cycle corresponds to the final period of agricultural intensification at the Ross Colony.

GEOLOGIC HISTORY

The Mendocino Plateau and the Coast Ranges have evolved over many millions of years. As one moves west from the Sierra Nevada, California geology becomes progressively younger. According to Alt and Hyndman (1975:19), the Coast Ranges began to form during the late Jurassic period, approximately 150 million years ago. This was caused largely by the subduction of the Pacific Plate beneath the North American Plate. When these two plates collided, marine sediments were scraped off of the Pacific Plate as it submerged and pushed the sediments against the North American Plate. Consequently, new land was added to the western edge of North America (Alt and Hyndman 1975:5). The movement of marine sediments against the North American plate ended roughly 80 million years ago. The San Andreas Fault began moving approximately 40 to 50 million years ago (Alt and Hyndman 1975:20), when the continental crust bonded to the rock beneath it after subduction had ceased.

Miocene

Howard (1951) suggests that the pre-Miocene folding and faulting mentioned above are responsible for the variety of topographic detail in western California. The Coast Ranges, during the early Miocene, were part of a rolling coastal basin, lower in altitude than today. During this period the basin was subject to a great deal of sedimentation, because of periodic inundation by the ocean as the sea levels changed and erosion of the Sierra Nevada peneplain. The structural framework of the Coast Ranges consists mainly of the marine sediments scraped off of the Pacific Plate as it jammed up against and submerged beneath the North American Plate (Alt and Hyndman 1975). Ernst (1979:191) refers to this as "the capping crust of one or more paleopacific plates." Some intrusive igneous formations associated with movement along the San Andreas Fault also occur here. In the early

Miocene, further orogenic activity took place, mainly thrust faulting and uplifting. This activity established much of the composition, direction, and location of the present Coast Ranges (Howard 1951). During the middle and late Miocene, uplifting and erosion continued in this area, interrupted briefly by volcanic activity in the Petaluma area.

Pliocene

In the early Pliocene, shallow seas still filled the Miocene depositional basins in the Coast Ranges area. Prentice (1989:169) provides evidence of a large embayment between Fort Ross and Gualala during the Pliocene. The shoreline of this embayment seems to have been approximately ten km farther east than the present shore. A long, rugged land mass separated the interior from marine basins in the west. Throughout the Pliocene, erosion reduced the Miocene mountains and filled in the broad valleys between them, producing a true peneplain (Howard 1951). At the end of the Pliocene the entire Coast Ranges region was uplifted. Folding of younger sediments occurred and some strata were completely overturned. These newly uplifted ranges were immediately subject to erosion resulting in the deposition of coarse sediments well into the Pleistocene.

Pleistocene

Erosion continued during the early Pleistocene, resulting in continued filling of lower areas and the development of a relatively mature topography. In the mid-Pleistocene, considerable orogenic activity took place. New folds developed and block-faulting occurred on a large scale. The rapid uplifting in the mid-Pleistocene caused massive landslides. Much of the present coastline, raised out of the sea during the Miocene and Pliocene, was formed at this time (Howard 1951), and subsequently modified by the Holocene sea level rise, described above. This mid-Pleistocene activity was the last major orogenic activity in the area. Although much of this landscape has endured to modern times (Huffman and Armstrong 1980), subsequent erosion, subsidence, sea level rise, and faulting dominated by the San Andreas have also shaped present day western California. The San Francisco Bay was formed by local subsidence during the late Pleistocene that continued into the early period of human occupation (Alt and Hyndman 1975; Howard 1951; Louderback 1951; Schenck 1926). A massive landslide approximately one km from Fort Ross has been dated to the Pleistocene (Prentice 1989:96). Many features in the San Andreas rift zone, such as the displacement of Fort Ross Creek, the sag ponds in Fort Ross State Historic Park and near Plantation, fault scarps, and scarred trees, are due to post-Pleistocene geologic/tectonic activity.

CONTEMPORARY GEOLOGY

The tortured geologic history of this region has resulted in a jumbled mixture of rocks, minerals, and geologic formations in Sonoma County. A simplified version of the region's complicated geology is presented here (e.g. figure 5.2). Weaver (1943) also describes the geology of this region. The Sonoma County coast is made up of two distinct geologic core complexes: 1) the Early Cretaceous granitic intrusives and older metamorphic rocks (the Salinian Block) to the west of the San Andreas Fault, and 2) the Jurassic-Cretaceous eugeosynclinal assemblage (the Franciscan Formation) to the east of the fault (Page 1966:255). These core complexes are typically overlain with more recent sedimentary, and in some places, plutonic formations.

Salinian Block

Classic Salinian Block core formations of Mid-Cretaceous hornblende-biotite, quartz diorite and granodiorite are found just south of the study area at Bodega Head, Point Reyes, and the Farallon Islands (Compton 1966:286). The presence of true "Salinian" rocks is not mentioned specifically by Compton (1966), Page (1966), or Taliaferro (1951). Nonetheless, the presence of Salinian Core complex related rocks in the Fort Ross region is inferred from available geologic maps (Armstrong 1980a, b; Blake et al. 1971) that reveal Salinian complex Cretaceous and Tertiary sedimentary rocks west of the San Andreas Fault from just south of Fort Ross to the Gualala River. While there is some spilite (sodic basalt) near Black Point (Armstrong 1980a, 1980b; Blake et al. 1971), the majority of the rocks to the west of the San Andreas Fault are well-bedded sandstone and mudstone conglomerates containing potassium feldspar (Armstrong 1980a, 1980b; Blake et al. 1971). Many of the metamorphic rocks typical of the Salinian Block such as the gneisses, schists, quartzites, marbles, and granulites found in the Sur Formation, are not found here. Along the California coast these later formations frequently are overlain with quaternary marine terrace deposits.

Franciscan Formation

The majority of the land area in the Fort Ross region lies to the east of the San Andreas Fault and is considered part of the Franciscan Formation. Page (1966:258) describes the Franciscan Formation as ". . . a vast, diverse assemblage of eugeosynclinal rocks with unsystematic structure and without the regional metamorphism and granitic plutons of the other [Salinian] complex (Page 1966:258)." This formation has undergone tremendous, unsystematic disturbance throughout its existence.

Sandstone. The most common rock type found in the Franciscan Formation is sandstone, mainly graywacke. The sandstone beds generally range from 0.3 to 3 m in thickness. The sand grains in Franciscan graywackes are angular and medium in size. The majority of the sand grains are plagioclase and quartz, with particles of greenstone, chert, shale, and schist (Page 1966:258). Bailey et al. (1964:30) find that Franciscan graywackes average approximately thirty-five percent feldspar. Page (1966:258) believes that "the graywacke sediments are very immature, were derived by rapid erosion, and were deposited swiftly without normal wave action, probably in part by mass flows and turbidity currents."

Shale. According to Page (1966:258) shales make up approximately ten percent of the Franciscan Formation. Shale typically occurs between graywacke beds or locally thicker units. These shales are mainly gray to black, silty, brittle, and fissile.

Conglomerate. Conglomerate is uncommon in the Franciscan Formation. It typically occurs in lenses in graywacke and shale sequences. Conglomerate clasts include: quartzite, siliceous porphyritic-aphanitic rocks, granitic cobbles, black, red, and green chert, greenstone, and rocks containing jadeite or glaucophane (Page 1966:258). This indicates destruction and redeposition of older facies of the Franciscan Formation, which is consistent with the general geologic history mentioned above.

Volcanics. According to Bailey et al. (1964:6) Franciscan volcanic rocks, termed greenstones, are widespread and comprise approximately ten percent of the total assemblage. Most of these greenstones are "pillows, tuffs, or breccias resulting from submarine eruptions, but some massive units may be intrusive." Plagioclase and augite are the most common minerals. Olivine is rare. The composition of most of these greenstones has been altered through reaction with sea water.

Cherts. Page (1966:259) states that "Franciscan cherts are distinctive, thin bedded, green or red, closely jointed rocks commonly associated with the greenstones." These cherts are composed mainly of chalcedonic quartz without clastic grains. Franciscan chert usually contains a few scattered fossilized Radiolaria tests. Volcanic rocks are commonly found near these cherts. Bailey et al. (1964:65-68) believe that these cherts are actually chemical precipitates formed by the reaction of lavas exposed to sea water. They conclude that Franciscan cherts were formed by the contribution of silica to sea water from lava at a depth of 3900 m or more. At that depth water attains a temperature of approximately 350 degrees centigrade without boiling and can dissolve large quantities of silica. The dissolved silica would then precipitate as a gel as the water cools (Page 1966:259). The

vast majority of stone tools and debitage found archaeologically in the study area are of red, green, and gray Franciscan cherts.

Limestone. Some limestone occurs within the region. Franciscan limestone is usually encountered in small, discontinuous bodies. Generally light or white in color, it sometimes contains lenses of gray chert. This limestone is fine grained and contains tests of pelagic Foraminifera, calcareous algae, corals, and Pelecypods (Page 1966:259). The relationship of Franciscan limestones to volcanic rocks is not yet fully understood. Some believe that these limestones represent reef and lagoonal deposits on old volcanic piles. Others believe this limestone was deposited by chemical precipitation of lime into seawater by hot, subaqueous lava. Page (1966:259) states that the lava might have infused lime into the sea water, and heat may have caused precipitation of the lime by driving off carbon dioxide. Larger deposits can be found near Elk and Laytonville (Hart 1978:7).

Metamorphics. Relatively uncommon kinds of metamorphic rocks are characteristic of the Franciscan Formation (Page 1966:259). The presence of these types of metamorphic rocks indicates ". . . periods of rapid convergence and profound underflow of the Franciscan terrane . . . " (Ernst 1979:192). Glaucophane-bearing rocks, jadeitized graywacke, and eclogite occur in widely distributed lenses with larger masses in the eastern parts of the Fort Ross region. These rocks were probably formed under high pressure at only moderate temperatures (Page 1966:259). This geologic condition can occur through rapid burial and uplift, or great tectonic stresses. Both of these effects are consistent with the proposed geologic history of the area.

Glaucophane appears in a variety of rocks, including blueschist. Over fifty blueschist blocks have been mapped in the Gualala River drainage (Prentice 1989:178). Glaucophane-bearing rocks seem to be formed isochemically from basalts and graywackes (Ernst 1965).

Some jadeite occurs in the Fort Ross region. Much of this jadeite is of low quality and hardly distinguishable from the graywacke that it replaces (Page 1966:259). Jadeite is often confused with the more common green Franciscan chert found on beaches and in streams in the region.

Eclogite is sparsely distributed in the study area. Usually occurring as lumps or masses within other rocks as a result of tectonic activity (Page 1966:260), eclogite has sparked considerable debate concerning its source. Some believe eclogite originated in the mantle, others believe it is crustal, derived from purely tectonic pressures (Coleman et al. 1965).

Serpentine. Ultramafic rocks, especially serpentine, are commonly found in the Franciscan Formation. Some serpentine localities seem to be the result of molten intrusions. The majority of serpentines in the study area appear to be non-molten or cold intrusions. According to Page (1966:290) "cold intrusion is indicated by [the] lack of contact metamorphism and typical igneous contacts, and by the sheared, slickensided structure of the masses." The likely source of these ultramafic rocks is the mantle, which probably immediately underlies the Franciscan Formation.

Ohlson Ranch Formation

The Franciscan Formation rocks in the Fort Ross region are locally overlain with marine terrace deposits of the Ohlson Ranch Formation. This formation developed during the Pliocene and now lies in the northwestern portion of Sonoma County. The Ohlson Ranch Formation consists primarily of poorly-exposed, fine-grained siltstones, sandstones, and conglomerates. Prentice cites paleontological and depositional evidence demonstrating that it was deposited in a low-stress, marine environment, such as a bay or inlet (Prentice 1989:165).

Economic Mineral Deposits

There has been limited exploitation of economic minerals within the boundaries of this region. A coal mine, established under an agreement between William Benitz and the Fort Ross Coal Mine Company, operated on a ten-year lease beginning in 1863 (Tomlin 1991:29). This mine has yet to be accurately relocated, although John McKenzie (retired Ranger/Curator of Fort Ross State Historic Park) has marked the former entrance of the mine with a metal stake. An abandoned manganese mine remains near the confluence of Turner Canyon and the South Fork of the Gualala River. Chromite deposits have been exploited at the Laton Mine, located in "The Cedars" near the head of Austin Creek. Mercury is known to be in the area to the north of the Laton Mine. This area also contains magnesite deposits. The Kashaya Pomo inhabitants of the area valued highly cooked magnesite beads. Local European inhabitants and the Kashaya themselves, however, seem to have been unaware of the local magnesite deposits (Stewart 1943). The study area has a number of gravel pits. Serpentine, present in the Fort Ross region, is known to contain asbestos. There is no indication, however, of asbestos exploitation in western Sonoma County.

SOILS

The soils of the study area have been thoroughly examined and mapped by the California State Cooperative Soil-Vegetation Survey (DeLapp and Powell 1979a; DeLapp et al. 1978). The type of soil in a given area varies greatly with relation to slope, exposure, and available parent material. Soils in this area range from less than 30 cm in depth to greater than 2 m in depth. The majority of the soils are between 60 cm and 1 m in depth. As would be expected, these soils reflect their Franciscan Formation heritage. The most common soils are derived from sandstone and shale. A number of less common soil types derived from conglomerate and metamorphic rocks are also found in the region. Most of the soil types are moderately acidic, very few are neutral or slightly alkaline. The soils are typically light to dark brown, but range from lateritic reddish brown to light gray. (For a more detailed description of soil types in the region refer to Soil-Vegetation Maps; 61D-3, 61C-4, and 63A-2, published by the Pacific Southwest Forest and Range Experiment Station.)

The depth, slope, and water retention of these soils helps determine the plant life they can support. For example, serpentine soils are typically shallow, retain little water, and are moderately to steeply sloping. They usually support chaparral or grassland plant communities. Few plants other than certain specially adapted species grow in these soils. The dense redwood and mixed evergreen forests covering much of the Fort Ross region are found on deeper, moister, more fertile soils.

BOTANY

A wide variety of native plant species and distinct plant communities occur in the region. Many of these plants were used by the prehistoric and historic inhabitants of the area for a variety of purposes including food, medicines, and tools (Barrett 1952, Chestnut 1902, Gifford 1967, Loeb 1926; Goodrich, Lawson and Lawson 1980). For a list of selected species and their uses see appendix 3.1.

Botanical History

Over the past 2,000 years the composition of these species has undergone considerable fluctuation. Based on palynological analysis of sediment cores from Lake Oliver and Lower Lake, near Plantation, West (1988:14) has interpreted three different forest compositions. The earlier redwood-dominated forest compositions had a significant shrub understory consisting mainly of wax myrtle, bracken ferns, and heath family (Ericaceae) plants. Following this was a period of relative increase in redwood, cypress, and yew pollen values, and a dramatic decrease in shrub (Ericaceae) and herb pollen values. West also provides evidence, based on carbon-dated charcoal found in his sediment cores, of at least one significant wildfire around 1620 B.P. The period following the second general period exhibits an increase in Douglas fir and exotic pollen, indicating the advent of Historic period logging and grazing practices (West 1988).

A number of plant species that are not native to California are found in the study area (see appendix 3.1). Most of these introduced species are native to Europe (Munz and Keck 1973). They were introduced by settlers primarily as fodder for domesticated animals, crops, or decoration (Jepson 1925). Certain exotic species have been very successful in California and have subtly changed the state's botanic character. European grasses, for example, have outcompeted and largely replaced native grass species in the Fort Ross region and throughout the state. West (1988:12) documents the introduction of exotic plant species near Fort Ross during the Historic period. During this same period Douglas fir and especially redwoods were intensively harvested. The introduction of cattle also seems to have contributed to an increase in European grasses (West 1988:12). These anthropogenic disturbances greatly altered the flora of the region.

Botanic Associations

We have divided the flora of the study area into twelve basic plant communities after Munz and Keck (1973) (see table 3.1). The term community as used here refers to "an aggregation of living organisms having mutual relationships among themselves and to their environment" (Munz and Keck 1973). These plant communities often grade into one another across the landscape and range in density from closed-canopy forests to relatively open oak savannahs or even open grassland. Many individual species can be found in more than one specific plant community, however the communities discussed here distinguish themselves by having a number of species more or less restricted to them such as dominants or indicator species (Munz and Keck 1973).

The distribution of plant communities in the Fort Ross region and California as a whole is complex and varied. The positioning of these communities on the landscape is by no means haphazard. A number of edaphic and climatic factors including salinity, rainfall, exposure, and soil type help determine the plant community that will be found in a given area (Munz and Keck 1973).

In order to simplify the botanical picture at Fort Ross and to facilitate the analysis of vegetation/site associations in chapter 4, areas covered by some of the relatively discrete plant communities listed in table 3.1, and described below, have been placed in broader categories. The plant communities dominated by pure, closed-canopy stands of coniferous species such as those found in the Closed-Cone Pine Forest, Redwood Forest, Douglas Fir Forest, and Northern Coastal Coniferous Forest are identified as "Coniferous Forest." Areas of closed-canopy forest dominated by a mix of coniferous and broad-leafed species, including

oaks, such as those found in Mixed Evergreen Forest, Northern Oak Woodland, and Foothill Woodland are defined as "Mixed Forest–with oaks." Areas of mixed forest in which oaks are not present are described as "Mixed Forest–without oaks." Plant communities of diffuse, open canopy and/or patchy forest are identified as "Savannah." "Grassland" connotes areas devoid of forest including grassland, cultivated fields, and bare patches. Chaparral and northern coastal scrub communities are called "Scrub."

Many of the plant communities discussed below have disjunct distributions and often occur as islands within one another. Their respective distributions can be greatly dissected with irregular lines of contact and often have numerous transitional areas due to the variety of topographic and climatic regimes occurring in the region (Munz and Keck 1973). Plant communities with greater moisture demands are commonly found in more sheltered areas and fog zones. Plants better adapted to drier conditions, on the other hand, grow in steeper, more exposed areas with poorer soils. For example, north-facing slopes are often covered by different plant communities than south-facing slopes due to the degree of exposure and the amount of water that remains in the soil after evaporation. Kniffen (1939), referring to the Southwestern Pomo area, states that "in the deep valleys along the perennial streams, on the well-protected north slopes, tree growth is heavy. On the higher slopes with southerly exposures there are numerous and good-sized natural openings where the vegetation cover is grass and shrubs rather than trees." As one moves toward the ocean, different constraints, such as tolerance to salinity, are placed on plant communities.

Of course, differing levels of salinity tolerance occur within the plant communities closest to the ocean. The plant community with the greatest tolerance for salinity can be found, not surprisingly, in the rocky intertidal area on the open coast and protected outer coast areas (after Ricketts et al. 1985). Plants that can tolerate a lesser degree of salinity and exposure are found in the Coastal Strand, Northern Coastal Scrub, Coastal Prairie, and Closed-Cone Pine Forest communities. These communities are arranged one behind the other along the coast on the slopes, quaternary terraces, cliffs, and the few beaches between the moist forests and the sea. As one moves inland the level of salinity decreases in two ways. Less salt spray is carried inland, and the salts that do arrive in the more inland areas are diluted by rainfall. Typically the Closed-Cone Pine Forest occurs on the coastal side of the Redwood, Douglas Fir, and Mixed Evergreen Forests. The Northern Coastal Scrub and Coastal Prairie communities are usually found sandwiched between the conifer forests and the Coastal Strand (Kniffen 1939, Munz and Keck 1973).

Table 3.1

PLANT COMMUNITIES FOUND IN THE FORT ROSS REGION

Rocky Intertidal

Coastal Strand

Northern Coastal Scrub

Coastal Prairie

Closed-Cone Pine Forest

Redwood Forest

Douglas Fir Forest

Northern Coastal Coniferous Forest

Mixed Evergreen Forest

Northern Oak Woodland

Foothill Woodland

Chaparral

After Munz and Keck 1973; Ricketts et al. 1985.

In general, the plant communities requiring the greatest amounts of water such as Redwood Forest, Douglas Fir Forest, and Mixed Evergreen Forest are arranged more or less parallel to the coast in the first ridge system (and farther inland northwards), along larger watercourses, in the higher elevations inland, and in relatively protected areas that retain moisture such as deep canyons and north-facing slopes. Plant communities adapted to the more xeric conditions of the interior such as Northern Oak Woodland, Foothill Woodland, and Chaparral are found inland—beyond, or in, more exposed areas within the moister forests. The exposed, south-facing slopes with poorer soils and in more lightly watered ranges of hills support those communities most highly adapted to xeric conditions, Chaparral and Grassland.

The twelve plant communities listed in table 3.1 are basic plant species associations, as described by Munz and Keck (1973), and many species in them are not necessarily constrained to a specific community. Their description here is intended to give the reader a sense of the complexity of the organization of these communities on the landscape, their exploitation by indigenous people, and their relations to climate and other factors such as exposure and soils. Generally moving inland from the ocean to the mountainous areas, the plant communities are described below.

Rocky Intertidal. The rocky intertidal plant community consists almost exclusively of red (*Protista*; *Rhodophyta*), brown (*Protista*; *Phaeophyta*), and green (*Protista*; *Chlorophyta*) seaweeds. Ricketts et al. (1985) divide the rocky intertidal area into four discrete zones: Zone 1, the Uppermost Horizon; Zone 2, the High Intertidal; Zone 3, the Middle Intertidal; and Zone 4, the Low Intertidal. Seaweeds inhabit all of these zones, however, species diversity is greatest in zones 2, 3, and 4. Some of the seaweeds found in the Rocky Intertidal are listed in appendix 3.1. Two intertidal species of surfgrass (Zosteraceae), *Phyllospadix torreyi* and *P. scouleri*, also occur within the Fort Ross region.

Coastal Strand. Terrestrial plants that can tolerate the greatest amount of salinity and consequently can survive closest to the ocean are included in the Coastal Strand community. Plants in this community grow on the sandy beaches and dunes scattered along the coast for the entire length of the state. These plants tend to be low or prostrate and are often succulent and late flowering. Average rainfall ranges from 381 to 1778 mm, with much fog and wind. The Coastal Strand plant community was exploited for a variety of purposes by indigenous peoples (see appendix 3.1). Some representative plants include: tree lupine (*Lupinus arboreus*), beach strawberry (*Fragaria chiloensis*), Douglas's bunchgrass (*Poa douglasii*), and beach morning glory (*Convolvulus soldanella*).

Northern Coastal Scrub. The Coastal Strand grades into the Northern Coastal Scrub and/or Coastal Prairie plant associations farther inland. Northern Coastal Scrub extends from southern Oregon to San Mateo County (Munz and Keck 1973). This plant community is typically sandwiched between the Coastal Strand and the Northern Coastal Coniferous Forest up to about 150 m in elevation. Rainfall averages from 635 to 1905 mm, with much fog and wind. This scrub is usually under two meters in height and can be quite dense. Nonetheless, Northern Coastal Scrub is often closely associated with large areas of Coastal Prairie. Some common Northern Coastal Scrub plants include: coyote brush (*Baccharis pilularis*), northern bush monkeyflower (*Mimulus auranticus*), California blackberry (*Rubus ursinus*), cow parsnip (*Heracleum lanatum*), and salal (*Gaultheria shallon*).

Coastal Prairie. Coastal Prairie can be found from the San Francisco Bay area northwards on the marine terraces and the western slopes of the outer and middle coast ranges up to about 1200 m in elevation (Munz and Keck 1973). Average rainfall ranges from 635 to 1016 mm, with much fog and wind. This plant community was originally dominated by native bunch grasses and flowering herbs, but has now been partly superseded by introduced annual grasses. In coastal areas Coastal Prairie often intergrades with Northern Coastal Scrub (Munz and Keck 1973). Indigenous people seem to have exploited many Coastal Prairie plants (see appendix 3.1). Some typical Coastal Prairie plants include: western fescue (*Festuca occidentalis*), California oatgrass (*Danothia californica*), Pacific reedgrass (*Calamagrostis nutkaensis*), Pacific hairgrass (*Deschampsia caespitosa*), coast sedge (*Carex tumulicola*), coast brodiaea (*Brodiaea pulchella*), wild iris (*Iris douglasiana*), blue-eyed grass (*Sisyrinchium bellum*), Mariposa lily (*Calochortus lureus*), and coast lupine (*Lupinus formosus*).

Closed-Cone Pine Forest. Throughout much of the Fort Ross region the coastal scrub and prairie are separated from the redwood, Douglas fir, and mixed evergreen forests by stands of Closed-Cone Pine Forest. These forests are found from Santa Barbara County to the Mendocino plains in the north, from sea level to around 365 m in elevation. Munz and Keck (1973) state that "northward it [Closed-Cone Pine Forest] is on the seaward side of the redwoods in barren soils." Trees 10 to 30 m tall grow in these relatively dense forests. Rainfall averages from 508 to 1524 mm, with much fog. This plant community does not seem to contain many species exploited by indigenous people (c.f. Barrett 1952, Chestnut 1902, Gifford 1967). Some of the common Closed-Cone Pine Forest plants include: Bishop pine (*Pinus muricata*), beach pine (*Pinus contorta*), and pigmy cypress (*Cupressus pygmaea*).

Redwood Forest. Redwood forests are found from southern Oregon to central Monterey County, from 3 to 915 m in elevation on the seaward slopes of the outer coast ranges. Rainfall ranges from 889 to 2540 mm, with frequent, dense fog. Redwoods can get exceedingly tall, as high as 110 m, and usually grow in dense stands (Munz and Keck 1973). The redwood forests, described in anthropological literature as "gloomy" and unproductive (Kniffen 1939), contain many species of plants used extensively by indigenous people such as the preferred acorn producer, the tan oak, (*Lithocarpus densiflora*), and medicinal plants such as redwood sorrel (*Oxalis oregona*), white alder (*Alnus rhombifolia*), and California nutmeg (*Torreya californica*) (Barrett 1952, Gifford 1967; see appendix 3.1). Some typical Redwood Forest plant species include: coast redwood (*Sequoia sempervirens*), Douglas fir (*Pseudotsuga menziesii*), Pacific wax-myrtle (*Myrica californica*), California huckleberry (*Vaccinium ovatum*), salal (*Gaultheria shallon*), coast rhododendron (*Rhododendron californicum*), sword fern (*Polystichum munitum*), western trillium (*Trillium ovatum*), western yew (*Taxus brevifolia*), and Yerba de Selva (*Whipplea modesta*).

Douglas Fir Forest. Douglas Fir Forest communities are scattered through Marin and Sonoma counties, but mainly occur from Mendocino County northwards. This type of forest is usually found to the east of the Redwood Forest on east- and north-facing slopes (Munz and Keck 1973). In the Fort Ross Region it occurs almost as far west as the coast and is often mixed in amongst stands of redwoods. Its trees can get up to 60 m in height; and rainfall ranges from 635 to 1651 mm, with much fog. Some plants from this community were exploited by indigenous people, especially the ubiquitous tan oak and the madrone (*Arbutus menziesii*) (see appendix 3.1). Typical Douglas Fir Forest plants include: Douglas fir (*Pseudotsuga menziesii*), tan oak (*Lithocarpus densiflora*), giant chinquapin (*Castanopsis chrysophylla*), and sugar pine (*Pinus lambertiana*).

Northern Coastal Coniferous Forest. Northern Coastal Coniferous Forest can be found in the outer coast ranges from Mendocino County north. Restricted patches are found as far south as Sonoma County, from sea level to 300 m. Rainfall ranges from 1016 to 2794 mm, with frequent fog. The forests are dense, with much undergrowth and trees between 45 and 60 m tall. The yew tree (*Taxus brevifolia*), found in these (and other conifer forests), was very important to the indigenous people for food, medicine, and especially bows (Barrett 1952, Gifford 1967, Kniffen 1939, Loeb 1926). Common plants of this community include: grand fir (*Abies grandis*), Douglas fir (*Pseudotsuga menziesii*), bigleaf maple (*Acer macrophyllum*), western hemlock (*Tsuga heterophylla*), and western yew (*Taxus brevifolia*).

Mixed Evergreen Forest. Mixed Evergreen Forest is typically found along the inner edge of the Redwood Forest and on higher hills within it from 150 to 760 m in elevation (Munz and Keck 1973). Occurring mainly in the North Coast Ranges, this community can be found as far south as the northern Santa Lucia Mountains. Rainfall ranges from 635 to 1651 mm, with some fog. Many of the plants in this type of forest can also be found in Redwood Forest and Northern Oak Woodland communities. Indigenous people extensively exploited many plants in this community, especially the oak species. Trees in this relatively dense forest grow as high as 30 m, often with dense underbrush and small islands of Coastal Prairie Grassland. Some typical Mixed Evergreen Forest plants include: tan oak (*Lithocarpus densiflora*), madrone (*Arbutus menziesii*), Douglas fir (*Pseudotsuga menziesii*), giant chinquapin (*Castanopsis chrysophylla*), laurel (*Umbellaria californica*), bigleaf maple (*Acer macrophyllum*), canyon live oak (*Quercus chrysolepis*), California black oak (*Quercus kelloggii*), hazelnut (*Corylus californica*), mountain dogwood (*Cornus nuttallii*), Parry ceanothus (*Ceanothus parryi*), and blueblossom (*Ceanothus thyrsiflorus*).

Northern Oak Woodland. Northern Oak Woodland is found in the North Coast Ranges from Humboldt and Trinity counties in the north to Napa County in the south. This community occurs inland from the Redwood Forest and up to an altitude of 915 to 1525 m. Rainfall averages from 635 to 1016 mm, with little fog. Trees reach 8 to 23 m high in relatively open woodland without significant undergrowth. Many of the plants in this community were exploited by indigenous people (appendix 3.1). Common Northern Oak Woodland plant species include: Oregon oak (*Quercus garryana*), California black oak (*Quercus kelloggii*), canyon live oak (*Quercus chrysolepis*), interior live oak (*Quercus wislizinii*), bigleaf maple (*Acer macrophyllum*), buckeye (*Aesculus californica*), and common manzanita (*Arctostaphylos manzanita*).

Foothill Woodland. Foothill Woodland communities occur on the inner Coast Ranges, from Trinity County to Santa Barbara County, at elevations from 120 to 915 or even 1525 m. Rainfall averages from 381 to 1016 mm, with little or no fog. Trees are 5 to 20 m in height, in either dense or open woodland, with scattered brush and grassland. Indigenous people exploited a number of the plants in this community. Representative species of the Foothill Woodland plant community include: digger pine (*Pinus sabiniana*), Coulter pine (*Pinus coulteri*), blue oak (*Quercus douglasii*), coast live oak (*Quercus agrifolia*), valley oak (*Quercus lobata*), laurel (*Umbellaria californica*), buckeye (*Aesculus californica*), California coffeeberry (*Rhamnus californica*), buck brush (*Ceanothus cuneatus*), and yerba santa (*Eriodictyon californicum*).

Chaparral. Chaparral is typically found on dry slopes and ridges in the Coast Ranges from Shasta County south, and grows in rocky, gravelly, or heavy soils (Munz and Keck 1973). Rainfall averages from 355 to 635 mm, with no fog. An almost impenetrable, broad-leafed, sclerophyll vegetation type, chaparral is well suited to the drier conditions of the interior. It usually ranges from 1 to 3 m in height. Many of the plant species in this community were exploited by indigenous people. Typical Chaparral plants include: chamise (*Adenostoma fasciculatum*), toyon (*Heteromeles arbutifolia*), California coffeeberry (*Rhamnus californica*), scrub oak (*Quercus dumosa*)), mountain mahogany (*Cercocarpus betuloides*), flannel bush (*Fremontia californica*), ceanothus (*Ceanothus spp.*), manzanita (*Arctostaphylos spp.*), and vinegarweed (*Trichostema lanatum*).

ZOOLOGY

The occurrence and habits of selected vertebrate animal species are described below. For lists of commonly occurring animals' scientific names, common names, and uses by indigenous people refer to appendices 3.2 through 3.6. Some vertebrate animal species in the Fort Ross region are associated with specific plant communities, while others are less constrained, exploiting a variety of plant communities and habitats. A number of animal species, once common in the region, have been severely impacted or extirpated in historic times.

Zoological History

The paleontology of this region is poorly known. Nonetheless, it can be generally inferred that the Pliocene Clarendonian, Hemphillian, and Blancan faunas including giant tortoises, cranes (*Grus conferta*), flamingos (*Phoenicopteridae*), rabbits (*Hypolagus*), mice (*Cupidinimus, Peromyscus, Pliotomodon*), ground sloths (*Megalonychidae*), hyaenoid dogs (*Aelurodon, Osteoborus, Borophagus*), foxes (*Vulpes vafer*), mustelids (*Cernictus*), large cats (*Pseudaelurus*), mastodons (*Gomphotherium simpsoni*), horses (*Nannipus, Hipparion, Neohipparion, Pliohippus, Equus*), rhinoceroses (*Teleoceras*), peccaries (*Prosthennops*), camels (*Pliauchenia, Paracamelus*), and antelope (*Merycodus, Spenophalos*) may have once roamed the Sonoma County landscape (Stirton 1951).

It is also likely that the Pleistocene Irvingtonian and Rancholabrean faunas including Emydid turtles, geese (*Branta canadensis*), murres (*Uria aalge*), ground squirrels (*Spermophilus [Citellus]*), gophers (*Thomomys*), mice and rats (*Perognathus, Peromyscus, Neotoma, Microtus*), ground sloths (*Megalonyx, Nothrotherium, Paramylodon*), the dire wolf (*Canis dirus*), sabre-toothed cats (*Dinobastis, Smilodon*), mammoths (*Mammuthus columbi*), horses (*Equus*), tapirs (*Tapirus*), camels (*Camelops minidoke, C. hesternus, Tanupolama*), deer (*Odocoileus*), antelope

(*Tetrameryx irvingtonensis, Breameryx*), musk ox (*Eucatherium*), and bison (*Bison antiquus, Bison latifrons*) once wandered Sonoma County (Stirton 1951).

At the time Europeans arrived the vertebrate fauna of the region was essentially the same as it is today, with a few notable exceptions. During the period of Russian occupation grizzly bears, elk, wolves, and sea otters could still be observed in the local area (Khlebnikov 1976:124-25). All of these species were extirpated during the Russian and subsequent American ranch periods. Many other animals mentioned by Khlebnikov are still common in the area. It should be noted that a lone sea otter was sighted in Fort Ross Cove in 1987 (Ranger Bill Walton, personal communication). Sea otters may be slowly repopulating the North Coast of California.

CONTEMPORARY ZOOLOGY

The fauna of the Fort Ross region is rich and varied. Animals in this region can be roughly divided into marine, aquatic, and terrestrial groups. The aquatic animals are arguably the more restricted group since they are confined to watery environments such as the coastline and freshwater streams and rivers. The terrestrial animals tend to be more free ranging, with a few notable exceptions.

Invertebrates

Rocky shores, which predominate the north coast of California, support a diverse array of crustaceans, mollusks, and other invertebrates, as well as a variety of fish and sea mammals (see appendix 3.2). Many of these animals were used by the indigenous Pomo and Miwok people of the region. The intertidal invertebrates harvested by natives (barnacles, limpets, mussels, abalone, sea urchins, turban snails, and chitons) are restricted to the rocky intertidal zones found throughout the area (see appendix 3.2). Highly-prized, hard-shelled clam species, such as the Washington clam (*Saxidomus nuttalli*), the giant Washington clam (*Saxidomus giganteus*), and Nuttal's cockle (*Clinocardium nuttali*) were used as raw material for shell beads. The shells were gathered and/or traded from Bodega Bay (Gifford 1967:21; Stewart 1943:61), since the bivalves favor large, sandy or muddy flats that are unavailable near Fort Ross. Another economically important mollusk, the purple olive (*Olivella biplicata*), is found commonly in the small beach areas of the region.

A wide variety of terrestrial invertebrates inhabit the region. Many different species of insects including ants, butterflies, moths, beetles, bees, and wasps abound in this area of Sonoma County. The larvae of some of these insects such as the army worm (*Pseudaletia unipuncta*) and yellow jackets (*Vespula*

sp.) served as food resources (Barrett 1952:108-109). A variety of arachnids (spiders, mites, ticks, and scorpions) are found in western Sonoma County. The majority of the arachnids in the area are quite harmless. However, the black widow (*Latrodectus mactans*), brown recluse, common scorpion (*Vejovis* sp.), and the black-legged tick can all cause health problems. The bites of the brown recluse, black widow, and common scorpion can be quite painful and, under extreme circumstances, deadly. The black-legged tick carries Lyme disease.

Fish

Many different species of fish are found in the Fort Ross region. Barrett (1952:103) states that "practically all species of fish were used as food." Most of the marine fish species preferred by the Kashaya Pomo (Gifford 1967; see appendix 3.3) such as rockfish, cabezon, and greenling are inhabitants of rocky shores. These fish were usually caught by hook and line (Gifford 1967:19; Loeb 1926), whereas surf fish, such as smelt and surf perch, were caught in nets (Gifford 1967:19). Gifford (1967:19) also reports that tide pools were drugged in order to catch perch, coal fish, and eels. Anadromous fish such as coho, chinook, and pink salmon and steelhead can still be found in the Gualala and Russian rivers (Moyle 1976). Salmon and other fish were obtained using a variety of methods including spears, harpoons, nets, and weirs (Barrett 1952:149-56; Kniffen 1939:356-59; Loeb 1926:167-69). Salmonids represent a valuable food resource and were heavily exploited, when available, by indigenous peoples in the prehistoric and historic periods (Baumhoff 1963; Gifford and Kroeber 1937; Loeb 1926). Another anadromous fish species, the lamprey, was exploited as well (Loeb 1926). The Pomo used many different fresh water fish (Kniffen 1939; Loeb 1926), especially around Clear Lake. In the Fort Ross region, however, the diversity of fresh water fish is somewhat limited. Trout, minnows, suckers, and sculpins are the most common in the major rivers (Russian and Gualala) and in the streams (McGinnis 1984; Moyle 1976). Sturgeon are found in the lower reaches of the Russian River (Moyle 1976). Smaller rivers and streams were often dammed and drugged with plant preparations in order to obtain the fish (Barrett 1952:149-50).

Amphibians

The herpetofauna of the region includes three newt species, seven salamander species, one toad, four frog species, three turtle species, five lizard species, and thirteen snake species (see appendix 3.4). This is somewhat depauperate, compared to the rest of the United States (Stebbins 1985). Amphibians are, as a rule, constrained to moist environments. The newts (*Taricha granulosa, T. rivularis,* and *T. torosa*), three of the salamander species (*Ambystoma gracile*, *Dicamptodon ensatus*, and *Rhyacotriton olympicus*), and all of the frogs and the toad (*Bufo boreas*, *Hyla regilla*, *Rana aurora*, *R. catesbiana*, and *R. boylei*) must lay their eggs in water in order to reproduce. These animals, with the exception of the newts and the toad, are all found close to ponds or streams. The newts and the toad are relatively resistant to desiccation and can be found considerable distances from water. Four salamander species found in western Sonoma County belong to the family Plethodontidae (*Aneides ligubris*, *A. flavipunctatus*, *Batrachoseps attenuatus*, and *Ensatina eschscholtzi*). Plethodontids are lungless and can lay their eggs on land. This allows these animals to inhabit much of the region. They simply require moisture and shelter of rocks, logs, or leaf litter. According to ethnographic sources (Barrett 1952; Gifford 1967; Loeb 1926), amphibians were not eaten, but were sometimes used for medicine or poisoning.

Reptiles

Reptiles seem to have been utilized like amphibians. They "were shunned except upon rare occasions" (Barrett 1952:105). Some lizards and snakes were used as medicine and/or charms. The lizards found in the Fort Ross region include two fence lizards (*Sceloporus graciosus* and *S. occidentalis*), a skink (*Eumeces skiltonianus*), and alligator lizards (*Elgaria coerulea* and *E. multicarinata*). All of these lizards are widely distributed, with *S. graciosus* being found at elevations above 150 m. The snake species occurring in the region (see appendix 3.4) are widely distributed, in general. Rattlesnakes (*Crotalus viridis*) are usually found in the interior, to the east of the first ridge system. The California mountain king snake (*Lampropeltis zonata*) is generally found in chaparral. Turtles seem to have been the only reptiles used as a food resource (Barrett 1952:105; Gifford 1967:19). The only turtle commonly found in the region is the Pacific pond turtle, *Clemmys marmorata*. These turtles typically inhabit larger streams, rivers, and ponds.

Birds

Over 200 species of birds can be seen in the Fort Ross region. Many of these birds were exploited for food, feathers, bones, and other purposes (see appendix 3.5). A wide variety of pelagic and shore waterfowl are found including sea ducks (scoters), sandpipers, murres, and guillemots. Gifford (1967:18-19) notes that pelicans, willets, cormorants, and scoters were not eaten. He also states that sea gulls were eaten only when food was scarce (Gifford 1967:18). Barrett (1952:100) states that gulls were not eaten at all in the

interior. Simons (1990:40-41) notes that the short-tailed albatross (*Diomedea albatrus*) was extirpated from the Fort Ross region and California's north coast in general during the Historic period due to overhunting by feather traders. According to Barrett (1952:100-101), most ducks and wading birds were eaten. Gifford (1967) does not mention many water birds at all.

Both Barrett (1952:101-102) and Gifford (1967:19) state that no owls, vultures, eagles, or hawks were eaten. These birds are widely distributed in the region. They were exploited primarily for their feathers, used as ornamentation and medicine, and for their bones, which were used for whistles and charms (Barrett 1952:101-102; Gifford 1967:18; Loeb 1926:154,167). Owls are associated with bad luck, child stealing, and death (Gifford 1967:18).

Smaller birds such as sparrows, thrushes, and doves were all eaten (Gifford 1967:18). Quail and woodpeckers were prized for their head plumage, which was used to decorate feathered baskets (Barrett 1952:98-99; Gifford 1967:18-19). These smaller terrestrial species are quite common. Woodpeckers prefer mixed forests, whereas quail prefer savannah or chaparral. Many of the aforementioned bird species prefer specific microhabitats occurring throughout western Sonoma County. Since the birds mentioned here are able to fly to and from their preferred habitats, most species are widely distributed in the region.

Mammals

A variety of mammals live in the Fort Ross region (see appendix 3.6). Many of them were used as sources of food, hides, bones, sinew, and antlers (Barrett 1952; Gifford 1967; Loeb 1926). Elk (*Cervus elaphus*) and deer (*Odocoileus hemionus*) were probably the most important sources. Elk prefer relatively dense forests and savannah, and were locally extirpated by the late 1800s (Gifford 1967:16). Deer are still commonly found in savannah, mixed forest, grassland, and chaparral habitats. A variety of taboos were related to the hunting of deer (Gifford 1967; Loeb 1926).

Marine mammals can also be encountered in the region. Harbor seals (*Phoca vitulina*) haul out onto the sandbar at the mouth of the Russian River, near Jenner. Sea lions (*Eumetopias jubatus*, and *Zalophus californianus*) are sighted frolicking in the waves in Fort Ross Cove. Gray whales (*Eschrichtius robustus*) can be seen offshore in the spring and fall during their migration to and from Alaska and Mexico. Occasionally, porpoises are spotted offshore. According to Loeb (1926) marine mammals were used by the coastal Pomo when they could be obtained, usually by hunting of sea lions and seals, and strandings of whales and porpoises. Gifford (1967:17) reports, however, that the Kashaya Pomo did not kill or eat seals or sea lions. He also reports that sea otters (*Enhydra lutris*) were not hunted until the arrival of the Russians (Gifford 1967:16).

Many of the smaller species of animals such as rabbits and rodents were hunted for food and hides (Gifford 1967:16-17; Loeb 1926). Gifford notes that the backbones of these smaller animals were pounded when they were cooked in order to keep the animals straight (Gifford 1967:16-17). Larger animals such as black bear, mountain lion, and bobcat, which are still present in a variety of habitats today, were hunted for food and/or hides (Gifford 1967; Loeb 1926). Most of the mammals in the local area have preferred microhabitats, but can often be found in many different habitats due to their relatively high mobility. Some of the smaller rodents are a little more specialized. Voles and gophers are usually found in open, grassy areas. One small rodent found in the Fort Ross region, the red tree vole (*Arborimus longicaudus*), eats only new conifer needles, and is restricted to stands of Douglas fir.

CONCLUSION

The Fort Ross region is a topographically complex area with a long and tortured geologic history. Raw material suitable for stone tools (chert, sandstone) is readily available. Sources of other economically important materials such as obsidian and hard-shelled clams are relatively close. The area around Fort Ross contains diverse plant and animal resources, many of which were exploited fully by the prehistoric and historic inhabitants (Barrett 1952; Baumhoff 1963; Gifford 1967; Kniffen 1939; Loeb 1926). The areas richest in resources exhibit the greatest species diversity, including key plants such as oak trees. These preferred habitats of economically-important species appear to be the rocky intertidal, mixed forest with oaks, savannah, and grassland (see appendices 3.1-3.6). Humans, especially during the Historic period, have profoundly influenced the natural environment of the region through the extirpation or exploitation of several local vertebrate species, extensive lumbering, and the introduction and cultivation of non-native plants and domesticated animals.

CHAPTER FOUR

AN ARCHAEOLOGICAL OVERVIEW

OF THE FORT ROSS REGION

IN THIS CHAPTER, WE present a historical overview of the archaeology of the Fort Ross region. The primary purpose is to describe proposed subsistence-settlement models for the southern North Coast Ranges. Some scholars maintain that small family units practiced extensive seasonal rounds during much of the annual cycle, aggregating into interior villages many kilometers from the coast in the winter. Others suggest the development of a larger, more complex, central-based village settlement system. We summarize the current data and initiate a subsistence-settlement analysis of the 455 sites recorded to date in this region.

From the outset we note the sporadic tempo of archaeological research in the Fort Ross region prior to the 1970s; research was limited in scope and brief in execution. The earliest archaeological work was undertaken in conjunction with ethnographic studies of coastal Pomo societies (Barrett 1908; Stewart 1943; Gifford 1967). Yet with the exceptions of Meighan's (1967) subsurface testing of two ethnographic "villages" in 1951 and Von der Porten's (1964) testing of four coastal sites in the early 1960s, few excavations (beyond the Ross stockade complex) or systematic surveys took place. This contrasts sharply with the adjacent coastal region south of the Russian River, especially from Bodega Bay to Tomales Bay, where a number of early surveys (Nelson 1909; Peter 1938) and extensive excavations (Fredrickson 1962; Beardsley 1954; Greengo 1955) were completed (see

Alvarez and Fredrickson 1989).

In the 1970s with the advent of cultural resource management studies, the tempo of archaeological research in the Fort Ross region accelerated (see Stewart 1980:3.22-3.27). Large sections of the coastal strip north of the Russian River were surveyed under the auspices of the California Department of Parks and Recreation (DPR) and other government agencies which initiated broad-scale inventories of their properties (Pritchard 1970; Thompson and Fredrickson 1979; Bramlette and Fredrickson 1990; Farris 1986a). In addition, some interior locations were investigated as part of DPR surveys (Alvarez 1991), timber sale inventories of the California Department of Forestry and Fire Protection (Foster 1983a, 1983b, 1987), and as archaeological surveys of proposed housing projects (Fredrickson 1974a, 1974b; King 1974a, King 1974b). The cultural resource management studies to date have emphasized intensive survey of specific project areas and limited subsurface testing of some sites (see Fredrickson 1984a:526). Few large-scale, areal excavations of prehistoric or historic age native sites have been initiated in the region.

THE EARLY YEARS

The archaeological investigation of the Fort Ross region was initiated in the early decades of this century by anthropologists from U.C. Berkeley. Trained primarily as ethnographers, these scholars interviewed native elders on the location of prehistoric and historic villages as part of their research on coastal Pomo societies. A primary research problem was to examine cultural adaptations to the steep, rocky coast and mountainous terrain of the southern North Coast Ranges. At issue was the resource productivity of the narrow, foggy coastal strip and adjacent redwood belt that extended anywhere from eight to thirty-two kilometers into the interior (Kroeber 1925:225).

The early consensus of most ethnographers was that the southern North Coast Ranges provided a relatively meager resource base for native peoples. Barrett (1908:24) first noted that the dense redwood belt provided few economic resources for hunter-gatherers. Alfred Kroeber (1925:225-34) expanded upon this theme, arguing that the food supply of the coastal Pomo was inferior to interior Pomo groups located along the Russian River and Clear Lake. Not only did he perceive the redwood belt as being largely barren and unproductive, but he characterized the rocky reefs and rocky intertidal zones of the coastline as providing only a "fair" amount of food. According to Kroeber, the paucity of resources could only have supported a low population density. Similar views have been echoed by Kniffen (1939:383-84) and Gifford (1967:1).

Most of the above studies suggested that some form of annual cycle was practiced that involved seasonal movements from coastal camps to interior villages. For example, Kniffen (1939:384) argued that the coastal Pomo had to "scour the country to provide their livelihood from a variety of sources." He postulated an annual cycle in which the local population was dispersed into small family groups for most of the year, except during the winter when they aggregated into winter villages. Since the effects of European colonization were largely ignored by early ethnographers (see Kroeber 1925:v-vii), there was little attempt to differentiate late prehistoric from early historic settlement patterns.

The Mendocino Coast

Anthropological studies of the Mendocino coast directly north of the Fort Ross region support some aspects of the above scenario. Like the Fort Ross region, this area is characterized by a steep continental shelf, rocky reef and intertidal habitats, high wave-stress shores, and extensive redwood forests. Here ethnographic descriptions of the Northern Pomo and Central Pomo indicate a seasonal use of the coastline before the mid-nineteenth century (McLendon and Oswalt 1978:283). Few coastal villages are reported north of the Gualala River (Barrett 1908:20), and most permanent or winter villages appear to have been situated far inland (up to 32 km from the coast) to the east of the redwood belt (Stewart 1943:34; Bean

and Theodoratus 1978:289).

Recent archaeological fieldwork at Albion Head in Mendocino County by Thomas Layton and Dwight Simons suggests some time depth exists for the seasonal exploitation of the Albion coastline. In a detailed analysis of artifactual and faunal remains from five coastal sites, they suggest that small groups from the interior or southern coastal homelands visited the coast to hunt sea mammals, and to gather shellfish and specific plant foods (Layton 1990:52-57; Simons 1990:37-50). Short-term camps appear to have been occupied during the spring and/or summer months on the basis of various seasonality indices. At the end of the summer season, the coastal visitors are thought to have returned to interior winter villages located some distance from the coast. Layton (1990:188) suggests that some of these winter villages may have been located in the Little Lake Valley, more than 20 km overland from the coast. Layton and Simons's findings correspond closely with ethnographic accounts of Northern Pomo seasonal residential movements.

Greg White's (1989, 1991) ongoing study of coastal sites in the MacKerricher State Park north of Fort Bragg suggests a somewhat more complex settlement system. In the MacKerricher Phase (A.D. 0-350), White (1991, personal communication) suggests that year-round occupations of coastal sites took place based on the exploitation of both coastal and terrestrial resources, especially steller sea lions. His excavations in the summer of 1989 revealed oval-shaped house structures with numerous subfloor pits. In the Sandhill Phase (A.D. 1300-1850) there is evidence for a shift to short-term, early fall occupation in which fisherpeople systematically stripped intertidal rocks for mussels (White 1989:141). After the seasonal mussel harvests, the camps appear to have been abandoned as people probably continued their annual cycle or possibly moved to nearby winter villages.

The Sonoma Coast

When one turns to the Sonoma County coast north of the Russian River, the archaeological evidence of a small, residentially mobile population "scouring the landscape" in a resource poor environment is questionable. We believe the Fort Ross region proved to be an enigma to early anthropologists. While its physical environment resembles that of the Mendocino coast, the density of ethnographically described "old" villages and campsites compares more favorably to the rich, protected estuarine environments of Bodega Bay and Tomales Bay to the south.

Samuel Barrett undertook the most comprehensive study of ancestral village and camp locations in his interviews with Pomo elders in the years 1903-1907. In his first monograph, Barrett (1908) described each site as recalled by native informants, and plotted its location on a master map of the entire Pomo linguistic territory. Barrett apparently relied primarily on informants for locational information, as he did minimal field checking of sites. Only about fifteen "old villages" and twenty "old campsites" were recalled by Northern and Central Pomo informants for the coastal region extending 85 km north of the Gualala River to Pudding Creek (north of Fort Bragg) and about 12 km into the interior (Barrett 1908:foldout map). In contrast, the Kashaya Pomo could point to the locations of fifty-six "old villages" and thirty-four "old camp sites" in the Fort Ross region stretching 50 km from the Russian River to the Gualala River. Figure 4.1 shows the locations of Barrett's "old villages" and "old campsites" in the same region, while table 4.1 cross references the site numbers in that figure with Kashaya place names for the villages and camps.

The majority of the "old villages" in the Fort Ross region are found within about a 5 km distance of the ocean (see figure 4.1); fifteen are dispersed along the coastal terrace, fourteen are along the first ridge system, and ten are found along the second ridge system. The remainder (seventeen) are disseminated in interior habitats in the watersheds of the Middle Fork of the Gualala River and Austin Creek. A little more than half of the "old camps" (n=18) are found on the coastal terrace, with the rest dispersed across the different ridge systems of the region.

C. Hart Merriam, who visited the Kashaya Pomo in August 1905, compiled a list of "Kachiah" names for villages, rancherias, and campsites in Sonoma County (Merriam 1977:43-59). In Merriam's description of these sites, he noted that many were recorded by Barrett (1908). Later ethnographers, such as Kroeber (1925:plate 36) and Kniffen (1939:382), relied primarily on Barrett's settlement data with only some modifications in spelling Kashaya names. No attempt was made to field check Barrett's map until E. W. Gifford and Omer Stewart initiated extensive, nonsystematic, reconnaissance surveys.

Gifford worked with the Pomo in 1915-1918, 1934, and 1950, and it appears that much of his field checking was undertaken in 1950 with Herman James, a Kashaya Pomo consultant. While some villages were misplaced (see Gifford 1967:8), in general Gifford and James's fieldwork indicated a relatively high degree of precision in Barrett's site locations. Gifford (1967:7-9) described several village sites that consist of clusters of "housepits" ranging from 3 to 6 m in diameter, midden refuse containing shellfish debris and cooking stones, and dark organic soils (sites #37, #66, #67, #68, #71 in figure 4.1 and table 4.1).

Omer Stewart appears to have undertaken much

of his reconnaissance work in 1935 in the hinterland of the Ross stockade. His ethnographic and archaeological fieldwork indicated that most villages were located about 1.5 to 5 km from the coast along the upper slopes and tops of the first ridge system. He believed that few permanent villages were situated on the coastal terrace, and that most sites found here were camping places for gathering sea food (Stewart 1943:50). He located several of Barrett's "old villages" [#75, #71, #77, and #76 in figure 4.1 and table 4.1; recorded as sites 18, 23, 25, and 27 in Stewart's map (1943:28)], which were assigned permanent California state trinomial numbers by the University of California Archaeological Survey in 1948 (CA-SON-176, -180, -182, and -184, respectively). He also recorded information on several sites near the Ross stockade that had not been previously described by Barrett. These were also assigned trinomial numbers: CA-SON-174, -175, -177, -178, -179, -181, -183, and -185 [listed as sites 16, 17, 19, 20, 21, 24, 26, and 28 respectively, in Stewart's map (1943:28)]. All of these "village" sites contained one or more "house" depressions, measuring several meters in diameter, diverse artifact assemblages, and midden deposits.

A Central-Based Village System

The implications of Barrett's (1908), Gifford's (1967), and Stewart's (1943) studies were threefold.

1) Population Density. The density of villages and camp locations recorded by these investigators suggested a relatively high population density for the Fort Ross region. Clearly the settlement pattern recorded for the Kashaya Pomo contrasted markedly with the number of coastal villages found in the Northern Pomo and the Central Pomo territories. The site density of the former region comared more favorably with that reported for the Bodega Bay and Tomales Bay region in the 1940s and early 1950s (see Beardsley 1954:20). Here, along the protected shores of these southern estuaries, were located many large coastal sites that consisted primarily of thick, shell deposits.

2) Resource Productivity. The poverty of resources in the Fort Ross region was probably overstated by Kroeber (1925) and Kniffen (1939). A dark, gloomy, impenetrable redwood belt does not parallel the Sonoma County coast. Rather a mixed forest/woodland/grassland mosaic exists along the interior ridge systems composed of different plant communities that contain a variety of economic resources (see chapter 3; also Baumhoff 1963:197). Stewart (1943:55) stressed that Pomo people would place their village communities in locations best suited to take advantage of different habitats in the local region. He noted that by extending territorial boundaries in an east/west orientation, Kashaya Pomo groups in the coastal province could exploit:

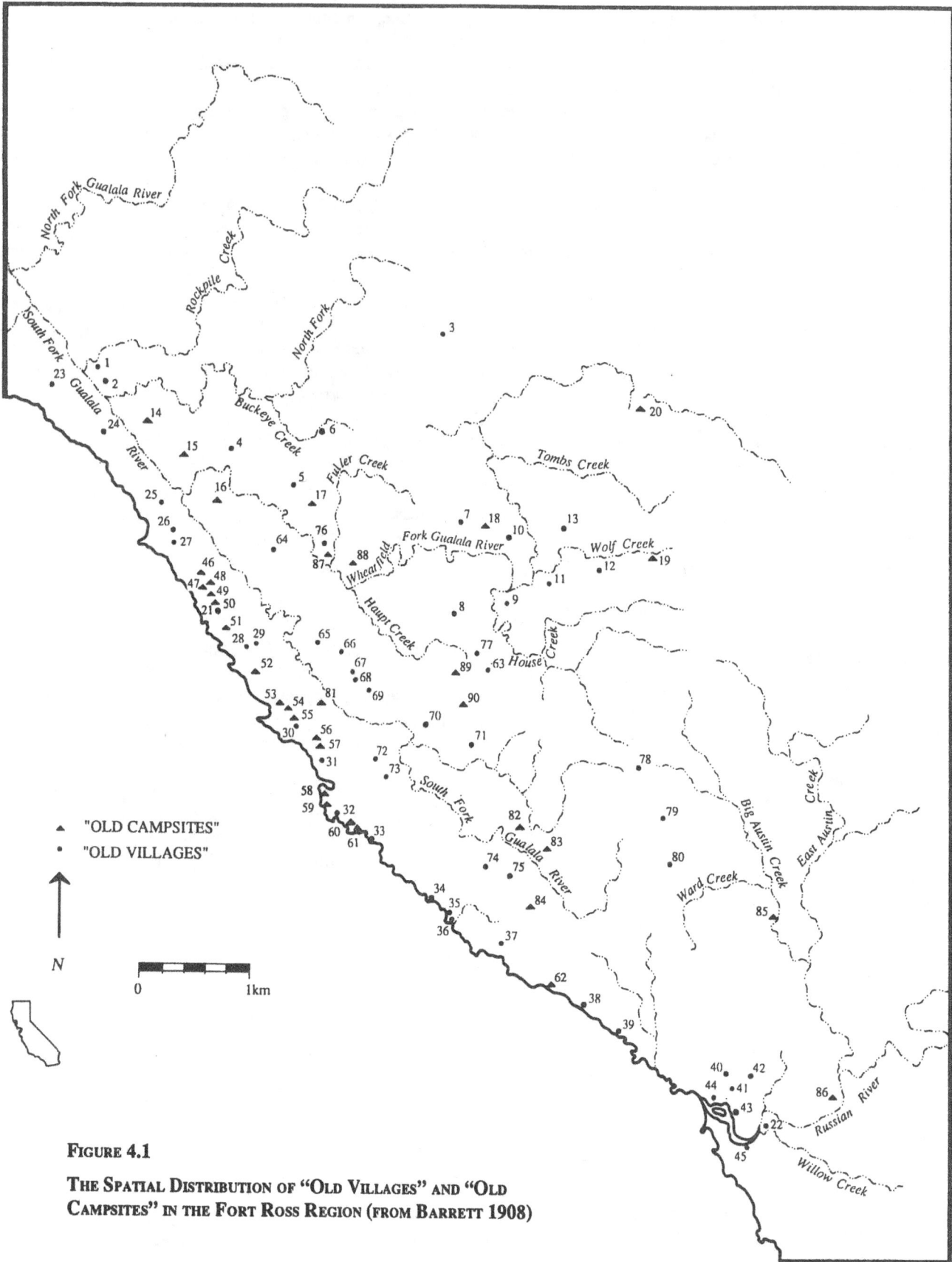

FIGURE 4.1

THE SPATIAL DISTRIBUTION OF "OLD VILLAGES" AND "OLD CAMPSITES" IN THE FORT ROSS REGION (FROM BARRETT 1908)

the ocean beach, the wind-swept grassy coastal shelf, the redwood and tan-oak forested hills; these including the numerous and fairly extensive clearings on ridges and near interior streams that are small counterparts of the hills and valleys of the Russian River province (Stewart 1943:55).

3) Settlement Hierarchies. Both Gifford (1967:7) and Stewart (1943:50) suggested that the settlement system of the Kashaya Pomo consisted of relatively permanent villages in the hills close to the coast and camp sites along the coastal terrace (see also Gifford and Kroeber 1937:118). Gifford (1967:8), relying extensively on his consultant Herman James, suggested that the ridge top villages were used primarily in the winter, and that small camps were established on the coastal terrace during the summer. Meighan's (1967) excavations of a coastal site (Kapacinal, #30 in figure 4.1, later recorded as CA-SON-256) and an interior village (Atcacinateawalli, #66 in figure 4.1, later recorded as CA-SON-369) tended to support this interpretation. Meighan's (1967:47) analysis of the two artifact assemblages suggested significant "occupational" differences between the sites.

A difference in seasonal living patterns appears to be the major factor involved and this is strongly demonstrated in the mound analyses. When at the inland village, the people spent more time hunting deer and other land animals. On the coast, shellfish and sea mammals formed the subsistence of the group. This difference may be reflected in the different types of projectile points; apparently a heavier point, made of local chert, was used in hunting sea mammals (Meighan 1967:47).

Unfortunately, Meighan (1967:47) was inclined to rule out temporal differences between the sites since "ethnographic information indicates that the sites were used by the same group of people."

Stewart (1943:50) inferred that clusters of sites may represent former village communities. He proposed that political relations between villages could be defined in archaeological contexts by the presence or absence of large depressions that may represent former assembly houses. He assumed that villages containing assembly houses were the abodes of important chiefs (1943:50). Based on discussions with Kashaya informants, especially Rosa Sherd, a Kashaya woman born at Dukacal (Stewart 1935b), he defined a two-tiered hierarchy of settlements along the ridge tops consisting of large principal villages with assembly houses, and smaller hamlets in the nearby hinter-

land that lacked such structures (see also Kniffen 1939:389). Five villages were identified as exhibiting large depressions that may have once served as the foundations of assembly houses. They include Lalaka, Seepinamatci, Hibuwi, and Dukacal (#71, #75, #76, and #77 in figure 4.1), as well as the village of Bacel, which Barrett did not describe. Bacel [shown as site 24 in Stewart's (1943:28) map] appears to be located near the village of Tcumati (#64 in figure 4.1). Ten villages are listed that exhibit evidence of only house pits and not depressions associated with assembly houses. These are Tcumati, Mutcawi, Atcacinatcawalli, Kalecadim, Tcalamkiamali, Tadona, Kobotcitcakali, Tanam, Kaletcumaial, and Tsapuwil (site #64, #65, #66, #67, #68, #69, #72, #78, #79, #80, respectively in figure 4.1).

In figure 4.2, we plot the spatial pattern of villages with and without assembly houses identified by Stewart (1943). The principal villages are distributed on ridge tops in a roughly linear configuration (approximately north/south) that parallels the coast. Hamlets are dispersed to the east and west of the principal villages on the first, second, and third ridge systems. The spatial distribution suggests four or five village communities whose principal villages are spaced between 4.2 and 8.6 km apart. The territories of the village communities appear to have been oriented in an east/west direction to take advantage of the diverse foods and raw materials that extend from rocky intertidal habitats to the open woodlands of the interior (Stewart 1943:55). We refer to this model as the central-based village system, since principal villages and associated hamlets were centrally located to allow easy access to the different plant communities in the region.

LATER ARCHAEOLOGICAL STUDIES

The next documented archaeological fieldwork in the region was undertaken by Edward Von der Porten of Santa Rosa Junior College. During the period of 1962 to 1964, Von der Porten and his field crews recorded four coastal sites near Timber Cove and Stillwater Cove, 2.4 to 5.3 km northwest of the Ross stockade along Highway 1. Excavation units (5' by 5') were placed in at least two of the sites designated as Fort Ross #2 and #4. Field notes from the project (Von der Porten 1964) indicate that a "house floor" of crushed fire debris was uncovered at Fort Ross #2, as well as a wide range of artifacts including obsidian and chert flakes, pestle fragments, an *Olivella* bead, clam disk beads, bone awls, projectile points, a "fish hook" made from a bent nail, and historic ceramics. Fort Ross #4 is a shell midden measuring 30 by 46 m in size where subsurface testing yielded a number of flakes and some bifaces of obsidian and chert, nails,

Table 4.1.

KASHAYA PLACE NAMES FOR SITES IN FIGURE 4.1

Site # in Figure 4.1	Kashaya Name	Site Type	Description in Barrett 1908 (page #)
1	Kubahmoi	village	225
2	Kabeteyo	village	225
3	Kawante limani	village	225
4	Kobate	village	225
5	Camli	village	225
6	Makawica	village	225
7	Mahmo	village	225
8	Matiwi	village	225
9	Kawamtcaeli	village	225
10	Bimukaton	village	225
11	Hiwalhmu	village	226
12	Duwiditem	village	226
13	Bulakowi	village	226
14	Tcayahkaton	camp	226
15	Dutsakol	camp	226
16	Katmatci	camp	226
17	Kabatui	camp	226
18	Tsunno	camp	226
23	Kabaputcemali	village	229
24	Seeton	village	229
25	Tcapida	village	229
26	Kalinda	village	229
27	Kowical	village	229
28	Duwimatcaeli	village	230
29	Ohomtol	village	230
30	Kapacinal	village	230
31	Tabatewi	village	230
32	Kabesilawina	village	230
33	Tcitono	village	230
34	Tcitibidakali	village	230
35	Sulmewi	village	230
36	Otonoe	village	230
37	Metini	village	230-1
38	Baceyokaili	village	231
39	Powicana	village	231
40	Tsukantitcanawi	village	231
41	Kalemalato	village	231
42	Kataka	village	231
43	Tsubatcemali	village	232
44	Tcamuka	village	232
45	Acatcatiu	village	232
46	Kadjusamali	camp	233
47	Tulekaleyo	camp	233

Table 4.1 con't.

KASHAYA PLACE NAMES FOR SITES IN FIGURE 4.1

Site # in Figure 4.1	Kashaya Name	Site Type	Description in Barrett 1908 (page #)
48	Tcikobida	camp	233
49	Tontotcimatci	camp	233
50	Suldjo tumali	camp	233
51	Pacukitmawali	camp	233
52	Matimali	camp	233-4
53	Hemalakahwalau	camp	234
54	Batsatsal	camp	234
55	Duwikalawakali	camp	234
56	Bacewi	camp	235
57	Sohoibida	camp	235
58	Tcitibidakali	camp	235
59	Tatcbida	camp	235
60	Ledamali	camp	235
61	Dikata	camp	235
62	Amayalatci	camp	235
63	Potol	village	235-6
64	Tcumati	village	236
65	Mutcawi	village	236
66	Atcacinatea walli	village	236
67	Kalecadim	village	236
68	Tcalamkiamali	village	236
69	Tadono	village	236
70	Tatcumawali	village	237
71	Lalaka	village	237
72	Kobotcitcakali	village	237
73	Kicaiyi	village	237
74	Tcamokome	village	237
75	Seepinamatci	village	237
76	Hibuwi	village	237
77	Dukacal	village	237
78	Tanam	village	237
79	Kaletcumaial	village	237
80	Tsapuwil	village	238
81	Koomtcobotcali	camp	238
82	Tanahimo	camp	238
83	Capetome	camp	238
84	Matcoko	camp	238
85	Kabebateli	camp	238
86	Hatciwina	camp	238
87	Tcaikosadotcani	camp	238
88	Nekawi	camp	238-9
89	Tatcaka	camp	239
90	Tekalewi	camp	239

worked glass artifacts, pestles, and hammerstones (see Von der Porten 1964).

The first systematic archaeological surveys in the Fort Ross region were undertaken in the 1970s. Most of these projects have been small in scope, often involving the survey of cultural resources in road alignments, in proposed residential developments, and in properties slated for timber harvests. Below we briefly describe five areas where large-scale surveys have been complete (see figure 3.1).

1) Navarro Ranch Land Development Project. Located in mountainous terrain northwest of Cazadero, Fredrickson (1974a) initially examined the site potential of the 841 ha project area by making field checks on foot. He divided the project area into zones of high sensitivity, moderate sensitivity, and low sensitivity. King (1974a) then undertook a survey of the project area, giving priority to highly sensitive zones that had high probabilities of containing sites, but examining other, less sensitive zones as well. A total of six sites, eighteen bedrock petroglyphs, and several isolated surface finds were recorded. The six sites are lithic scatters exhibiting primarily flakes and debitage of chert and some obsidian, as well as occasional ground stone tools (King 1974a:2-3). The petroglyphs were ground and pecked into schist boulders in the style of cupules, line groups, and deep grooves. Individual petroglyph boulders contained as many as 43 cupules. Interestingly, the petroglyph boulders are all clustered in the northern section of the project area in the Ward Creek drainage (King 1974a:3-6).

2) Gualala Land Development Project. This project involved survey in the rugged terrain of the South Fork of the Gualala River near Creighton Ridge, about 5 km east of the Ross stockade complex. Similar to the Navarro project, Fredrickson (1974b) first field checked the 6.5 sq km project area to identify parcels with high potential for sites (high sensitivity). King (1974b) then surveyed the area, giving priority to those parcels of high sensitivity, but also field checking other parcels. A total of fourteen sites, primarily lithic scatters and some petroglyphs, were recorded. Descriptions of these sites will be presented in chapter 5.

3) Fort Ross State Historic Park. Substantial fieldwork is now being undertaken in the near hinterland of the Ross stockade by archaeologists from the California Department of Parks and Recreation, Sonoma State University, Santa Rosa Junior College, and U.C. Berkeley. An area measuring 2.8 sq km has been intensively surveyed in the Fort Ross State Historic Park. Subsurface testing has been initiated at several sites. The results of this fieldwork are included in chapter 5.

4) Stillwater Cove Regional Park. This 23 ha regional park, located between the Fort Ross State Historic Park and Salt Point State Park on the coast, was surveyed in 1979 by crews from Sonoma State University (Thompson and Fredrickson 1979). The project included the assistance of a Kashaya Pomo tribal scholar, Otis Parrish. Parrish believes that some coastal locations may have been inhabited year-round given the abundance of intertidal resources such as abalone (Thompson and Fredrickson 1979:3,8). A mixed strategy reconnaissance was employed to survey the park, with priority given to zones of high sensitivity. Three sites (CA-SON-687, -688, -689) were relocated. Two additional sites (CA-SON-1183, -1184) were recorded. All of the sites are shell middens containing various proportions of mussels, chitons, clams, abalone, and limpets, as well as some chert and obsidian artifacts (Thompson and Fredrickson 1979:10-12).

5) Salt Point State Park. Considerable archaeological fieldwork has taken place in this 20.24 sq km state park during the last twenty years. The boundaries of the park include an extensive stretch of coastline, as well as the coast-facing side of the first ridge system directly west of the modern hamlet of Plantation.

In October 1969, William E. Pritchard of the Department of Parks and Recreation, commenced an archaeological survey of the park. He recorded a total of forty-seven sites: three Euro-American sites from the American period, twenty-five shell middens, and nineteen lithic scatters (Pritchard 1970:31). Two groups of shell middens were identified. One group (n=21) consists of small middens (130 sq m or less in size) situated on sea cliffs, in the lee of rock outcrops or on the southern slopes of stream banks. The other group (n=4) includes large middens (1022 sq m or more in size) located well back into the tree line several hundred meters from the beach. Pritchard interpreted the small shell middens as single family camps where marine foods were processed, and the larger sites as more intensive occupation areas of more extensive populations (e.g., "villages"). Employing ethnographic analogies of the coast Yuki and Pomo, Pritchard (1970:30) believed the shell middens were used primarily in the summer months, although he was unsure about the "economic significance of the larger villages." Pritchard found evidence that the lithic scatters, located primarily on the sea cliff edge and coastal terrace, may have predated the shell middens. The measurements of the hydration rims of two obsidian artifacts suggest a relatively early date for the lithic scatters (Pritchard 1970:32).

In the fall and winter of 1987, and spring of 1988 an intensive survey was conducted in Salt Point State Park by field crews from Sonoma State University to assess the potential effects of burn management

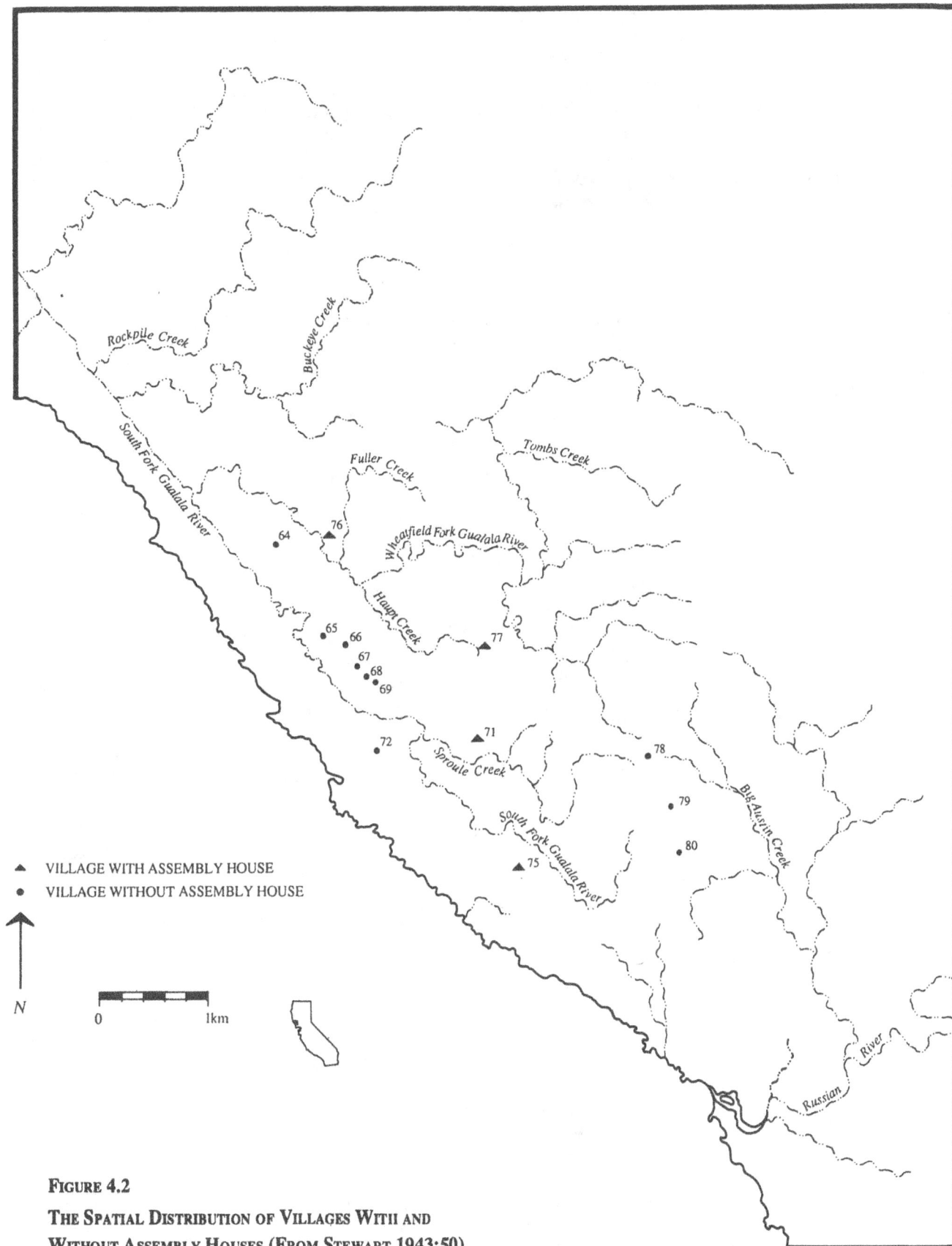

FIGURE 4.2

THE SPATIAL DISTRIBUTION OF VILLAGES WITH AND
WITHOUT ASSEMBLY HOUSES (FROM STEWART 1943:50)

practices on archaeological resources. A 4.05 sq km area was intensively surveyed along the coastal strip and lower elevation terraces (Bramlette and Dowdall 1989:142). The sites originally found by Pritchard were relocated, and new sites were recorded. A total of 126 prehistoric sites were relocated or recorded (Bramlette and Dowdall 1989:142). The site density (31 sites/sq km) is probably one of the highest yet recorded in the coastal regions of northern California (Bramlette and Fredrickson 1990:5). Prehistoric sites include shell deposits on the coastal terrace usually within 50 m of a primary drainage. Many of these shell deposits contain a low density of lithic artifacts. Other sites are lithic scatters situated on coastal bluffs or on the leeward side of sandstone stacks (Bramlette and Dowdall 1989:143). The results of obsidian hydration analysis tend to confirm Pritchard's hypothesis concerning the earlier occurrence of lithic scatters. The earliest lithic scatters date back as early as 4500 years ago, while most of the shell deposits date to within the last 2000 to 3000 years (Bramlette and Fredrickson 1990:5).

One site (CA-SON-473) was excavated by Francis A. Riddell in 1981 near the parking lot at Gerstle Cove. A 426 by 36 m area was sampled by excavating a combination of soil auger holes and seven 1 by 1 m units. The analysis of the materials, conducted by Dowdall (1988), suggests the place was used seasonally for processing marine foods. Mussel, barnacle, abalone, limpet, and chiton make up the majority of the shell refuse in descending order of total shell weight. Some obsidian, chert, quartzite, basalt, and schist debitage (n=299) and a few flaked stone tools (n=11) were recovered. Twenty-one cobbles, three pestles, and three millingstone fragments were also analyzed. Only three pieces of rodent and fish bones were identified. Obsidian sourcing indicates that the majority came from Napa Valley and Annadel. Only a few pieces of obsidian were sourced to Mt. Konocti, and none came from the Borax Lake flow (see Dowdall 1988).

SUMMARY: THE CENTRAL-BASED VILLAGE MODEL

The results to date of fieldwork in the Fort Ross region suggest the following central-based village settlement model. Along the ridge tops and high slopes near the coast one expects to find large sites with housepits, midden deposits, and diverse artifact assemblages. These sites may have functioned as relatively permanent, central-based villages from which people exploited foods and raw materials in nearby coastal and interior habitats. The settlements may have been organized into small village communities composed of principal villages with chiefs and assembly houses and smaller outlying hamlets.

In the outlying hinterland beyond the ridge top villages, one expects to find a variety of special purpose sites where foraging parties and task groups exploited various food resources and raw materials. In Salt Point State Park, a variety of small shell deposits and lithic scatters are found on the coastal terrace, possibly representing the remains of special purpose activities involving maritime food gathering and processing. Larger sites containing extensive middens, which may represent the remains of villages, are found on the coastal facing slope of the first ridge system. Other settlement data from the Navarro and Gualala land development projects, situated deep in the hinterland of the South Fork of the Gualala River and Austin Creek drainages, include lithic scatters and petroglyphs that may reflect special purpose activities involving hunting, plant processing, and ceremonies.

A SUBSISTENCE-SETTLEMENT ANALYSIS OF SITES IN THE FORT ROSS REGION

In the remainder of this chapter, we present a preliminary evaluation of the central-based village model employing information from all known, recorded sites in the Fort Ross region. Our overview includes all the archaeological site record forms currently on file at the Northwest Information Center, Sonoma State University. This region, as defined in chapter 3, sets the boundaries for site inclusion. A total of 455 sites have been recorded in these boundaries.

We recognize several problems in undertaking this analysis, and the inherent weaknesses in our data set. The site forms, and kinds of information recorded, varied greatly from the earliest (1935) to the most recent (1990). In addition, the data provided by the site investigators also show significant variance. As the focus of the researcher changed, so did the emphasis on the variables recorded. In some cases, site form updates are available and are used. In many instances, data has to be extrapolated from the narrative and/or from other relevant form information. Often, data on pertinent variables are inconsistent, not available, or available in only a very gross fashion. A good example of this is assigning the prehistoric/protohistoric/historic moniker to the site. Investigators often guess at the age of sites in the field prior to any rigorous chronological analyses of site constituents, thus making the chronological assessments reported in site forms somewhat dubious. The "site type" variable also presents problems. Site types are not clearly or consistently defined on the site forms and, in many cases, multi-purpose uses are identified without priority. However, a significant data base does exist, and given the above caveats we proceed with it.

The universe of 455 sites in the Fort Ross region provides 441 sites with records; the remaining 14 sites that lack documentation are excluded. Additionally, 43 sites defined as Euro-American in origin are excluded from the analysis. The remaining 398 sites comprise the regional data base (appendix 4.1). These sites are analyzed as like temporal sites without regard to the pre/proto/historic identifier listed on the site form. Variables examined include site type, environmental zone, site location, and area.

Site Type

The analysis of the data on site type segregates sites as follows: shell middens (50.5%), rock shelters (2.2%), habitation sites (16.1%), lithic scatters (21.5%), and other–petroglyphs, quarries, cupule rocks, bedrock mortars (9.8%). While habitation sites represent only 16% of the total sites, special purpose or limited activity sites account for 84% of the total. This may indicate that the residents of the habitation sites utilized many special purpose loci both near and at some distance from their residential bases. Assuming that the individuals who used the special purpose sites also resided in the Ross region, each habitation site was associated with, on the average, six special purpose sites. Of course, this ratio does not take into account the temporal relationships or overall use durations of the different site types.

Only thirty-one of the sites evidenced features (pits and/or depressions): twenty-nine of those sites are habitation sites and two are shell middens. Features are associated with almost 40% of all habitation sites (29 out of 74).

Site Size

A review of site size, as measured in square meters, reveals considerable variation in the areal extent of different site types. It should be noted that two sites, CA-SON-1204 and CA-SON-1205, aggregations of Salt Point sites, are not included in this analysis. The average size and size range of each site type is as follows: shell middens ($\bar{x}$=1988; sd=6597; one standard deviation is 0 to 8567); rock shelters ($\bar{x}$=6870; sd=20377; one standard deviation is 0 to 27247); habitation sites ($\bar{x}$=5162; sd=11025; one standard deviation is 0 to 16187); lithic scatters ($\bar{x}$=5307; sd=10049; one standard deviation is 0 to 15356); and other sites ($\bar{x}$=3007; sd=4773; one standard deviation is 0 to 7780).

These findings suggest that habitation sites, lithic scatters, and rock shelters tend to vary more in size than any other site types. The three site types are characterized by assorted sized sites that range from very small (less than 50 sq m) to very large (68,000 sq m).

Environmental Zone

Each site in the regional data base is assigned an environmental zone code based on the aggregated plant community descriptions provided in chapter 3. With the exception of mixed forest-without oak, sites are found in all other environmental zones: conifers (8.6%), mixed forest-with oak (22.6%), grassland (57.1%), savannah (10.9%), and scrub (.8%). Almost sixty percent of the sites are located in a grassland zone and an additional twenty-three percent in a mixed forest-with oak zone. This suggests that the vast majority of the sites (80%) are situated in areas of greatest plant and animal resources (mixed forest-with oak) and/or on the boundary between differing resource areas (grasslands). Less than one percent of the sites are located in the scrub zone.

For each site type, the proportion found in each environmental zone is as follows: shell midden–13.4% conifer, 12.6% mixed forest-with oak, 8.2% savannah, 64.5% grassland, and 1.3% scrub; rock shelter–30% conifer, 20% mixed forest-with oak, 0% savannah, 50% grassland, and 0% scrub; habitation site–1.4% conifer, 20.5% mixed forest-with oak, 13.7% savannah, 64.4% grassland, and 0% scrub; lithic scatter–4% conifer, 30.3% mixed forest-with oak, 15.2% savannah, 50.5% grassland, and 0% scrub; other site types–2.2% conifer, 51.1% mixed forest-with oak, 13.3% savannah, 33.3% grassland, and 0% scrub. Ninety-nine percent of the habitation sites are located in the three most productive zones: mixed forest-with oak, grassland, and savannah. While at least half of all shell middens, lithic scatters, rock shelters, and habitation sites are located in the grassland zone, half of the other site types (petroglyphs, quarries, cupule rocks, bedrock mortars) are found in a mixed forest-with oak zone, suggesting activities such as hunting, plant processing, quarrying, and ceremonies.

For each environmental zone, the proportion of each site type is as follows: conifers–77.5% shell midden, 7.5% rock shelter, 2.5% habitation, 10% lithic scatter, and 2.5% other; mixed forest-with oak–29.3% shell midden, 2% rock shelter, 15.1% habitation, 30.3% lithic scatter, and 23.2% other; savannah–38% shell midden, 0% rock shelter, 20% habitation, 30% lithic scatter, and 12% other; grassland–56% shell midden, 1.9% rock shelter, 17.7% habitation, 18.8% lithic scatter, and 5.6% other; scrub–100% shell midden. Of interest, almost eighty percent of all sites located in the conifer zone are shell middens, perhaps suggesting that shelter or access to wood was a main requisite in selecting some coastal shellfish processing sites.

Site Location

Analysis of the sites in the data base also includes a review of three site locations: coastal (the coastal strip, estuarine areas, coastal terraces, and lower ridge slopes up to about 125 m in elevation), ridge (ridge slopes over 125 m in elevation and ridge tops in the first ridge system inland from the coast), and hinterland (all lands inland from the first ridge system). In a few cases, second ridge system sites, when near the first ridge system, are coded as ridge sites. The boundaries between coastal, ridge, and hinterland locations are not discrete, and, in many cases, the site location code is estimated. For the regional data base, 65.9% of the sites are found in coastal locations, 9.6% in ridge locations, and 24.5% in the hinterland.

The data show great discrepancies in the size of sites found in coastal, ridge, and hinterland locations. The average and range of site sizes (in square meters) are as follows: coastal locations ($\bar{x}$=1641; sd=5588; one standard deviation is 0 to 7229); ridge locations ($\bar{x}$=7872; sd=11,229; one standard deviation is 0 to 19,101); and hinterland locations ($\bar{x}$=5705; sd=11,208; one standard deviation is 0 to 16,913). Two trends in the size of habitation sites can be observed. First, sites in coastal locations tend to be smaller, on the average, than those in ridge and hinterland areas. Second, sites in ridge and hinterland locations exhibit a greater range of size variation than those recorded in coastal locales. In the latter, habitation sites average about 4242 sq meters (sd=11,303; one standard deviation is 0 to 15,454), while at ridge and hinterland locations they average respectively, 7141 sq meters (sd=9352; one standard deviation is 0 to 16,493) and 6986 sq meters (sd=10,653; one standard deviation is 0 to 17,639).

Site type also varies with site location. For each site location, the proportion of each site type found is as follows: coastal–65.5% shell midden, 3.2% rock shelter, 13.9% habitation, 13.9% lithic scatter, and 3.5% other; ridge–41.9% shell midden, 0% rock shelter, 32.6% habitation, 23.3% lithic scatter, and 2.3% other; hinterland–11.1% shell midden, 0% rock shelter, 15.7% habitation, 42.6% lithic scatter, and 30.6% other. Over half of the sites found in coastal locations are shell middens, while almost half of all hinterland sites are lithic scatters. These results are not unexpected; they reflect area/resource specific activities: shellfish processing at the coast, plant processing and hunting in the interior.

For each site type, the proportion found in each location is as follows: shell midden–87.1% coastal, 7.7% ridge, and 5.2% hinterland; rock shelter–100% coastal; habitation–58.1% coastal, 18.9% ridge, and 23% hinterland; lithic scatter–43.4% coastal, 10.1%

ridge, and 46.5% hinterland; other–24.4% coastal, 2.2% ridge, and 73.3% hinterland. Of interest is the location of the other site types: seventy-three percent are in the hinterland and only two percent are found on the first ridge system. This suggests very specific locational requirements exist for site types including petroglyphs, cupule rocks, bedrock mortars, and quarries. Of the twenty-nine habitation sites with pit/depression features, nine are coastal, nine are hinterland, and eleven are ridge locations.

CONCLUSION

In summary, a preliminary analysis of the Fort Ross region archaeological sites supports some aspects of the central-based village model. A few large habitation sites are located in areas of great resource productivity and/or on the boundary between diverse resource zones. Supporting these habitation sites are a variety of special purpose sites that probably represent loci where seafoods were gathered and processed, terrestrial game, seeds, and nuts were harvested, chert nodules were quarried, and ceremonial activities performed. On the average, six special purpose loci are found for each habitation site recorded in the region. Also, the sites on the coastal strip and coastal terrace are somewhat smaller than those in ridge and hinterland locations. Shell middens and rock shelters tend to be most commonly found in coastal locations, while lithic scatters tend to be most frequently found in coastal and hinterland locations and are rarely found along the first ridge system. Interestingly, petroglyphs, quarries, cupule rocks, and bedrock mortars also are rarely located on the first ridge system.

The greatest discrepancy between the central-based village model and the findings of our site record analysis concerns the location of habitation sites. According to Stewart (1943:50), villages should be found primarily on the first ridge system and not on the coast. However, our admittedly limited analysis suggests that habitation sites, as defined by site record information, are commonly found on the coastal terrace and the first ridge system, as well as in the outlying hinterland. The results of our analysis tend to emulate more closely the settlement distribution of "old villages" as defined by Barrett (1908; figure 4.1). An important distinction is that our analysis suggests that habitation sites on the coast tend to be smaller than those found on the first ridge system or in the hinterland.

In general, the data analysis supports the three main implications of Barrett's, Gifford's, and Stewart's studies as discussed earlier. First, the 74 habitation sites and 324 special purpose sites located to date in the Fort Ross region suggest a relatively high site density that may translate into a high population density for some temporal periods. Some of these sites tend to be large; 103 of them measure greater than 1,000 square meters in size. Second, we estimate that eighty percent of the sites are located in areas of greatest resource productivity and/or on the boundaries of varied resource zones, suggesting the utilization of a diverse resource base. Finally, the ratio of special purpose sites to habitation sites (6:1) suggests some type of central-based village system supported by resource-specific activity areas. The habitation sites may have served as bases from which people exploited the diverse plant communities in the region.

CHAPTER FIVE

AN ARCHAEOLOGICAL ANALYSIS

OF THE FORT ROSS STUDY AREA

IN THE PREVIOUS CHAPTER, we presented a central-based village model for the Fort Ross region. We found some support for the model when we synthesized settlement information from the regional data base of recorded sites. We recognize, however, that some of the data derived from site records are too coarse-grained to evaluate the model with any precision. Site record forms generally provide reliable information on site locations, site sizes, and prevalent site constituents, as well as brief descriptions of the on-site environment. They are much less useful in providing detailed information on chronology, specific artifact types, and faunal remains. Since chronological control is critical for employing the direct historical approach, the study of diachronic changes in subsistence-settlement patterns for the entire region is not possible at this time.

We now turn our attention to an ongoing archaeological investigation of the Fort Ross Study Area. The purpose of this investigation is to provide controlled archaeological data for undertaking a diachronic study of subsistence-settlement changes in the hinterland of the Ross Colony. Since the summer of 1988, a collaborative research team composed of scholars from the California State Department of Parks and Recreation, Sonoma State University, Santa Rosa Junior College, and U.C. Berkeley have been undertaking fieldwork in this area. We plan to focus much of our research efforts in this study area over the next few years.

The Fort Ross Study Area is a five by ten km rectangle in the heart of the ethnographically described Kashaya Pomo territory. The study area includes a five km stretch of coastline with the Ross stockade at its central point and a ten km stretch of interior habitats directly east of the stockade (see figure 5.1). Essentially, the study area is a coastal/inland slice that samples the environmental diversity of the broader region. The topography consists of a rocky coastline with a small cove (Fort Ross Cove) near the stockade, a relatively narrow coastal terrace that extends about one km at its widest point, and two ridge systems (Campmeeting Ridge and Creighton Ridge) that parallel the coast. Between the first and second ridge systems, which rise to 490 and 512 m above sea level at their respective highest points, is a steep valley drained by the South Fork of the Gualala River. The valley parallels the coast about five km inland from the Ross stockade. The geology of the study area is illustrated in figure 5.2.

Many of the plant communities of the broader region described in chapter 3 are distributed in a clinal pattern across the study area (figure 5.1). The coastal facing ridge (Campmeeting Ridge) contains closed-cone pine forests at lower elevations and redwood forests in the steep drainages that pour into the ocean (conifers only in figure 5.1). The lower elevations of this ridge also contain coastal grassland and coastal scrub. In the upper and exposed elevations of Campmeeting Ridge, as one moves out of the fog belt,

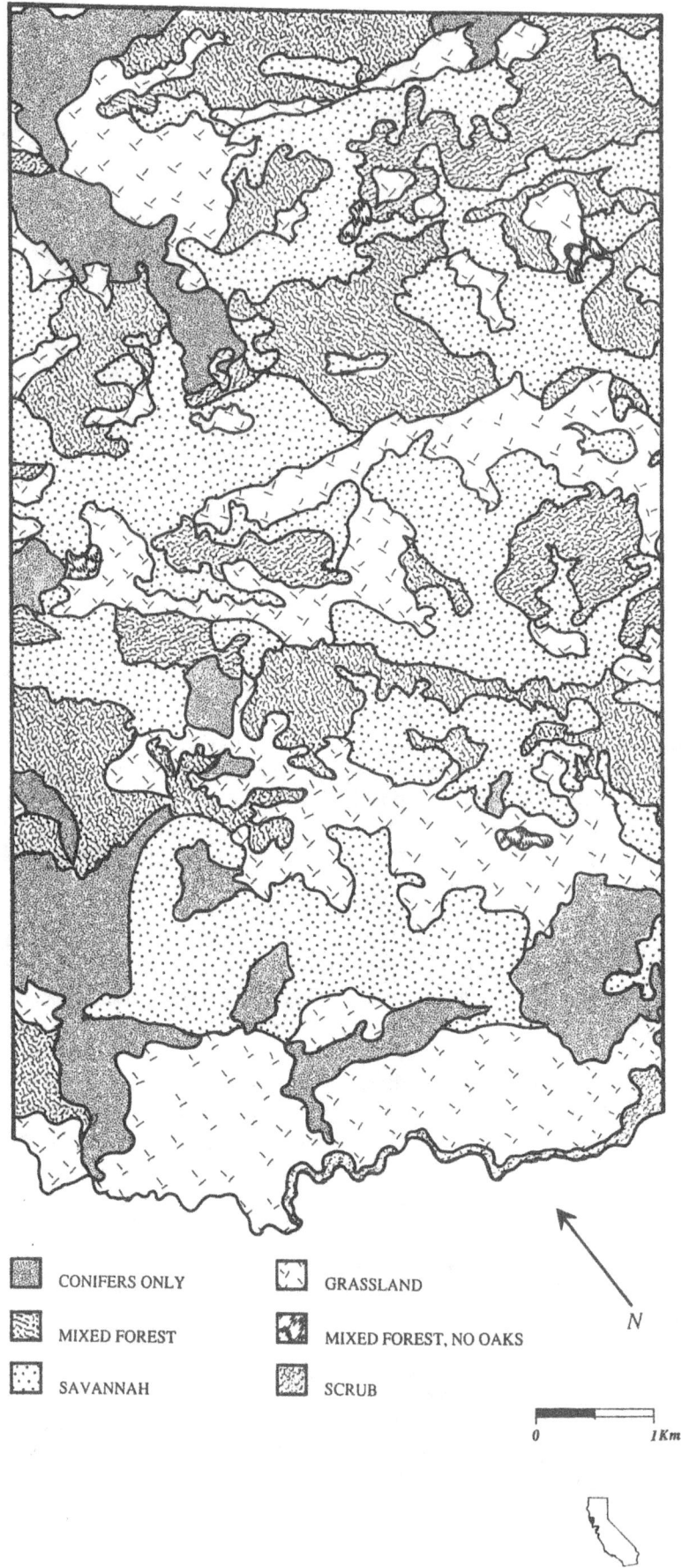

FIGURE 5.1
PLANT COMMUNITIES
OF THE FORT ROSS
STUDY AREA

CONIFERS ONLY   GRASSLAND

MIXED FOREST   MIXED FOREST, NO OAKS

SAVANNAH   SCRUB

N

0   1 Km

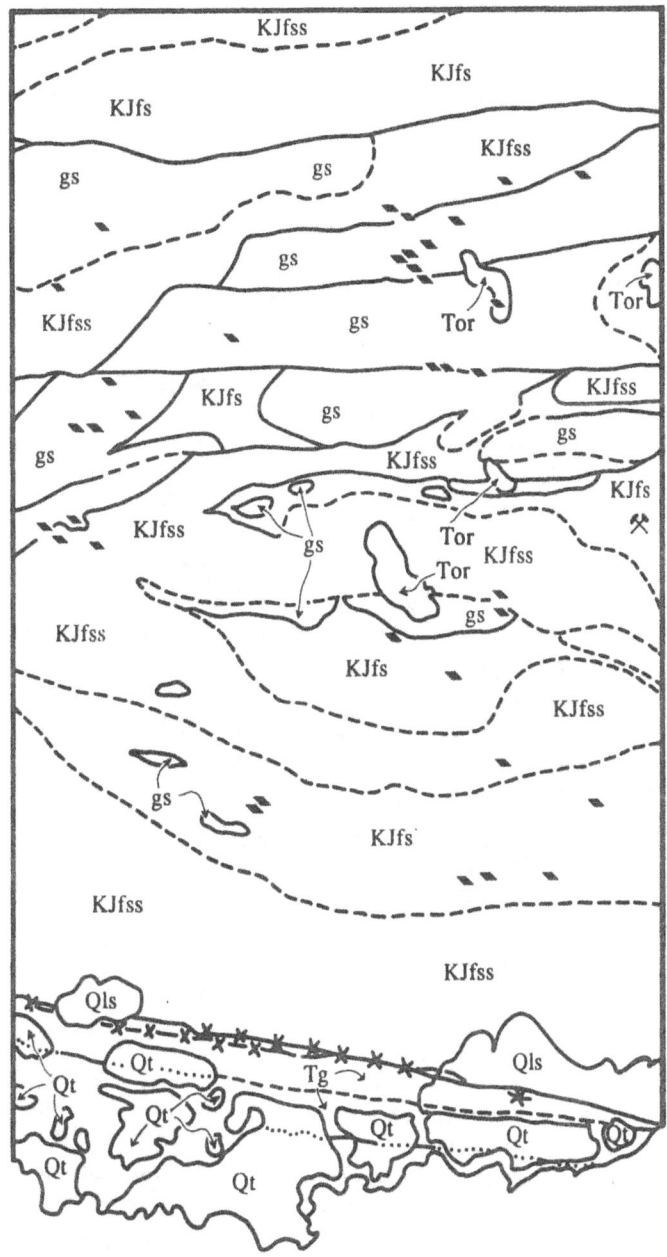

FIGURE 5.2
GEOLOGIC MAP OF
THE FORT ROSS
STUDY AREA

Legend:

- HIGH GRADE METAMORPHIC ROCK
- MINE (Mg)
- SAN ANDREAS FAULT TRACE
- Qt QUARTERNARY TERRACE
- Qls QUARTERNARY LAND SLIDE
- Tg TERTIARY GRAVEL
- Tor TERTIARY OHLSON RANCH FORMATION
- gs GREENSTONE
- KJfs CRETACEOUS/JURASSIC FRANCISCAN SHALES
- KJfss CRETACEOUS/JURASSIC FRANCISCAN SANDSTONES

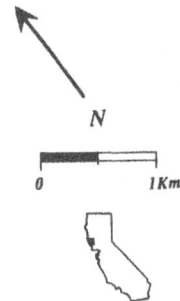

N

0   1 Km

the dominant vegetation is open savannah that contains oak and Douglas fir. On the other side of Campmeeting Ridge, out of the fog belt, the summers are both drier and warmer. Mixed forests with oaks and grasslands flourish along the South Fork of the Gualala and up the slopes of the second ridge (Creighton Ridge).

In this chapter we summarize previous fieldwork conducted in the study area and describe survey and excavation work being undertaken by our collaborative research team. Results of an analysis of archaeological remains in the Fort Ross State Historic Park are discussed. We present counts of artifact types and faunal remains, calculate diversity indexes, and employ a regional chronology to date survey sites. In the final section, we describe diachronic developments in the subsistence-settlement patterns of native sites in the hinterland of the Ross Colony.

PREVIOUS AND ONGOING FIELDWORK

Fifty-four sites have been recorded for the study area to date (figure 5.3). All site records are on file at the Northwest Information Center, Sonoma State University. The earliest archaeological fieldwork took place in the 1930s and 1940s by Omer Stewart and F. H. Bauer whose reconnaissance located several large sites. In the 1970s and 1980s intensive surveys took place in two parcels: a 6.5 sq km area of the interior along drainages of the South Fork of the Gualala (Fredrickson 1974b, King 1974b), and a 2.8 sq km parcel in the Fort Ross State Historic Park. Each of these survey areas is described below.

Reconnaissance Work along the First Ridge

Stewart and Bauer recorded thirteen sites in the study area. Of these, Stewart described four large "villages" along Campmeeting Ridge (CA-SON-176, -177, -178, -179) and three "villages" on the lower slopes of the first ridge (CA-SON-174, -175, -231). Stewart observed house pits, deep midden deposits with shellfish refuse and darkened soil, and diverse artifact types on these sites. Bauer also identified six shell deposits along the coastal terrace and lower slopes of the first ridge (CA-SON-188,-230,-232,-233,-234,-235) (figure 5.3). These sites are characterized by dark "midden" soils, high densities of shellfish remains, and various lithic artifacts.

In 1989 we relocated two of Stewart's ridge top "village" sites (CA-SON-179,-177). We have not yet re-recorded, mapped, or surface collected these sites. An attempt by Sonoma State University crews to relocate CA-SON-176 proved unsuccessful. It is possible that this site was not accurately located by Stewart, or that another nearby site (CA-SON-1793) that exhibits a house depression may actually be the original site (Allison 1989).

Other sites recorded on the top or lower slopes of Campmeeting Ridge or the coastal terrace outside the original boundaries of the Fort Ross State Historic Park include CA-SON-1393,-1525,-1091, and -1452 (figure 5.3). CA-SON-1393 is a small oval scatter of chert flakes found south of the ridge top villages of CA-SON-178 and -179. CA-SON-1525, a moderate scatter of Franciscan chert and obsidian artifacts near CA-SON-177, was recorded by Richard Jenkins as part of a timber harvest project. CA-SON-1091 is a shell midden located north of Kolmer Gulch, while CA-SON-1452 is a cupule rock containing twelve cupules southeast of the Ross stockade on the exposed coastal terrace.

The Gualala River Hinterland Survey

Eighteen sites have been recorded along the South Fork of the Gualala River near Creighton Ridge (figure 5.3). Fourteen sites are found in the 6.5 sq km project area of the Gualala Land Development surveyed by Fredrickson (1974b) and King (1974b). The site density, about 2.1 sites/sq km, is probably conservative since some zones of low site potential were not surveyed intensively. Two sites are recorded as habitation sites. CA-SON-999 contains one house pit, measuring six m in diameter, various chipped stone artifacts, a handstone and other groundstone tools, and a midden deposit. CA-SON-1425, a large artifact scatter covering 6000 sq m, is also recorded as a possible habitation site. Another site (CA-SON-1001) is described as a large chert quarry containing many flakes, cores, hammerstones, and preforms. An additional eleven sites (CA-SON-1000,-1002,-1003,-1005,-1007, -1008,-1009,-1011,-1012,-1013,-1325) are defined as lithic scatters, varying in size from 100 sq m to more than 45,000 sq m, that contain flakes and debitage and occasional chipped stone tools, such as projectile points. Groundstone implements, such as handstones, pestles, and milling slabs, are recorded for some (CA-SON-1000,-1002,-1005,-1008,-1011). The final class of sites include four cupule rocks (CA-SON-1004,-1006,-1010,-1423). CA-SON-1004 and -1010 contain one and four cupules pecked into schist bedrock boulders. CA-SON-1006 is a "series of cupules on top of a brown schist boulder," while CA-SON-1423 consists of forty-seven separate cupules (King 1974b:3).

Survey of the Fort Ross State Historic Park

Since the 1970s, fieldwork has been ongoing in the near hinterland of the stockade compound in the Fort Ross State Historic Park. The original boundaries of the park encompassed a 2.8 sq km area of coastal terrace near the Ross stockade and the lower slope of the first ridge to an elevation of 305 m above sea level. In 1990, the Save the Redwoods League

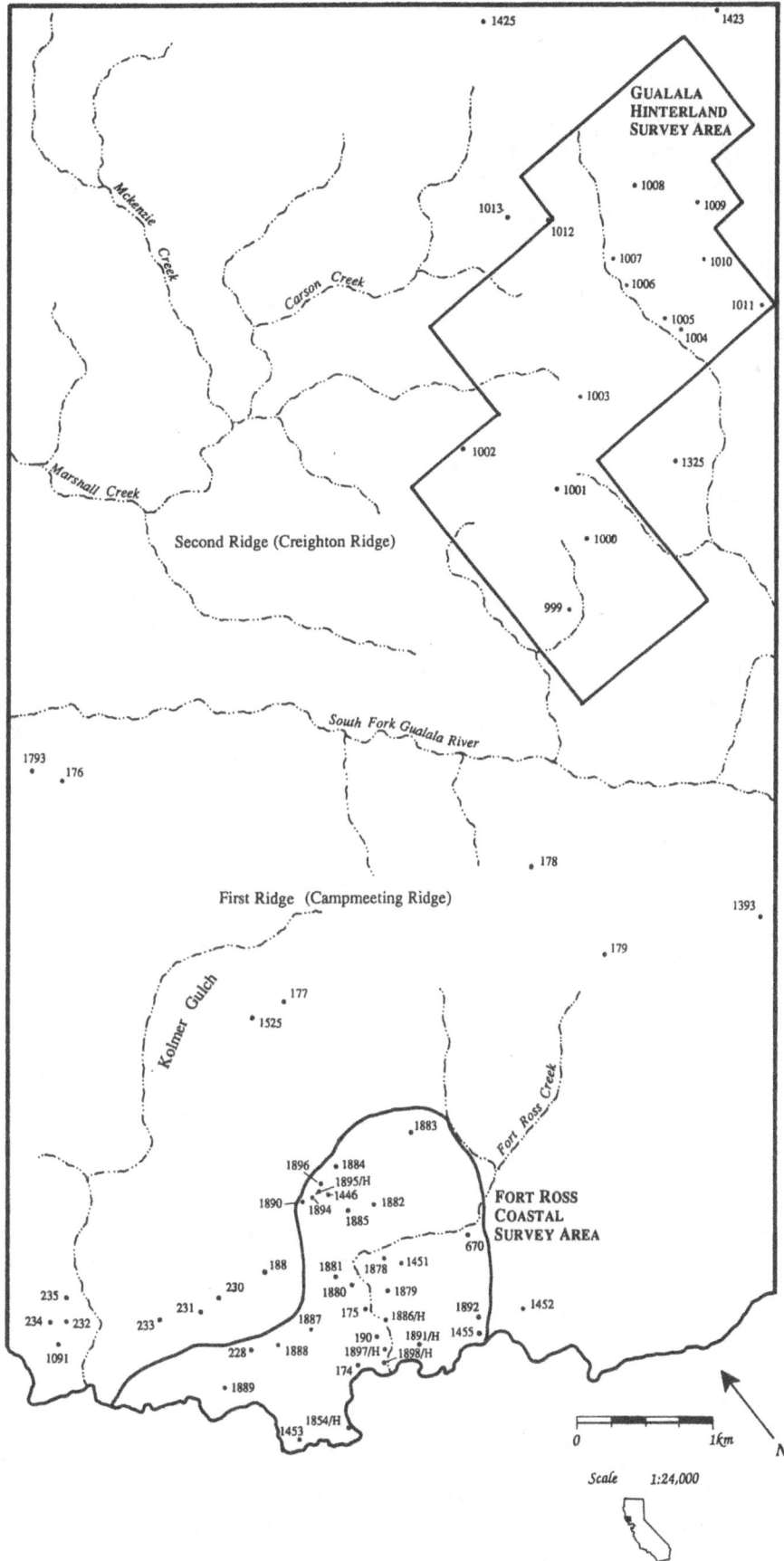

FIGURE 5.3

THE SPATIAL DISTRIBUTION OF SITES IN THE FORT ROSS STUDY AREA

purchased an additional 8.73 sq km of land that incorporates most of the study area north of the Ross stockade to the top of Campmeeting Ridge. The land, donated to expand the Fort Ross State Historic Park and to protect its viewshed, contains several of Stewart's "villages" (CA-SON-177,-179,-231), Bauer's shell middens (CA-SON-188,-230,-233), as well as CA-SON-1525. In the summers of 1988 and 1989, field crews from U.C. Berkeley completed an archaeological survey within the original boundaries of the state park. We began the systematic survey of the new acquisition to the park in 1991 and plan to continue this fieldwork over the next few years.

Field Methods

A standard surface pedestrian survey was employed to detect archaeological remains in the Fort Ross State Historic Park. We divided the original park property into twelve survey blocks (designated by the letters A-L) that centered around the stockade. Survey crews, each consisting of four to five people, walked consecutive transects back and forth across each block. Crew members, spaced ten meters apart, scanned the ground surface for evidence of artifacts, faunal remains, mounds, depressions, other surface features, and soil color changes. All evidence of past human activities, such as isolated artifacts, was noted on transect forms.

Clusters of artifacts and/or one or more features were defined as sites. We employed the guidelines of the California Archaeological Inventory Handbook of the Office of Historic Preservation to define sites. These guidelines are as follows (p. 2):

> For the purposes of the California Archaeological Inventory, a 'site' is defined as the location of associated artifacts and features, regardless of temporal placement or complexity. Minimally, a 'site' must meet two criteria: 1) It must consist of at least three associated artifacts or a single feature. 'Isolates' (less than three associated artifacts) will not be assigned a Trinomial Designation. If a record has been filled out for an isolate, this will be kept at the appropriate Information Center for future researchers' use. 2) A site must be at least 45 years of age. The age of the site may be determined by artifactual evidence, documentary evidence or similarity of the site to others which have firm dating.

Each site detected in the Fort Ross survey was assigned a field designation that included the block letter, transect number, and site number (in the consecutive order as recorded on the transect). For example, field number A-3-2 is the second site detected on the third transect of block A. For each site detected, crew members filled out the Archaeological Site Record form, mapped the boundaries of the site and any pertinent surface features using a Silva compass and metric tape, and collected a representative sample of archaeological materials from across the surface. A site datum (0N0E) was established in a central location from which segmented collection transects, divided into 1 by 2 m collection units, were laid out in the four cardinal directions. Each segmented collection transect extended from the site datum to the outer edge of the site. The southwest corner of each collection unit was designated as the unit datum. Its coordinates were defined by the distance north/south and east/west of the site datum (e.g., 4N0E, 0N6E). Archaeological materials collected from each unit were bagged and provenienced as a separate lot. In some cases, artifacts were point provenienced and surface collected from across the surface of sites.

In 1990, the site record forms for the Fort Ross survey sites were submitted to the Northwest Information Center, Sonoma State University. Each site was then assigned a permanent trinomial designation (e.g., CA-SON-1889).

Survey Sites

Thirty sites were recorded or relocated within the original boundaries of the Fort Ross State Historic Park. Table 5.1 presents the trinomial site numbers, field designations, and recorder for each site.

Euro-American Sites. Three sites represent the remains of primarily Euro-American structures or broader settlement complexes. CA-SON-190 refers to the entire stockade complex, including the Mad-Shui-Nui locus adjacent to the north palisade walls. CA-SON-1891H is the foundation of a potato warehouse that was constructed south of the stockade prior to A.D. 1859. The third, CA-SON-1446H, is the remains of a brick foundation or chimney near the Old Russian Orchard. The site may represent the location of a four-room house and adjoining kitchen built by the Russians.

Native American Sites. The remaining twenty-seven sites appear to have been used primarily by Native Americans in prehistoric, protohistoric, and/or historic times. The site density for the park is 9.6 sites/sq km. As outlined in table 5.1, twenty-two of the Native American sites were recorded or re-recorded by U.C. Berkeley field crews. Subsurface testing was initiated at one site, CA-SON-1898/H, by U.C. Berkeley crews, while two other sites (CA-SON-670, -1896) were excavated in the past by DPR or Sonoma State University crews.

The other five Native American sites (CA-SON-175, -1451, -1453, -1454/H, -1455) were not re-recorded or surface collected by U.C. Berkeley crews.

Table 5.1.

SURVEY SITES RECORDED IN THE FORT ROSS STATE HISTORIC PARK

Trinomial Designation (CA-SON-)	Field Designation	Recorder
174	Site 16	Stewart 1935/U.C. Berkeley 1989
175	Site 17	Stewart 1935/Pilling 1949
190	Stockade	Pilling 1950
228	228	Bauer 1949/U.C. Berkeley 1989
670	670	Stillinger 1977/U.C. Berkeley 1988
1446H	1446H	Farris and Parkman 1984
1451	1451	Parkman 1984
1453	1453	Farris 1984
1454/H	1454/H	Schulz 1984
1455	1455	Farris 1984
1878	A-5-1	U.C. Berkeley 1988
1879	A-13-1	U.C. Berkeley 1988
1880	B-3-1	U.C. Berkeley 1988
1881	B-5-1	U.C. Berkeley 1988
1882	Traci	U.C. Berkeley 1988
1883	D-3-1	U.C. Berkeley 1988
1884	D-7-1	U.C. Berkeley 1988
1885	B. Walton	U.C. Berkeley 1988
1886/H	Chapel 2	U.C. Berkeley 1989
1887	E-2-1	U.C. Berkeley 1989
1888	E-6-1	U.C. Berkeley 1989
1889	I-2-1	U.C. Berkeley 1989
1890	K-4-1	U.C. Berkeley 1989
1891H	L-1-1	U.C. Berkeley 1989
1892	L-8-1	U.C. Berkeley 1989
1894	Locus 4	U.C. Berkeley 1988
1895/H	Locus 3	U.C. Berkeley 1988
1896	Locus 2	U.C. Berkeley 1988
1897/H	NAVS	U.C. Berkeley 1989
1898/H	FRBS	U.C. Berkeley 1988/1989

As described below, CA-SON-175, often designated as the original "Metini" site, has received little attention since it was first recorded in 1935 by Omer Stewart. CA-SON-1451 is a small lithic scatter surface collected by DPR archaeologists in 1984. The results of a recent subsurface testing program at CA-SON-1453 and CA-SON-1454/H by Sonoma State University and Santa Rosa Junior College are currently being written up. CA-SON-1455 was extensively investigated in 1984 by DPR archaeologists.

Before describing the Fort Ross sites, we first discuss the methods employed for analyzing artifacts and faunal remains, for calculating diversity indexes, and for generating a local chronology.

THE ANALYSIS OF ARTIFACTS AND FAUNAL REMAINS

Archaeological materials collected from Fort Ross survey sites during the summers of 1988 and 1989 were processed and analyzed in the Archaeological Research Facility's laboratories at U.C. Berkeley. Students in the field school course (Anthropology 133) and in the follow-up laboratory course (Anthropology 134) sorted materials into the following groups: chipped stone artifacts, ground stone tools, fire-cracked/ground stone fragments, historic artifacts (ceramics, glass, metal), other artifacts (shell, bone), and faunal remains.

1) Chipped Stone Artifacts. U.C. Berkeley students initially classified chipped stone artifacts by raw material types and artifact classes. Kent Lightfoot and Ann Schiff checked each identification for accuracy and consistency. The primary raw material types include obsidian from four sources in the southern North Coast Ranges (Annadel, Mt. Konocti, Borax Lake, and Napa Valley), chert, and schist.

The classification of chipped stone artifacts follows the guidelines published by the California Office of Historic Preservation (see Jackson et al. 1988). Chipped stone tools include bifaces (symmetrically shaped, bearing flake scars on both sides), unifaces (symmetrically shaped, bearing flake scars on one side), and battered cobbles or hammerstones (evidence of pecking or battering along body of artifact). Projectile points are classified into the point types described below. Flakes exhibiting secondary modification along the lateral edges are classified as edge-modified flakes. The modification may be due to use-related damage or the purposeful alteration of the lateral edge.

Flakes not exhibiting lateral edge modification are treated as chipping debris resulting from different stages of lithic reduction. Six categories of lithic debris are defined after Jackson et al. (1988): biface thinning flakes, primary cortical flakes, secondary cortical flakes, interior flakes, cores, and shatter. Biface thinning flakes exhibit large remnant platform scars and longitudinal cross-sections. Primary cortical flakes are those initially removed from the surface of cores. The dorsal side contains little or no evidence of flake scars and a high percentage of cortex. Secondary cortical flakes are characterized by dorsal surfaces exhibiting one or two flake scars and moderate cortex. Interior flakes exhibit multiple dorsal flake scars and little or no cortex. They are sometimes referred to as "thinning flakes." Cores are nodules (usually of chert or obsidian) from which flakes are detached. They are unmodified (not used as tools once they are discarded). Shatter refers to workshop debris resulting from core reduction and/or tool production where no attributes characteristic of true flakes exist (i.e., bulb of percussion, striking platform).

2) Ground Stone Tools. Ground stone tools are shaped by grinding, pecking, and polishing. U.C. Berkeley students initially identified ground stool tools by raw material type and tool type. All identifications were checked by Kent Lightfoot and Ann Schiff. The primary raw materials include basalt, graywacke, and sandstone. The common tool types include handstones (or manos), pestles, hopper mortars, slab millingstones, and net weights. Handstones are hand-sized, convex-shaped tools that exhibit a grinding edge on at least one surface. Pestles are elongated tools, ground into the shape of a cylinder that exhibit battering along the distal and/or proximal end. Hopper mortars are slabs that exhibit a centrally-placed, shallow, concave depression. Slab millingstones are large, flat slabs that exhibit a grinding surface on one or both surfaces. Net weights are hand-sized cobbles in which characteristic grooves have been pecked or ground into the distal and proximal ends.

3) Fire-cracked/Ground Stone Fragments. A significant percentage of the lithic assemblage from some Fort Ross survey sites consists of broken pieces of rounded cobbles. Most of the pieces appear to have been fired at high temperatures and then quickly cooled, (probably in water) to produce fire-cracked rocks. We believe many of these artifacts are broken fragments of groundstone tools, such as handstones or millingstones that were recycled as cooking stones. Others may simply be beach cobbles used as cooking stones. We define this rather enigmatic category as fire-cracked ground stone fragments.

4) Historic Artifacts. All glass, ceramic, and metal artifacts from Fort Ross survey sites were analyzed by Margaret Purser of Sonoma State University. The glass fragments are identified by function and type; most are flat glass, probably from window panes, and moldblown dark olive green or black colored alcoholic beverage bottles. Ceramics are defined by ware and vessel form. They include white improved earthenware, creamware, pearlware, Chinese coarse opaque porcelain (or porcellaneous stoneware), and industrial porcelain. Vessel forms consist primarily of cups and bowls. Metal artifacts are classified into functional categories. The majority are nails and spikes.

5) Other Artifacts. Few artifacts manufactured from shell and bone were recovered from sites. These include primarily clam shell disk beads.

6) Faunal Remains. The identification of mollusk remains and animal bones from the surface of sites is hindered by poor preservation, and the fragmentary condition of many specimens from trampling and other surface disturbances. U.C. Berkeley students initially sorted the mollusk remains into the following broad classes: abalone, chiton, limpet, turban snail, dogwinkle, periwinkle, hooked slipper snail, *Olivella*, and barnacles. The fragmentary nature of many specimens, in combination with their eroded, weathered surfaces, precludes the identification of the remains into more specific categories (i.e., genus and/or species). The calculation of Minimum Number of Individuals (MNIs) is based on diagnostic elements (see Waselkov 1987:154-161). Kent Lightfoot calcu-

lated the mollusk MNIs for the survey sites. Abalone MNIs are calculated by counting the number of whorl elements present, since each individual exhibits only one whorl. Chiton MNIs are computed by counting the number of plates and dividing by eight, since each individual is characterized by eight plates. Limpet MNIs are figured by counting the number of limpet caps. Turban snail, dogwinkle, periwinkle, hooked slipper snail, and *Olivella* MNIs are calculated by counting the number of apertures in the mollusk assemblage for each gastropod class. Barnacle MNIs are estimated by dividing the number of pieces by 20 to standardize our counts with those derived by Swiden (1986:56) in her analysis of the mollusks excavated from CA-SON-1455.

We recognize that our estimates of mollusk MNIs on Fort Ross sites are both conservative and tentative. Surface disturbances cause one to greatly underestimate the counts of MNIs. Many mollusk pieces collected from the surface are so fragmentary that diagnostic elements cannot be identified. The most critical problem is that fragile, thin-shelled, mollusk species (such as mussels) tend to be underrepresented in comparison to more durable, thick-shelled species (such as limpets). This problem should be kept in mind in considering the results below.

Mammal and bird bones are the only other faunal remains recovered from the surface of survey sites. Since surface sediments were not screened through fine mesh, the collection methodology is biased against the recovery of small faunal remains (or artifacts) such as fish skeletal elements. Thomas Wake classified the mammal and fish bones by taxon and element (when possible), and he noted whether the bones exhibited evidence of modification (cut marks, burning, scavenging marks). Given the fragmentary nature of the surface assemblage only broad taxa were defined in most cases (large mammal, medium mammal, etc.).

THE CALCULATION OF
DIVERSITY INDEXES

Diversity indexes are heuristic measures for comparing the relative diversity of archaeological materials from different site assemblages. We calculate diversity indexes for Fort Ross survey sites to evaluate the relative range of activities or tasks that took place at archaeological places. We assume that the diversity of artifact or faunal classes on a site represents, in a crude manner, the range of tasks performed there. A site containing a great variety of tool classes or faunal categories is assumed to represent a place

where a diverse range of activities took place. In contrast, a site with few artifact classes or limited faunal diversity is assumed to represent a place where a restricted range of activities took place. Of course, this assumption holds only for those activities that produce artifactual materials or faunal remains that are recoverable in archaeological contexts.

In evaluating the central-based village settlement model for the study area, we expect, all other factors being equal, that relatively permanent villages should exhibit high diversity indexes in comparison to other, more limited activity loci. Of course, all other factors are never equal in archaeology. One must interpret diversity indexes with great caution.

A critical consideration is the use-duration of an archaeological place. Lightfoot and Jewett (1986:19) define the use-duration as the "total aggregate of time that a specific location is used, regardless of the functional nature of that use." Binford (1982) describes how optimal places may be reused by the same or different people over extended lengths of time. Some archaeological places may have different economic potentials during the annual cycle. A place used as a short-term residential camp during one part of the year may function as a food processing station in another. The end result is a palimpsest of archaeological remains of considerable diversity. Thus, an archaeological place with a long use-duration may produce, at least theoretically, diversity indexes comparable to a village location, even though the place was never used, at any one time, as more than a short-term camp or processing station.

Sample size also critically effects diversity indexes. As Kintigh (1984; 1989) shows, there is a strong tendency for large assemblages to exhibit more diversity than small assemblages simply because there is a greater chance for large assemblages to contain a greater variety of items. Since the sample sizes of artifact and faunal assemblages from Fort Ross survey sites vary greatly, as detailed below, the sample size problem is a significant concern. Some sites may exhibit higher diversity indexes than others simply because we collected many more artifact and faunal specimens from them.

We calculate two diversity indexes, richness and evenness, for chipped stone artifacts, ground stone tools, and mollusk assemblages. We do not include counts of fire-cracked/ground stone fragments in the calculations. Diversity indexes are not computed for animal bones given their very limited occurrence on Fort Ross sites. Richness or R is simply the number of classes of lithic artifacts or mollusk remains collected from a site. The greater the number of classes, the more diverse the assemblage (see Kintigh 1984:44-

49). Evenness is the J score, initially used by ecologists to measure "the evenness of the distribution of counts across the categories" (see Kintigh 1988:48). The J score has been employed to evaluate the diversity of archaeological assemblages in the American Southwest (Whittlesey and Reid 1982; Kintigh 1989:31-39) and in southern New England (Lightfoot 1985:300-303; Lightfoot et al. 1987). The J score is calculated as follows (see Kintigh 1987:29):

$$H = \frac{n \log (n) - \sum_{i=1}^{k} f_i \log (f_i)}{n}$$

$$Hmax = \log (k)$$

$$J = \frac{H}{Hmax}$$

Where: f = frequency of category i
        k = number of categories
        n = sample size

The J score ranges from 0 to 1, with 0 representing the least diverse archaeological assemblage and 1 representing the most diverse or varied assemblage.

We employ Kintigh's (1988) DIVERS computer program to calculate indexes of richness and evenness. The program addresses the problem of sample size by simulating numerous trial runs using a Monte Carlo approach. For each site with a given sample size, a large number of simulated assemblages is computed based on the underlying frequency distribution of the entire Fort Ross assemblage. The program produces a mean and ninety percent confidence interval for evaluating actual diversity indexes for each site. One can then evaluate critically whether a site's diversity index is greater or lower than expected given a specific sample size. In controlling the effects of sample size, the key consideration is to examine diversity indexes for sites relative to the expected distribution of the simulated trials, rather than the absolute values per se. For example, a J score calculated for a large assemblage may be relatively high (i.e., .7) but in comparison to other simulated assemblages of that same size it may be smaller than expected (below the ninetieth percentile). In contrast, a J score computed for a moderate-sized assemblage may be a smaller absolute value (i.e., .6), but in comparison to other simulated assemblages of that same size it may be greater than expected (in the ninety-fifth percentile, or in the upper five percent of all trials).

THE CONSTRUCTION OF LOCAL CHRONOLOGY

We employ Fredrickson's (1974c:49; 1984a:485) regional chronology to designate the Prehistoric, Protohistoric, and Historic periods that are necessary to use the direct historical approach. The prehistory of the region is divided into the PaleoIndian period (10,000 B.C.-6000 B.C.), the Lower Archaic (6000 B.C.-3000 B.C.), the Middle Archaic (3000 B.C.-1000 B.C.), the Upper Archaic (1000 B.C.-A.D. 500), and the Lower Emergent (A.D. 500-A.D. 1500). The Protohistoric period is defined as the Upper Emergent (ca A.D. 1500-A.D. 1812) in the Ross region, when the earliest contacts with native peoples were made by Spanish and English explorers in nearby coastal Marin County. The Historic period, when Europeans first settled the local region and sustained contact took place with native peoples, begins with the construction of the Ross Colony in A.D. 1812.

The dating of survey sites is based on three sets of chronological data: obsidian hydration, projectile point types, and historic ceramic and glass types.

Obsidian Hydration. The principal method for dating survey sites is the measurement of hydration bands on obsidian artifacts. Since the surface of obsidian absorbs water over time, estimates on the length of time a surface has been exposed to the local environment can be made by measuring the width of the hydration layer in microns. Generally, the thicker the hydration layer, the greater the passage of time. Unfortunately, the specific rate of hydration over time is very complicated, varying significantly with local obsidian flows and local environmental factors such as temperature (see Origer 1987:1-5; Tremaine 1989:1-6).

Over the last ten years, a tremendous amount of research has been undertaken on the hydration properties of four different obsidian sources in the southern North Coast Ranges: Annadel near Santa Rosa, Borax Lake and Mt. Konocti near Clear Lake, and Glass Mountain in Napa Valley (Fredrickson 1987, 1989; Jackson 1989; Tremaine and Fredrickson 1988; Tremaine 1989; Origer 1987; and Origer and Wickstrom 1982). In particular, the Obsidian Hydration Laboratory, Sonoma State University, has been at the forefront of developing an obsidian hydration chronology for the southern North Coast Ranges with specific application to the interior of Sonoma County.

We employ Sonoma State University's obsidian hydration chronology to date survey sites in the study area. The vast majority of obsidian on Fort Ross sites derive from one of the above four obsidian sources. Obsidian is relatively ubiquitous on survey sites, and at least a few obsidian artifacts were recovered from most sites we surface collected. All obsidian samples were analyzed by the Obsidian Hydration Laboratory, Sonoma State University.

To aid in the chronological placement of Fort Ross sites, we employ Tremaine's (1989:69-70) comparison constants derived from induced obsidian experiments to compare the hydration band measurements of obsidians from the four major sources. Hydration band measurements are calibrated to the hydration rates of the Annadel flow by multiplying Napa Valley and Mt. Konocti readings by .77, and Borax Lake measurements by .62.

We recognize that obsidian hydration is best used as a relative dating method. Obsidian hydration measurements can be employed to rank, in an ordinal temporal scheme, the age of sites from oldest to youngest; for defining the relative use-duration of a location (short-term or long-term); and for assigning "units of contemporaneity" (Fredrickson 1984b; Tremaine 1989:6). Our research problem, however, necessitates a temporal scheme that is refined enough to distinguish cultural change in the Prehistoric, Protohistoric, and Historic periods. To develop this capability, we use the regression equation devised by Origer (1987:55-59) for the hydration rate of Annadel obsidian. The hydration rate is based on the association of Annadel obsidian artifacts in radiocarbon dated contexts from six sites in the southern North Coast Ranges. The equation provides a rough approximation of the hydration band measurements in microns that correspond to the periods outlined above. They are as follows: Lower Archaic (6.6-5.3 microns), Middle Archaic (5.2-4.1 microns), Upper Archaic (4.0-2.9 microns), Lower Emergent (2.8-1.7 microns), Upper Emergent (1.6-1.0 microns), and the Historic period (1.0 micron or smaller). The temporal placement of sites is based on the mean and standard deviation of the hydration readings. Histograms are generated for each site to examine the frequency distribution of hydration measurements. In cases where distinct clusters of measurements exist, the mean and standard deviation of the readings for each cluster are calculated. In such a manner we attempted to define the relative use-duration of individual sites.

We stress that the obsidian hydration chronology employed in this analysis is tentative. Future research on obsidian hydration rates will most certainly refine Tremaine's (1989) comparison constants for obsidians from southern North Coast Ranges sources. Future research will probably also modify the regression equation of Origer (1987) to fine tune the hydration rate of Annadel obsidian for the temporal periods outlined above. A potentially serious problem is our application of a hydration rate developed primarily for interior Sonoma County to the cooler environment of the coast. Cooler temperatures tend to retard the hydration rates of most obsidians. Origer's (1987:48)

research suggests that rates of hydration for Annadel and Napa Valley obsidians are slower on the coast than the interior. Additional research will eventually be undertaken to refine the hydration rates of obsidians from different sources found at coastal sites.

Projectile Point Types. The classic method for dating survey sites in the southern North Coast Ranges is based on projectile point seriations (Beardsley 1954; Baumhoff 1982; Levulett and Hildebrandt 1987:31-37; Origer 1987; White et al. 1982). The majority of projectile points recovered from survey sites can be classified into four basic types after Origer (1987).

1. Corner-Notched. This type is a small triangular point whose basal portion is marked by corner notches. The point is assumed to date to the Upper Emergent and Historic periods (from A.D. 1500) (see Origer 1987:32). In Origer's (1987:47) study of ninety corner-notched points of Annadel obsidian, the hydration measurements range from .9 to 2.2 microns ($\bar{x}$=1.3, sd=.26).

2. Serrated. These small points are characterized by distinctive square, rounded or pointed serrations along the blade. The general shape is straight, parallel, or slightly expanding stems. They are thought to be diagnostic of the Lower Emergent period (see Origer 1987:34-35). In Origer's (1987:47) analysis of eighty-six serrated points of Annadel obsidian, the hydration readings range from 1.2-2.2 microns ($\bar{x}$=1.6, sd=.24).

3. Shouldered Lanceolate. This is a large point demarcated by its leaf- or lanceolate-shaped body. The triangular blade narrows to a convex base. It is probably a dart point. Locally known as an "Excelsior" point, large numbers in Sonoma County appear to date to the Upper Archaic period, although its temporal range is considerably greater (Origer 1987:36). An analysis of forty-three shouldered lanceolate points of Annadel obsidian yielded hydration measurements from 1.5 to 4.8 microns ($\bar{x}$=2.6, sd=.67) (Origer 1987:47).

4. Large Side/Corner-Notched. These large points are characterized by a triangular shape with relatively parallel sides. The basal portion contains either side notches or corner notches. The shape of the base may be convex. Dating of this point is rather approximate, but traditionally it is believed to be found on early Upper Archaic and Middle Archaic sites (Origer 1987:35-36). In Origer's (1987:47) study of ten large side/corner-notched points of Annadel obsidian, hydration measurements range from 1.2-2.8 microns ($\bar{x}$=2, sd=.51).

Historic Artifacts. Ceramic and bottle sherds provide another means of dating survey sites to the Historic period (or even Upper Emergent period). The majority of the glass recovered from survey sites (moldblown glass, dark olive-green in color, from alcoholic beverage containers) appears to have been manufactured in the nineteenth century (prior to 1910). The majority of the ceramics from survey sites (white improved earthenware and porcelain) could date from the early nineteenth to the early twentieth centuries. The dating of some ceramic artifacts was complicated by the fragmentary condition and eroded surface of the sherds.

FORT ROSS SURVEY SITES

Below we describe each of the thirty sites recorded in the Fort Ross State Historic Park. To facilitate our presentation of survey data, we summarize pertinent information in the following tables for the twenty native Californian sites surface collected by U.C. Berkeley crews. Please note that CA-SON-1897/H and CA-SON-1898/H are not included since they will be described in detail in Volume 2 of the Archaeology and Ethnohistory of Fort Ross, California series.

Table 5.2 presents data on site size, the total surface area collected (sq m), the sample fraction (percent of site area surface collected), lithic and mollusk densities, and the diversity indexes for lithic and mollusk assemblages. Lithic densities are calculated by dividing the total number of lithics by the area surface collected on sites. Mollusk densities are determined by dividing the total MNIs by the area surface collected. Tables 5.3 and 5.4 are the counts and percentages, respectively, of lithic artifact classes. Tables 5.5 and 5.6 are the counts and percentages of lithic raw material types. Tables 5.7 and 5.8 present the counts and percentages of mollusk MNIs for each site collected. Table 5.9 lists the counts of beads, glass sherds, historic ceramics, metal artifacts, and animal bones. Table 5.10 summarizes the study of the obsidian hydration analysis. More specific information on the catalog numbers and proveniences of lithic artifacts; mollusk MNIs; mammal and bird bones; glass, ceramic, and metal materials; and selected beads are listed in appendices 5.1, 5.2, 5.3, 5.4, and 5.5, respectively. Illustrations of diagnostic artifacts are presented in appendix 5.6.

Table 5.2

SIZE, SAMPLE FRACTION, LITHIC AND MOLLUSK DENSITIES,

AND DIVERSITY INDEXES OF FORT ROSS SITES

Site #	Size (m²)	Sample Area (m²)	Sample Fraction (%)	Lithic Density (n/m²)	Mollusk Density (MNI/m²)	Diversity Indexes			
						Lithics		Mollusks	
						R(%)	J(%)	R(%)	J(%)
174	346	10	3	.2	.6	3(38)	.367(38)	3(67)	.439(76)
228	4536	pp*	-	-	0	8(3)	.492(0)	-	-
670	3750	24	23	.67	.08	2(7)	.198(5)	4(96)	.579(96)
1878	2107	86	4	.2	0	12(94)	.806(98)	2(53)	.276(53)
1879	1.8	1.8	100	0	0	-	-	-	-
1880	2024	46	2	.65	.65	10(72)	.763(87)	7(93)	.617(98)
1881	471	8	2	1.0	2.7	4(8)	.406(5)	5(63)	.480(65)
1882	54	18	33	.05	.3	-	-	4(90)	.577(96)
1883	8247	960	12	.46	.02	15(56)	.823(98)	7(99)	.672(100
1884	3044	126	4	.67	.03	11(68)	.735(65)	4(99)	.602(99)
1885	919	56	6	.05	.16	7(44)	.650(57)	7(100)	.80(100)
1886	94	22	23	9.86	32.86	11(11)	.658(0)	9(15)	.395(0)
1887	.23	.23	100	0	0	-	-	-	-
1888	85	22	26	1.04	2.14	4(0)	.470(1)	7(79)	.67(100)
1889	189	8	4	.37	2.37	8(80)	.649(59)	5(38)	.447(40)
1890	871	2	.02	3.0	3.0	6(63)	.592(59)	4(92)	.540(89)
1892	120	12	10	.92	6.9	7(88)	.667(92)	5(6)	.494(54)
1894	155	-	-	-	-	8(39)	.665(48)	-	-
1895	203	32	16	.06	.34	4(59)	.470(59)	5(92)	.692(99)
1896	400	39	10	.18	.87	-	-	6(72)	.684(99)

* pp = point provenience

CA-SON-174

Brief History. Omer Stewart originally recorded the site in 1935. It is depicted in his map (1943:28) as site 16. The site was re-recorded, mapped, and surface collected by a U.C. Berkeley crew in the summer of 1989.

Location. CA-SON-174 is situated 250 m southwest of the Ross stockade and across the old highway from the Call's ranch house (figure 5.3). It sits on the cliff edge of the coastal terrace overlooking the ocean in coastal prairie grass.

Site Description. The 346 sq m area contains three large depressions, a cluster of sandstone blocks, and scattered shellfish refuse (figure 5.4). The two easternmost depressions measure about 8 m in diameter, the westernmost about 6 m in diameter. The sandstone blocks are remnants of the first Fort Ross schoolhouse built in November 1884. In 1938, the original schoolhouse was dismantled, moved, and

Table 5.3

LITHIC COUNTS FROM FORT ROSS SURVEY SITES

Site	BC	BI	BT	CO	EM	FC/GF	HA	HM	IF	HS	NW	PC	PE	PP	SC	SH	SM	UN	T
174	1	0	2	0	1	0	0	0	0	0	0	0	0	0	0	0	0	0	4
228	2	1	5	2	4	0	0	0	23	1	0	0	0	0	0	1	0	0	39
670	0	0	1	0	0	16	0	0	0	3	0	0	0	0	0	0	0	0	20
1878	0	3	3	3	9	2	1	0	4	2	0	4	0	2	1	4	1	0	39
1879	0	0	0	0	0	1	0	0	0	1	0	0	0	0	0	0	0	0	2
1880	0	1	5	3	4	7	0	0	4	3	0	1	0	0	2	2	1	0	33
1881	0	0	0	1	0	2	0	0	0	0	0	0	0	0	1	5	2	0	11
1882	0	0	0	0	0	1	0	0	0	0	0	0	0	0	0	0	0	0	1
1883	2	17	20	35	30	296	5	0	51	28	1	4	3	5	15	44	4	0	570
1884	0	1	2	5	6	58	1	0	6	0	1	3	0	4	2	13	0	1	103
1885	0	0	2	1	3	6	0	0	3	0	0	0	0	1	4	2	0	1	23
1886	5	1	0	4	24	122	0	0	30	14	0	4	1	2	9	1	0	0	217
1887	0	0	0	0	0	0	0	0	0	0	0	0	0	0	0	0	0	0	0
1888	0	0	5	0	5	2	0	0	8	0	0	0	0	0	3	0	0	0	23
1889	0	1	1	1	5	5	0	0	2	1	0	0	1	0	0	0	0	1	18
1890	0	0	2	0	1	0	0	0	1	0	0	0	0	1	1	3	0	0	9
1892	1	0	1	0	2	6	1	0	1	0	0	0	0	0	1	2	0	0	15
1894	0	1	2	2	2	1	0	1	5	0	0	0	0	0	2	6	0	0	22
1895	2	0	0	1	0	4	0	0	1	0	0	0	0	0	1	0	0	0	9
1896	0	0	0	0	0	7	0	0	0	0	0	0	0	0	0	0	0	0	7

Legend:

BC = battered cobble	IF = interior flake
BI = biface	NW = net weight
BT = biface thinning flake	PC = primary cortical flake
CO = core	PE = pestle
EM = edge-modified flake	PP = projectile point
FC/GF = fire-cracked/ground stone fragment	SC = secondary cortical flake
HA = hammerstone	SH = shatter
HM = hopper mortar	SM = slab millingstone
HS = handstone	UN = uniface

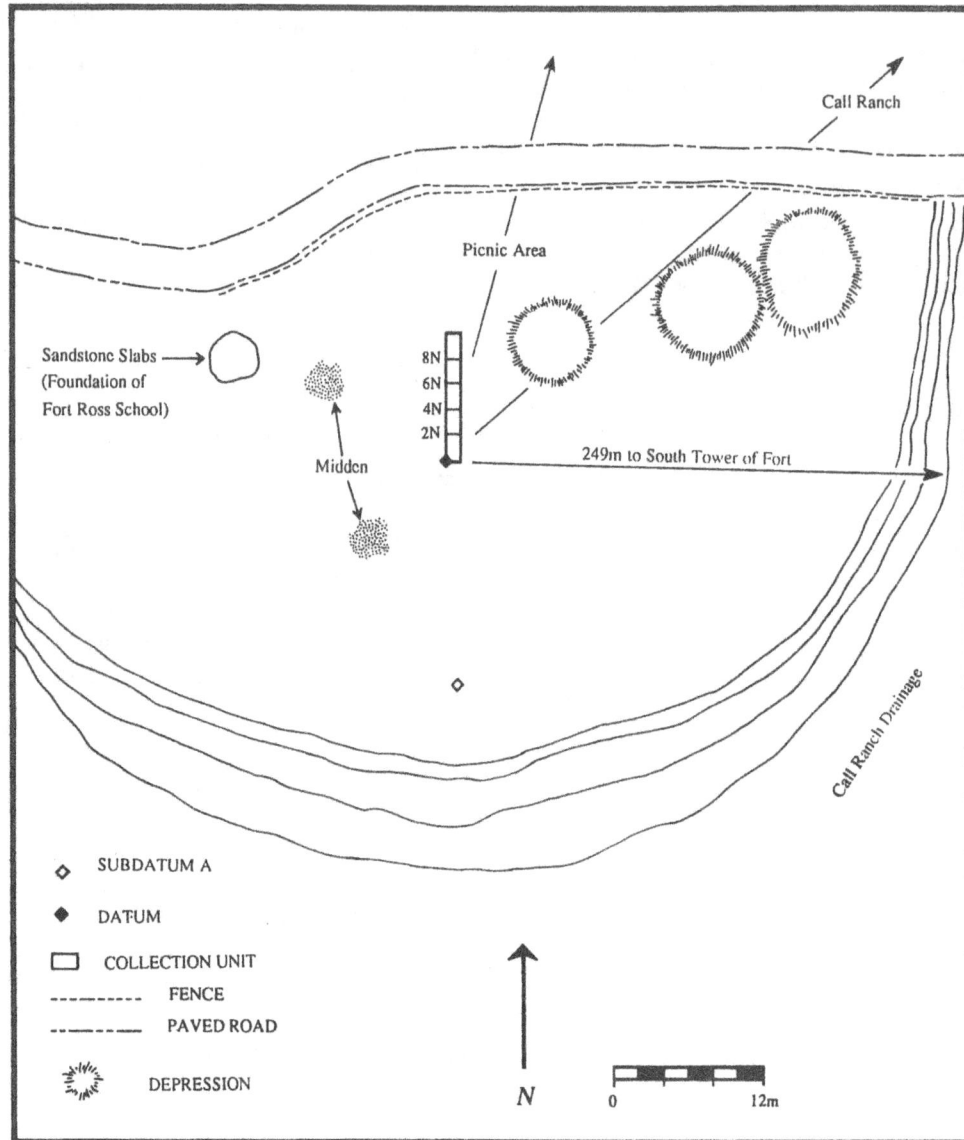

Figure 5.4

Site Map of CA-SON-174

reassembled at the present location of the Fort Ross School near Seaview. In 1973, the structure was again moved to the nearby Sonoma County park of Stillwater Cove where it can be viewed today (Tomlin 1991).

Collection Strategy. About 3% of the site's surface area was collected. A segmented transect containing five 1 by 2 m units was laid out north of the site datum (figure 5.4). Additional surface materials, scattered widely along the southern edge of the site, were point provenienced and collected.

Lithic Artifacts. Only four lithic artifacts were collected: 1 battered cobble, 2 biface thinning flakes, and 1 edge-modified flake. Three were manufactured from obsidian and one from chert. The lithic density (not including point provenienced material) is .2 artifacts/sq m.

Historic Artifacts. Glass sherds from seven different vessels were identified. These include 2 moldblown colorless glass containers; 1 moldblown olive green wine bottle; 3 flat glass specimens probably from window panes; and the base sherd of a square-shaped, black glass container embossed with the letters "ER." The latter is a "Hostetter's Stomach Bitters" bottle. The surface collection yielded the fragments of 2 ceramic vessels. One is represented by 2 sherds of the handle of a white improved earthenware pitcher, large cup, or serving vessel. The vessel is very hard ("ironstone" weight), white and covered by a thin clear glaze. The other ceramic vessel is represented by the rim of a thin, whitish-blue bowl (1.4 mm thick) of Chinese porcellaneous stoneware. The exterior is decorated with a blurred cobalt design below the rim. Metal artifacts include the fragments

Table 5.4

PERCENTAGE OF LITHIC TYPES AT FORT ROSS SURVEY SITES

Site	BC	BI	BT	CO	EM	FC/GF	HA	HM	IF	HS	NW	PC	PE	PP	SC	SH	SM	UN
174	25	0	50	0	25	0	0	0	0	0	0	0	0	0	0	0	0	0
228	5	3	13	5	10	0	0	0	60	2	0	0	0	0	0	2	0	0
670	0	0	5	0	0	80	0	0	0	15	0	0	0	0	0	0	0	0
1878	0	8	8	8	22	5	3	0	10	5	0	10	0	5	3	10	3	0
1879	0	0	0	0	0	50	0	0	0	50	0	0	0	0	0	0	0	0
1880	0	3	15	9	12	22	0	0	12	9	0	3	0	0	6	6	3	0
1881	0	0	0	9	0	18	0	0	0	0	0	0	0	0	9	46	18	0
1882	0	0	0	0	0	100	0	0	0	0	0	0	0	0	0	0	0	0
1883	0	3	3	6	5	52	1	0	9	5	0	2	1	1	3	8	1	0
1884	0	1	2	5	6	56	1	0	6	0	1	3	0	4	2	12	0	1
1885	0	0	9	3	14	27	0	0	14	0	0	0	0	3	18	9	0	3
1886	2	0	0	2	11	57	0	0	14	7	0	2	0	1	4	0	0	0
1887	0	0	0	0	0	0	0	0	0	0	0	0	0	0	0	0	0	0
1888	0	0	22	0	22	8	0	0	35	0	0	0	0	0	13	0	0	0
1889	0	5	5	5	29	29	0	0	12	5	0	0	5	0	0	0	0	5
1890	0	0	22	0	11	0	0	0	11	0	0	0	0	11	11	34	0	0
1892	7	0	7	0	12	41	7	0	7	0	0	0	0	0	9	28	0	0
1894	0	4	9	9	9	4	0	4	24	0	0	0	0	0	2	6	0	0
1895	22	0	0	11	0	45	0	0	11	0	0	0	0	0	11	0	0	0
1896	0	0	0	0	0	100	0	0	0	0	0	0	0	0	0	0	0	0

Legend:

BC = % battered cobble

BI = % biface

BT = % biface thinning flake

CO = % core

EM = % edge modified flake

FC/GF = fire-cracked/ground
           stone fragment

HA = % hammerstone

HM = % hopper mortar

HS = % handstone

IF = % interior flake

NW = % net weight

PC = % primary cortical flake

PE = % pestle

PP = % projectile point

SC = secondary cortical
           flake

SH = % shatter

SM = % slab millingstone

UN = % uniface

of two square iron spikes and nails, two iron tongue hinge valves used with a padlock, and other unidentifiable pieces.

Faunal Remains. Mollusk MNIs include three chitons, two mussels, and one barnacle. The density of mollusks (not including point provenienced material) is .6 MNIs/sq m. The surface collection also yielded 13 mammal bones and teeth, including a tibia and scapula of a cow (*Bos taurus*), 2 mandibles and the second lower premolar tooth of elk (*Cervus elaphus*), a tibia from a mule deer (*Odocoileus hemionus*), and the remains of unidentified large mammals (6 long bones, 1 unidentified bone element). The elk mandibles are both from the left side of the body, suggesting that at least two individuals are represented in the surface assemblage. The two elements of a *Bos taurus* exhibit evidence of cut marks.

Table 5.5

COUNTS OF LITHIC RAW MATERIAL TYPES

AT FORT ROSS SURVEY SITES

Site	BA	CH	GW	OB	QU	SA	SC	T
174	0	1	0	3	0	0	0	4
228	0	13	0	21	0	5	0	39
670	11	0	0	1	0	8	0	20
1878	2	31	0	0	1	5	0	39
1879	0	0	0	0	0	2	0	2
1880	1	9	0	13	0	10	0	33
1881	0	3	0	3	1	4	0	11
1882	0	0	0	0	0	1	0	1
1883	19	161	7	62	4	312	5	570
1884	0	35	0	5	2	59	2	103
1885	0	12	0	5	0	6	0	23
1886	13	65	6	7	2	123	1	217
1887	0	0	0	0	0	0	0	0
1888	0	15	0	6	0	2	0	23
1889	0	6	0	5	0	7	0	18
1890	0	6	0	3	0	0	0	9
1892	0	5	1	2	0	7	0	15
1894	0	7	0	10	0	2	3	22
1895	0	1	0	2	0	6	0	9
1896	1	0	0	0	0	5	1	7

Legend: BA = basalt   QU = quartz

CH = chert   SA = sandstone

GW = graywacke   SC = schist

OB = obsidian   T = Total Count

Table 5.6

PERCENTAGE OF LITHIC RAW MATERIAL TYPES AT FORT ROSS SURVEY SITES

Site	BA	CH	GW	OB	QU	SA	SC	%
174	0	25	0	75	0	0	0	100
228	0	33	0	54	0	13	0	100
670	55	0	0	5	0	40	0	100
1878	5	80	0	0	3	12	0	100
1879	0	0	0	0	0	100	0	100
1880	3	27	0	40	0	30	0	100
1881	0	27	0	27	9	37	0	100
1882	0	0	0	0	0	100	0	100
1883	3	28	1	11	1	55	1	100
1884	0	34	0	5	2	57	2	100
1885	0	52	0	22	0	26	0	100
1886	6	30	2	3	1	57	1	100
1887	0	0	0	0	0	0	0	0
1888	0	65	0	26	0	9	0	100
1889	0	33	0	28	0	39	0	100
1890	0	67	0	33	0	0	0	100
1892	0	33	7	13	0	47	0	100
1894	0	32	0	45	0	9	14	100
1895	0	11	0	22	0	67	0	100
1896	14	0	0	0	0	72	14	100

Legend:　BA = % basalt　CH = % chert　GW = % graywacke　OB = % obsidian

　　　　QU = % quartz　SA = % sandstone　SC = % schist

Table 5.7

COUNTS OF MOLLUSK MNIs FOR FORT ROSS SURVEY SITES

Site	AB	BA	CH	LI	TU	DO	OL	MU	PE	HS	OT	T
174	0	1	3	0	0	0	0	2	0	0	0	6
228	0	0	0	0	0	0	0	0	0	0	0	0
670	1	0	1	2	1	0	0	0	0	0	0	5
1878	0	0	0	2	0	0	0	1	0	0	0	3
1879	0	0	0	0	0	0	0	0	0	0	0	0
1880	1	1	1	5	15	0	0	6	0	1	0	30
1881	0	2	1	15	2	0	0	3	0	0	0	23
1882	0	1	1	0	2	0	0	2	0	0	0	6
1883	1	1	2	11	3	0	0	6	0	1	0	25
1884	0	1	1	1	0	0	0	1	0	0	0	4
1885	0	1	2	1	1	1	0	3	1	0	0	10
1886	2	9	13	537	95	12	6	32	0	5	12	723
1887	0	0	0	0	0	0	0	0	0	0	0	0
1888	0	1	7	17	12	0	0	8	1	1	0	47
1889	0	1	1	21	6	0	0	3	0	0	0	32
1890	0	1	1	0	1	0	0	3	0	0	0	6
1892	0	1	3	45	12	0	0	22	0	0	0	83
1894	0	0	0	0	0	0	0	0	0	0	0	0
1895	0	2	2	3	2	0	0	2	0	0	0	11
1896	0	2	6	9	5	0	1	11	0	0	0	34

Legend:

AB = abalone　BA = barnacle　CH = chiton　LI = limpet　TU = turban　DO = dogwinkle

OL = Olivella　MU = mussel　PE = periwinkle　HS = hooked slipper shell　OT = other　T = total count

Table 5.8

PERCENTAGE OF MOLLUSK MNIs AT FORT ROSS SURVEY SITES

Site	AB	BA	CH	LI	TU	DO	OL	MU	PE	HS	OT	%
174	0	17	50	0	0	0	0	33	0	0	0	100
228	0	0	0	0	0	0	0	0	0	0	0	0
670	20	0	20	40	20	0	0	0	0	0	0	100
1878	0	0	0	66	0	0	0	34	0	0	0	100
1879	0	0	0	0	0	0	0	0	0	0	0	0
1880	3	3	3	17	51	0	0	20	0	3	0	100
1881	0	9	4	65	9	0	0	13	0	0	0	100
1882	0	17	17	0	33	0	0	33	0	0	0	100
1883	4	4	8	44	12	0	0	24	0	4	0	100
1884	0	25	25	25	0	0	0	25	0	0	0	100
1885	0	10	20	10	10	10	0	30	10	0	0	100
1886	0	2	2	74	13	2	1	4	0	1	1	100
1887	0	0	0	0	0	0	0	0	0	0	0	0
1888	0	2	15	36	26	0	0	17	2	2	0	100
1889	0	3	3	66	19	0	0	9	0	0	0	100
1890	0	17	17	0	17	0	0	49	0	0	0	100
1891	0	0	0	0	0	0	0	0	0	0	0	0
1892	0	1	3	54	15	0	0	27	0	0	0	100
1894	0	0	0	0	0	0	0	0	0	0	0	0
1895	0	18	18	28	18	0	0	18	0	0	0	100
1896	0	6	18	26	15	0	3	32	0	0	0	100

Legend: AB = % abalone   LI = % limpet   OL = % Olivella   HS = % hooked slipper shell
         BA = % barnacle   TU = % turban   MU = % mussel   OT = % other
         CH = % chiton   DO = % dogwinkle   PE = % periwinkle

Table 5.9

COUNTS OF OTHER ARCHAEOLOGICAL MATERIALS AT FORT ROSS SURVEY SITES

Site	GB	DB	GV	CV	ME	AB
174	0	0	7	2	15	13
228	0	0	1	0	0	0
670	0	0	0	0	0	0
1878	0	0	3	3	0	0
1879	0	0	0	0	0	0
1880	1	0	2	2	0	14
1881	0	0	0	0	0	2
1882	0	0	0	0	0	0
1883	0	0	2	0	0	1
1884	0	0	0	1	0	0
1885	0	0	0	1	0	0
1886	0	1	4	3	0	28
1887	0	0	0	0	0	0
1888	0	0	0	0	0	4
1889	0	0	0	0	0	0
1890	0	0	0	0	0	5
1892	0	1	0	0	0	0
1894	0	0	0	0	0	0
1895	0	0	4	1	0	3
1896	0	0	0	0	0	1

Legend: GB = glass bead   DB = clam disk bead   GV = minimum number of glass vessels
         CV = minimum number   ME = metal artifact   AB = animal bone
              of ceramic vessels

Table 5.10

OBSIDIAN HYDRATION DATA FOR THE FORT ROSS SITES

All Readings Are Calibrated for the Hydration Rate of Annadel Obsidian

Site	N	M	SD	Min	Max	Range	Multiple Clusters or Outliers
174	2	1.65	.15	1.5	1.8	(1.5 -1.8)	no
228	12	2.82	.69	1.7	3.8	(2.1 -3.5)	no
670	1	1.7	0	1.7	1.7		no
1878	0						
1879	0						
1880	9	2.04	1.46	.8	5.2	(.6 -3.5)	yes
1881	2	1.20	.10	1.1	1.3	(1.1-1.3)	no
1882	0						
1883	16	1.52	.50	.8	2.6	(1.0 -2.0)	no
1884	3	1.01	.16	.9	1.2	(.8 -1.2)	no
1885	5	1.82	.49	1.4	2.5	(1.4 -2.2)	no
1886	5	1.44	.39	1.0	2.0	(1.0 -1.8)	no
1887	0						
1888	3	1.4	.14	1.2	1.5	(1.3 -1.5)	no
1889	4	1.9	.75	1.4	3.2	(1.1 -2.6)	yes
1890	2	1.97	.87	1.1	2.8	(1.1 -2.8)	no
1892	2	1.30	.10	1.2	1.4	(1.2 -1.4)	no
1894	5	1.58	.67	.8	2.7	(.9 -2.2)	no
1895	1	1.2	0	1.2	1.2		no
1896	17	.85	.12	.7	1.2	(.7 -1.0)	no

Legend: N = number of obsidian hydration readings Min = minimum hydration measurement in microns
M = mean hydration measurement in microns Max = maximum hydration measurement in microns
SD = standard deviation in microns Range = +/- standard deviation

Diversity Indexes. The diversity of chipped stone artifact and ground stone tool classes is lower than expected for a similar sized sample. The richness and J scores for the lithic classes are 3 (thirty-eighth percentile) and .367 (thirty-eighth percentile), respectively. The diversity of mollusks is somewhat greater. The richness and J scores for the mollusks MNIs are 3 (sixty-seventh percentile) and .439 (sixty-seventh percentile), respectively.

Chronology. CA-SON-174 yielded only two obsidian hydration measurements (table 5.11). The average of the two measurements is 1.65 microns (sd=.15; one standard deviation range: 1.5-1.8 microns), suggesting an approximate late Lower Emergent or early Upper Emergent date. Of course, the sample size is so small that this estimate is very tentative.

The historic artifacts suggest a later nineteenth century date. The moldblown glass containers suggest a pre-1910s date of manufacture. Hostetter's Bitters bottles were produced from A.D. 1858 to ca. A.D. 1910. The weight and style of the white improved earthenware handle indicates a somewhat later manufacturing date, possible sometime during the 1860s through the 1900s. The metal spikes are machine made and could range in date from the mid-1800s to the 1940s.

Interpretation. The coastal terrace on which CA-SON-174 sits has witnessed a long use-duration that spans several hundreds of years. The archaeological place may have been sporadically used as early as the late Lower Emergent period based on two obsidian hydration measurements. The age of the three depressions remains unknown and will require further archaeological investigation. Nevertheless, we feel the major occupation of CA-SON-174 may have taken place immediately after the withdrawal of the Russians from Fort Ross. Glenn Farris directed an archaeological excavation directly across the old highway from CA-SON-174 to mitigate the effects of a

Table 5.11

OBSIDIAN HYDRATION DATA FOR CA-SON-174

Lab #	Catalog #	Source	Hydration (microns)	Comparison Constant (microns)
78	F- 6/2/89-4-L:1	Napa Valley	1.9	1.5
79	F- 6/2/89-5-L	Annadel	1.8	1.8
80	F- 6/5/89-17-L:1	?	No Visible Hydration	

leach line. His project unearthed a variety of native artifacts including glass projectile points, glass trade beads, obsidian and chert flakes, various buttons, and an 1854 U.S. dime with a hole drilled in one edge (Farris 1986a:20-21). The analysis of the glass beads suggests a date sometime during the 1840s and 1850s (Glenn Farris, personal communication). It is possible that CA-SON-174 was part of larger village where Kashaya Pomo people stayed while working as agricultural laborers on William Benitz's Ross ranch (see chapter 6). By the late nineteenth century, the archaeological place was reused as the site of a small school, and as an extension of the front yard of the Call Ranch house, which was built in 1878 (Kaye Tomlin, personal communication). The low density and diversity of remains from this site may reflect intensive collecting of artifacts from the surface by school children and other interested parties over the years

CA-SON-175

Brief History. Barrett (1908:230-231) identifies this site as the historic village of "Metini" (site #37 in figure 4.2). Omer Stewart recorded the site in 1935, and designated it as site 17 in his map (Stewart 1943:28). It was re-recorded in 1949 by A. Pilling and C. Meighan. Gifford (1967:9) also describes the "Metini" site.

Location. The site is located 110 m directly north of the Ross stockade on the coastal terrace in coastal prairie grass.

Site Description. Gifford (1967:9) describes the site as consisting of a large central depression, which he interpreted as the remains of a "dance-house," surrounded by twelve to fifteen smaller "house pits." Pilling and Meighan (1949) estimate that the size of the site is about 18,241 sq m. They note that plowing of the site area has obliterated most of the smaller surface depressions. Today, only the large pit depression is clearly visible on the surface. Mollusk debris, animal bones, and artifacts are found along the eastern edge of the site.

Collection Strategy. As far as we know, the site has yet to be mapped in detail and surface collected in a systematic manner. O'Connor (1984:12) notes in passing, however, that the site was investigated by archaeologists in 1970. If so, then no report of their findings has been written up.

Interpretation. Little is known about the historic village that Barrett first designated as "Metini." Some evidence suggests, however, that the village may actually post-date the Russian occupation of Fort Ross. Glenn Farris (1986a:16) notes that the site is marked as an Indian Rancheria in the 1859 Plat map of the Muniz Rancho (Matthewson 1859). Stewart (1935a) records on the original site form that the village probably dates to ca. A.D. 1850.

CA-SON-190 (Stockade Compound)

Brief History. As outlined in chapter 2, considerable archaeological work has taken place in the stockade compound and directly outside the northern palisade walls. While most of this research has focused on the Russian activity here, some of the excavations unearthed lithic tools, artifacts manufactured from glass (i.e., projectile points), and glass beads that suggest a Native American presence (see Treganza 1954:18; Smith 1974:7-9:45). Smith (1974:2-6) hypothesizes that this material may reflect an earlier Kashaya Pomo village that was abandoned when the stockade complex was first constructed by the Russians. She suggests that the original Metini village was then moved to a new location some distance from the fort.

A recent excavation along the southeastern perimeter of the stockade wall sheds some light on Smith's hypothesis. Directed by Thomas Origer and Allan Bramlette of Sonoma State University in 1989, field crews excavated along the original alignment of the wall, as well as outside the wall proper. The purpose of the fieldwork was to evaluate the impact of reconstructing the palisade wall for the third time in this section of the compound. In the final report, Margaret Purser, Vickie Beard, and Adrian Praetzellis (1990) describe obsidian and chert debitage, three projectile points (including a corner-notched point), six bifaces, a core, and various ground and battered stones from the excavation. Approximately 235 grams of shellfish, dominated by abalone, were also collected.

Chronology. Purser et al. (1990) submitted 54 obsidian specimens to Thomas Origer for hydration readings (table 5.12). The results suggest an extended use-duration in the southeastern section of CA-SON-190, spanning well back into prehistory. The mean of

Table 5.12

Oʙsɪᴅɪᴀɴ Hʏᴅʀᴀᴛɪᴏɴ Dᴀᴛᴀ ғᴏʀ ᴛʜᴇ Sᴏᴜᴛʜᴇᴀsᴛ Sᴇᴄᴛɪᴏɴ ᴏғ CA-SON-190*

Lab #	Source	Hydration (microns)	Comparison Constant (microns)
1	Annadel	1.2	1.2
2	Annadel	1.4	1.4
3	Annadel	1.5	1.5
4	Annadel	1.7	1.7
5	Annadel	1.5	1.5
6	Annadel	-	-
7	Napa Valley	3.4	2.6
8	Napa Valley	3.9	3.0
9	Napa Valley	2.9	2.2
10	Annadel	2.7	2.7
11	Annadel	2.9	2.9
12	Annadel	2.5	2.5
13	Napa Valley	3.8	2.9
14	Napa Valley	2.8	2.2
15	-	-	-
16	Annadel	1.8	1.8
17	Annadel	1.8	1.8
18	Napa Valley	3.8	2.9
19	Napa Valley	2.9	2.2
20	Napa Valley	2.4	1.8
21	Annadel	3.5	3.5
22	Napa Valley	3.1	2.4
23	Napa Valley	4.3	3.3
24	Napa Valley	4.4	3.4
25	Annadel	3.1	3.1
26	Annadel	2.3	2.3
27	Annadel	2.9	2.9
28	Napa Valley	3.4	2.6
29	Annadel	2.5	2.5
30	Annadel	1.8	1.8
31	Annadel	2.7	2.7
32	Annadel	1.6	1.6
33	Annadel	-	-
34	Napa Valley	3.4	2.6
35	Napa Valley	3.7	2.8
36	Konocti	2.6	2.0
37	Konocti	2.6	2.0
38	Konocti	3.4	2.6
39	Konocti	2.1	1.6
40	Konocti	2.3	1.8
41	Konocti	6.0	4.6
42	Borax Lake	3.1	1.9
43	Borax Lake	3.4	2.1
44	Borax Lake	3	1.9
45	Borax Lake	8.4	5.2
46	Annadel	-	-
47	Borax Lake	8.1	5.0

con't. on next page

Table 5.12 con't.

OBSIDIAN HYDRATION DATA FOR THE SOUTHEAST SECTION OF CA-SON-190*

Lab #	Source	Hydration (microns)	Comparison Constant (microns)
48	Konocti	4.9	3.8
49	Konocti	4.4	3.4
50	Konocti	4.8	3.7
51	Borax Lake	4.9	3.0
52	Borax Lake	5.0	3.1
53	Borax Lake	3.6	2.2
54	Annadel	-	-

* (from Purser et al. 1990: 88-89)

Figure 5.5

Histogram of Obsidian Hydration Measurements for CA-SON-190

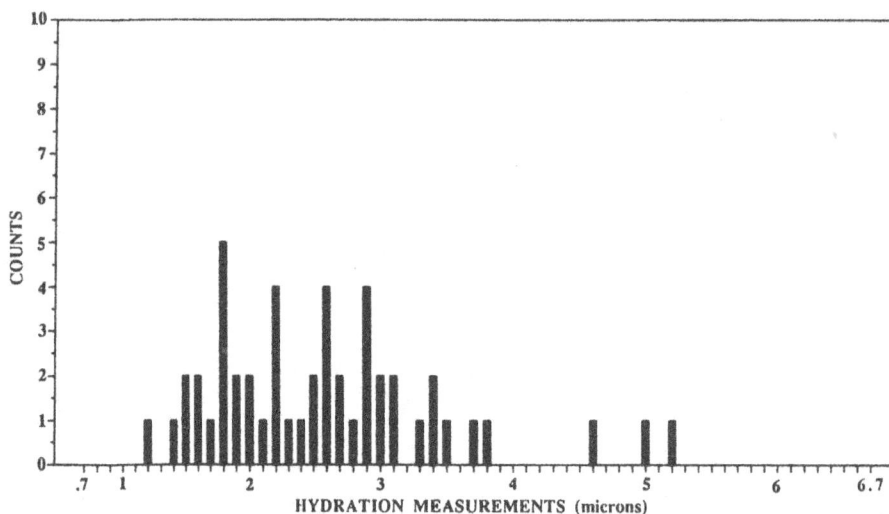

the measurements for the entire sample is 2.57 microns (sd=.87). A histogram of the hydration measurements suggests two separate clusters of readings (see figure 5.5). Recalculations of the mean and standard deviation for each cluster indicate 1) an early Middle Archaic date (n=3; $\bar{x}$ = 4.93 microns; sd=.25; one standard deviation range: 4.7-5.2 microns) and 2) a later Upper Archaic through early Upper Emergent date (n=46; $\bar{x}$=2.42 microns; sd=.65; one standard deviation range: 1.8-3.1 microns).

Interpretation. Current evidence does not support the hypothesis that the stockade complex was constructed over a recently abandoned Pomo village. The recent excavation reported by Purser et al. (1990) indicates a broad lithic scatter may underlie the stockade complex. However, this scatter appears to date well into prehistory and was abandoned some time before the Russians settled the Ross Colony. In turn, we believe the native artifacts recovered from Mad-Shui-Nui, the locus of CA-SON-190 along the northern palisade walls, probably date to the Russian occupation. These artifacts include glass projectile points, glass scraping tools, and glass beads (Smith 1974:45-52). Paintings of the stockade complex in 1828

(Duhaut-Cilly 1946) and in 1841 (Vozensenksii's "Ross Settlement" in Blomkvist 1972:105-106) clearly portray small "Russian-style" houses along the northern wall of the compound. Glenn Farris (personal communication) believes these structures may have been used as general housing for unmarried men. The ethnicity of these men is unknown at this time.

CA-SON-228

Brief History. The site was originally recorded by Bauer in 1949. In the summer of 1989, a U.C. Berkeley field crew re-recorded, mapped, and surface collected the site.

Location. CA-SON-228 is in coastal prairie grasslands of the coastal terrace (figure 5.3).

Site Description. The site consists of a broad, dispersed lithic scatter covering about 4536 sq m. No faunal remains were reported.

Collection Strategy. Given the broadly dispersed pattern of lithics, segmented collection transects were not employed. Rather, artifacts from across the site were point provenienced and collected.

Lithic Artifacts. Thirty-nine artifacts were

collected. The majority are interior flakes (60%), followed by biface thinning flakes (13%), edge-modified flakes (10%) cores (5%), battered cobbles (5%), shatter (2%), and handstones (2%) (tables 5.3 and 5.4). The most common raw material type is obsidian (54%), followed by chert (33%), and sandstone (13%) (tables 5.5 and 5.6). No lithic densities are calculated.

Historic Artifacts. The surface assemblage includes one sherd of colorless container glass, possibly moldblown.

Faunal Remains. None were collected.

Diversity Indexes. The assemblage of chipped stone artifacts and ground stone tools exhibits a much lower diversity than expected for a Ross site with a comparable sample size. The richness and J scores for the lithic classes are 8 (third percentile) and .492 (0 percentile), respectively.

Chronology. Obsidian hydration measurements on 12 artifacts are listed in table 5.13. The mean of the measurements is 2.82 microns (sd =.69). The range of one standard deviation is 2.1-3.5 microns, suggesting an Upper Archaic to Lower Emergent date.

Interpretation. CA-SON-228 is a broadly dispersed, low-density lithic scatter distributed along the coastal terrace. It appears that the archaeological place was sporadically used over the last two thousand years to perform a limited range of activities involving the production, use, or discard of interior flakes, biface thinning flakes, edge-modified flakes, and cores.

CA-SON-670

Brief History. Initial excavations were undertaken as part of a spring field class under the direction of David Fredrickson in 1971 to mitigate the effects of constructing a group campground on the site (Stillinger 1975). Further excavations were undertaken at the site by California State Parks and Recreation (DPR) archaeologists in 1979 and 1985. The 1985 excavation, directed by Breck Parkman and Glenn Farris and staffed with volunteers from the Santa Cruz Archaeological Association, evaluated the impact of a proposed septic tank in the campground. In the summer of 1988, U.C. Berkeley field crews recorded a small locus 30 m south of the main site. Further excavations were undertaken in 1990 by Thomas Origer and field crews from Santa Rosa Junior College as part of the expansion of camp facilities.

Location. CA-SON-670 is situated in a mixed evergreen forest on the lower slopes of the first ridge system at an elevation of 70 m above sea level (figure 5.3). The San Andreas Fault runs along the southern edge of the site.

Site Description. The main site, a 3750 sq m area, sits in a small, protected valley overlooking Fort Ross Creek. In the original site form on file at the Northwest Information Center, Stillinger notes the foundations of buildings probably built as part of a historic logging operation. The southern locus recorded in 1988 is an elliptical-shaped area, measuring 104 sq m in area, near the Fort Ross Creek. The locus consists of a low density of ground stone tools, ground stone fragments, and mollusk remains.

Collection Strategy. A total of 7.8 cubic m was excavated in 1971. Excavation units were distributed across the site. The 1985 field crew excavated four 2 by 2 m units. The southern locus of Son 670 was surface collected in 1988 by laying out twelve 1 by 2 m units in the four cardinal directions from a central

Table 5.13

OBSIDIAN HYDRATION MEASUREMENTS FOR CA-SON-228

Lab #	Catalog #	Source	Hydration (microns)	Comparison Constant (microns)
81	H-6/7/89-1-L:1	Napa Valley	5.0	3.8
82	H-6/7/89-4-L:1	Napa Valley	3.4	2.6
83	H-6/7/89-9-L	Napa Valley	4.3	3.3
84	H-6/7/89-12-L:1	Borax Lake	5.9	3.6
85	H-6/7/89-13-L	Annadel	1.8	1.8
86	H-6/7/89-15-L	Annadel	2.6	2.6
87	H-6/8/89-20-L:1	Annadel	2.8	2.8
88	H-6/8/89-24-L	Napa Valley	4.9	3.8
89	H-6/8/89-29-L:2	Konocti	3.8	2.9
90	H-6/8/89-30-L	Annadel	1.7	1.7
91	H-6/8/89-32-L	Napa Valley	2.9	2.2
92	H-6/8/89-34-L	Napa Valley	3.4	2.6

datum point (figure 5.6). The collection represents a
23% sample of the surface area of the locus. Some
materials outside of collection units were also collected by point proveniencing their exact locations.

Lithic Artifacts. Stillinger (1975) analyzed the
lithic artifacts from the 1971 excavation. He identifies 2 battered cobbles, 4 choppers, 1 anvil, 5 large
bifaces, 2 scraper planes, 6 handstones, 2 net weights,
1 pestle, and 57 whole or fragments of projectile
points. In addition, Stillinger weighed a very large
number of flakes and other chipping debitage (total
chert debitage = 208.3 gr; total obsidian debitage =
16.39 gr). Counts of the debitage are not presented in
his report. The specific counts of projectile points are
19 shouldered lanceolate (Excelsior) points, 5 corner-
notched points, 3 serrated points, and 30 unidentifiable fragments.

The surface collection south of the main site
yielded 20 lithic artifacts. The bulk are fire-cracked/
ground stone fragments (80%) and handstones (15%),
as well as one biface thinning flake (5%) (tables 5.3
and 5.4). Of the raw materials represented, 55% are
basalt, 40% are sandstone, and only 5% are obsidian

(tables 5.5 and 5.6). The lithic density (not including
materials point provenienced) is .67 artifacts/sq m.

Historic Artifacts. Stillinger (1975) reports 15
glass beads, a large quantity of nails, and 40 glass
fragments from the 1971 excavation. Two projectile
points are manufactured from glass. No historic
materials were recovered in the locus south of the
main site.

Faunal Remains. Stillinger (1975) notes that
some animal bones (29.1 gr) and a large quantity of
shellfish refuse (383.8 gr) were recovered in the 1971
excavation, although it is not analyzed in his report.
The 1988 surface collection of the southern locus
produced 5 mollusk MNIs, including 2 limpets (40%),
1 turban snail (20%), 1 chiton (20%), and 1 abalone
(20%) (tables 5.7 and 5.8). The mollusk density is .08
MNIs/sq m. No animal bones were recovered in the
surface collection.

Diversity Indexes. Since Stillinger's (1975) report does not provide counts of lithic debitage and
flakes, diversity indexes are calculated only for the
small surface assemblage south of the main site. The
diversity of chipped stone artifacts and ground stone

Figure 5.6

**Site Map of
CA-SON-670
(Southern Locus)**

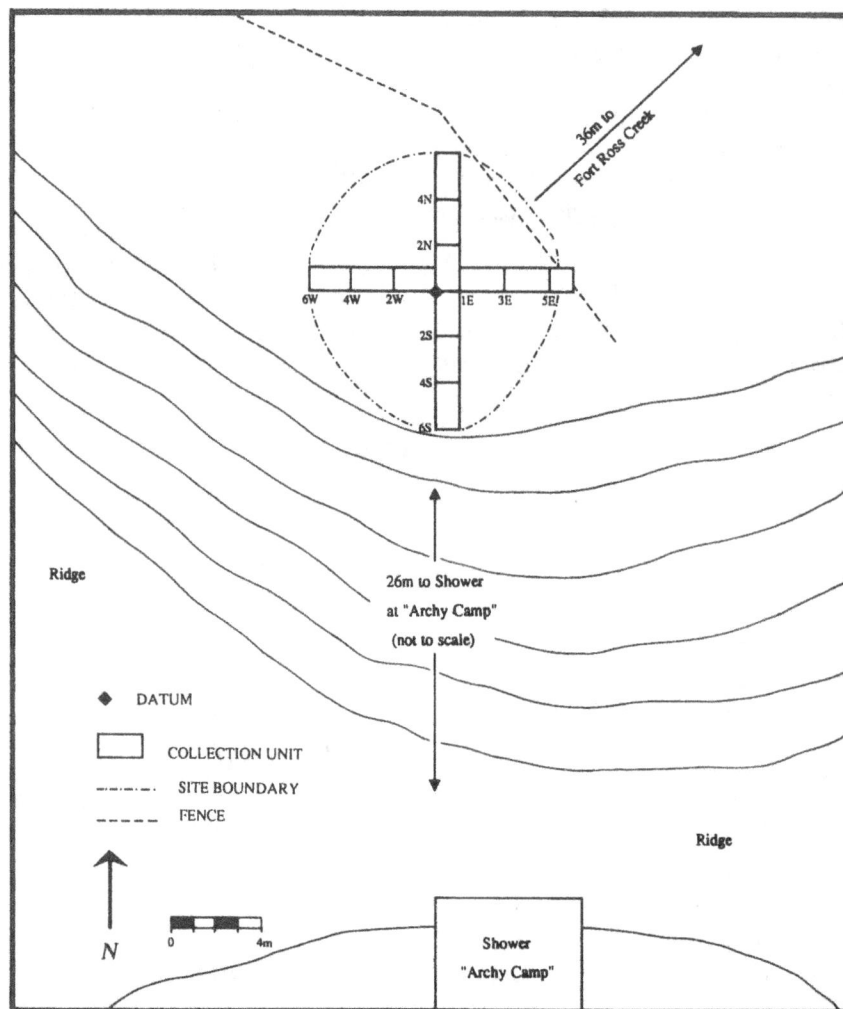

tools is lower than expected for a similar sized assemblage. The richness and J scores for lithic classes are 2 (seventh percentile) and .198 (fifth percentile), respectively. The diversity of the mollusk assemblage is greater. The richness and J scores for mollusk MNIs, respectively, are 4 (ninety-sixth percentile) and .579 (ninety-sixth percentile).

Chronology. Stillinger (1975) suggests a long use-duration for this archaeological place involving at least three different cycles of occupation over time. The first occupation is based on the association of ground stone tools and shouldered lanceolate projectile points in the lower levels of some excavation units. The projectile points suggest roughly a Late Archaic or early Lower Emergent date. The one biface thinning flake of Annadel obsidian (catalog # A-6/7/88-15-L:1) from the southern locus of CA-SON-670 exhibits a hydration layer measuring 1.7 microns. This very tentative evidence suggests a late Lower Emergent date.

The second cycle of occupation appears to be by native peoples during the Historic period given the presence of glass beads, glass projectile points, and corner-notched points. Preliminary indications suggest this occupation took place during Russian times (1812-1841) and/or in the early ranching phase (1841-1867) (Farris 1986a:20).

The third occupation is that of James Dixon and Charles Fairfax's logging operation established at Fort Ross in A.D 1867 (chapter 6). Stillinger's (1975) analysis of the nail types recovered from CA-SON-670 suggests that this occupation postdates A.D. 1870. The 1876 U.S. Coast Survey map of the Fort Ross region, on file in the Bancroft Library, U.C. Berkeley, illustrates a mill complex in the vicinity of CA-SON-670. One structure is situated in the exact location of the site. Kaye Tomlin (personal communication) believes that the Dixon/Fairfax mill, originally established in Kolmer Gulch in 1867, was moved to the vicinity of CA-SON-670 in 1870. The lumber mill was located just off the boundary line of the current state park. The structure built at CA-SON-670 was probably used to house workmen. Tomlin (personal communication) also notes that James Dixon's house, known as the "White House," was located further up Fort Ross Creek and was part of the mill complex.

Interpretation. Many questions remain about the occupation history of CA-SON-670. It appears that the archaeological place is characterized by extensive use-duration possibly spanning back to the Late Archaic period. Stillinger (1975) reports a relatively diverse range of lithic artifacts suggesting that a variety of activities took place here. However, it is not clear what range of native activities occurred during the earliest occupation, and what took place in the Historic period. It is possible that the site represents a substantial hamlet occupied by Pomo/Miwok peoples working at the Ross Colony. This hypothesis will be the subject of future work.

The locus south of the main site appears to be a special purpose location where vegetable processing and possibly cooking were taking place. A by-product of the stone boiling method in baskets is the deposition of many fire-cracked rocks. It appears that native peoples recycled former (possibly exhausted) ground stone tools for use as cooking stones. The ground stone tools were probably broken into fragments, heated, and submerged into cool water, a process that created multiple ground stone remnants with the characteristics of fire-cracked rocks.

CA-SON-1446H

Brief History. The site was recorded and excavated by Glenn Farris, Breck Parkman, and a DPR crew in 1984. This site is also described as locus 1 of Son 1446H.

Location. CA-SON-1446H is situated on the lower slope of the first ridge (elevation 146 m above sea level) in savannah grassland (figure 5.3). As part of the original Russian Orchard, the site is located on the San Andreas Fault line.

Site Description. The site is characterized by Russian bricks distributed over a 20 sq m area.

Collection Strategy. The excavation involved the shallow, areal exposure of bricks *in situ.*

Lithic Artifacts. Some obsidian flakes were recovered.

Historic Artifacts. A number of whole Russian bricks as well as brick fragments, representing four different brick styles, were mapped. Other historic artifacts include iron spikes and nails, earthenware ceramic sherds, and three glass beads.

Faunal Remains. Large mammal bones were recovered in the excavation.

Interpretation. Glenn Farris and Breck Parkman (personal communications) believe the brick and artifact scatter represents the remains of a four-room house and kitchen built by the Russians near their orchard. The house and kitchen are described in the Sutter Inventory of Fort Ross (1841), in the Vallejo Inventory of Fort Ross (1841), and in Duflot de Mofras's (1842) description of Fort Ross. The Sutter and Vallejo Inventories describe a kitchen and a "new" four-room house that measures 9.6 m by 8.5 m and is covered with planks. Duflot de Mofras describes a kitchen, measuring 5 sq m, next to a new house covered with thin boards (see Farris 1984).

CA-SON-1451

Brief History. The site was recorded by Breck Parkman in 1984.

Location. CA-SON-1451 is located in a dirt road that leads to the group campground (CA-SON-670). The site sits on the coastal terrace in open, coastal prairie grassland.

Site Description. CA-SON-1451 is a small lithic scatter measuring 75 sq m. Parkman (1984) notes that the site may be larger, but that poor visibility in the deep prairie grass makes it difficult to determine the boundaries of the lithic scatter.

Collection Strategy. Artifacts were collected from the exposed road bed.

Lithic Artifacts. Six chert flakes were collected.

Historic Artifacts. None were reported.

Faunal Remains. One *Olivella* shell was collected.

Interpretation. The scatter of lithics along the coastal terrace, although more limited in its spatial distribution, is similar to CA-SON-228. The age of CA-SON-1451 is not known since no diagnostic projectile points or obsidian artifacts have yet been recovered there.

CA-SON-1453

Brief History. The site was initially recorded by Glenn Farris and a crew of DPR archaeologists in 1984. Beginning in the spring semester of 1988, field crews from Santa Rosa Junior College, under the direction of Thomas Origer, undertook the mapping, surface collection, and subsurface testing of CA-SON-1453. A full report of their findings is in progress. The information presented below is tentative awaiting the analysis of the excavated materials.

Location. The site extends along the eroding sea cliffs of the coastal terrace in coastal prairie grassland (figure 5.3).

Site Description. CA-SON-1453 consists of a broad, low-density lithic scatter extending over a 10,000 sq m area.

Collection Strategy. Artifacts were first point provenienced and collected from the surface of the site. A number of 1 by 2 m units (STUs or surface testing units) were then laid out across the site in transects and excavated to a 10 cm depth. Finally, some units were excavated completely to sterile underlying deposits.

Lithic Artifacts. The majority of the lithics observed on the surface are chert and obsidian flakes and debitage, with some ground stone tools and schist battered cobbles. Origer (personal communication) reports that a similar range of artifact classes was recovered in excavation units.

Historic Artifacts. None were observed on the surface.

Faunal Remains. Few mollusk remains or animal bones were found on the surface.

Chronology. Nine obsidian artifacts have been analyzed by the Obsidian Hydration Laboratory, Sonoma State University. We thank Eric Allison for sharing this information with us. The hydration measurements for each specimen will be listed in a forthcoming Sonoma State University report. Suffice it to say that the mean of the hydration measurements, after converting all readings to the Annadel hydration rate using Tremaine's comparison constants, is 3.02 microns (sd =.95). The range of one standard deviation is 2.1 to 4.0 microns, suggesting a long use-duration from the early Upper Archaic to the Middle Lower Emergent.

Interpretation. While a full interpretation of CA-SON-1453 awaits the final report, the site appears to be very similar to CA-SON-228. It is a broad, diffuse lithic scatter that extends along the coastal terrace. Similar to CA-SON-228, it exhibits a long use-duration that begins at a relatively early date, possibly as early as 1000 B.C.

CA-SON-1454/H

Brief History. Jeanette Schulz initially recorded the site with a crew of DPR archaeologists in 1984. Beginning in the spring of 1988, field crews from Santa Rosa Junior College and Sonoma State University, under the directions of Thomas Origer and David Fredrickson, respectively, initiated an intensive study of the site. The fieldwork includes mapping the site, systematically collecting surface artifacts, and excavating a number of 1 by 2 units. A full report of this work is forthcoming.

Location. CA-SON-1454/H sits on the coastal cliffs overlooking Fort Ross Cove (figure 5.3). It is located directly east of CA-SON-1453 on the coastal terrace in coastal prairie grassland.

Site Description. The site is an extensive lithic scatter, covering an area of about 15,000 sq m that contains several boulders with cupules. One sandstone outcrop contains 25 cupules; another, 17 cupules; and a third, 2 cupules (see Schulz 1984). A small discrete locus of shell fragments is also found along the edge of the bluff. Historic features, probably associated with a loading chute and storage area, are also found here. A stump of a spar-pole is believed to have been part of the original chute (Schulz 1984).

Collection Strategy. Surface artifacts were point provenienced during the mapping of the site in 1989. Similar to CA-SON-1453, a number of 1 by 2 m excavation units were laid out in transects across the site. Some were STUs (surface testing units), while others are characterized as VTUs (vertical testing units) in which sediments are excavated down to sterile, underlying deposits.

Lithic Artifacts. Primarily chert and obsidian flakes and debitage are found on the surface. Origer (personal communication) reports that the great bulk of materials recovered from excavation units are flakes and debitage. Some ground stone tools, including a few handstones and a sandstone mortar were also recovered. He notes that biface fragments, while present, are rare. A few net weights were also identified from or near the shell deposit.

Historic Artifacts. Fragments of mill cut redwood lumber are scattered across part of the site, as well as several metal artifacts (iron rings or eye-bolts, a length of rusted chain) that are probably associated with the loading chute. One brown glass bottle fragment was also noted on the surface.

Faunal Remains. None were noted on the surface. Origer (personal communication) reports few faunal remains in excavation units with the exception of the small discrete shell deposit near the edge of the bluff. The erosion of the bluff into the ocean is rapidly destroying the shell deposit.

Chronology. One hundred and twenty-six obsidian artifacts have been analyzed by the Obsidian Hydration Laboratory, Sonoma State University. We thank Eric Allison for generously sharing the results with us. The specific hydration data will be presented in the forthcoming excavation report. Using this data, we calculated that the mean of the hydration measurements, corrected to the hydration rate of Annadel obsidian, is 2.19 microns (sd=1.0). A histogram (see figure 5.7) of these measurements exhibits two distinct outliers of 6.2 and 6.7 microns, suggesting an Early Archaic date sometime around 6000 B.C. The mean of the rest of the measurements is 2.12 microns (sd=.84). The range of one standard deviation is 1.3 to 3.0 microns, suggesting an extended use-duration in the late Upper Archaic to the early Upper Emergent.

Interpretation. While a full account of CA-SON-1454/H is forthcoming in the excavation report, Origer (personal communication) believes that lithic production was taking place, but probably not the manufacture of bifaces, since few fragments are found. He also notes that the presence of ground stone tools suggests activities involving the mashing and grinding of plant products and other raw materials. Finally, Origer suggests that the broad, diffuse lithic scatter is probably the result of many different kinds of tasks taking place in the area over an extended period of time.

We note the similarities between CA-SON-228, CA-SON-1453, and CA-SON-1454/H. All are extensive lithic scatters on the coastal terrace with long use-durations. CA-SON-1454/H differs from the other two sites in its small shell deposit, its cupule rocks, and its historic artifacts and features.

The loading chute and lumber storage area were constructed by James Dixon in A.D. 1867 or 1868 (Tomlin 1991:31). The original chute, constructed of wood, was built to facilitate the loading of lumber onto ships. On December 9, 1898 the wooden chute blew down in a terrific storm that created havoc along the north coast of California. Winds were clocked up to 96 miles per hour at Point Reyes (Tomlin 1991:39). In 1899, a wire-rigged chute was built to replace the wooden one. The wire chute operated at Fort Ross until 1921 when the chute, donkey engine, anchor chains, cars and rails were sold to the Salsig Lumber Company who moved the equipment to nearby Timber Cove (Tomlin 1991:43).

CA-SON-1455

Brief History. The site, originally designated as Fort Ross Campground #1, was recorded in 1984 by Glenn Farris. Since an access trail from the nearby campground was impacting the site, a crew of DPR archaeologists under Farris's direction excavated a portion of CA-SON-1455. The following description of the site is taken from the excavation report (Farris 1986a).

Location. CA-SON-1455 is located next to a rock overhang approximately .8 km south of the Ross stockade (figure 5.3). The site is on the edge of the rocky coastal terrace, adjacent to a small creek that flows into the Pacific Ocean.

Site Description. The site, a small shell midden measuring about 500 sq m, sits on a small bench next to a large boulder-bedrock outcrop. The archaeological deposits, consisting of dark, charcoal-stained soil, shellfish refuse, and some lithics, vary in depth from .5 to 1.18 m.

Collection Strategy. Surface artifacts were mapped with a transit and collected. A four-inch-barrel auger was then used to test the depth of the site. This was followed by the excavation of four 1 by 1 m units to bedrock. All sediments were passed through 1/8" mesh.

Lithic Artifacts. The majority of the lithic assemblage consisted of 540 chert flakes and debitage analyzed by Mark Hylkema (1986). They include 225 interior flakes, 114 pieces of shatter, 108 biface thinning flakes, 61 secondary cortical flakes, 16 primary cortical flakes, 7 edge-modified flakes, 6 cores, 2 bifaces, and 1 drill. In addition, Farris (1986a:25-37) reports 151 "hammerstones" (rounded rocks from the beach probably used as hammer and anvil stones that showed some evidence of battering), 1 handstone, 2 net weights, and 63 obsidian flakes and tools, including two corner-notched projectile points.

Historic Artifacts. One white cane glass bead was recovered.

Faunal Remains. The mollusk remains were

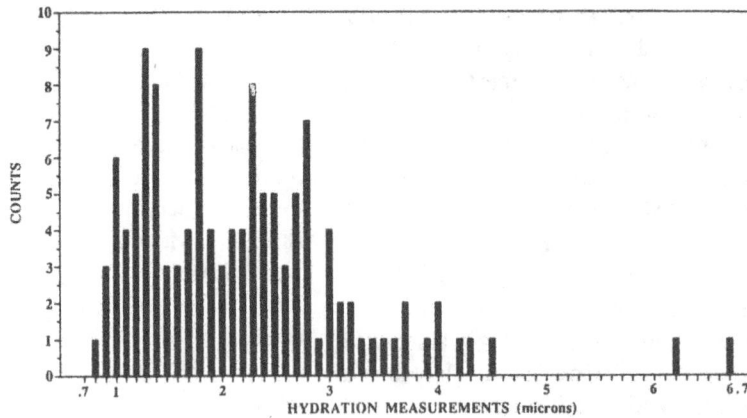

Figure 5.7

Histogram of Obsidian
Hydration Measurements
for CA-SON-1454/H

analyzed by Christina Swiden (1986). The bulk of the mollusk MNIs is composed of limpets (70%), followed by mussels (12%), turban snails (10%), hooked slipper shells (3%), other gastropods (2%), and barnacles (2%). Clams and abalone made up less than 1% of the shell assemblage. Although *Haliotis* shells made up a small percentage of the mollusk assemblage, one of the notable features unearthed was a layer composed of numerous *Haliotis* shells, presumably marking a living floor. One *Olivella* bead was also recovered.

Great numbers of fish bones were recovered. They account for 97% of the vertebrae found in the site. Unfortunately, the remains are not adequately diagnostic to determine genus and species (Farris 1986a:44). Few mammal bones were observed, and these were fragmentary at best. The majority include artiodactyls (primarily *Odocoileus hemionus*) and rodents. One bone was worked into a point. Farris (1986a:44) also reports the caudal end of a sacrum of an adult sea lion (*Zalophus californianus*).

Diversity Indexes. We calculated diversity indexes for the chipped stone artifacts and ground stone tools tallied above. One must be cautious about comparing these to other survey sites since they were computed from an excavated assemblage. We expect that surface assemblages may be somewhat less diverse than excavated assemblages given the greater impact of surface disturbances (unauthorized collecting of artifacts such as projectile points and beads) and poorer preservation. Interestingly, the results suggest that CA-SON-1455 is much less diverse than expected for a survey site with a relatively large sample size. The richness and J scores are 12 (0 percentile) and .613 (0 percentile), respectively. Since Swiden (1986) does not present MNI counts, but only percentages, diversity indexes are not calculated for the mollusk assemblage.

Chronology. CA-SON-1455 is the best dated site in the Fort Ross Study Area. Four samples of charcoal and one abalone were submitted to the radiocarbon laboratory at U.C. Riverside (Farris

1986a:33). The radiocarbon dates are as follows: 450±80 B.P. (charcoal), 460±100 B.P. (*Haliotis*), 510±70 B.P. (charcoal), 1120±100 B.P. (charcoal), and 150 B.P. (charcoal).

Forty-one obsidian artifacts were submitted to the Obsidian Hydration Laboratory, Sonoma State University (table 5.14). The results suggest a late Lower Emergent to Historic period use of the site. The mean of the measurements, calibrated to the Annadel hydration rate, is 1.18 microns (sd=.52). The range of one standard deviation is .7 to 1.7 microns.

Interpretation. Farris (1986a:51) interprets CA-SON-1455 as a "small seafood processing station." The site appears to have been reused by small groups collecting shellfish, fish, and other marine foods primarily during protohistoric and historic times. The radiocarbon dates and corner-notched point suggest a significant period of use around A.D. 1500 (Farris 1986a:51). In addition, the obsidian hydration measurements and glass bead indicate the site was sporadically used during the Russian occupation of Fort Ross.

CA-SON-1878

Brief History. The site was first recorded in the summer of 1988 by a U.C. Berkeley field crew. The site was assigned the field number, A-5-1.

Location. CA-SON-1878 sits on the intersection of the coastal terrace and lower slope of the first ridge overlooking Fort Ross Creek (figure 5.3). The vegetation is primarily coastal prairie grassland that grades into a mixed evergreen forest.

Site Description. This extensive site, measuring 2107 sq m, contains a diverse range of lithic artifacts, historic materials, and some mollusk remains. A small ranch shed enclosing a water barrel is on the northern boundary of the site. A depression, probably made by a bulldozer, is found in the northwest corner of the site (figure 5.8). We noted, in a field visit to the site in the fall of 1990, slight depressions not previously mapped, in the southern section of the site.

Table 5.14

OBSIDIAN HYDRATION DATA FOR CA-SON-1455

Lab #	Source	Hydration (microns)	Comparison Constant (microns)
1	Napa Valley	2.0	1.5
2	Napa Valley	1.0	.8
3	Napa Valley	1.3	1.0
4	Napa Valley	1.1	.8
5	Napa Valley	1.0	.8
6	Konocti	2.0	1.5
7	Napa Valley	1.9	1.5
8	Napa Valley	1.3	1.0
9	Napa Valley	1.1	.8
10	Napa Valley	1.1	.8
11	Napa Valley	-	-
12	Napa Valley	1.0	.8
13	Napa Valley	1.0	.8
14	Annadel	1.6	1.6
15	Napa Valley	3.9	3.0
16	Konocti	1.1	.8
17	Napa Valley	-	-
18	Napa Valley	-	-
19	Napa Valley	1.7	1.3
20	Napa Valley	1.3	1.0
21	Napa Valley	1.6	1.2
22	Napa Valley	1.1	.8
23	Konocti	-	-
24	Borax Lake	3.3	2.0
25	Annadel	-	-
26	Borax Lake	1.2	.7
27	Napa Valley	1.0	.8
28	Annadel	1.0	1.0
29	Napa Valley	1.1	.8
30	Annadel	2.5	2.5
31	Konocti	1.1	.8
32	Konocti	2.3	1.8
33	Annadel	.9	.9
34	Napa Valley	1.7	1.3
35	Napa Valley	.9	.7
36	Napa Valley	2.0	1.5
37	Napa Valley	1.2	.9
38	Napa Valley	2.3	1.8
39	Napa Valley	1.2	.9
40	Annadel	1.3	1.3
41	Napa Valley	1.2	.9

(after Farris 1986a:49)

Collection Strategy. From a central datum, 1 by 2 m collection units were laid out in the four cardinal directions (figure 5.8). Forty-three units were surface collected (a 4% sample of the entire site area). Some materials were point provenienced and collected outside the units.

Lithic Artifacts. A total of 39 lithic artifacts were surface collected. The most common are edge-modified flakes (22%), followed by interior flakes (10%), shatter (10%), primary cortical flakes (10%), bifaces (8%), biface thinning flakes (8%), cores (8%), fire-cracked/ground stone fragments (5%), handstones (5%), and projectile points (5%). A hammerstone (3%), a secondary cortical flake (3%), and a slab milling stone (3%) were also collected (tables 5.3 and 5.4). One of the projectile points is classified as a large side-notched point. The majority of the lithics were produced from chert (80%) and sandstone (12%). Two artifacts were manufactured from basalt (5%), and one from quartz (3%) (tables 5.5 and 5.6). The density of lithics (not including those point provenienced) is .2 artifacts/sq m.

Historic Artifacts. The surface assemblage includes the sherds of three moldblown glass containers. One is colorless glass that has been modified by hard percussion. It exhibits a bulb of percussion. Another sherd is from a light blue-green colored container of solarized glass. The third sherd is from

Figure 5.8

**Site Map of
CA-SON-1878**

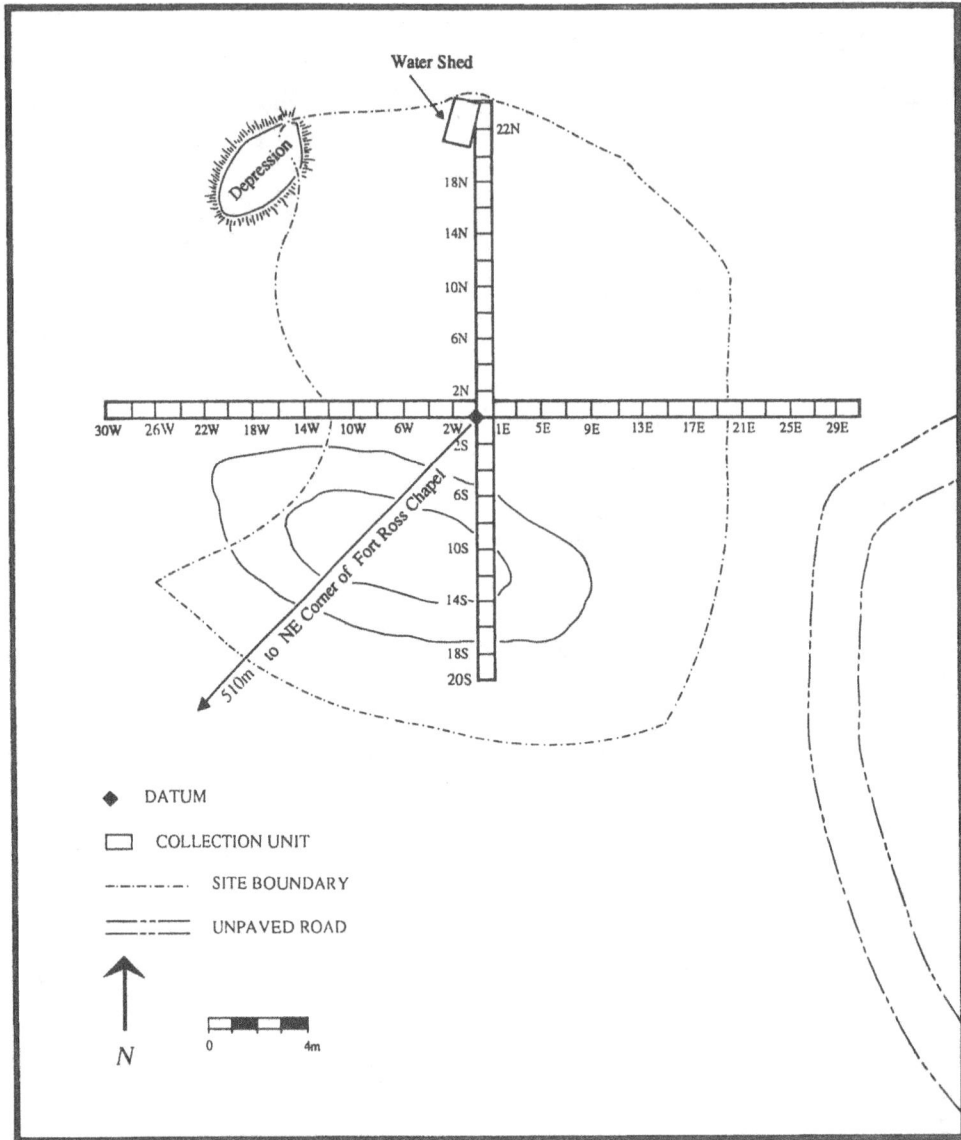

the base of a light olive green alcoholic beverage bottle. The edge exhibits evidence of intentional chipping, possibly to sharpen it.

Sherds from three ceramic vessels were also recovered. One is the footring sherd of porcelain bowl that is very white with a clear glaze. The second vessel is represented by a footring sherd of a Chinese porcellaneous stoneware bowl. The body is whitish-blue with cobalt blue linear decoration on the interior surface. The sherd appears to be heavily surf-worn. The third vessel is represented by the rim sherd of a creamware hollowware form that is both glazed and crazed. It may be a chamberpot.

Faunal Remains. Three mollusk MNIs were identified. They include 2 limpets and 1 mussel (tables 5.7 and 5.8). None of these were recovered in collection units (mollusk density = 0/sq m). No animal bones were recovered.

Diversity Indexes. The diversity of lithic artifacts is much greater for CA-SON-1878 then expected for a similar sized sample. The richness and J scores are 12 (ninety-fourth percentile) and .806 (ninety-eighth percentile). The calculation of diversity indexes for mollusk MNIs is rather dubious given the extremely small sample size. The richness and J scores for the mollusk MNIs are 2 (fifty-third percentile) and .276 (fifty-third percentile).

Chronology. The dating of this site is rather ambiguous. No obsidian artifacts were recovered. The identifiable projectile point suggests a relatively early prehistoric age. The historic materials suggest an early to late nineteenth century date. From the moldblown glass one can infer a pre-1910s date of manufacture, while the solarized container glass indicates the addition of manganese or "glassmaker's bleach," which suggests a date between 1870 and

1910. The opaque porcelain was first manufactured in the mid-nineteenth century and continued to be produced through the turn of the twentieth century. The dates for the Chinese porcellaneous stoneware span from the 1760s through the 1800s, and some versions of the same decorative patterns are still in use today (Purser, personal communication).

Interpretation. CA-SON-1878 is a large scatter characterized by a high diversity of artifact classes but a low density of surface materials. It may represent an archaeological place with a relatively short use-duration where a diverse range of activities took place. We believe it may be a native hamlet where a few families resided for a short while in the Historic period. The worked glass artifacts provide some support for this interpretation.

CA-SON-1879

Brief History. The site was first recorded in the summer of 1988 by a U.C. Berkeley field crew. The original site designation was A-13-1.

Location. CA-SON-1879 is situated on the coastal terrace overlooking Highway 1 in prairie grassland (figure 5.3).

Site Description. The site is a sandstone boulder in which nine cupules have been pecked (figure 5.9). Each depression measures about 7 cm in diameter and 2-2.5 cm in depth.

Lithic Artifacts. Two artifacts, a handstone and a fire-cracked/ground stone fragment, both manufactured out of sandstone, were collected near the cupule rock. No other archaeological materials were observed in the nearby vicinity.

Interpretation. The site is a small cupule rock which commands a good view of the ocean as well as of CA-SON-175. The date of the site is unknown.

CA-SON-1880

Brief History. The site is first mentioned by Gifford (1967:9) who describes its location as due north of CA-SON-175. He notes that John McKenzie, then curator of the Fort Ross State Historic Park, showed him several "grooved stone sinkers" and a round-tipped chert projectile point. A U.C. Berkeley field crew first recorded the site in the summer of 1988. It was assigned the field designation of B-3-1.

Location. The site is located on the coastal terrace in coastal prairie grassland about 400 m due north of the stockade (figure 5.3). Fort Ross Creek is 120 m due east.

Site Description. CA-SON-1880 is an extensive scatter of artifacts and faunal remains covering about a 2024 sq m area. The western boundaries of the site were determined by shovel probes given the thick grassland that impeded a clear view of the ground. The subsurface of the site is characterized by very dark, organic sediments. A midden deposit consisting of mollusk remains, animal bones, and fire-cracked/ground stone fragments extends along the eastern edge of the site where it drops off into the Fort Ross Creek. Rodent activity has brought some materials to the surface. No clearly defined surface depressions

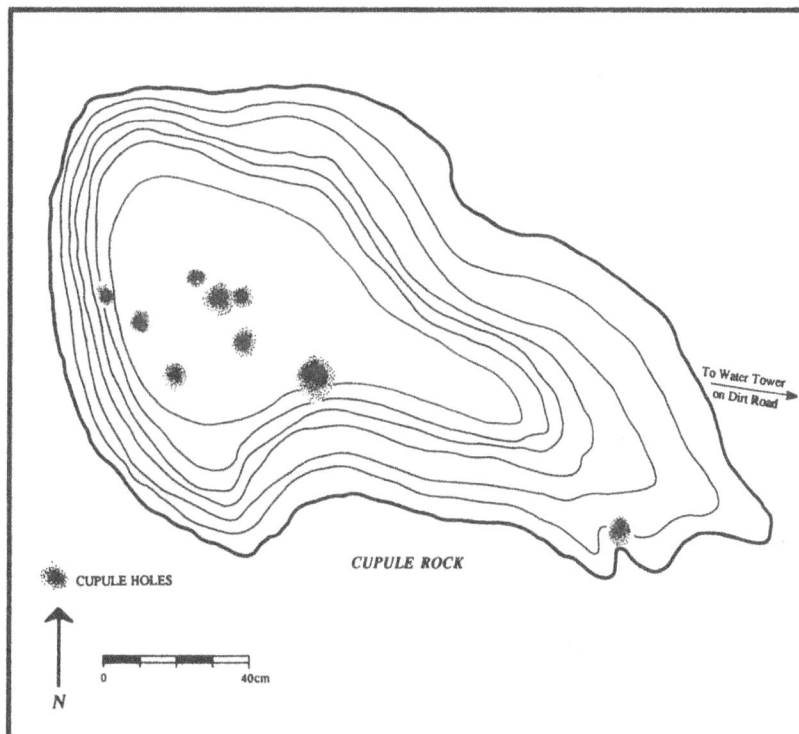

Figure 5.9
Map of Cupule Rock
at CA-SON-1879

To Water Tower
on Dirt Road

CUPULE HOLES

CUPULE ROCK

0   40cm

N

were recorded, although the thick grass precludes a very detailed survey for surface features.

Collection Strategy. Twenty-three collection units were laid out from four different datums (site datum, subdatums A, B, C) distributed across the site (figure 5.10). The collection represents a 2% sample of the entire site area. The grass sod was excavated from each unit to provide a clear view of the site's surface.

Lithic Artifacts. Thirty-three artifacts were recovered from the collection units (density = .65 artifacts/sq m). The largest quantity of artifacts were classified as fire-cracked/ground stone fragments (22%), followed by biface thinning flakes (15%), edge-modified flakes (12%), interior flakes (12%), handstones (9%), cores (9%), secondary cortical flakes (6%), shatter (6%), one biface (3%), one primary cortical flake (3%), and one slab millingstone (3%) (tables 5.3 and 5.4). Obsidian (40%) was the most common raw material, then sandstone (30%), chert (27%), and basalt (3%) (tables 5.5 and 5.6).

Historic Artifacts. The surface assemblage includes one white opaque glass bead. Six glass sherds of a dark olive-green moldblown wine bottle were recovered. Another glass vessel is represented by the base sherd of a light olive-green container. This sherd is burned and exhibits evidence of retouching along its edge. Sherds from two ceramic vessels were also recovered. These include one sherd of a very white porcelain, and the rim sherd of a white-bodied earthenware cup or bowl that exhibits evidence of burning.

Faunal Remains. Thirty mollusk MNIs were identified at CA-SON-1880 (density = .65 MNIs/sq m). Almost half of the mollusk individuals are black turban snails (51%). The remainder are mussel (20%), limpets (17%), barnacle (3%), chiton (3%), hooked slipper shell (3%), and abalone (3%) (tables 5.7 and 5.8).

Identifiable animal bones include 1 naviculocuboid, 1 mandible, and 1 astragalus of mule deer (*Odocoileus hemionus*), and the second lower premolar

Figure 5.10

**Site Map of
CA-SON-1880**

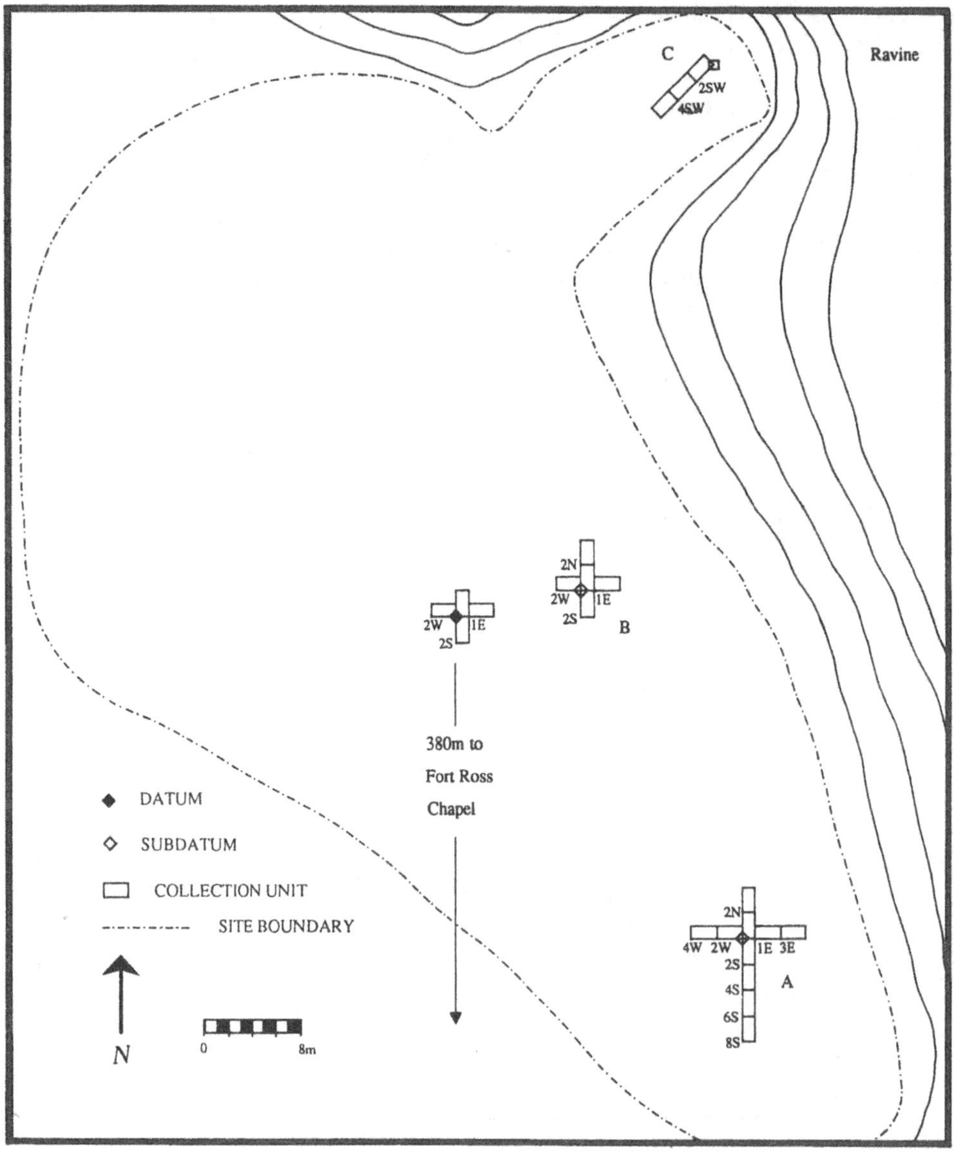

of an elk (*Cervus elaphus*). Also recovered in the surface collection were 6 long bones of large mammals, 2 vertebrae of large mammals, an unidentified element of a large mammal, and the scapula of a medium mammal. None of the skeletal elements exhibit evidence of cut marks or burning.

Diversity Indexes. The diversity of lithics from CA-SON-1880 is somewhat higher than expected in a similar sized sample. The richness and J scores are 10 (seventy-second percentile) and .763 (eighty-seventh percentile), respectively. The diversity of mollusk remains are higher than expected for a similar sized assemblage. The richness and J score are 7 (ninety-third percentile) and .617 (ninety-eighth percentile).

Chronology. Nine hydration rim measurements were taken on obsidian artifacts from CA-SON-1880 (table 5.15). The mean of the measurements is 2.04 microns (sd=1.46). A histogram of the measurements indicates an outlier and two distinct clusters (figure 5.11). The outlier is 5.2 microns, suggesting an early Middle Archaic date. The first cluster (n=3) is characterized by a mean of 2.9 microns (sd=.35). The range of one standard deviation is 2.5-3.2 microns, pointing to an Upper Archaic and early Lower Emergent date. The other cluster (n=5) has a mean of .9 micron (sd=.1). The range of one standard deviation is .8-1.0 microns, indicating a date near the beginning of the Historic period. The presence of the glass bead and worked glass artifact tends to corroborate the latter date. The sherds from the moldblown wine bottle may date prior to 1910 given the absence of turnmolding. On the other hand, it may be just a cheaper bottle produced at a later date (Purser, personal communication).

Interpretation. CA-SON-1880, a large site not far from the Ross stockade, is composed of a diverse assemblage of artifacts and faunal remains. An extensive use-duration, dating back to 3000 B.C., appears to characterize this archaeological place. We believe the few, early lithics may be part of a broader, diffuse lithic scatter, similar to others found along the coastal terrace (i.e., CA-SON-228, -1453, -1454/H). The later manifestation, which composes the great bulk of the site, may be a historic native hamlet, probably dating to the Russian occupation of Fort Ross and possibly into early ranch times.

CA-SON-1881

Brief History. The site was first recorded by a U.C. Berkeley field crew in the summer of 1988. The field number assigned to the site is B-5-1.

Location. Located on the upper coastal terrace in mixed conifer woodland, the site is about 150 m northwest of CA-SON-1880 (figure 5.3).

Site Description. A midden deposit with considerable shellfish debris and some lithic artifacts, CA-SON-1881 covers about a 471 sq m area on a small tributary of Fort Ross Creek. The material is eroding down the face of the creek bed.

Collection Strategy. A site datum was established at the bottom of the creek bed from which four 1 by 2 m units were surface collected. Another subdatum (A) was placed at the top of the low cliff face from which four 1 by 2 m units were collected (figure 5.12). The collection represents 2% of the entire site area. Some materials were point provenienced and collected outside of collection units.

Lithic Artifacts. Only 11 lithic artifacts were recovered from the site. These include 5 pieces of shatter, 2 pieces of slab millingstones, 2 fire-cracked/ground stone fragments, a core, and a secondary cortical flake (tables 5.3 and 5.4). Sandstone (37%),

Table 5.15
OBSIDIAN HYDRATION DATA FOR CA-SON-1880

Lab #	Catalog #	Source	Hydration (microns)	Comparison Constant (microns)
2	B-6/8/88-1-L:1	Napa Valley	1.4	1.1
3	B-6/8/88-1-L:2	Annadel	No Visible Hydration	
4	B-6/8/88-2-L:4	Napa Valley	1.1	.8
5	B-6/8/88-2-L:5	Napa Valley	1.1	.8
6	B-6/8/88-2-L:6	Annadel	2.7	2.7
7	B-6/8/88-2-L:7	Napa Valley	-	-
8	B-6/8/88-3-L:1	Annadel	2.6	2.6
9	B-6/8/88-11-L:1	Annadel	5.2	5.2
10	B-6/8/88-15-L:1	Konocti	1.2	.9
11	B-6/8/88-15:L:2	Napa Valley	1.2	.9
12	B-6/8/88-24-L:1	Napa Valley	4.4	3.4
13	B-6/8/88-26-L:1	Annadel	-	-

Figure 5.11

Histogram of Obsidian Hydration Measurements for CA-SON-1880

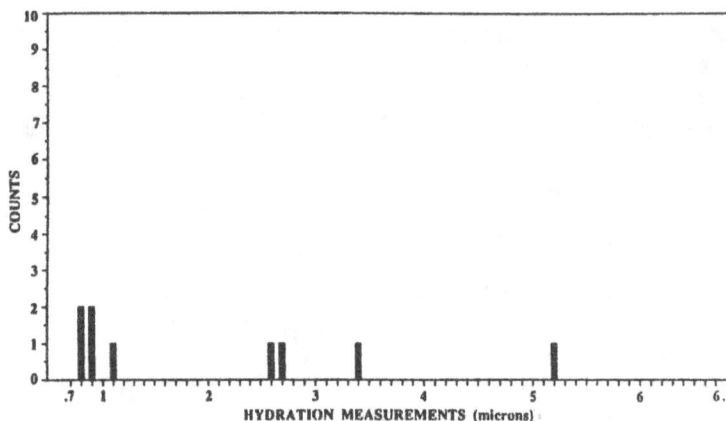

chert (27%), obsidian (27%), and quartz (9%) were represented (tables 5.5 and 5.6). The lithic density (not including those point provenienced) is 1 artifact/sq m.

Historic Artifacts. None were observed.

Faunal Remains. Twenty-three mollusk MNIs were identified for CA-SON-1881. They include limpets (65%), mussels (13%), black turban snails (9%), barnacles (9%), and one chiton (4%) (tables 5.7 and 5.8). The mollusk density (not including point provenienced material) is 2.7 MNIs/sq m.

Animal bones recovered in the surface collection include the second phalanx of a large bird and the long bone of a large mammal. The long bone exhibits evidence of both cut marks and burning.

Diversity Indexes. The diversity of chipped stone artifacts and ground stone tools is lower than expected for a similar sized Fort Ross assemblage. The richness and J scores are 4 (eighth percentile) and .406 (fifth percentile). The diversity of mollusk MNIs is greater than average for a similar sized sample. The richness and J scores are 5 (sixty-third percentile) and .480 (sixty-fifth percentile).

Chronology. Two obsidian hydration readings suggest an Upper Emergent date (table 5.16). The readings, standardized to the hydration rate of Annadel obsidian, are 1.1 and 1.3 microns respectively.

Interpretation. The site appears to be a place where food processing activities took place given the high density of mollusk remains and the presence of fire-cracked/ground stone fragments and slab millingstones. The site may date to the Upper Emer-

gent period, although this interpretation is very tentative given the tiny sample of obsidian hydration readings.

CA-SON-1882

Brief History. The site was recorded in the summer of 1988 by U.C. Berkeley crews and designated in the field as the "Traci" site.

Location. CA-SON-1882 sits on the lower slope of the first ridge in savannah grassland/mixed evergreen forests at an elevation of 134 m (figure 5.3).

Site Description. A small discrete shell midden, covering a 54 sq m area, the site exhibits a low density of mollusk remains and lithic artifacts.

Collection Strategy. Nine 1 by 2 m units, representing a 33% sample of the surface area, were collected from a centrally placed site datum (figure 5.13).

Lithic Artifacts. One artifact, a fire-cracked/ground stone fragment, was collected, resulting in a lithic density of only .05 artifacts/sq m.

Historic Artifacts. None were observed.

Faunal Remains. Six MNIs were identified in the shellfish assemblage collected from the site. They include 2 mussels, 2 black turban snails, 1 chiton, and 1 barnacle. The density of mollusks is .3 MNIs/sq m. No animal bones were recovered.

Diversity Indexes. Diversity indexes were only calculated for the mollusk assemblage. The diversity of mollusk MNIs is greater than expected for a similar sized Fort Ross assemblage. The richness and J scores is 4 (ninetieth percentile) and .577 (ninety-sixth percentile), respectively.

Table 5.16

OBSIDIAN HYDRATION DATA FOR CA-SON-1881

Lab #	Catalog #	Source	Hydration (microns)	Comparison Constant (microns)
14	B-6/9/88-2-L:1	Napa Valley	1.4	1.1
15	B-6/9/88-9-L:1	Borax Lake	2.1	1.3

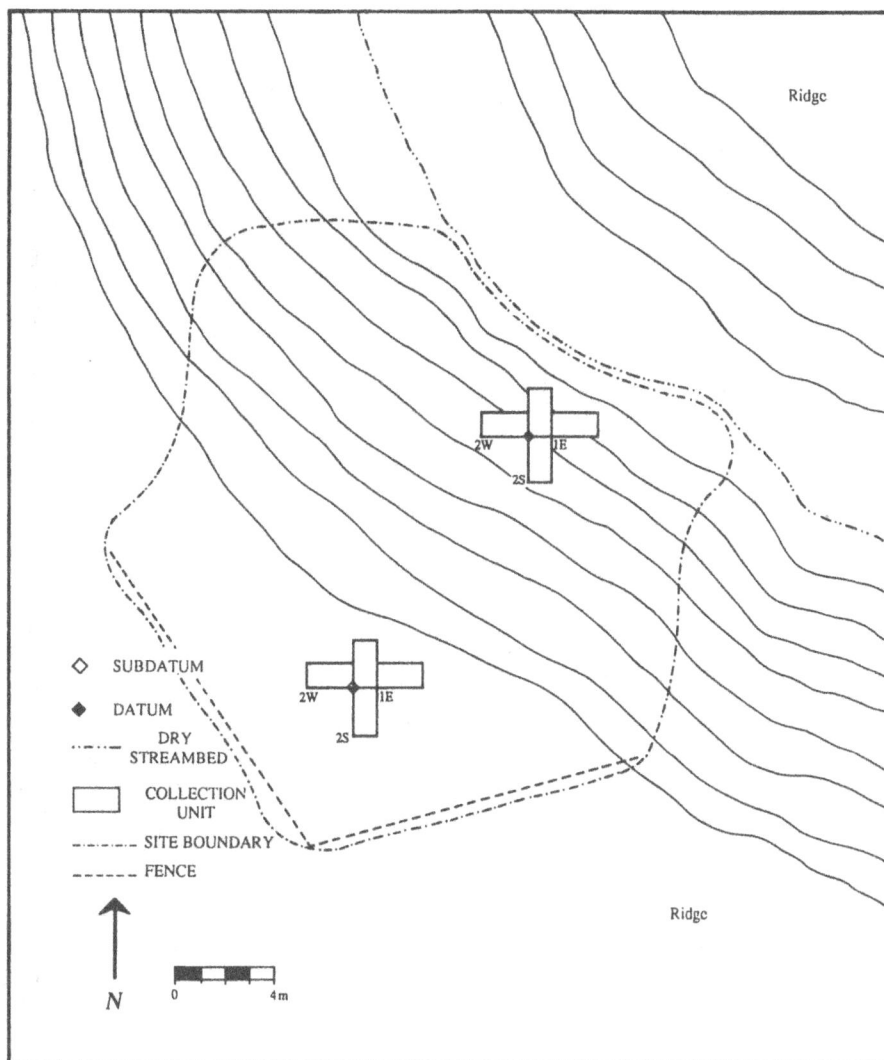

Figure 5.12

Site Map of CA-SON-1881

Chronology. No chronological data is presently available for this site.

Interpretation. The Low-density shell deposit is probably a small, short-term food processing location. The age is unknown.

CA-SON-1883

Brief History. The site was first recorded by a U.C. Berkeley survey crew in 1988 and assigned the field number, D-3-1.

Location. CA-SON-1883 is situated on a bench in the upper slope of the first ridge in a mixed savannah grassland and evergreen forest. The site, at an elevation of 268 m above sea level, is the highest yet recorded in the Fort Ross State Historic Park. It affords a spectacular view of the coastline and coastal terrace below. A permanent spring is located 154 m southwest of the site.

Site Description. CA-SON-1883, a very extensive elliptical-shaped artifact scatter covering 8247 sq

m, is characterized by two spatial components (figure 5.14). The first is a midden deposit of mollusk remains, some lithics, and a dark, charcoal-stained soil in the south and west sections of the site, where the surface banks downhill. The other component is in the upper slope of the north and east sections of the site. It contains an extensive lithic scatter and some burned daub. Handstones and fire-cracked/ground stone fragments are very common here. No features were clearly detailed, but the surface has been greatly impacted by logging activities in the past. A skid trail runs through the middle of the site.

Collection Strategy. Archaeological materials were collected from about 12% of the surface area. A collection cross of fifty-six 1 by 2 m units was laid out from the site datum. Additional 4 by 4 m units were collected to augment the sample of the collection cross. Fifty-three 4 by 4 m units were collected in the southwest, southeast, and northeast quadrants of the site (figure 5.14). Some additional materials were

Figure 5.13

**Site Map of
CA-SON-1882**

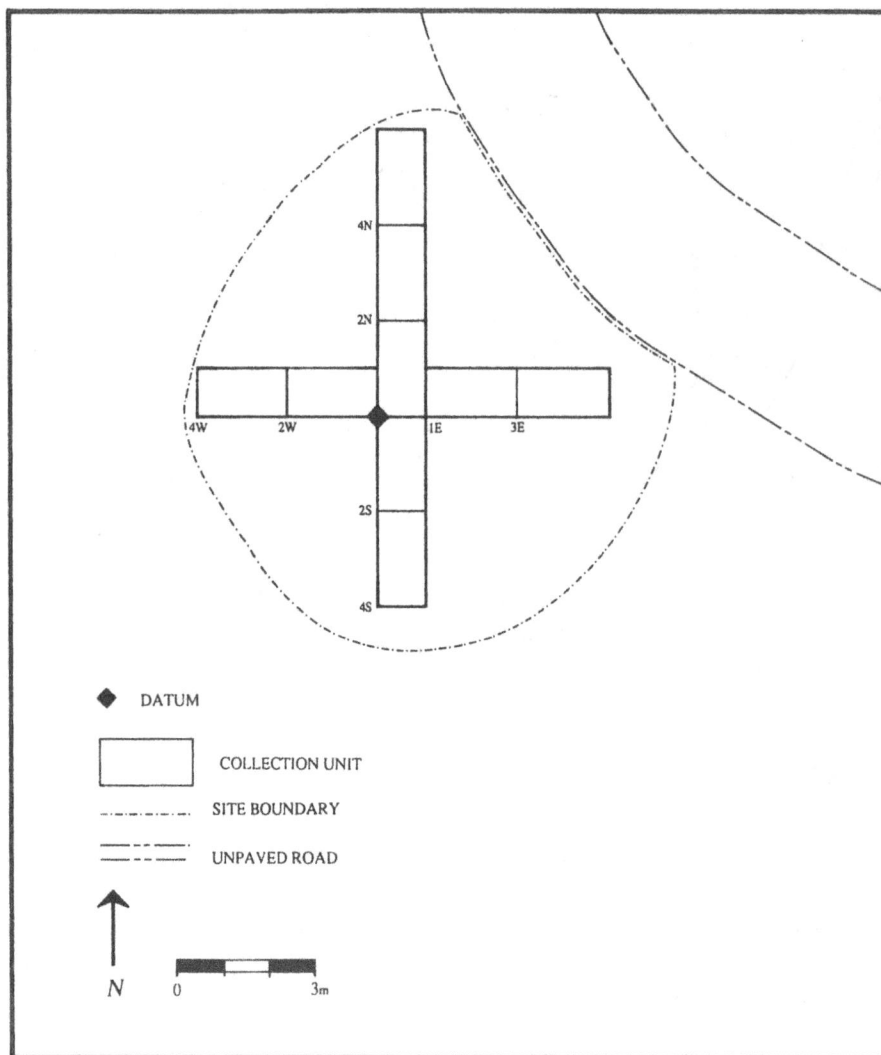

point provenienced and collected outside the units.

Lithic Artifacts. Five hundred and seventy artifacts were analyzed. The majority are fire-cracked/
ground stone fragments (52%), followed by interior
flakes (9%), shatter (8%), cores (6%), edge-modified
flakes (5%), handstones (5%), biface thinning flakes
(3%), bifaces (3%), secondary cortical flakes (3%),
primary cortical flakes (2%), projectile points (1%),
hammerstones (1%), pestles (1%), and slab
millingstones (1%) (tables 5.3 and 5.4). The projectile point types include 1 corner-notched point, 3
shouldered lanceolate points, and 1 large side-notched
point. A diverse range of raw materials are represented, including sandstone (55%), chert (28%), obsidian (11%), basalt (3%), graywacke (1%), quartz
(1%), and schist (1%) (tables 5.5 and 5.6). The
density of lithic artifacts, not including those point
provenienced outside collection units, is .46 artifacts/
sq m.

Historic Artifacts. Two sherds of a moldblown,
dark olive-green alcoholic beverage bottle were re-

covered. Another sherd of flat glass, blue-green in
color, was also collected. It exhibits evidence of
concoidal wear or impact scarring.

Faunal Remains. Twenty-five MNIs were identified for the mollusk assemblage. They include
limpets (44%), mussels (24%), black turban snails
(12%), chitons (8%), one barnacle (4%), one hooked
slipper shell (4%), and one abalone (4%) (tables 5.7
and 5.8). The mollusk density is .02 MNIs/sq m.

One long bone fragment of an unidentifiable
large mammal was recovered in the surface collection. The bone exhibits evidence of burning.

Diversity Indexes. The diversity of lithic classes
at CA-SON-1883 is greater than expected for a Fort
Ross assemblage of this size. The richness and J
scores are 15 (fifty-sixth percentile) and .823 (ninety-
eighth percentile), respectively. The diversity of
mollusk MNIs is much greater than expected for a
comparable sized assemblage. The richness and J
scores are 7 (ninety-ninth percentile) and .672 (100th
percentile).

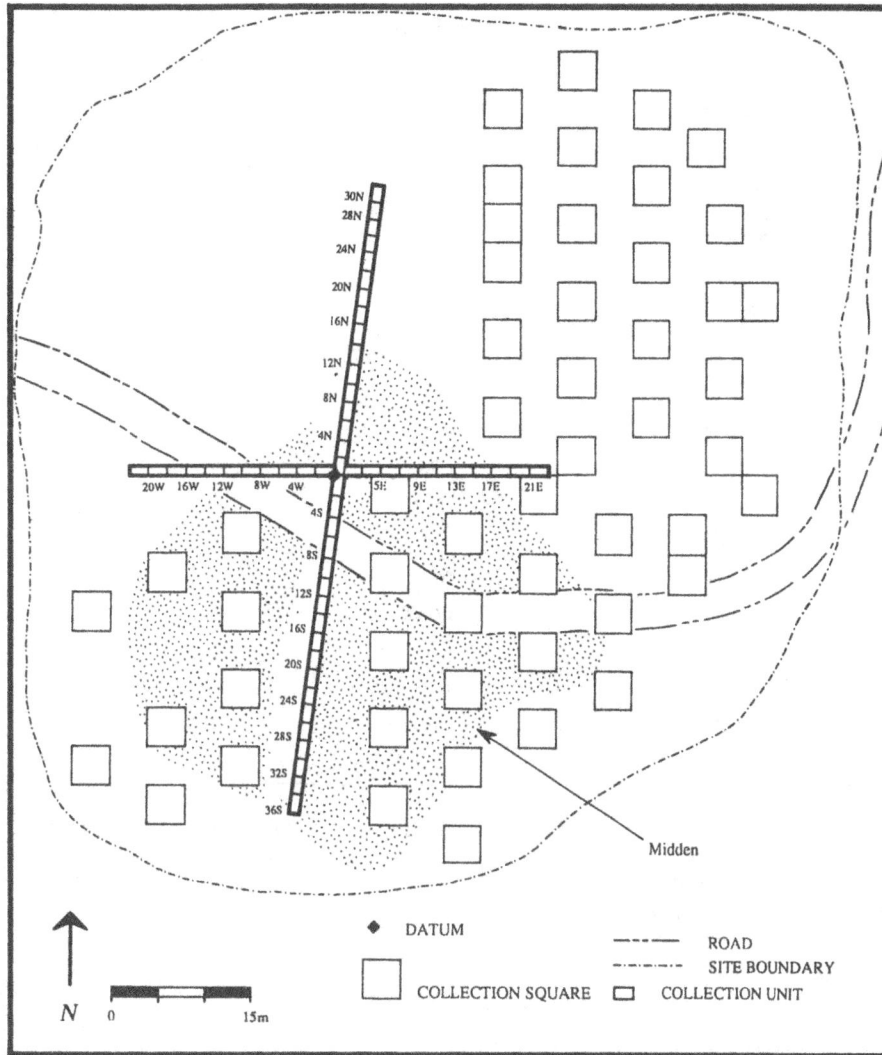

Figure 5.14

Site Map of
CA-SON-1883

Chronology. The mean hydration measurement for 16 obsidian artifacts is 1.52 microns (sd=.50). The range of one standard deviation is 1.0-2.0 microns, suggesting a date range of the Lower Emergent to the Upper Emergent. The obsidian hydration data are listed in table 5.17. Also, the projectile-point types suggest a prehistoric age for the site, possibly extending back to the Upper Archaic. The historic materials on the site are probably associated with historic logging activities in the local area.

Interpretation. The location, areal size, and diversity of artifacts and faunal remains are similar to the ridge top "villages" described by Stewart (1943). The site appears to be a major residential base occupied in prehistoric times, probably sometime in the Lower Emergent. While no features (i.e., "house pits") are visible on the surface, logging activities have greatly altered the landscape. We observed and collected fired clay (daub) from the north section of the site that is similar to that associated with pithouses

in the American Southwest. We believe the daub may represent architectural materials used in the construction of subterranean structures on the site.

CA-SON-1884

Brief History. The site was first recorded in the summer of 1988 by a U.C. Berkeley field crew. It was designated as D-7-1 in the field.

Location. CA-SON-1884 is situated on a bench in the mid-slope of the first ridge at an elevation of 207 m above sea level (figure 5.3). The nearby vegetation communities include savannah grassland and mixed evergreen forest. A permanent spring is located on the site.

Site Description. The site is an elliptical-shaped area of 3044 sq m with two spatial components (figure 5.15). A midden deposit containing shellfish refuse and considerable numbers of fire-cracked/ground stone fragments is distributed along the lower and southern section of the site. The northern and upper section is

Table 5.17

OBSIDIAN HYDRATION DATA FOR CA-SON-1883

Lab #	Catalog #	Source	Hydration (microns)	Comparison Constant (microns)
16	D-6/8/88-11-L:3	Borax Lake	3.8	2.4
17	D-6/8/88-19-L:1	Napa Valley	2.0	1.5
18	D-6/9/88-4-L:3	Napa Valley	3.4	2.6
19	D-6/9/88-7-L:1	Annadel	1.7	1.7
20	D-6/9/88-9-L:1	Napa Valley	1.5	1.1
21	D-6/9/88-14-L:1	Annadel	1.2	1.2
22	D-6/10/88-11-L:2	Borax Lake	1.3	.8
23	D-6/10/88-14-L:2	Konocti	2.5	1.9
24	D-6/10/88-16-L:5	Annadel	1.3	1.3
25	D-6/10/88-17-L:1	Konocti	1.8	1.4
26	D-6/10/88-20-L:1	Napa Valley	1.5	1.1
27	D-6/13/88-2-L:1	Borax Lake	3.2	2.0
28	D-6/13/88-8-L:1	Konocti	2.1	1.6
29	D-6/14/88-7-L:7	Napa Valley	2.3	1.8
30	D-6/14/88-11-L:2	Annadel	.9	.9
31	D-6/14/88-42-L:6	Napa Valley	1.3	1.0

characterized by a lithic scatter.

Collection Strategy. A collection cross containing sixty-three 1 by 2 m units was laid out from the site datum. Some materials were also point provenienced and collected outside the units.

Lithic Artifacts. One hundred and three artifacts were analyzed, including a number of fire-cracked/ ground stone fragments (56%), shatter (12%), edge-modified flakes (6%), interior flakes (6%), cores (5%), projectile points (4%), primary cortical flakes (3%), biface thinning flakes (2%), secondary cortical flakes (2%), a biface (1%), a hammerstone (1%), a uniface (1%), and a net weight (1%) (tables 5.3 and 5.4). The projectile point types include 3 shouldered lanceolate points and 1 corner-notched point. The dominant raw material is sandstone (57%), followed by chert (34%), obsidian (5%), quartz (2%), and schist (2%) (tables 5.5 and 5.6). The lithic density is .67 artifacts/sq m.

Historic Artifacts. One base fragment of an industrial porcelain electrical insulator cylinder was collected.

Faunal Remains. Four MNIs were identified from the mollusk assemblage. They include 1 mussel, 1 chiton, 1 limpet, and 1 barnacle. The mollusk density is .03 MNIs/sq m.

No animal bones were recovered.

Diversity Indexes. The diversity of chipped stone artifacts and ground stone tool classes is somewhat

higher than expected for a similar sized assemblage. The richness and J scores are 11 (sixty-eighth percentile) and .735 (sixty-fifth percentile), respectively. The diversity of mollusk MNIs is higher than expected for similar, small-sized assemblages. The richness and J scores are 4 (ninety-ninth percentile) and .602 (ninety-ninth percentile), respectively.

Chronology. The mean hydration measurement for three obsidian artifacts is 1.01 microns (sd=.16). The range of one standard deviation is .8-1.2 microns, suggesting a later Upper Emergent and Historic period date. The obsidian hydration data are listed in table 5.18. The projectile point types suggest a similar or somewhat earlier date.

Interpretation. The spatial structure of CA-SON-1884 resembles that of CA-SON-1883 with a northern lithic scatter and a southern midden area. While the density of both artifacts and shellfish refuse is low, the diversity of different classes of materials is relatively high, suggesting a variety of tasks were performed at the location. The site exhibits characteristics similar to ridge top hamlets described by Stewart (1943). The dating is somewhat ambiguous, given the small sample of obsidian artifacts obtained. We interpret the site as a native hamlet probably used during the transition from the Upper Emergent to the Historic periods.

CA-SON-1885

Brief History. The site was fist recorded in the summer of 1988 by a U.C. Berkeley field crew. It was

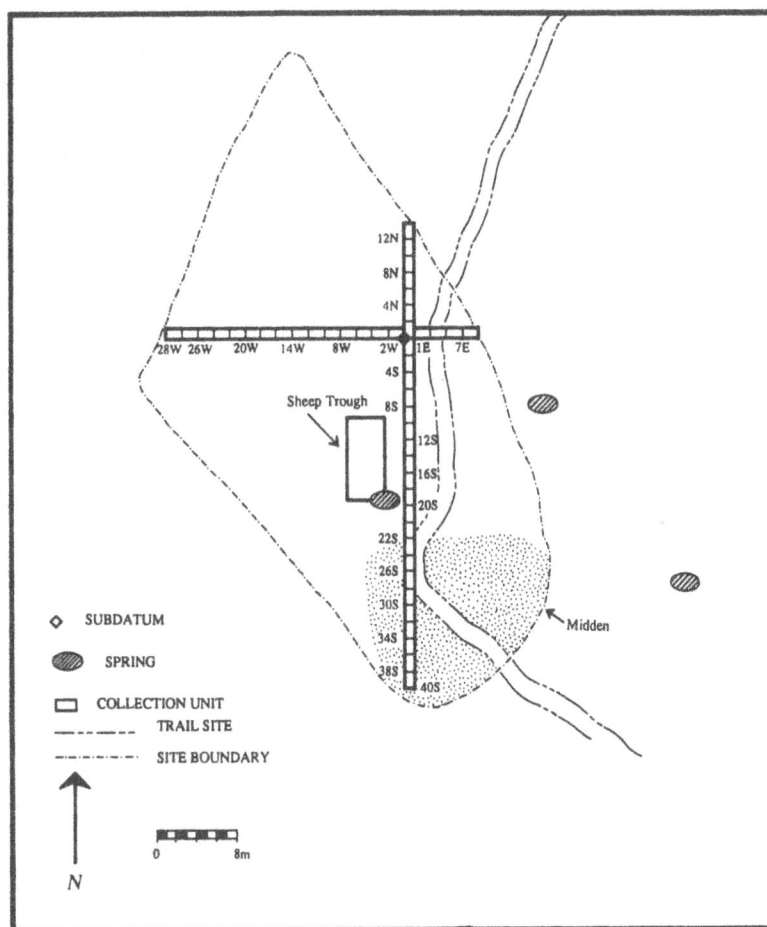

Figure 5.15

Site Map of CA-SON-1884

designated the "Bill Walton" site, named after the intrepid park ranger who introduced us to the site.

Location. CA-SON-1885 is situated in the lower slope of the first ridge in mixed savannah grassland and evergreen forest. It sits on an uplifted fault scarp of the San Andreas Fault at an elevation of 134 m.

Site Description. The site is a small, oval-shaped shell midden that covers about 919 sq m.

Collection Strategy. A 6% sample of the site was surface collected by laying out twenty-eight 1 by 2 m units along the four cardinal directions from the site datum (figure 5.16). Some materials were point provenienced and collected outside of collection units.

Lithic Artifacts. Twenty-three artifacts were collected, including fire-cracked/ground stone fragments (27%), secondary cortical flakes (18%), interior flakes (14%), edge-modified flakes (14%), biface thinning flakes (9%), shatter (9%), one uniface (3%), one projectile point (3%), and one core (3%) (tables 5.3 amd 5.4). The projectile point is classified as a corener-notched point. The lithic raw materials include chert (52%), sandstone (26%), and obsidian (22%) (tables 5.5 and 5.6). The lithic density, not including materials point provenienced, is .05 artifacts/sq m.

Historic Materials. Two sherds of a polychrome

Table 5.18

OBSIDIAN HYDRATION DATA FOR CA-SON-1884

Lab #	Catalog #	Source	Hydration (microns)	Comparison Constant (microns)
32	D-6/15/88-15-L:1	Konocti	1.6	1.2
33	D-6/15/88-16-L:1	Napa Valley	1.2	.9
34	D-6/15/88-39-L:4	Borax Lake	1.4	.9
35	D-6/15/88-41-L:1	Napa Valley	-	-

pearlware cup were recovered. The base sherds exhibit a flaring footring, are very white in body and very porous. The clear lead glaze is puddled and crazed. A dark green floral motif pattern is handpainted on the interior surface, while a red foliate pattern is painted on the exterior.

Faunal Remains. Ten mollusk MNIs were identified including 3 mussels, 2 chitons, 1 barnacle, 1 limpet, 1 dogwinkle, 1 turban snail, and 1 periwinkle (tables 5.7 and 5.8). The mollusk density is .16 MNIs/ sq m. No animal bones were recovered.

Diversity Indexes. The diversity of chipped stone artifact and ground stone tool classes is about average for an assemblage of this size. The richness and J scores are 7 (forty-fourth percentile) and .650 (fifty-seventh percentile), respectively. The diversity of mollusk MNIs is much higher than expected for a similar sized assemblage. The richness and J scores are 7 (100th percentile) and .800 (100th percentile), respectively.

Chronology. The five obsidian hydration readings average 1.82 microns (sd=.40). The range of one standard deviation is 1.4-2.2 microns, suggesting a Lower Emergent to early Upper Emergent date. The obsidian hydration data are listed in table 5.19. The corner-notched point supports the late prehistoric date. Pearlware ceramics were introduced in the mid-1760s, but continued to be produced through the middle and later nineteenth century.

Interpretation. The site appears to be a small camp used for processing local resources such as shellfish. The midden deposit appears to have been produced in late prehistoric times.

CA-SON-1886/H

Brief History. The site was first recorded by U.C. Berkeley archaeologists in the summer of 1989. In the field the site was designated as the "Chapel 2" site.

Location. This site is located 50 m due east of the reconstructed Fort Ross chapel. CA-SON-1886/H is

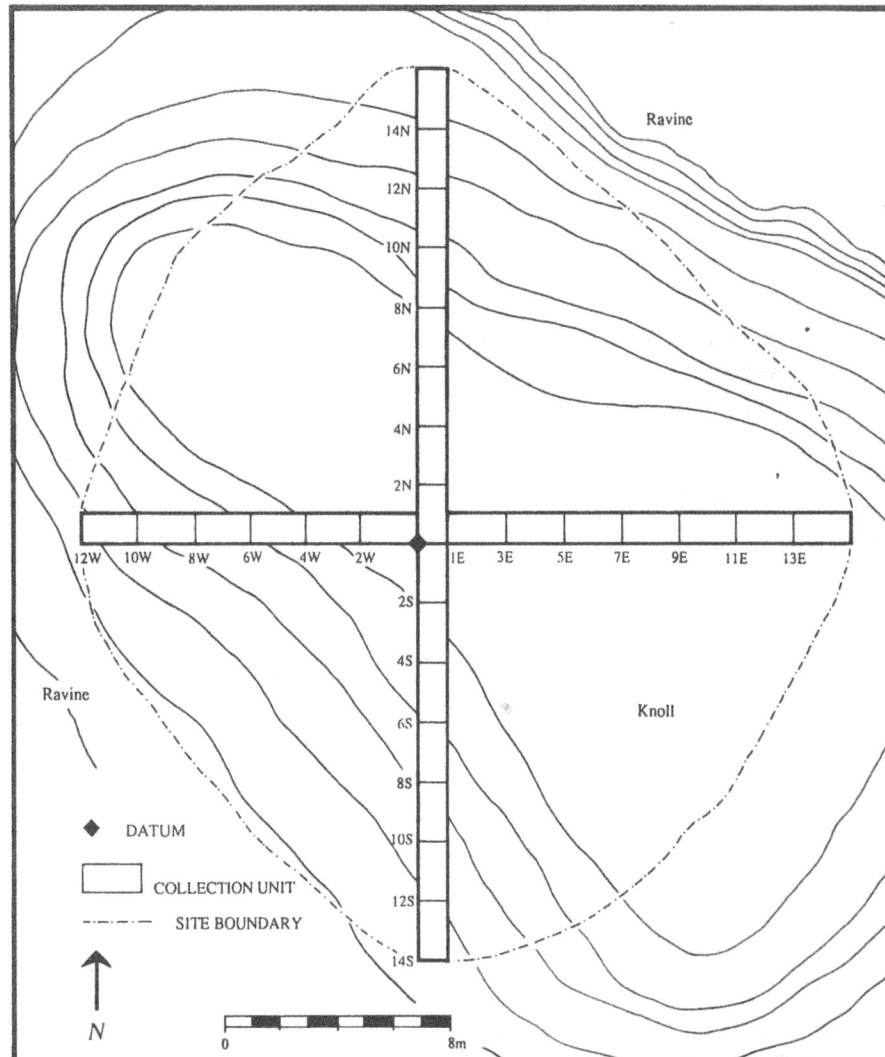

Figure 5.16

Site Map of CA-SON-1885

Table 5.19

OBSIDIAN HYDRATION DATA FOR CA-SON-1885

Lab #	Catalog #	Source	Hydration (microns)	Comparison Constant (microns)
76	C-6/6/88-48-L:1	Napa Valley	3.3	2.5
77	C-6/6/88-48-L:2	Napa Valley	2.2	1.7
102	C-6/6/88-35-L:6	Napa Valley	1.9	1.5
103	C-6/6/88-35-L:7	Napa Valley	2.6	2.0
104	C-6/6/88-35-L:8	Borax Lake	2.2	1.4

on a small shelf overlooking Fort Ross Creek about halfway down the steep embankment on which the stockade sits. The site extends across the entire shelf (10 by 12 m).

Site Description. CA-SON-1886/H is an elliptical-shaped midden about 94 sq m in size. The compact site is characterized by dense concentrations of shell, many lithic artifacts, and very dark, charcoal-stained soil. No surface features were observed.

Collection Strategy. A 23% sample of the total surface area was collected. Eleven 1 by 2 m units were laid out in a collection cross (figure 5.17).

Lithic Artifacts. From the eleven units, 217 lithic artifacts were identified yielding a density of 9.86 artifacts/sq m. The major lithic classes include fire-cracked/ground stone fragments (57%), interior flakes (14%), edge-modified flakes (11%), handstones (7%), secondary cortical flakes (4%), primary cortical flakes (2%), cores (2%), battered cobbles (2%), and projectile points (1%) (tables 5.3 and 5.4). The projectile point types include a corner-notched point and an undiagnostic triangular point. A diverse range of raw materials is represented, including sandstone (57%), chert (30%), basalt (6%), obsidian (3%), graywacke (2%), schist (1%), and quartz (1%) (tables 5.5 and 5.6).

Shell Bead. One clam disk bead was recovered.

Historic Artifacts. Sherds from four glass vessels were collected. One is a fragment of flat glass that is colorless, patinated, and probably from a window pane. The second is colorless moldblown glass container. The third is an olive-green moldblown glass container. The fourth is burned glass that could not be identified. The fragments of three ceramic vessels were collected. One is the body sherd of a white-bodied creamware vessel that is soft and chalky in texture. The surface exhibits a clear crazed glaze with no bluish or yellowish tint. The second vessel is represented by the body sherd of a buff-colored creamware with a yellowish (clear) lead glaze. The third vessel is represented by a white creamware sherd. None of the ceramic vessel forms can be identified.

Faunal Remains. Seven hundred and twenty-three MNIs were counted for the mollusk assemblage. The majority (74%) are limpets (n=537). The others are black turban snails (13%), mussels (4%), dogwinkles

(2%), chitons (2%), barnacles (2%), *Olivella* (1%), and hooked slipper shells (1%). About 1% of the mollusks are land snails. Also, abalone is present (tables 5.7 and 5.8). The mollusk density is 32.86 MNIs/sq m.

Twenty-eight mammal bones and teeth were recovered in the surface collection. Mule deer (*Odocoileus hemionus*) skeletal elements (a third lower molar, an astragalus, a metacarpal, two humeri, a naviculo-cuboid, and a fibula) are the most common. The mule deer humeri are both from the left side of the body, signifying that at least two individuals are represented in the surface assemblage. Other identifiable mammal elements include the mandible of a rabbit (*Sylvilagus bachmani*), the third phalanx of a cow (*Bos taurus*), the radius of a sea otter (*Enhydra lutris*), the metacarpal of a sheep (*Ovis aries*), the radius of a harbor seal (*Phoca vitulina*), the tarsal of the California sea lion (*Zalophus californianus*), and the ilium of a gopher (*Thomomys bottae*). Other skeletal elements that could not be identified as belonging to a specific species include thirteen long bones and a cranium of large-sized mammals. Of the bone elements, only one humeri of the mule deer exhibited evidence of cut marks. Evidence of burning was observed on the radius of the sea otter and three of the long bones from large-sized mammals.

Diversity Indexes. The assemblage of chipped stone artifacts and ground stone tools is much less diverse than expected for a similar sized sample. The richness and J scores are 11 (eleventh percentile) and .658 (0 percentile), respectively. The mollusk assemblage is also much less diverse than expected for similar sized sample. The richness and J scores are 9 (fifteenth percentile) and .395 (0 percentile), respectively.

Chronology. The average hydration measurement of 5 obsidian artifacts is 1.44 microns (sd=.39). The range of one standard deviation is 1.0-1.8 microns, suggesting a late Lower Emergent to late Upper Emergent date. The obsidian hydration data are presented in table 5.20. The corner-notched point tends to corroborate the results of the obsidian hydration analysis. The thin, patinated "window"

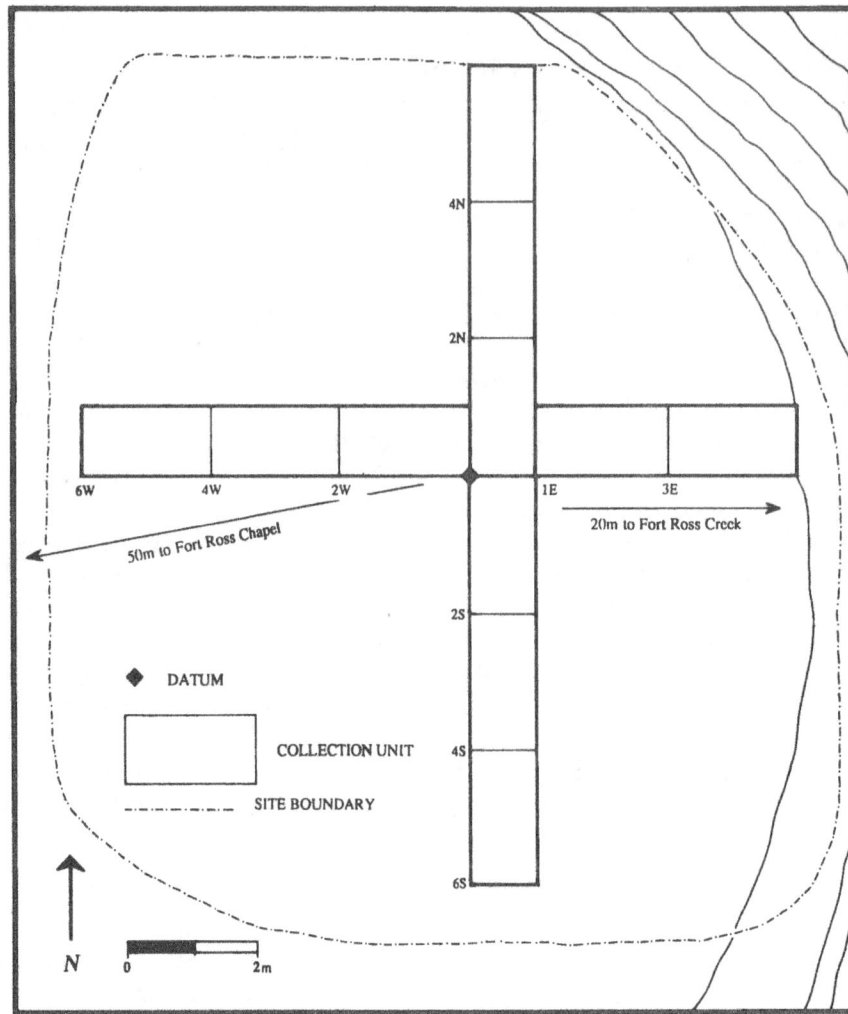

Figure 5.17

Site Map of

CA-SON-1886/H

Table 5.20

OBSIDIAN HYDRATION DATA FOR CA-SON-1886/H

Lab #	Catalog #	Source	Hydration (microns)	Comparison Constant (microns)
93	L-6/2/89-3-L:9	Konocti	No Visible Hydration	
94	L-6/5/89-6-L:2	Borax Lake	1.7	1.0
95	L-6/5/89-6-L:3	Annadel	1.3	1.3
96	L-6/5/89-6-L:3	Napa Valley	2.6	2.0
97	L-6/5/89-13-L:1	?	1.8	-
98	L-6/5/89-13-L:1	Borax Lake	1.8	1.1
99	L-6/5/89-13-L:2	Annadel	1.8	1.8

glass looks early. Purser (personal communication) estimates a date of sometime between the 1860s to 1880s. The moldblown bottle glass indicates a pre-1910s manufacture.

Interpretation. CA-SON-1886/H exhibits the highest density of lithics and mollusk remains of the survey sites examined. On the other hand, the assemblages are relatively limited in the kinds of materials present. Many fire-cracked/ground stone fragments are present, presumably from cooking activities. The low diversity indexes calculated for the chipped stone artifacts and ground stone tools reflect the relatively large number of interior flakes and edge-modified flakes. The low diversity indexes for the mollusk remains correspond to the great concentration of limpets on the site. The site exhibits the greatest diversity of mammal remains from any of the survey sites that we surface collected, including domesticated species (cow and sheep), terrestrial game (mule deer) and sea mammals (California sea lion, harbor seal, and sea otter). We believe that this archaeological place has experienced a complex occupational history that spans much of the Upper Emergent and Historic periods, most probably during the Russian occupation of the Ross Colony, or even in early Ranch times. At certain times it may have been a special purpose processing locus, at other times it may have functioned as a small residential base. John McKenzie, based on his interviews with the Call family, identified the site as the residence of the last Pomo family (Lucari and Mary) at Fort Ross in the early 1900s (McKenzie 1963:1-2).

CA-SON-1887

Brief History. The site was first recorded by a U.C. Berkeley crew in the summer of 1989. The site was assigned the field number, E-2-1.

Location. CA-SON-1887 sits on the coastal terrace in coastal prairie grassland (figure 5.3).

Site Description. The site consists of two cupules pecked into the surface of a small sandstone outcrop boulder (figure 5.18). One cupule is 8 cm in diameter

and 5 cm deep; the other measures 7 cm in diameter and 2 cm deep. No artifacts were observed in the nearby vicinity.

Interpretation. The site is a cupule rock located on the coastal terrace with a good view of the ocean. The age of the site is unknown.

CA-SON-1888

Brief History. The site was first recorded in the summer of 1989. It was designated as E-6-1 in the field.

Location. CA-SON-1888 sits on the coastal terrace in coastal prairie grassland (figure 5.3). The site is on a low rise overlooking Clam Beach Creek.

Site Description. An elliptical-shaped shell midden, the site covers about an 85 sq m area.

Collection Strategy. A 26% sample of the site's surface area was collected. Eleven 1 by 2 m units were laid out in a collection cross (figure 5.19).

Lithic Artifacts. Twenty-three lithic artifacts were analyzed. They include interior flakes (35%),

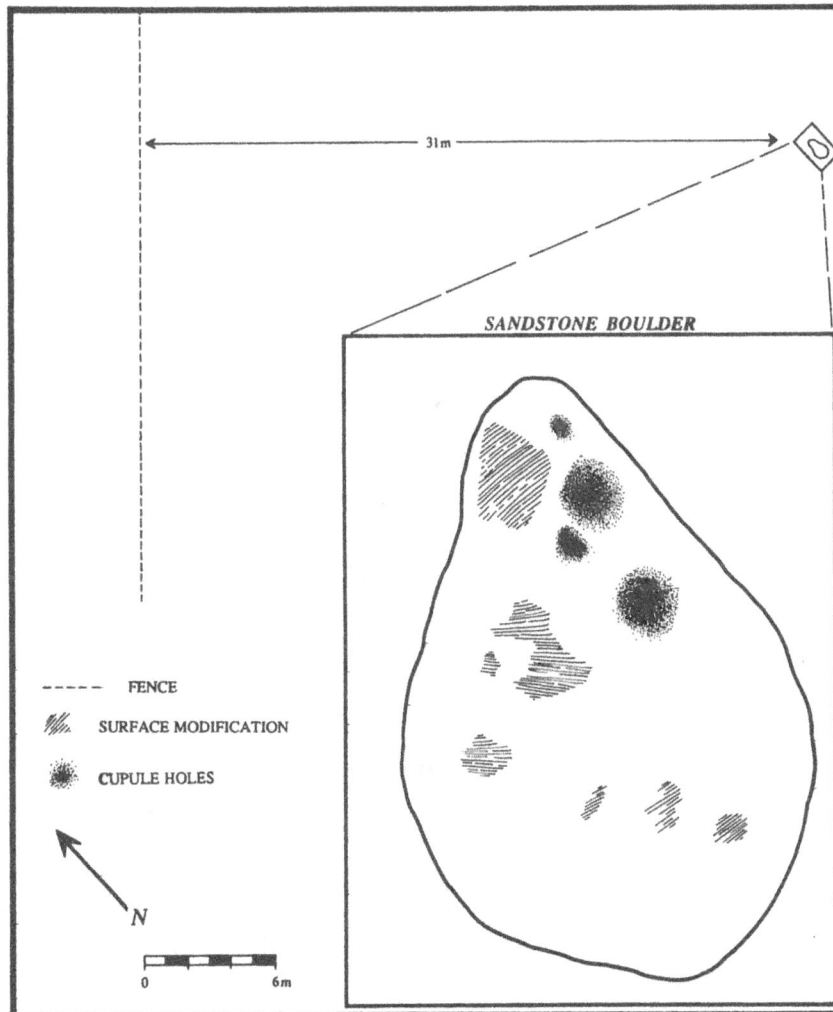

Figure 5.18

Map of Cupule Rock at CA-SON-1887

SANDSTONE BOULDER

31m

- - - - -   FENCE

///   SURFACE MODIFICATION

···   CUPULE HOLES

N

0   6m

Figure 5.19

Site Map of

CA-SON-1888

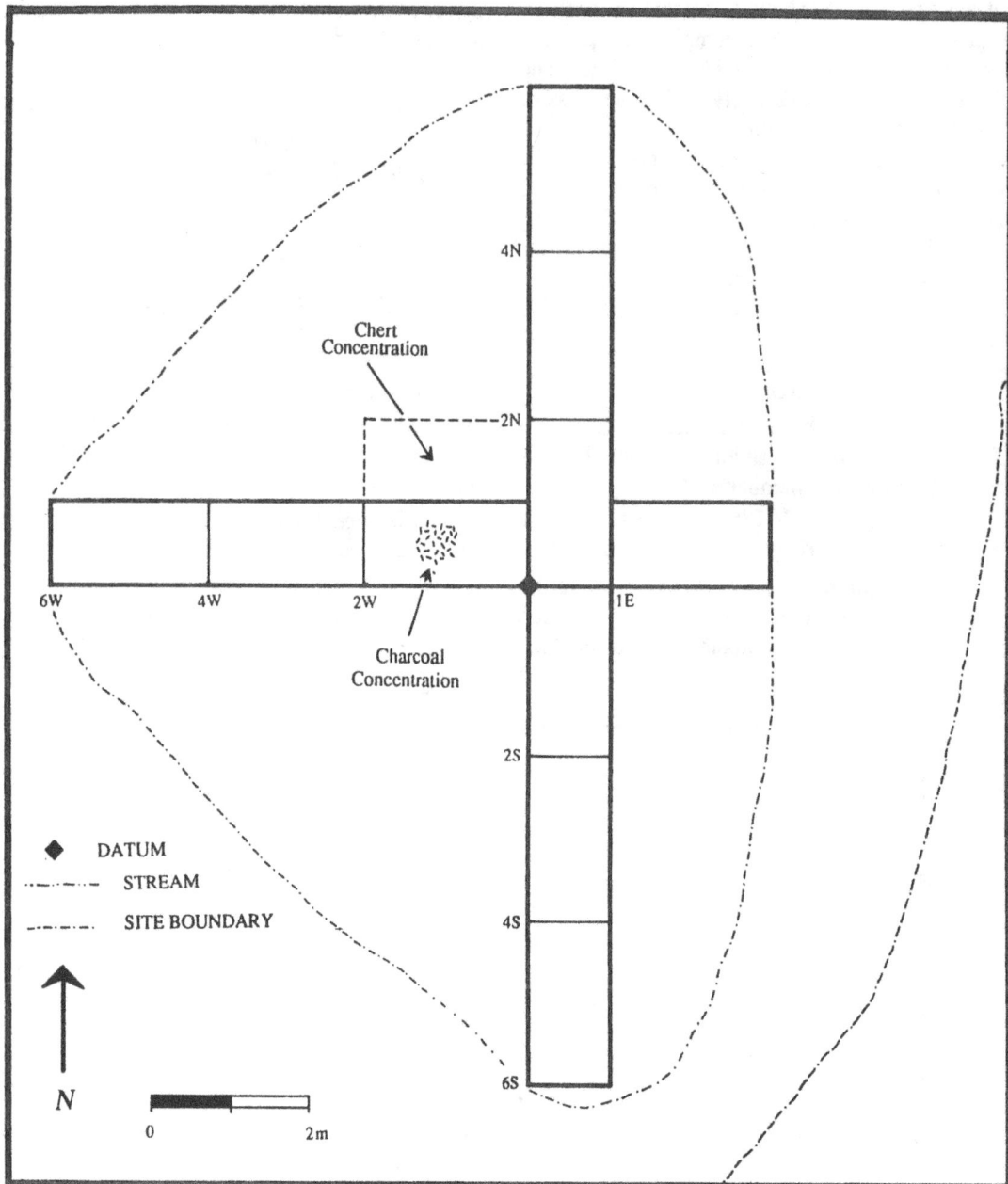

edge-modified flakes (22%), biface thinning flakes (22%), secondary cortical flakes (13%), and fire-cracked/ground stone fragments (8%) (tables 5.3 and 5.4). The majority are manufactured from chert (65%). Other raw materials include obsidian (26%) and sandstone (9%) (tables 5.5 and 5.6). The lithic density is 1.04 artifact/sq m.

Historical Materials. None were observed.

Faunal Remains. Forty-seven MNIs were identified in the mollusk assemblage. They include limpets (36%), black turban snails (26%), mussels (17%), chitons (15%), a periwinkle (2%), a horned slipper shell (2%), and a barnacle (2%) (tables 5.7 and 5.8). The mollusk density is 2.14 MNIs/sq m.

Animal bones (n=4) collected from the surface

could be identified only as large-sized mammals. The skeletal elements include a vertebra, a long bone, a scapula, and a rib. None of the elements exhibit evidence of cut marks; only one is burned.

Diversity Indexes. The chipped stone artifact and ground stone tool classes on CA-SON-1888 are much less diverse than expected for a similar sized survey assemblage. The richness and J scores are 4 (0 percentile) and .470 (first percentile), respectively. On the other hand, the mollusk assemblage is more diverse than expected for a similar sized sample. The richness and J scores are 7 (seventy-ninth percentile) and .67 (100th percentile), respectively.

Chronology. The average of three obsidian hydration readings is 1.4 microns (sd=.14). The range of

Table 5.21

OBSIDIAN HYDRATION DATA FOR CA-SON-1888

Lab #	Catalog #	Source	Hydration (microns)	Comparison Constant (microns)
37	E-6/7/89-8-L:1	Annadel	1.5	1.5
38	E-6/7/89-8-L:1	Annadel	1.5	1.5
39	E-6/7/89-10-L:2	Napa Valley	1.6	1.2

one standard deviation is 1.3-1.5 microns, suggesting an Upper Emergent date. The obsidian hydration data are presented in table 5.21.

Interpretation. This small site appears to have been characterized by a limited range of activities involving the exploitation of coastal resources such as shellfish. It seems to have been used primarily in the Upper Emergent.

CA-SON-1889

Brief History. The site was first recorded in the summer of 1989 by a U.C. Berkeley survey crew. The site was designated as I-2-1 in the field.

Location. CA-SON-1889 sits on the exposed coastal terrace in coastal prairie grassland (figure 5.3). The site is on the lee side of a rock outcrop (sandstone stack).

Site Description. An elliptical shaped shell midden measuring 189 sq m, the site is bordered on the north by a large rock outcrop and on the south by a small drainage (figure 5.20). A relatively dense concentration of shell and some lithic artifacts are dispersed across the surface.

Collection Strategy. Four 1 by 2 m units were laid out in a collection cross, representing about a 4% sample of the site's surface area. Other materials were point provenienced and collected outside the collection units.

Lithic Artifacts. Eighteen lithic artifacts were analyzed. These include edge-modified flakes (29%), fire-cracked/ground stone fragments (29%), interior flakes (12%), one biface (5%), one biface thinning flake (5%), one core (5%), one handstone (5%), one

pestle (5%), and one uniface (5%) (tables 5.3 and 5.4). The raw material types include sandstone (39%), chert (33%), and obsidian (28%) (tables 5.5 and 5.6). The lithic density is .37 artifacts/sq m.

Historical Materials. None were observed.

Faunal Remains. Thirty-two MNIs were identified for the mollusk assemblage. They include limpets (66%), black turban snails (19%), mussels (9%), a chiton (3%), and a barnacle (3%) (tables 5.7 and 5.8). The mollusk density is 2.37 MNIs/sq m.

No animal bones were recovered in the surface collection.

Diversity Indexes. The diversity of chipped stone artifacts and ground stone tools is somewhat higher than expected for a similar sized assemblage. The richness and J scores are 8 (eightieth percentile) and .649 (fifty-ninth percentile), respectively. The diversity of the mollusk assemblage is somewhat less than expected for a comparable sample size. The richness and J scores are 5 (thirty-eighth percentile) and .447 (fortieth percentile), respectively.

Chronology. The mean of four obsidian hydration readings is 1.9 microns (sd=.75). The obsidian hydration data is presented in table 5.22. A histogram indicates that the 3.2 microns measurement is clearly an outlier (figure 5.21). Without this outlier the mean of the measurements is 1.5 microns (sd=.05). The range of one standard deviation is 1.4 to 1.5 microns. The results suggest a long use-duration for CA-SON-1888 beginning as early as the late Upper Archaic. The major use of this site probably took place in the Upper Emergent.

Table 5.22

OBSIDIAN HYDRATION DATA FOR CA-SON-1889

Lab #	Catalog #	Source	Hydration (microns)	Comparison Constant (microns)
40	I-6/8/89-1-L:1	Napa Valley	2.0	1.5
41	I-6/8/89-3-L	Konocti	-	-
42	I-6/8/89-8-L:1	Borax Lake	5.1	3.2
43	I-6/8/89-8-L:2	Napa Valley	1.8	1.4
44	I-6/8/89-11-L:2	Konocti	1.9	1.5

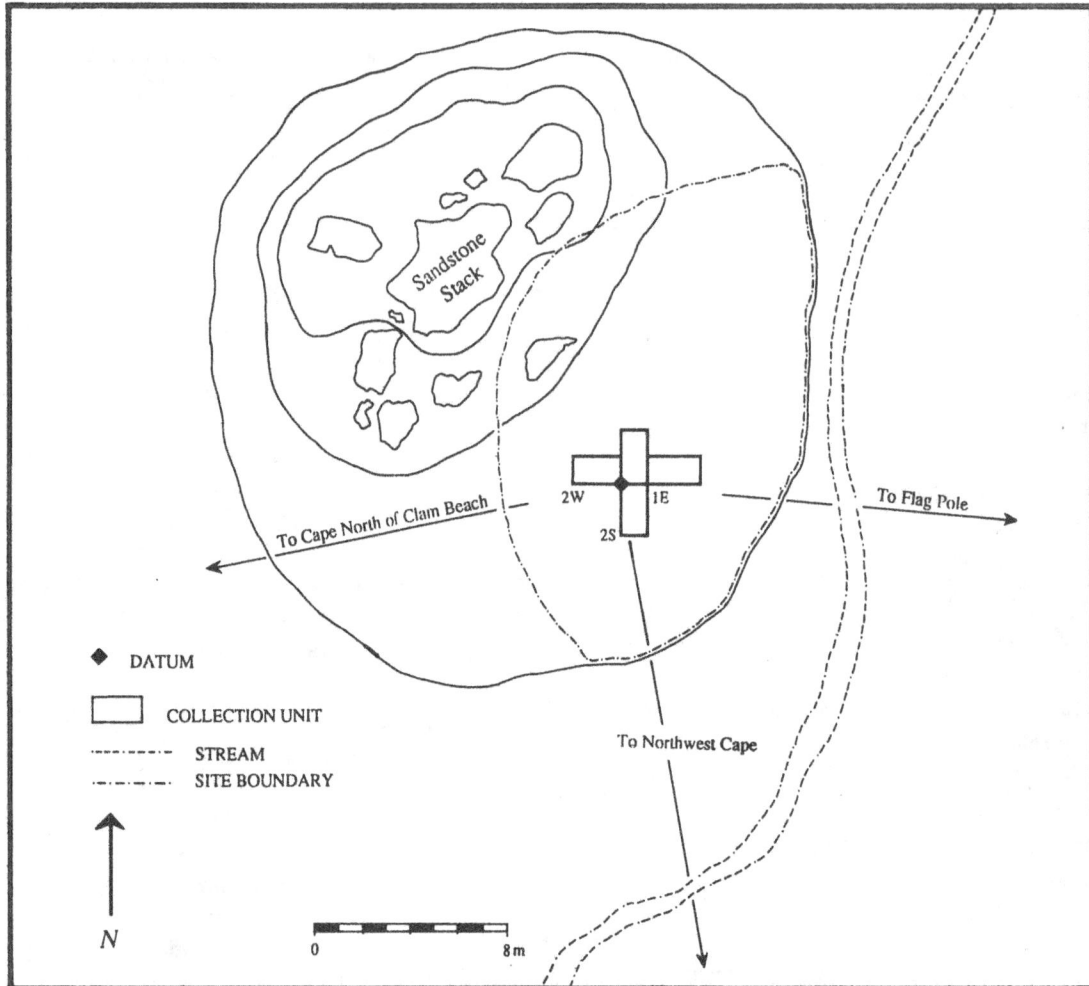

Figure 5.20   Site Map of CA-SON-1889

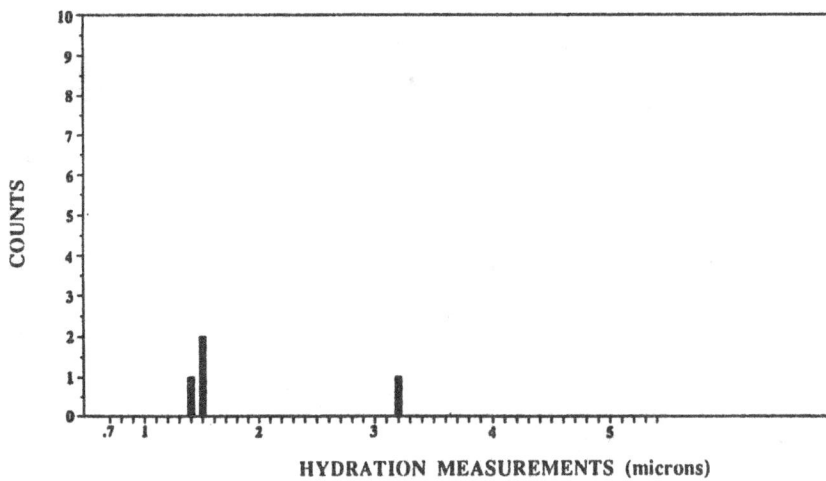

Figure 5.21   Histogram of Obsidian Hydration Measurements for CA-SON-1889

Interpretation. The relatively diverse range of artifacts and shellfish types at CA-SON-1889 suggest it may have served as a residential base for a small group of people exploiting maritime resources. The processing and cooking of both shellfish and vegetable products probably occurred here. The archaeological place may have an extended use-duration, but the shell midden appears to date primarily to the Upper Emergent.

CA-SON-1890

Brief History. The site was first recorded by a U.C. Berkeley survey crew in the summer of 1989. It was assigned the field number, K-4-1.

Location. CA-SON-1890 is situated on the lower slope of the first ridge in a mixed evergreen forest (figure 5.3).

Site Description. The site consists of an elliptical midden area (871 sq m) characterized by black organic soil, shellfish debris, and lithics. Thick grass precludes a clear view of the surface.

Collection Strategy. Given the thick grass cover, only one 1 by 2 m unit was collected, about a .02% sample of the surface. The sod was removed to obtain a clear view of the surface. Other materials, brought to the surface by rodents, were point provenienced and collected outside the unit.

Lithic Artifacts. Nine artifacts were identified, including shatter (34%), biface thinning flakes (22%), a projectile point (11%), an edge-modified flake (11%), an interior flake (11%), and a secondary cortical flake (11%) (tables 5.3 and 5.4). The projectile point is classified as a shouldered lanceolate point. Raw materials include chert (67%) and obsidian (33%) (tables 5.5 and 5.6). The lithic density for the collection unit is 3 artifacts/sq m.

Historical Artifacts. None were observed.

Faunal Remains. Six MNIs were identified, including 3 mussels, one barnacle, 1 chiton, and 1 turban snail. The mollusk density is 3 MNIs/sq m.

Animal bones (n=5) include the scapula of a mule deer (*Odocoileus hemionus*), the molar of a sheep (*Ovis aries*), and three long bones of large-sized mammals. None exhibit evidence of cut marks, while two of the long bones are burned.

Diversity Indexes. The diversity of chipped stone artifacts and ground stone tools is above average for an assemblage of this size. The richness and J scores are 6 (sixty-third percentile and .592 (fifty-ninth percentile), respectively. The diversity of mollusk MNIs is also above average. The richness and J scores are 4 (ninety-second percentile) and .540 (eighty-ninth percentile).

Chronology. The mean of two hydration measurements is 1.97 microns (sd=.87), tentatively indicating a date sometime in the late Upper Archaic to Upper Emergent (table 5.23). The shouldered lanceolate projectile point also suggests a similar range of time.

Interpretation. CA-SON-1890 appears to be another small midden deposit where a moderate range of activities took place sometime during late prehistoric times. Given the very small surface area collected, it is difficult to say much about the site at this time.

CA-SON-1891H

Brief History. John McKenzie, retired curator/ranger, first pointed out the location of the site to us in 1988. The site was first recorded by a U.C. Berkeley crew in the summer of 1989. It was assigned the field number, L-1-1.

Location. CA-SON-1891H sits on the eastern side of Fort Ross Cove (figure 5.3).

Site Description. The site consists of a 20 by 26 m rectangular, smoothed dirt platform (figure 5.22). Some metal artifacts are scattered in the local vicinity.

Collection Strategy. The few artifacts visible on the surface were point provenienced and collected.

Lithic Artifacts. One edge-modified flake was collected.

Historical Artifacts. A square nail, nail fragments, and unidentified metal fragments were collected.

Faunal Remains. None were observed.

Interpretation. The site appears to be the founda-

Table 5.23

OBSIDIAN HYDRATION DATA FOR CA-SON-1890

Lab #	Catalog #	Source	Hydration (microns)	Comparison Constant (microns)
45	K-6/14/89-1-L	Borax Lake	4.6	2.8
46	K-6/15/89-2-L:1	Annadel	1.1	1.1

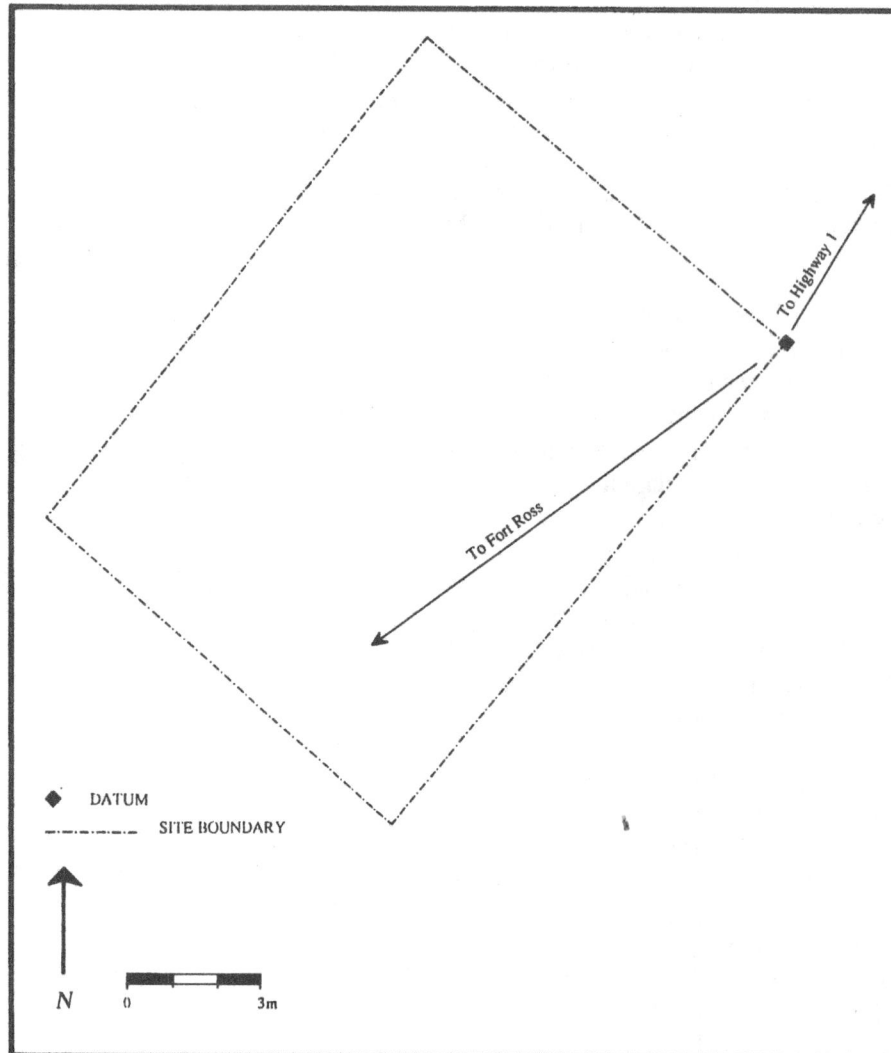

Fgure 5.22
Site Map of
CA-SON-1891/H

tion of a potato "warehouse" constructed sometime during the early to mid-nineteenth century. The 1859 plat map of the Muniz Rancho clearly marks the site as a "potato warehouse" (Matthewson 1859). The 1876 U.S. Coast Survey map of the region, on file in the Bancroft Library, shows a structure on the site. The storage structure was probably used by William Benitz in the 1840s or 1850s.

CA-SON-1892

Brief History. The site was first recorded in 1989 by a U.C. Berkeley survey crew. The site was designated in the field as L-8-1.

Location. The site is on a small bench at the base of a drainage that dissects the coastal terrace near CA-SON-1455 in the Fort Ross Campground (figure 5.3).

Site Description. CA-SON-1892 is a shell midden buried under about one m of overburden. The site, exposed in the cut of the campground road, consists of a 20–40 cm thick deposit of dark soil, shellfish refuse and some lithics. The road exposes a 12 m long slice of the midden (figure 5.23). We estimate that the size of the midden is roughly 120 sq m.

Collection Strategy. Six 1 by 2 m collection "profiles" were set up along the 12 m road cut. Materials were collected from the surface of these profile units. Materials were also collected from the base of the profile where they had eroded out of the wall.

Lithic Artifacts. We identified 15 artifacts, including fire-cracked/ground stone fragments (41%), pieces of shatter (12%), edge-modified flakes (12%), a battered cobble (7%), a biface thinning flake (7%), a hammerstone (7%), an interior flake (7%), and a secondary cortical flake (7%) (tables 5.3 and 5.4). The majority were produced from local sandstone (47%), followed by chert (33%), obsidian (13%), and graywacke (7%) (tables 5.5 and 5.6). The lithic density for only the surface profiles is .92 artifacts/sq m.

Shell Bead. A clam disk bead was collected.

Historical Materials. None were observed.

Faunal Remains. Eighty-three MNIs were identified from CA-SON-1892. The largest numbers are limpets (54%), followed by mussels (27%), black turban snails (15%), chitons (3%), and one barnacle (1%) (tables 5.7 and 5.8). The mollusk density for only the surface profiles is 6.9 MNIs/sq m.

No animal bones were recovered in the surface collection.

Diversity Indexes. The diversity of chipped stone artifacts and ground stone tools is higher than expected for an assemblage of this size. The richness and J scores are 7 (eighty-eighth percentile) and .667 (ninety-second percentile), respectively. The diversity of mollusk MNIs is somewhat less than expected. The richness and J scores are 5 (6th percentile) and .494 (fifty-fourth percentile), respectively.

Chronology. The hydration readings for two artifacts of Annadel obsidian are 1.2 and 1.4 microns (table 5.24), suggesting an Upper Emergent date.

Interpretation. The site, similar to CA-SON-1888, appears to be a small coastal camp or residential base where a moderate range of activities took place in late prehistoric times.

of the Fort Ross Road.

Site Description. CA-SON-1894 is a diffuse lithic scatter covering about a 155 sq m area.

Collection Strategy. Artifacts were collected along the road cut.

Lithic Artifacts. Twenty-two artifacts were collected. These include pieces of shatter (28%), interior flakes (24%), secondary cortical flakes (9%), biface thinning flakes (9%), cores (9%), edge modified flakes (9%), a biface (4%), a fire-cracked/groundstone fragment (4%), and a hopper mortar (4%) (tables 5.3 and 5.4). The raw materials include obsidian (45%), chert (32%), schist (14%), and sandstone (9%) (tables 5.5 and 5.6).

Historic Artifacts. None were observed.

Faunal Remains. None were observed.

Diversity Indexes. The diversity of chipped stone artifacts and ground stone tools is somewhat less than expected for an assemblage of this size. The richness and J scores are 8 (thirty-ninth percentile) and .665 (forty-eighth percentile), respectively.

Chronology. Five obsidian artifacts (table 5.25) produced a mean hydration rim width of 1.58 microns (sd=.67). The range of one standard deviation is .9 to

Table 5.24

OBSIDIAN HYDRATION DATA FOR CA-SON-1892

Lab #	Catalog #	Source	Hydration (microns)	Comparison Constant (microns)
47	L-6/28/89-6-L:2	Annadel	1.2	1.2
48	L-6/28/89-10-L:2	Annadel	1.4	1.4

CA-SON-1894

Brief History. The site was first recorded in the summer of 1988 by a U.C. Berkeley field crew. It was designated in the field as Locus 4 of CA-SON-1446H.

Location. The site is located on the lower slope of the first ridge near the Old Russian Orchard in savannah grassland. The site parallels the south side

2.2 microns, suggesting use sometime during the Lower to Upper Emergent periods.

Interpretation. CA-SON-1894 is a diffuse lithic scatter found in the lower slope of the first ridge. Lithic artifacts appear to have been deposited in both late prehistoric and early historic times near the Old Russian Orchard.

Table 5.25

OBSIDIAN HYDRATION DATA FOR CA-SON-1894

Lab #	Catalog #	Source	Hydration (microns)	Comparison Constant (microns)
1	C-6/14/88- 2L:1	Napa Valley	1.0	.8
2	C-6/14/88- 2L:2	Napa Valley	1.3	1.0
3	C-6/14/88- 2L:3	Konocti	2.2	1.7
4	C-6/14/88- 2L:4	Borax Lake	4.3	2.7
5	C-6/14/88- 2L:6	Annadel	1.7	1.7

Figure 5.23

Site Map of

CA-SON-1892

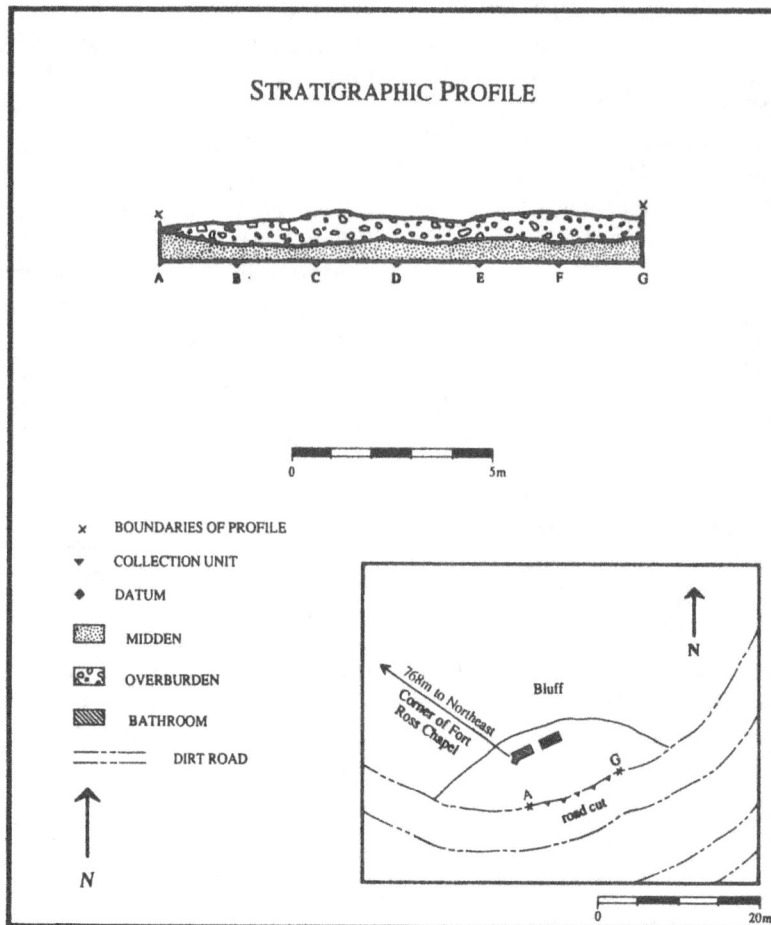

STRATIGRAPHIC PROFILE

× BOUNDARIES OF PROFILE

▼ COLLECTION UNIT

◆ DATUM

▦ MIDDEN

▨ OVERBURDEN

▧ BATHROOM

—·—·— DIRT ROAD

768m to Northeast Corner of Fort Ross Chapel

Bluff

road cut

CA-SON-1895/H

Brief History. The site was described by Breck Parkman and Glenn Farris in 1984 who designated it as Locus 2 of CA-SON-1446H. The site is also known as the North Orchard Site. We first recorded the site in the summer of 1988.

Location. The site is located in the lower slope of the first ridge adjacent to the Old Russian Orchard (figure 5.3). The local vegetation community is mixed savannah grassland.

Site Description. CA-SON-1895/H, a midden deposit containing primarily shell, dark soil, and some lithics, covers a 203 sq m area.

Collection Strategy. A 16% sample of the site's surface area was collected by laying out sixteen 1 by 2 m units in a collection cross (figure 5.24). Some materials were also point provenienced and collected outside the units.

Lithic Artifacts. Nine lithic artifacts were identified, including 4 fire-cracked/ground stone fragments, 2 battered cobbles, 1 core, 1 interior flake, and 1 secondary cortical flake (tables 5.2 and 5.3). The raw materials represented include sandstone (67%), obsidian (22%), and chert (11%) (tables 5.5 and 5.6).

The lithic density for only the collection units is .06 artifacts/sq m.

Historic Materials. Sherds from four different glass vessels were collected. They include 1 black, moldblown alcoholic beverage bottle, 1 mamelon (base) of a dark olive-green wine bottle, 1 dark olive-green alcoholic beverage bottle, and 1 small glass sherd that may be worked. A ceramic sherd of a white European-style porcelain hollowware was also recovered.

Faunal Remains. Eleven MNIs were identified, including 3 limpets, 2 black turban snails, 2 mussels, 2 chitons, and 2 barnacles (tables 5.7 and 5.8). The mollusk density is .34 MNIs/sq m.

Animal bones (n=3) include the vertebra of a cow (*Bos taurus*), the metacarpal of a mule deer (*Odocoileus hemionus*), and a fragment of a cranium of a large mammal. None of the bone elements exhibit evidence of cut marks or burning.

Diversity Indexes. The diversity of chipped stone artifacts and ground stone tools is somewhat greater than expected for a sample this size. The richness and J scores are 4 (fifty-ninth percentile) and .470 (fifty-ninth percentile), respectively. The diversity of mollusk MNIs is greater than expected. The richness and

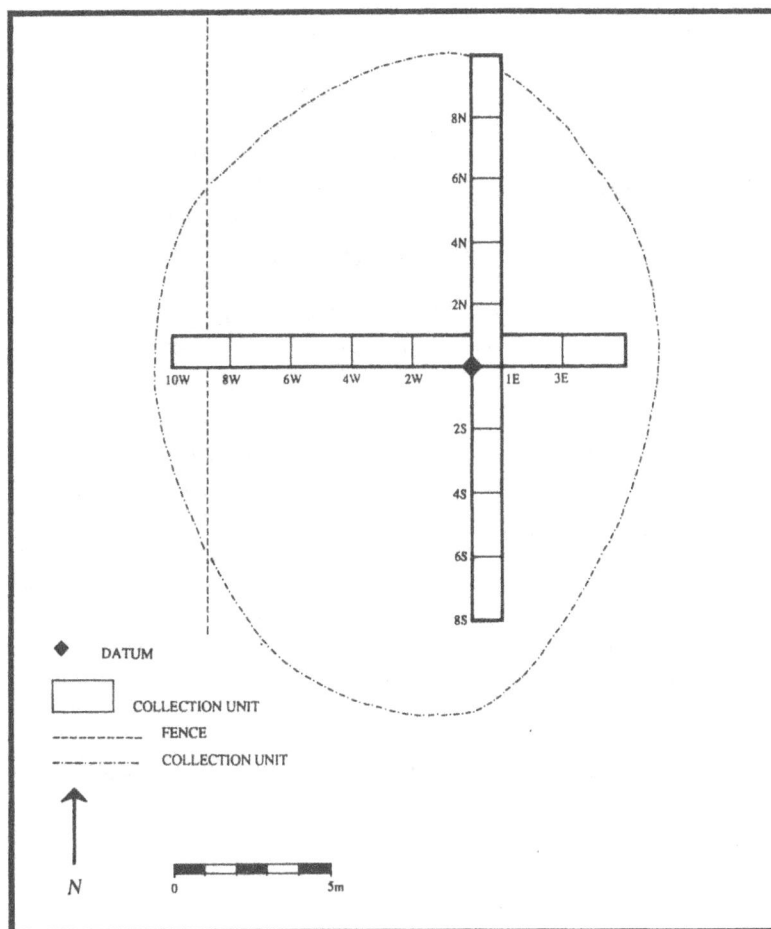

Figure 5.24
Site Map of
CA-SON-1895/H

J scores are 5 (ninety-second percentile) and .692 (ninety-ninth percentile), respectively.

Chronology. The single hydration measurement is from the secondary cortical flake (catalog # C-6/06/88-18-L) of Annadel obsidian. Its hydration band is 1.2 microns thick. The other obsidian artifact from the site exhibited a weathered surface whose hydration band could not be measured. The black moldblown beverage bottle is of a style that dates from the 1820s to the 1880s (Purser, personal communication).

Interpretation. This midden deposit appears to be a place where cooking and food processing activities took place. Its age is not clear. Use of it may date from late prehistoric to the early historic times when the Russians established the adjacent orchard.

CA-SON-1896

Brief History. The site, first described by Breck Parkman in September of 1984, was originally designated as Locus 3 of CA-SON-1446H. Parkman directed a crew of ten volunteers from the Santa Cruz Archaeological Society in mapping, surface collecting, and excavating a small sample of the site (Parkman 1990a). We decided to record it as a separate site in the

summer of 1988. It was designated in the field as Locus 3 or C-6-1.

Location. CA-SON-1896 sits upon a protected hilltop overlooking CA-SON-1895 and the Old Russian Orchard site on the lower slope of the first ridge (figure 5.3). The elevation is 171 m above sea level. The plant community associated with the site is savannah grassland and a mixed evergreen forest. The site is located close to a spring (Parkman 1990a).

Site Description. The archaeological deposit, which extends over about a 400 sq m area, is characterized by a dark, greasy midden containing a considerable number of faunal remains, lithics, and historic artifacts. Parkman's excavation demonstrates that the site is very shallow, ranging from 8-14 cm in depth, and rests on sterile sandstone bedrock. No features were noted in the excavation or on the surface of the site.

Collection Strategy. The 1984 investigation involved the excavation of seven 1 by 1 m units from the surface to the underlying bedrock. All sediments were screened through 1/8" mesh. A total of one cubic m of midden was excavated (Parkman 1990a). During our re-examination of the site in 1988, we noted some archaeological materials eroding down the hillslope. A collection cross of 1 by 2 m units was laid out and 19.5 units were collected (figure 5.25).

Lithic Artifacts. Sixty-six lithic artifacts were recovered during the 1984 excavation. They include 47 flakes and pieces of debitage, 2 edge-modified flakes, 11 fire-cracked/ground stone fragments, 2 handstones, 1 mid-section of an obsidian projectile point, 1 chert scraper, and 1 charmstone. The projectile point is serrated along the blade. The surface collection of the site in 1988 produced only 7 fire-cracked/ground stone fragments.

Historic Artifacts. The 1984 excavation yielded 8 glass beads (six white, 1 blue, and 1 red with a green center). Three glass sherds (1 green, 2 colorless) were also recovered in the excavation. No historic artifacts were collected from the surface in 1988.

Faunal Remains. Jeanette Schulz analyzed the shellfish remains from the excavation of CA-SON-1896. The majority of the MNIs include limpets (186), mussels (167), chitons (132), barnacles (71),

hooked slipper snails (41), and black turban snails (39). Other mollusk species, including abalone, are present in fewer numbers. Three clam shell disk beads were also recovered. Animal bones, identified by Dwight Simons, include 5 whole vertebrae of unidentified fish species, and the metapodial of a mule deer (*Odocoileus hemionus*).

The surface collection in 1988 yielded a total of 34 mollusk MNIs, including 11 mussels, 9 limpets, 6 chitons, 5 black turban snails, 2 barnacles, and 1 *Olivella* shell (tables 5.7 and 5.8). One animal bone, the axis of a large mammal that showed evidence of burning, was recovered in the 1988 surface collection.

Diversity Indexes. Diversity indexes were not generated for the lithic assemblages. An examination of the excavated materials will be undertaken in the near future to classify the flakes and debitage into categories that are consistent with the other Fort Ross sites. The survey assemblage contains no chipped stone artifacts or ground stone tools, only fire-cracked/ground stone fragments. The previous surface collec-

Figure 5.25

Site Map of CA-SON-1896

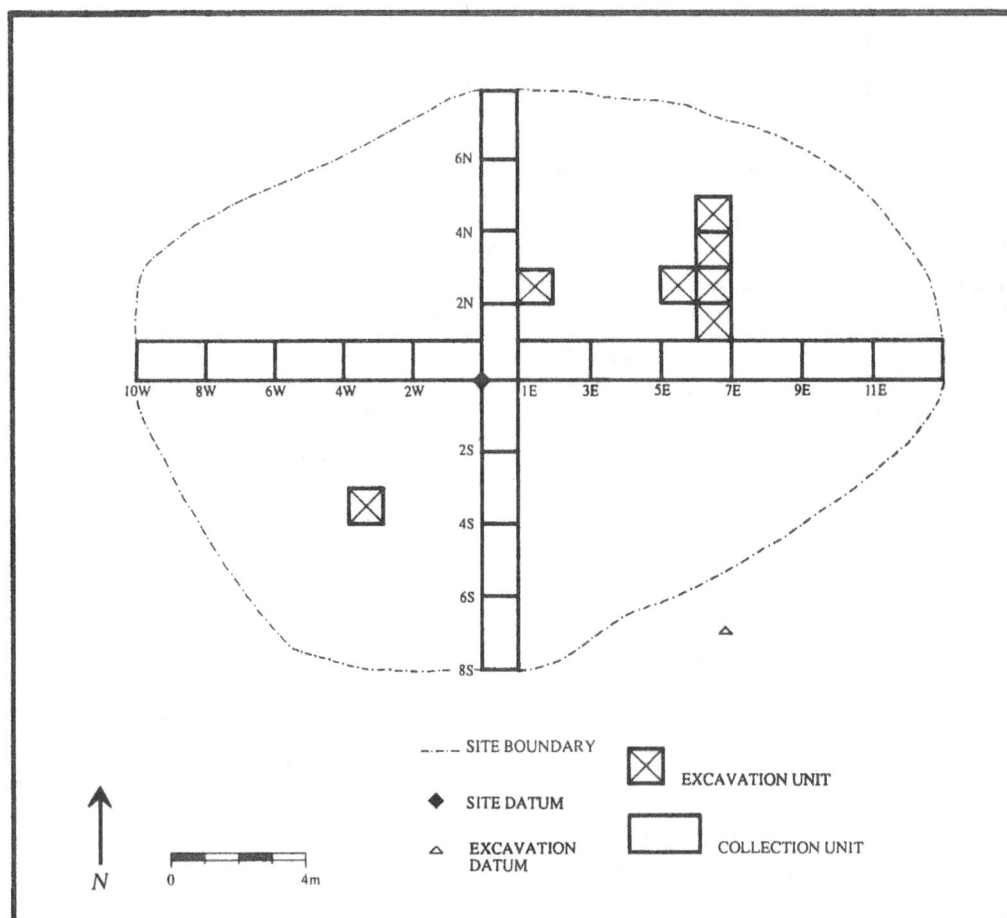

tion and excavation appears to have limited the artifact types found on the surface.

The mollusk assemblages from the 1984 excavation and 1988 survey are characterized by similar proportions of MNIs. Limpets, mussels, chitons, turban snails, and barnacles dominate both assemblages. The diversity of the 1988 assemblage is greater than expected for a similar sized surface sample. The richness and J scores are 6 (seventy-second percentile) and .684 (ninety-ninth percentile), respectively.

Chronology. A total of 18 obsidian artifacts from the 1984 excavation were submitted to Thomas Origer of the Obsidian Hydration Laboratory for analysis (table 5.26). The mean of the hydration readings is .85 microns (sd=.12). The range of one standard deviation is .7-1.0 microns, suggesting a historic date for the site. The glass trade beads strengthen this interpretation.

Interpretation. Parkman (1990a) concludes that CA-SON-1896 probably represents the remains of a historic Kashaya Pomo household encampment. He suggests they may have served as orchard workers for the Russians, but does not rule out occupation during early Ranch times as well. We concur with Parkman's interpretation.

CA-SON-1897/H

Brief History. We describe the Native Alaskan Village in chapter 1. Suffice it to say that this is a very large archaeological deposit (2800 sq m) south of the stockade complex where the native Alaskans resided while at the Ross Colony. Treganza (1954:18) is the first archaeologist to mention the site. In the summer of 1989 field crews from U.C. Berkeley recorded, mapped, and surface collected the site. Dr. Lewis Somers undertook a geophysical survey of the site. A full report of our findings will be presented in Volume 2 of the Archaeology and Ethnohistory of Fort Ross, California series.

For the purposes of this volume we discuss the results of the obsidian hydration analysis of 13 artifacts collected from across the site's surface. The data are presented in table 5.27. The mean of the readings is 2.05 microns (sd=.93). The range of one standard deviation is 1.1 to 3.0 microns, suggesting a Late Archaic to Upper Emergent date. Only one reading (.9 micron) indicates a Historic period date. The results suggest that a broad, diffuse prehistoric lithic scatter underlies the village. This lithic scatter also appears to underlie the stockade complex as well given the hydration measurements for CA-SON-190. Similar to CA-SON-228, CA-SON-1453 and CA-SON-1454/H, native peoples began to use the coastal terrace of Fort Ross at a relatively early date and continued to reuse it sporadically until late prehistoric times.

CA-SON-1898/H

Brief History. The Fort Ross Beach Site was first described by Treganza (1954:18). In the summers of 1988 and 1989, U.C. Berkeley crews

Table 5.26

OBSIDIAN HYDRATION DATA FOR CA-SON-1896 (from Parkman 1990a)

Lab #	Source	Hydration (microns)	Comparison Constant (microns)
1	Napa Valley	1.0	.8
2	Annadel	.9	.9
3	Annadel	.9	.9
4	Napa Valley	1.6	1.2
5	Napa Valley	.9	.7
6	Napa Valley	.9	.7
7	Napa Valley	1.0	.8
8	Annadel	.9	.9
9	Napa Valley	1.0	.8
10	Napa Valley	1.0	.8
11	Napa Valley	1.0	.8
12	Annadel	1.0	1.0
13	Annadel	.9	.9
14	Napa Valley	1.0	.8
15	Konocti	.9	.7
16	Annadel	1.0	1.0
17	Annadel	-	-
18	Napa Valley	1.0	.8

Table 5.27

OBSIDIAN HYDRATION DATA FOR CA-SON-1897/H

Lab #	Catalog #	Source	Hydration (microns)	Comparison Constant (microns)
52	KS-6/23/89-9-L:3	Annadel	4.2	4.2
53	KS-6/23/89-15-L:2	Annadel	1.9	1.9
54	KS-6/23/89-33-L:1	Annadel	2.8	2.8
55	KS-6/26/89-5-L:4	Annadel	1.7	1.7
56	KS-6/27/89-3-L:1	Annadel	1.2	1.2
57	KS-6/27/89-13-L:2	Napa Valley	-	-
58	KS-6/27/89-30-L	Napa Valley	4.5	3.5
59	KS-6/28/89-14-L	Annadel	2.2	2.2
60	KS-6/28/89-15-L	Annadel	1.7	1.7
61	KS-6/28/89-10-L:1	Annadel	2.0	2.0
62	KS-6/27/89-16-L	Annadel	1.1	1.1
63	KS-6/26/89-4-L:1	Annadel	2.2	2.2
64	KS-6/23/89-1-L	Napa Valley	1.2	.9
65	KS-6/16/89-2-L	Annadel	1.2	1.2

mapped, profiled, and excavated portions of the site. A full description will be presented in Volume 2 of the Archaeology and Ethnohistory of Fort Ross, California series.

DIACHRONIC CHANGES IN

SUBSISTENCE SETTLEMENT PATTERNS

The long-term land use patterns of native people in the Fort Ross Study Area follow similar diachronic trends as those observed elsewhere in the broader region. These trends include the early use of the coastal terrace, and the later manifestation of a well developed subsistence-settlement system in the Upper Emergent. The Upper Emergent settlement pattern fits many of the expectations of a central-based village settlement model. Some archaeological places are distinguished by complex occupational histories in which the nature of subsistence-settlement activities changed over time. In figure 5.26 we portray our estimates of the age and relative use-durations of survey sites using current data on obsidian hydration measurements, projectile point types, historic artifacts, and historic maps.

Early Lithic Scatters

Archaeological evidence to date indicates that the earliest human activities in the study area took place along the coastal terrace. Similar to the early settlement pattern described by Pritchard (1970), and Bramlette and Dowdall (1989) for Salt Point State Park, the earliest dated sites are coastal lithic scatters.

In the Fort Ross area, these scatters (CA-SON-228, -1453, -1454/H) tend to be broadly dispersed, low-density manifestations that contain a low diversity of lithic artifact classes. Interior flakes, biface thinning flakes, edge-modified flakes, shatter, and cores compose the bulk of the assemblages. Biface fragments are present in low numbers. At both CA-SON-1453 and 1454/H some ground stone tools and battered schist cobbles are also present.

The obsidian hydration analysis suggests that sporadic human use of the coastal terrace may have begun as early as 8000 to 6000 years ago. However, most data indicate the lithic scatters date primarily to the Upper Archaic and Lower Emergent (figure 5.26). The long use-durations of the sites coincide with significant changes taking place in the coastal morphology of the Fort Ross area due to post-Pleistocene sea level rise, coastal erosion and tectonic movements. The coastline was about 5 km west of its present location about 10,000 years ago (chapter 3). The early use of the coastal shelf occurred when sea level rise and coastal erosion were rapidly inundating the exposed continental shelf. The brisk rate of eustatic rise continued until about 7000 years ago. Subsequently, the present shoreline began to take shape, probably sometime in the Middle and Upper Archaic periods.

It is not clear what specific kinds of activities produced the lithic scatters. Nonetheless, we believe the entire coastal terrace can be characterized as an extensive, non-site manifestation (Thomas 1975). That is, a very broad, diffuse distribution of lithics appears to extend along the entire terrace. This early

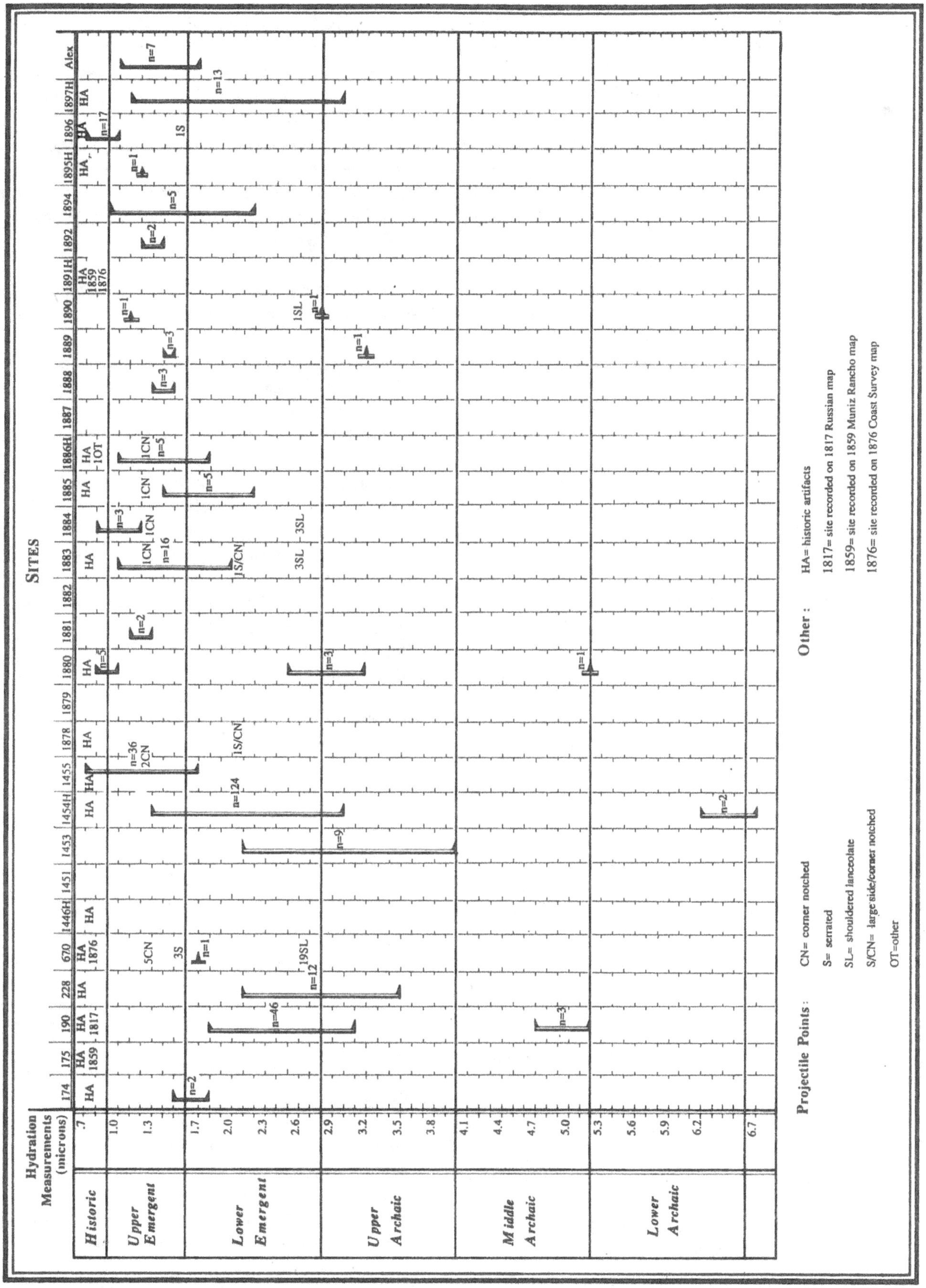

Figure 5.26   **Chronological Information on Fort Ross Survey Sites**

manifestation appears to underlie many of the settlements that were later established on the coastal terrace. For example, the Ross garrison (CA-SON-190) and the Native Alaskan Village (CA-SON-1897/H) are built upon an earlier lithic scatter that covers the coastal bluff overlooking the Fort Ross Cove. The bluff may have been used by native peoples as early as the Middle Archaic period. Other settlements on the coastal terrace that we suspect are placed upon earlier lithic scatters include the historic villages at CA-SON-174 and 1880, and the coastal camp at CA-SON-1889.

Non-site manifestations are often produced from foraging and hunting ventures over an extensive resource zone in which various tools are lost or discarded. Simons, Layton, and Knudson (1985:266) suggest that the earliest use of the coastal terrace in central Mendocino County, dating back to 11000 B.P., involved the hunting of terrestrial mammals. The patchy, coniferous forest may have been an ideal habitat for Roosevelt elk (*Cervus elaphus*) which would have attracted hunters to the region. The lithic scatters in the Fort Ross area may have resulted from a similar hunting pattern, as well as the exploitation of other available plant and animal resources. The ground stone implements and battered cobbles distributed across some scatters indicate that some raw materials, not yet identified in archaeological contexts, were being processed by mashing and grounding.

The current data do not suggest that the lithic scatters were a product of an early economy focused on maritime adaptations. The first unambiguous evidence of the exploitation of marine resources in the study area is quite late. The earliest dated shell midden is CA-SON-1885, a small processing station that may date to the middle Lower Emergent, about 1000 years ago (figure 5.26). A similar diachronic trend is described for Salt Point by Pritchard (1970) and Bramlette and Dowdall (1989). Bramlette and Fredrickson (1990) estimates that the earliest shell middens in Salt Point date to 2000-3000 years ago. However, Bramlette and Dowdall (1989) caution that early remains of a coastal economy (shellfish refuse, fish bones) may not have been preserved in the acidic soil of the coastal strip.

The late date of marine resources in archaeological deposits raises the age-old question of coastal archaeology. Is the paucity of early shell middens an accurate reflection of the late florescence of coastal adaptations in the region? Or is it the result of coastal sites being destroyed by rapid eustatic rise in the early Holocene, coastal erosion in the later Holocene, or the acidic soils of the Fort Ross region? The question is impossible to answer at this time. On one hand, this region may have been only used sporadically at an early date by interior based hunter-gatherer groups who produced the extensive lithic manifestations along the coastal terrace. On the other hand, it is possible that earlier coastal settlements were once established several kilometers seaward of the present coastline in the early and mid-Holocene. The early lithic manifestations that we observe today adjacent to the coast may have been deposited inland on a broad terrace that served as the interior hinterland of the coastal sites. Here coastal based hunter-gatherers may have exploited nearby terrestrial resources such as deer, elk, and seeds.

While purely conjectural at this time, the latter scenario is motivated largely by the recent excavation of the Duncan's Landing site (CA-SON-348) a short distance south of the Russian River (Schwaderer, Ferneau, and Parkman 1990). Here a stratified archaeological deposit, a three-meter-thick midden laden with shellfish debris and animal bones, is situated in a protected, rock overhang. The lower levels are dominated by clams and oysters, while the upper levels contain mostly mussels. The changes in mollusk frequencies probably reflect sea level rise and the transformation of nearby coastal landforms from protected sand beaches and estuarine areas to rocky intertidal habitats. Radiocarbon dates from the lower levels (240 cm below surface) of the deposit suggest that marine resources were being extensively collected as early as 8200 B.P. (Schwaderer, Ferneau, and Parkman 1990). Given the unique characteristics of the rock shelter, early hunter-gatherers may have made an extra effort to transport marine resources a few km inland to the protected location.

Central-Based Villages

Current evidence suggests that intensive occupation of the study area did not begin until the end of the Lower Emergent and the beginning of the Upper Emergent (figure 5.26). We note, however, that the coastal terrace and lower slope of the first ridge were probably never as intensively used by native peoples as the coastal strip of nearby Salt Point. The density of native sites at Salt Point (31 per sq km) is three times that of the Fort Ross State Historic Park (9.6 per sq km). The more expansive coastal terrace at Salt Point is distinguished by many more shell middens and lithic scatters.

By the Upper Emergent period, a relatively complex settlement pattern developed in the study area that supports some aspects of the central-based village model. We identify two sites, CA-SON-1883 and CA-SON-1884, in the Fort Ross State Historic Park that correspond in many ways to the ridge top "villages" recorded by Stewart (1943). Both sites are large (8247 sq m and 3044 sq m, respectively), contain a diverse range of artifact types and shellfish MNIs, and are spatially organized into discrete midden deposits and broad lithic scatters. Both sites are distinguished by relatively large numbers of fire-cracked/ground stone fragments. While no surface architectural features were observed, fired daub at CA-SON-1883 suggests the presence of subterranean structures. The kinds of activities that appear to have taken place on the sites include cooking, lithic manufacture, plant and animal food processing, and various domestic chores. The age of CA-SON-1883 is somewhat earlier, initially dating to the late Lower Emergent and persisting through most of the Upper Emergent. The earliest occupation of CA-SON-1884 may overlap the other village and then extend into early historic times (figure 5.26). However, we recognize that the small sample of obsidian hydration measurements from CA-SON-1884 may be a limiting factor in interpreting the full use-duration of this archaeological place.

We observed similar ridge top sites in the summer of 1988 southeast of the Fort Ross Study Area. The sites are located on private property on the very upper slope of Campmeeting Ridge. At the owner's request, we can not divulge the location of the sites. One site (the Alex site) we recorded, mapped, and surface collected. The other site (the Patch site) was only briefly visited. Both sites are located about 425 m above sea level, near freshwater springs, and command good views of the ocean below. We observed two spatial components on each site consisting of a discrete midden deposit of faunal remains and a broader lithic scatter. The Patch site contains a large surface feature 18-20 m in diameter that is centrally located with respect to three or four other smaller surface depressions. We submitted obsidian artifacts from the Alex site to the Obsidian Hydration Laboratory, Sonoma State University. The mean of the seven hydration readings is 1.37 microns (sd=.33). The range of one standard deviation is 1.-1.7 microns, suggesting a late Lower Emergent and Upper Emergent occupation (table 5.28).

The spatial distribution of "village" sites (CA-SON-176, -177, -178, -179, -231, -999, -1883, -1884, the Alex site, the Patch site) suggests they are centered along the coastal-facing slope and top of the first ridge (Campmeeting Ridge), although at least one (CA-SON-999) is found on the slope of the second ridge (Creighton Ridge) near a tributary of the South Fork of the Gualala River. All but one (CA-SON-231) are located in higher elevations above the cool fog and wind belt that marks the microclimate of the coastal terrace throughout much of the year. Most sites we recorded or visited are located near fresh water springs, and they usually afford a spectacular view of the coastline below. Three of the sites (CA-SON-1883, CA-SON-1884, and the Alex site) appear to be relatively contemporaneous, dating primarily to the Upper Emergent. The age of the other sites remains unknown. Whether these sites were used year-round or for only a portion of the year is not yet understood.

The village sites are dispersed relatively evenly along the first ridge system, about .5 to 2.5 km apart (figure 5.3). It is not yet possible to evaluate whether a settlement hierarchy exists of large sites with non-domestic architectural features (i.e., assembly houses) and smaller hamlets that lack such features. A full study of all the ridge top and ridge slope villages will first need to be undertaken to better estimate the size, surface features, and constituents of the sites. There is evidence, however, of substantial differences in the sizes of sites, especially when one considers the possibility that some small residential bases were being occupied during some part of the annual round on the coastal terrace and lower slope of the first ridge, as discussed below.

The ridge top and ridge slope village sites are ideally located to take advantage of both coastal and interior hinterland resources. The sites on the first ridge system are located no more than 5 km from rocky intertidal habitats, the coastal terrace, the South Fork of the Gualala River, or the second ridge system.

Table 5.28

OBSIDIAN HYDRATION DATA FOR THE ALEX SITE

Lab #	Catalog #	Source	Hydration (microns)	Comparison Constant (microns)
66	B-6/10/88-21-L:2	Annadel	-	-
67	B-6/10/88-22-L:1	Borax Lake	2.0	1.2
68	B-6/10/88-22-L:2	Annadel	1.6	1.6
69	B-6/10/88-22-L:3	Napa Valley	1.5	1.2
70	B-6/10/88-24-L:1	Napa Valley	1.5	1.2
71	B-6/10/88-29-L:1	Konocti	1.9	1.5
72	B-6/10/88-36-L	Napa Valley	1.2	.9
73	B-6/10/88-38-L	Annadel	2.0	2.0

From these residential bases, foraging parties or specialized task groups could, within a few hours, walk to a variety of resource patches. As described in chapter 3, these patches include the intertidal and coastal terrace habitats that contain shellfish, rocky reef fish, sea mammals, elk; the coastal-facing slope of the first ridge that supports tan-oak acorns; the Gualala River where salmon, steelhead trout, and rainbow trout run; and the second and third ridge systems that sustain deer, quail, and various kinds of acorns and seeds.

Archaeological investigations in the study area indicate that a variety of archaeological remains are found in these outlying resource patches. We have described a number of shell-bearing sites on the lower slope of the first ridge and on the coastal terrace that date to the Upper Emergent. These sites vary in size, in the diversity of artifacts and shellfish MNIs, and in the density of archaeological materials as described below.

1) Some sites on the coastal terrace appear to be small sea food processing stations located near the rocky intertidal zone. They include CA-SON-1455, CA-SON-1888, and CA-SON-1886/H. They are characterized by a very low diversity of lithic artifacts (only in the 1-11 percentile range of comparably sized assemblages), but a relatively high density of archaeological materials. Limpets dominate the mollusk MNIs at CA-SON-1455 and CA-SON-1886/H, while a more varied range of shellfish species are found on CA-SON-1888. All of these sites contain some skeletal evidence of terrestrial and/or sea mammal hunting.

2) Two sites (CA-SON-1881, CA-SON-1882) appear to be locations where small task groups stopped to process marine resources just out of the fog and wind. Situated on the lower slope of the ridge or the upper coastal terrace, they are similar to the seafood processing stations described above.

3) Two additional shell deposits on the coastal terrace (CA-SON-1889 and CA-SON-1892) may be residential bases or campsites used for some part of the annual cycle by small groups. These small sites, measuring no more than 190 sq m in size, are distinguished by a much higher diversity of lithic artifact classes (J score = fifty-ninth and ninety-second percentiles) than expected, a moderate density of lithics, a high density of mollusk MNIs, and low diversity of mollusk MNIs dominated by limpets. Similar to the village sites described above (CA-SON-1883 and CA-SON-1884), they are marked by relatively large numbers of fire cracked/ground stone fragments. The seasonal use patterns of the small coastal sites are unknown.

4) Still other sites (CA-SON-1885, CA-SON-1895/H, and CA-SON-1890) appear to be camp spots or residential bases above the fog belt on the lower slope of the first ridge. Somewhat larger in size (203 to 919 sq m), they are characterized by moderately high J scores for lithic classes (fifty-seventh to fifty-ninth percentile), low to moderate densities of archaeological remains, and a diverse range of mollusk MNIs including barnacles, chitons, black turban snails, and mussels, but few limpets. The seasonal use patterns of the sites are not yet understood.

The archaeological survey of the South Fork of the Gualala River by Fredrickson (1974b) and King (1974b) provides information on the settlement pattern in the interior hinterland. In addition to two possible residential bases (CA-SON-999, CA-SON-1425), the area contains a large chert quarry (CA-SON-1001), and a variety of lithic scatters, some of which King (1974b:4) identifies as possible campsites and plant processing stations. Others may be places used for hunting game or fishing along the river. King (1974b) suggests that these sites were used in prehistoric times, although more specific age estimates have not yet been generated. If some of these sites date from the Upper Emergent, then they may represent locations used by foraging parties and task groups from the nearby ridge top and ridge slope villages. Future work in the area will be undertaken to evaluate this expectation.

The petroglyphs found in the study area exhibit an intriguing spatial distribution. Four clusters of cupule rocks (CA-SON-1452,-1454/H,-1879,-1887) are dispersed along the coastal terrace with clear views of the ocean. Four clusters of cupule rocks (CA-SON-1004,-1006,-1010,-1423) are also found in the northern most section of the Gualala Land Development area. Three are distributed along the South Fork of the Gualala River, and the fourth (CA-SON-1423) is located along Ward Creek (King 1974b). A similar pattern is found in the nearby Navarro Land Development area where 18 petroglyphs, including cupule rocks, line groups, and deep grooves, are distributed in the northern section along Ward Creek (King 1974a).

The spatial pattern suggests that native peoples selected two kinds of locations for petroglyphs. One location, close to the ocean with a clear view of the water, was reserved primarily for cupule rocks. The other location, deep in the interior recesses of rugged mountain valleys, was employed to produce a variety of petroglyph types (cupules, line groups, deep grooves). Interestingly, no petroglyphs have yet been recorded along the first ridge system where the major villages are located (see chapter 4). This spatial distribution may be explained in many ways: it may reflect the lack of suitable sandstone or schist boulders along the first ridge, or more likely the paucity of intensive archaeological surveys along the ridge top.

It is also possible, however, that the petroglyphs were placed intentionally at the outer margins of the central-based village settlement system away from population centers. Ridge top villages, such as CA-SON-178 and CA-SON-179, are located at almost the center point of cupules carved in coastal bedrock boulders and petroglyphs found in interior valley locations (see figure 5.3). The locations may have been selected so that activities associated with the rocks could be conducted away from the populated villages and/or to distinguish the boundaries of the hinterland of local village groups. Of course, petroglyphs are notoriously difficult to date, so that this scenario remains highly speculative.

Parkman (1990b) has recently summarized current research on cupule rocks. He suggests that pitted boulders may have a long tradition (going back 7000 years or more) as "rain rocks" that were part of fertility ceremonies among some Mesoamerican and North American peoples. By Lower Emergent times (A.D. 500), it appears that a formalized style of cupules or cupule rocks had developed in the North Coast Ranges. Later cupule rocks, described as "baby rocks" by ethnographers, appear to have been locations where women in want of children would visit to perform fertility rites. Parkman (1990b:3) notes that these rites normally involved the "ritual collection and ingestion of powder from the rock" (see Barrett 1908; 1952; Loeb 1926).

Historic Native Settlements at Fort Ross

In addition to CA-SON-1884, which may date to the beginning of the Historic period, other native sites that exhibit historic components include CA-SON-174, -175, -670, -1455, -1878, -1880, -1886/H, -1895/H, -1896, -1897/H, and -1898/H. The last two sites compose the Native Alaskan Neighborhood and will not concern us here. We interpret the majority of these historic sites as villages, hamlets, or small residential bases where native Californians resided while serving as agricultural laborers for the Russians and/or for the William Benitz ranch. Some, such as CA-SON-670, may have been used throughout much of the period from A.D. 1812-1867. Others, such as CA-SON-174 and CA-SON-175, may date primarily to the 1840s and 1850s.

Two sites (CA-SON-1455 and CA-SON-1886/H) are exceptions to the above characterization. CA-SON-1445 is interpreted to be a seafood processing station used in both late prehistoric and historic times. CA-SON-1886/H may have functioned as either a small residential base or seafood processing station in late prehistoric and historic times. However, we are unclear as to whether native Alaskans, Creoles, native Californians, or some combination of the above were occupying CA-SON-1886/H in historic times. The

presence of sea otter, sea lion, cattle, sheep, and mule deer remains, the close proximity of the site to the Native Alaskan Neighborhood, and the common occurrence of chipped stone and ground stone tools similar to those found in Pomo/Miwok sites suggest it may have been occupied by mixed household(s) of native Alaskan hunters and Pomo/Miwok women, or reused by native Alaskans and native Californians at different times in its occupation. McKenzie (1963) suggests that the last occupants were a Pomo couple in the early 1900s.

THE EFFECTS OF RUSSIAN MERCANTILISM
ON NATIVE CALIFORNIANS

We now compare the historic native settlement pattern with that of the Upper Emergent to evaluate the nature and magnitude of cultural change brought about by the Russian colonization of Fort Ross. The archaeological evidence to date suggests that native responses involved a shift in the location of villages, the abandonment of seafood processing stations and camps near the colony, and changes in the local obsidian trade network. We suspect that these changes reflect modifications in the organizational structure of Pomo/Miwok communities. Surface assemblages of late prehistoric and historic residential sites are quite comparable, containing similar kinds of lithic artifacts and faunal remains. While some changes in food processing and diet were probably taking place, many aspects of native Californian material culture associated with lithic raw materials appear to have been quite resilient and resistant to change. It appears that a similar range of activities involving lithic materials was taking place on both Upper Emergent and Historic period sites. These developments are addressed separately below.

Location of Villages

A comparison of the Upper Emergent and Historic settlement patterns in the study area suggests that a significant shift took place in the location of major residential sites. Upper Emergent ridge top village locations, such as CA-SON-1883, and later CA-SON-1884, were abandoned. Historic villages and hamlets were subsequently located on the coastal terrace a short distance north of the Ross Colony. This settlement patterns indicates that population aggregation took place with the Russian colonization of Fort Ross, and that this process continued during the 1840s and 1850s when William Benitz continued to employ native laborers at his ranch (see chapter 6). Judging by the settlement data, the Russian-American Company was successful in recruiting local native peoples into the greater Fort Ross community. While the Russians relied primarily upon economic inducements (food and goods) to recruit native laborers, they occasionally employed coercive tactics in rounding up natives from outlying areas during the agricultural season as described in chapter 2.

Location of Coastal Sites

During historic times small coastal camps and seafood processing stations seem to have been abandoned. Of the ten small-shell middens found on the coastal terrace and lower slope of the first ridge, only three (CA-SON-1455, CA-SON-1886/H, CA-SON-1895/H) exhibit evidence of use after A.D. 1812. One appears to be a seafood processing station, while the other two may have functioned as small residential bases.

The abandonment of previously used coastal places may be the result of three factors. First, much of the coastal strip beyond the immediate boundaries of the native villages north of the stockade was probably in cultivation sometime between A.D. 1812 and 1841. Access to some favored coastal places, such as CA-SON-1889, CA-SON-1888, and CA-SON-1892, was probably restricted or hindered because of the broad distribution of wheat and barley fields across the coastal terrace. Second, since historic villages were now located closer to the intertidal zone, native collectors may have transported marine resources, such as mollusks, directly to the villages without first processing them at coastal locations. Third, the paucity of historic seafood processing sites may reflect a decline in use of some intertidal resources as new sources of foods were integrated into local native workers' diets.

Obsidian Exchange Network

The source of obsidian employed by native peoples at Fort Ross changed dramatically in historic times. A total of 329 obsidian artifacts from the study area have been analyzed by the Obsidian Hydration Laboratory, Sonoma State University. This includes 89 artifacts from the twenty survey sites summarized in table 5.10; 49 artifacts from CA-SON-190; 9 artifacts from CA-SON-1453; 126 artifacts from CA-SON-1454/H; 36 artifacts from CA-SON-1455; 13 artifacts from CA-SON-1897/H; and 7 artifacts from the Alex site. Of this total, 152 (46%) were sourced as Napa Valley, 131 (40%) as Annadel, and 23 each as Borax Lake (7%) and as Mt. Konocti (7%). Relatively few obsidian pieces were obtained from Clear Lake in contrast to the two sources almost directly east of Fort Ross (i.e., Annadel and Napa Valley).

In figure 5.27, we present a line-frequency distribution of hydration measurements for each obsidian source. Clearly, Borax Lake, and Mt. Konocti were minor sources of obsidian through time. They were most common between the upper Lower Emergent

and lower Upper Emergent periods (1.4-2.1 microns). Annadel obsidian peaks at 2.3, 2.6, 1.8, and 1.3 microns during the Lower Emergent and Upper Emergent. It remains relatively common through the Upper Emergent period, but then disappears during historic times (.9 micron). Napa Valley obsidian peaks at 2.6, 2.2, and 1.5 microns during the Lower and Upper Emergent periods, and then explodes in the Historic period at .9 micron. Evidently, Annadel obsidian was completely replaced by obsidian from Napa Valley with the colonization of Fort Ross. Some obsidian from Mt. Konocti was also obtained during historic times.

Farris (1989a:492) suggests that the flow of obsidian to the Kashaya Pomo was disrupted in historic times by the Spanish mission at Sonoma, as well as various Spanish ranchos established between Fort Ross and the obsidian sources. It appears that the Annadel source near Santa Rosa was completely cut off. In contrast, an exchange linkage continued in historic times that allowed Napa Valley obsidian to reach the natives of the Ross Colony.

Village Layout and Material Culture

In examining diachronic changes in material culture, we compare three village sites that overlap in their temporal distribution and are represented by relatively large surface assemblages. CA-SON-1883 dates primarily to the Upper Emergent period, CA-SON-1884 to the interface of the Upper Emergent and Historic periods, and CA-SON-1880 to the colonization of Fort Ross, and possibly later (see figure 5.26). We now compare the spatial structure, lithic artifacts, and faunal remains primarily from these sites.

Village Spatial Structure. The spatial layout of the three villages is similar. Discrete midden deposits, containing the majority of the mollusk remains, are located downhill of broader lithic scatters. A similar pattern is also observed at CA-SON-175 and the Alex site. We suspect the midden deposits represent discrete trash dumps where faunal remains and other garbage were tossed. The broader lithic scatters are probably residential areas where architectural features may be located. Here we speculate that a variety of lithic manufacture, cooking, food processing, and domestic chores took place.

While the sample size is small, there is a tendency for the earlier sites to be larger than the later ones. CA-SON-1883 and CA-SON-1884 measure 8247 and 3044 sq m, respectively, while CA-SON-1880 is only 2024 sq m. Other historic villages are comparatively small as well, including CA-SON-670 (3750 sq m), CA-SON-1878 (2107 sq m), CA-SON-1896 (400 sq m), CA-SON-174 (346 sq m), and CA-SON-1895/H (203 sq m). CA-SON-174 is probably somewhat larger however, since it extends across the highway near the Call Ranch house.

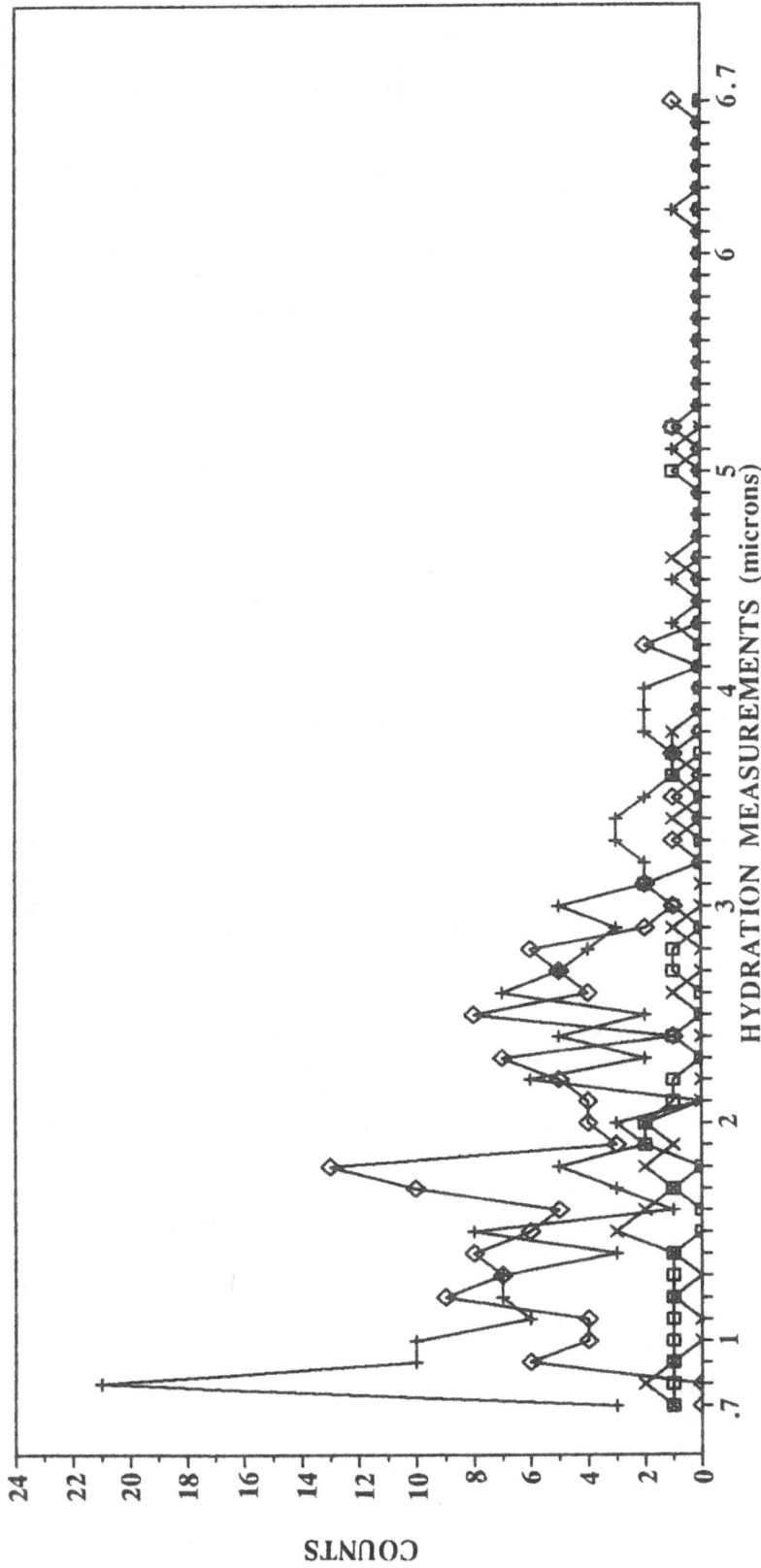

Figure 5.27

Frequency Distribution of Hydration Measurements for Obsidian from the Annadel, Borax Lake, Mt. Konocti, and Napa Valley Sources

The one exception is CA-SON-175 which is estimated to be about 18,241 sq m in size. This site has yet to be fully mapped and recorded, however.

It is not clear what the size differences signify between late prehistoric and historic villages. We recognize that site size is not a direct measurement of population, but only a reflection of how artifacts and faunal remains are distributed across the surface. The larger, late prehistoric sites may represent greater populations or simply reflect different land use practices in which material remains were deposited across the landscape. Yet the current data suggest that the historic native neighborhood north of the stockade was probably composed of small, multiple residential compounds. The number of households in the small villages and hamlets probably varied. Some small villages, such as CA-SON-175, may have been composed of 10 to 15 households, based on the number of "house pits" that Gifford (1967a) counted, while CA-SON-1896 (as well as CA-SON-1895/H) may have consisted of only one or two (Parkman 1990a).

The apparent differences in the sizes of Upper Emergent villages and Historic residential compounds may provide some insights into the process of population aggregation at Fort Ross. We suspect that the decision to participate in the economic activities of the Ross Colony took place at the level of individuals, families, and small groups. It appears that individual households and small groups may have responded differentially to Russian recruitment efforts, since the evidence does not suggest that entire village units moved intact to the Russian colony. While some individuals and families chose or were coerced to work at Fort Ross, other native peoples probably elected to hide in the outlying woods, well beyond the catchment zone where agricultural and wood cutting activities took place.

Lithic Artifacts. The three villages are characterized by a moderate density of lithics (.46 to .67 artifacts/sq m), and a diverse range of lithic classes. The most striking difference is in the percentage of fire-cracked/ground stone fragments. The earlier two sites are marked by very large numbers (53%-59% of the total lithic assemblage), while we collected relatively few from the latter village (22%). Other classes of lithic artifacts such as edge-modified flakes, interior flakes, cores, biface thinning flakes, bifaces, primary cortical flakes, secondary cortical flakes, and shatter are well represented on all three sites. Handstones and slab millingstones were collected only on CA-SON-1880 and CA-SON-1883.

The most common raw material on CA-SON-1883 and CA-SON-1884 is sandstone, a reflection of the large number of fire-cracked/ground stone fragments on these sites. Chert is the next most common raw material on these sites, followed by obsidian. The chert to obsidian ratio is 2.5/1 for CA-SON-1883 and 17/1 for CA-SON-1884. CA-SON-1880 is characterized by a smaller percentage of sandstone, more obsidian, and less chert. The ratio of chert to obsidian is .67/1.

The above comparison indicates a similar range of activities involving lithic raw materials was taking place at all three sites. Lithic production continued into historic times. The cooking method involving the immersion of hot rocks into water apparently continued into historic times, although the relative number of fire-cracked fragments decrease. This finding may indicate that other methods of cooking stews and gruels (traditional foods of the Kashaya Pomo) were being adopted, such as boiling foods directly over the fire using metal wares available from the Russians. It may also indicate that other kinds of foods were being consumed that were not cooked as stews. Traditional methods of plant food processing involving handstones and slab millingstones continued into historic times. Of course, the plant foods being processed may have changed as well.

The most significant difference is the greater abundance of obsidian than chert on CA-SON-1880, suggesting that historic changes in the obsidian exchange network, while affecting source availability, did not necessarily reduce the overall availability of obsidian into the study area after A.D. 1812. We recognize, however, that some of the obsidian found at CA-SON-1880 dates to the earlier lithic manifestation that covers the coastal terrace. Furthermore, we note that other historic sites with smaller surface assemblages vary in their ratio of obsidian to chert. Obsidian dominates at CA-SON-174, while chert is the major raw material type at CA-SON-1878. The excavations at CA-SON-670 and CA-SON-1896 indicate that while obsidian is common at both sites, chert is present in greater numbers (Stillinger 1975; Parkman 1990a).

Faunal Remains. The density of mollusk MNIs at CA-SON-1880 (.65 MNIs/sq m) is much greater than for both CA-SON-1883 and CA-SON-1884 (.02 and .03 MNIs/sq m). This difference may reflect a bias in the collecting strategy, where more collection units were placed in the midden deposit of CA-SON-1880 than either of the other villages. However, it may also indicate a greater volume of mollusks were brought back to residential compounds for processing. Such a pattern is not unexpected if small seafood processing stations were largely abandoned in historic times.

Diversity indexes indicate that a diverse range of mollusk classes are found on all three villages. However, each site is characterized by a slightly different combination of mollusk classes. At CA-SON-1883, limpets dominate, followed by mussels, turban snails, chitons, horned slipper shells, barnacles and abalone. At CA-SON-1884, an even distribution of limpets, mussels, chitons and barnacles is found. At CA-SON-1880, black turban snails dominate, followed by mussels, limpets, chitons, barnacles, and abalone. Whether these differences reflect changes in the popularity or availability of different mollusk classes over time is not known.

We caution that the above MNI counts are not direct indicators of the importance of specific mollusk classes in native diets. As mentioned previously, surface collections will tend to be skewed or biased in favor of hard shelled mollusk species. Furthermore, the nutritional values of different mollusk species must be taken into account. The caloric intake of one abalone is equivalent to many turban snails and limpets. A nutritional study of the mollusk classes must first be undertaken to calculate the equivalency values of different species to one another. This study will be initiated in the near future. For the purposes of this volume, we note that the collection of intertidal resources continued from Upper Emergent to historic times in the study area.

The limited number of mammal and bird bones recovered in surface collections precludes any detailed interpretation about their use in late prehistoric and historic contexts. It appears, however, that hunting terrestrial game, such as elk and deer, continued to be practiced by native Californians in historic times. Of those Upper Emergent period sites in which animal bones have been recovered and analyzed (i.e, CA-SON-174, -1880, -1886/H, -1895/H, -1896), deer and/or elk remains are represented on all the sites. Remains of domesticated animals (cow or sheep) are found on only three of the sites (CA-SON-174, CA-SON-1895/H, and CA-SON-1896).

CONCLUSION

The preliminary results of archaeological investigations to date indicate that the Russian colonization of Fort Ross had significant consequences for local Pomo/Miwok groups. One native response to the mercantile colony appears to have been manifested in the organizational structure of local communities. A change in the regional settlement pattern took place whereby Upper Emergent villages along the first ridge system were abandoned near Fort Ross. Population aggregation occurred north of the Ross stockade where small, multiple, residential compounds were established. It does not appear that entire village units moved intact to the Russian Colony, but that individual families and small groups responded differentially to Russian recruitment efforts. We speculate that this settlement change had significant implications for the sociopolitical organization of historic Pomo/Miwok communities. Traditional forms of tribal organization might have become strained as greater numbers of peoples from a variety of traditional village communities relocated to Fort Ross. This is especially true in the late 1830s when several hundred natives were serving as agricultural laborers.

A comparison of the archaeological assemblages from Upper Emergent ridge sites with historic residential compounds indicates both continuity and change in material culture. Surface assemblages from these sites are quite comparable, containing similar kinds of lithic artifacts and faunal remains. It appears that similar activities involving the production, use, and discard of lithics, the collection and processing of mollusks, and the hunting of terrestrial game such as deer and elk transcend both Upper Emergent and historic times. The location of seafood processing activities, however, may have shifted from small coastal stations and camps to the historic residential compounds. A decrease in the overall quantity of fire-cracked rocks may indicate that new methods of food preparation were being introduced. The remains of domesticated animals (cow and sheep) in the surface assemblages of several historic sites suggest that new foods were being cooked and consumed. While obsidian continued to be procured from Napa Valley and employed in the manufacture of chipped stone tools, moldblown glass from beverage bottles was being used as an alternative raw material source for manufacturing traditional native tool forms. Ceramics are present on some of the historic native compounds, but it is unclear whether they were used as containers or as a new source of raw materials for manufacturing ornaments or other native artifacts.

We stress, of course, that these findings are still very tentative since they are based largely on survey data. Excavation work yielding more refined archaeological data on faunal remains, artifacts, and architectural features of Upper Emergent and historic residences will most certainly modify and expand our interpretations.

CHAPTER SIX

A DIACHRONIC PERSPECTIVE OF THE

KASHAYA POMO FROM ETHNOHISTORIC OBSERVATIONS,

ETHNOGRAPHIC TEXTS, AND KASHAYA ORAL TRADITIONS

THIS CHAPTER CONSIDERS early ethnohistorical observations of native Californians at Fort Ross, later ethnographic studies of the Kashaya Pomo in the late nineteenth and early twentieth centuries, and Kashaya Pomo oral traditions as additional data sets for examining native responses to European and American colonial practices in the Fort Ross region. We address diachronic changes in native lifeways from A.D. 1814, when the first accounts were written, to A.D. 1953, when the last major ethnographic study of the Kashaya Pomo was completed. The criteria employed in this diachronic study are subsistence practices, material culture, sociopolitical organization, religious activities, and gender relations. Specifically, we compare and contrast the archaeological findings of the last chapter with eyewitness accounts of the Kashaya Pomo from the early nineteenth century to the mid-twentieth century. Is there corroborating evidence of changes in the organizational structure of historic Pomo communities and of both change and continuity in native material culture?

The chapter begins with a brief historical sketch of the Kashaya Pomo after the Russians abandoned the Ross Colony in A.D. 1841. We then summarize the different data sets (ethnohistorical observations, ethnographic texts, and native oral tradition) used in our diachronic study. This is followed by a consideration of each written account in terms of the criteria listed above. The final section examines the degree of corroboration between the different data sets when considering Kashaya Pomo history.

HISTORIC LAND USE PATTERNS
IN THE FORT ROSS REGION

The Kashaya Pomo people were greatly affected by changing Euro-American land use patterns in the region after the Russian colony was sold to John Sutter in A.D. 1841. The void left behind by the Russians was filled by Euro-American ranchers who turned the area into a patchwork of private properties. Beginning in 1841, Sutter employed several managers at Fort Ross (Robert T. Ridley, John Bidwell, and Samuel Smith) to remove supplies, livestock, and equipment left behind by the Russians to his Hock Farm near Marysville, California (Tomlin 1991:22-24). In 1843, William O. Benitz was appointed to oversee Sutter's property at Fort Ross. At about this time a conflict over ownership of the property developed. The Mexican Governor Pio Pico had awarded the Muniz Rancho, a massive land grant extending from the Russian River to north of Timber Cove, to Manuel Torres in 1845 (Tomlin 1991:25). Benitz, initially in partnership with Ernest Rufus, operated a ranch on the Muniz grant, eventually buying the 7191 ha rancho for $22,500 in 1855. The land dispute with

William Muldrow was not resolved until 1859 when Benitz paid $6000 to settle the suit (Tomlin 1991:28-29; Farris, personal communication).

The establishment of ranchos, such as the Benitz holding, in the 1840s and 1850s provided seasonal agricultural work for local native peoples. Bean and Theodoratus (1978:299) characterize this economic system as one of semi-peonage whereby native peoples provided a cheap source of labor to local ranchers in return for food or wages, protection, and a place to live. Oswalt (1964:4) notes that just about every ranch along the Sonoma County coast had a small rancheria associated with it at this time. A large Indian rancheria of between 100 to 161 people flourished on the Benitz rancho, while other native families were associated with Captain Stephen Smith's rancho near Bodega Bay, the German Rancho immediately north of the Muniz rancho, and the Kruse Ranch not far from Salt Point where a small rancheria of 20 to 30 Indians lived (Farris 1986a:15-16; Ross Census 1848; Haase 1952:50-51).

The Benitz holding is probably typical of the diversified ranching operations undertaken in the Fort Ross region in the mid to late nineteenth century. Benitz raised horses, cattle, and sheep; grew fields of wheat, oats, and potatoes; maintained an orchard of 1700 trees; and established a brewery (Spencer-Hancock 1980:24). In 1863, Benitz signed a ten-year lease with the Fort Ross Coal Mine Company that allowed them to mine coal, to harvest timber, and to build roads and houses on the rancho (Tomlin 1991:29). Benitz also signed another lease with the Ottilla Copper and Silver Mining Company in 1863 that permitted them to prospect for minerals and petroleum on the property.

William Benitz lived at the ranch with his family, several Mexican cowboys, and his work force of Pomo Indians. In a census taken on January 8, 1848, a total of 161 Indians were listed as part of the "Praesidio Ross" (Ross Census 1848). This included 62 men, 52 women counted as wives, and 47 children. Four of the men were listed as "chiefs" (Chief Tojon, Chief Noportegi, Chief Kolob-biscau, and Chief Cojoto). We believe the Indian rancherias were located at CA-SON-174 and CA-SON-175 as described in chapter 5. Benitz reportedly treated his native workers fairly while maintaining a rigorous work schedule. Native laborers were awakened at 6:00 A.M. for breakfast, labored until lunch at 11:30 A.M., and then continued to work until dinner at 6:00 P.M. Kennedy (1955:76-77) notes that the Indian workers received rations of whiskey with their lunch and dinner. Benitz paid his native workers with sacks of barley and peas.

William Benitz sold his ranch to James Dixon and his partner Lord Charles Fairfax in 1867 for $25,000 (Tomlin 1991:31). Dixon established a commercial timber operation in the local region that included the construction of a wooden loading chute and lumber storage yard at North Cove, the remains of which can still be seen on CA-SON-1454/H (chapter 5). The first lumber mill was established at Kolmer Gulch, and then later moved (probably around 1870) to Fort Ross Creek not far from the old Russian stockade (Tomlin personal communication). We believe that the structure illustrated at CA-SON-670 in the 1876 U.S. Coast Survey map is part of this mill complex (chapter 5).

By about 1870, Dixon had forced the Pomo workers off his property. Few Pomo people probably lived in the immediate area while Dixon operated his mill. In 1873, Dixon sold the property to George Washington Call who built the ranch house in 1878 near CA-SON-174 that can be visited today at the Fort Ross State Historic Park. At least one native couple is reported to have stayed on the Call ranch into the latter years of the nineteenth century (Farris 1986a:17; McKenzie 1963:1-2).

When Dixon forced the Pomo workers off their ancestral lands, it appears many of the native families shifted their residence to Charles Haupt's ranch on Skyline Ridge about 13 km southeast of Stewarts Point. Haupt was married to a Kashaya woman and welcomed the Pomo people to live on his property. Here they established the village of Potol (site #63 in figure 4.1). Oswalt (1964:4) indicates that some families may have also reoccupied the nearby ancient village of Dukacal (site #77 in figure 4.1), and that it became known as Abaloneville. Still other native families remained scattered across the region in small rancherias (Kennedy 1955:89).

By the turn of the century some Pomo families worked as migrant laborers in orchards along the Russian River during the spring, summer, and fall months. In the winter they returned home to their rancherias in the Fort Ross region (Bean and Theodoratus 1978:299; Oswalt 1964:4). Other Pomo men were employed in local lumber operations, while the women labored in ranch houses (Kennedy 1955:89). Haase (1952) indicates that by 1903 about half the Kashaya Pomo people were living at the old village of Danaga (site #21 in figure 4.1) near Stewarts Point while working in logging camps.

In 1914, at the request of the Kashaya Pomo people, the Bureau of Indian Affairs purchased property for a small reservation. Known as the Stewarts Point or Kashia Rancheria, the 16 ha property located about 5 km east of Stewarts Point on Miller Ridge was acquired for $1100 (Kennedy 1955:96). By 1919 most of the remaining Kashaya Pomo in the region had moved to the new reservation (Oswalt 1964:5). It remains the center of Kashaya Pomo culture today, even though some younger families live in nearby towns and cities (e.g., Santa Rosa) where more diversified economic opportunities exist.

KASHAYA POMO ETHNOHISTORY

A historical sketch of pertinent ethnohistorical accounts and ethnographic studies of the Kashaya Pomo in the Ross region follows.

Early Ethnohistoric Accounts

The Fort Ross Counter. We have found only a few eyewitness accounts of native peoples in the early years of the colony (1812-1830). An early account of the Indian village at Port Rumiantsev was recorded in December 1814 by Peter Corney (1896). Corney was chief officer on the merchant vessel *Columbia* owned by Inglis, Ellice and Company trading house in London, England. In 1814, the crew of the *Columbia* visited Port Rumiantsev during a trip to Spanish California to buy provisions for the Northwest Company's trade outposts on the Columbia River. The two most detailed accounts of the village at Port Rumiantsev were recorded in September 1818 by Vasilii M. Golovnin (1976 [1818]), a Russian naval captain, and Fedor Lutke (1989 [1818]) who accompanied Golovnin on his ship the *Kamchatka*. The two visitors describe a small Indian village not far from where their ship anchored at Port Rumiantsev. Lutke (1989:276 [1818]) noted that the Indian settlement was very small and fluid, with its population ranging between ten and fifty people depending upon the time of the year. The village probably remained relatively small through the early 1830s, as General Mariano Vallejo described it in 1833 as a settlement composed of a chief, known as Gualinela, and his band of forty-three men and women (Vallejo 1979:1 [1833]). There is no estimate on the size of the Indian community at Fort Ross in the early years. In his diary Golovnin (1976:160 [1818]) recorded that he visited the village at Fort Ross which consisted of a "collection of huts." Finally, Captain Otto Von Kotzebue (1830), a Russian naval officer who commanded the *Predpriatie* (*Enterprise*), visited the Ross settlement in September 1824 and made a few observations about the native workers.

More detailed ethnohistorical accounts of native peoples were recorded in the vicinity of Fort Ross in the 1830s. Ferdinand Petrovich von Wrangell, the chief manager of the Russian-American Company, visited Fort Ross in September 1833. Wrangell (1974 [1833]) described a trip along the Russian River during which a small Indian camp was visited. The most detailed account of the natives is provided by Peter Kostromitinov, (1976 [1830-38]) who served as the manager of the Fort Ross Counter from 1830 to 1838 (Tomlin and Watrous 1990:1). He recorded a number of observations about the lifeways of the natives living and working at the Ross Colony. Another excellent account of the Indian community was made by the French naval captain, Cyrille LaPlace, in August 1839. He described the nearby settlement where several hundred natives resided.

William Benitz's Ranch. Unfortunately, few accounts exist of the post-Russian rancherias in this region. Farris (1986a:14-15) recounts the brief observations made by the Swedish traveler, G. M. Waseurtz of Sandels, who visited Fort Ross in 1843. He described the native houses as "round, well-constructed and half underground." Sandels also noted that the Indians missed the Russians, were withdrawing from other white people, and denied their labor to Mexicans or Spanish because of past mistreatment. Kennedy's (1955:77) study of documents from the Benitz ranch days suggests that the Pomo adopted some innovations from the Mexican cowboys. These include cooking with lard and making flour tortillas, a food that remained a staple into the early 1950s. According to Kennedy (1955:80-82), the bulk of their diet, however, remained aboriginal foods including game, shellfish, and fish. Oswalt's (1964:4) study of the Kashaya language indicates that about 150 loanwords originated from Mexican cowboys at the Benitz Ranch, five times more loanwords than those originating from earlier Russian sources.

Charles Haupt's Ranch. An early observation of the Indian rancheria at Haupt's Ranch was recorded by Stephen Powers in the summers of 1871 or 1872 (Powers 1976). Powers interviewed Charles Haupt and spent an undisclosed amount of time observing the Indian group which he referred to as the Gua-la-la. Powers visited a number of Indian groups in northern and central California and published his observations in several articles in the *Overland Monthly* and *Atlantic* in 1872–1875, and later as a book, *Tribes of California*, in 1877. While Powers had no formal training in ethnography, and some of his interpretations have been dismissed by later anthropologists (see Kroeber 1925:ix), his observations of subsistence practices and material culture could be quite extensive and relatively detailed.

Later Ethnographic Studies

In the early twentieth century, university-trained ethnographers commenced their study of the native inhabitants of the Fort Ross region. The first ethnographer, Samuel Barrett (1908:54-68), divided the Pomo linguistic stock into seven distinct dialects (Northern, Central, Eastern, Southern, Southwestern, Southeastern, and Northeastern). The Southwestern Pomo are now usually referred to as the Kashaya Pomo. Further linguistic research indicates that these seven linguistic groups are diverse enough to represent members of a Pomo family of distinct languages (Oswalt 1964:7). Barrett (1908:227) initially defined the territory of the Kashaya Pomo as the coastline from the Gualala River in the north to Salmon Creek in the south. The eastern border followed the Gualala River and Fuller Creek in the north and the Austin Creek watershed in the south. Subsequent ethnographers have debated about the exact territory of the Kashaya Pomo. Kroeber (1925:plate 36) drew the southern border at Duncan's Landing; Stewart (1943:49) indicated it was either the Russian River or "Duncan's Point"; while Kniffen (1939:384) believed the area south of the Russian River was shared by the Kashaya Pomo and the Coast Miwok, their neighbors to the south. Stewart (1943:49) argued that the northern boundary of the Kashaya Pomo is Black Point, and that the coastal strip north of Black Point to the Gualala River was used primarily by Southern Pomo people. Oswalt (1964:2–3) supports Stewart's interpretation based primarily on linguistic evidence. It appears that the eastern boundary of the territory was never very exact, but rather an outlying hinterland that included the watershed of Austin Creek (Kniffen 1939:38; Oswalt 1964:3).

The majority of the ethnographies were undertaken by U.C. Berkeley graduate students trained in California ethnography by Alfred L. Kroeber. The goal of these ethnographic studies was to reconstruct "pristine" native lifeways in California as they functioned at the time of European contact. To filter out the recent effects of Euro-American influences, ethnographers interviewed tribal elders who would talk to them about the past. Employing this "memory culture" methodology, the ethnographers relied on tribal elders to portray traditional native lifeways as they remembered them in the middle to late nineteenth century.

The native elders interviewed by these ethnographers had resided in a number of villages during their lifetimes. While many of them resided on the Kashia Rancheria after 1919, the life histories of some informants indicate considerable residential mobility in the middle to late nineteenth century, with people moving to and from such settlements as Potol, Danaga, Dukacal, and Metini (see for example Gifford 1967:5-6; Stewart 1943:30-31; Barrett 1952:18). Since the fieldwork was conducted by various ethnographers over a half-century period, from 1903 to 1953, several generations of Kashaya Pomo tribal elders were interviewed.

The many shortcomings of Pomo ethnographies based on the "memory culture" methodology are described elsewhere (see McLendon and Oswalt 1978:276-77). For the purposes of this study we are concerned about two problems. First, the diachronic context of the ethnographic studies is not very precise. Since the intent of the fieldwork was not to describe contemporary rancherias as they appeared to the ethnographers, but rather to reconstruct native lifeways sometime in the past, it is difficult to determine whether the native practices being depicted date to the early twentieth, late nineteenth, or mid nineteenth centuries or even earlier based on oral tradition. Second, since the studies were based on interviews rather than participant observations, it is not clear whether the ethnographers observed firsthand the subsistence practices, foods, and material culture described in the reports.

The Ethnographers

Samuel Barrett. Barrett visited Haupt's Ranch sometime between 1903-1907 as part of his comprehensive analysis of Pomo culture that fulfilled the requirements for the first doctorate degree in anthropology from U.C. Berkeley (see Heizer 1975:29). The tribal elders that Barrett (1952:18) interviewed were born in the 1840s and 1850s. Barrett (1908:228-39) separated the Southwestern Pomo territory into two divisions of villages: the coast division (along the coastline) and the river division (along the South Fork of the Gualala River). This division has not been recognized by other ethnographers. As described in chapter 4, Barrett (1908) compiled an exhaustive list of former villages and campsites from his informants. He published a detailed account of Pomo buildings in 1916 that remains one the best descriptions of nineteenth and early twentieth century architectural styles to date, including photographs of various kinds of structures from the turn of the century. Later in his life, Barrett (1952) published an extensive study of Pomo material culture based on his earlier fieldwork and museum research.

C. Hart Merriam. Merriam visited some Kashaya Pomo people in August 1905, interviewing them about the location of ancestral villages and campsites (Merriam 1977). Index cards on file at the Lowie Museum of Anthropology, U. C. Berkeley, indicate that one of his Kashaya consultants was Gib Jarris (Merriam 1938). Merriam (1968:1-10) also compiled village names of the Southern Pomo and Coast Miwok peoples who became neophytes in the San Rafael Mission. Outside of a very brief description of the Bo'-yah or "Coast Pomo" (Merriam 1967:303-304), no ethnographic study of coastal Pomo in Mendocino or Sonoma counties was ever published by Merriam.

Alfred Kroeber. Kroeber (1925) wrote three chapters on the Pomo in his classic monograph, *Handbook of the Indians of California*. Much of his information, which includes details on the Kashaya

Pomo, probably was derived from Barrett's earlier study. However, Barrett (1952:19) insists that Kroeber did work with the Pomo, but that the informants were younger and less well versed in ancient customs than those he had interviewed.

Edwin Loeb. The next ethnography on coastal Pomo peoples was published by Loeb in 1926. Loeb's account includes information obtained by graduate students working under Alfred Kroeber in the winter of 1921, and from his fieldwork funded by a Guggenheim grant in 1924-1925. The relevance of the study to the Kashaya Pomo is somewhat limited, since it involved interviews with only two coastal Central Pomo peoples.

Edward W. Gifford. Gifford conducted fieldwork among the Kashaya Pomo from 1915 to 1918 as part of a statewide study of kinship systems (Gifford 1922), in 1934 as part of the culture element distribution survey (Gifford and Kroeber 1937), and in August 1950 (Gifford 1967). Gifford (1967) compiled information on ancient villages and campsites, native foods, and the cultural element list for the Kashaya Pomo.

Fred Kniffen. Kniffen, a geographer trained at U.C. Berkeley, published *Pomo Geography* in 1939 in which he compared Pomo groups from Clear Lake, the Russian River, and the Sonoma County coast. When he undertook his study of the Kashaya Pomo in the 1930s, about one hundred people resided at the Kashia Rancheria (Kniffen 1939:381). Kniffen (1939:384) noted that his informants disagreed with some of the earlier conclusions of Barrett and Kroeber.

Omer C. Stewart. Stewart (1943) conducted his ethnographic and archaeological fieldwork in the Ross region in 1935 on a research grant from the University of California Institute of Social Sciences. His objective was to fill "in a few lacunae" on the aboriginal culture as reported by Powers, Barrett, Kroeber, Loeb, and Gifford.

Mary Jean Kennedy. Kennedy was the last of the U.C. Berkeley ethnographers of Kroeber's legacy to work among the Kashaya Pomo. Edward Gifford served as her faculty advisor when she conducted fieldwork at the Kashia Rancheria in 1952-1953. Kennedy's (1955) study differs from the previous ethnographic research on two counts. First, the explicit goal of her research was not to reconstruct the aboriginal culture of the Kashaya Pomo, but rather to evaluate how it had changed over the last 150 years or so. She proposed to examine the process of acculturation among the Kashaya Pomo through their contact with Russians, Mexicans, and Americans. Second, she undertook an ethnographic study of the Kashia Rancheria as it functioned in the early 1950s.

Kennedy's acculturation study relied largely on previous ethnographic studies to reconstruct the aboriginal culture of the Kashaya. She then evaluated the nature of cultural change over time by analyzing ethnohistoric texts and by making detailed observations of native culture in the early 1950s. At the time of her study, the Kashia Rancheria consisted of twenty-one houses and less than one hundred people (Kennedy 1955:92).

Kashaya Pomo Oral Tradition

Robert Oswalt, a linguistic anthropologist trained at U.C. Berkeley, undertook a detailed study of the Kashaya Pomo language beginning in the late 1950s. During the course of his fieldwork, he transcribed word-for-word native accounts as told to him by Essie Parrish and Herman James. The native texts record historical observations, folklore, myths, and other stories that were part of Kashaya Pomo oral tradition. Oswalt translated and published the texts in 1964 in the monograph entitled *Kashaya Texts*.

More recent ethnographic research has been undertaken with the Kashaya Pomo by the Department of Anthropology, Sonoma State University. One study, directed by Shirley Silver, collected information on oral traditions and other aspects of Kashaya lifeways at the Kashia Rancheria in the 1970s (Breck Parkman, personal communication).

ANALYSIS OF THE
ETHNOHISTORIC TEXTS

In this section we compile information from the original texts that describes the foods, subsistence practices, material culture, sociopolitical organization, religious institutions, and gender relations of the Kashaya Pomo. In presenting the text, parentheses are used to denote words inserted by the original authors, while brackets are employed to denote words added by the translators or ourselves.

Peter Corney

Dates of Observation. December 1814.

Citation. Corney's accounts of his voyages in the Pacific were first published serially in a weekly literary magazine in London, 1821. These accounts were republished in an 1896 book entitled *Narrative of Several Trading Voyages from 1813 to 1818, Between the Northwest Coast of America, the Hawaiian Islands and China, with a Description of the Russian Establishments on the Northwest Coast* [Honolulu: Thomas G. Thrum].

Location. Indian village at Port Rumiantsev.

General Description of Village.

"On the 21st of December 1814 we sailed from Monterey towards Bodago [sic], in the Latitude 38 degrees 0', and Longitude 123 degrees, which we reached in Due Time. On the 24th we saw a large storehouse on shore; Mr. McDougal and myself went in quest of its owners; we found it locked, and then pulled up a lagoon, where we saw a number of Indians collected around a large fire. We landed, and found ourselves *above* an Indian village, for here they live underground, and we could hear their voices beneath us. Several old women and children made their appearance; we gave them some beads and by signs inquired where the Russians were; they pointed to the men round the fire, to whom we accordingly went up, and found them killing rabbits. Their mode of hunting them is to fire the grass for a considerable distance, and kill the rabbits as they are endeavoring to escape from the flame. The natives, on this part of the coast, appear to be a very harmless race. We inquired for the Russians, and they pointed to the northward. We then left them, and, on passing the village, some of our party had the curiosity to venture into their subterraneous abodes, but were obliged to make a hasty retreat, pursued by swarms of fleas, and an intolerable stench from a mass of filth" (Corney 1896:33-34).

Fedor Lutke

Dates of Observation. September 4 - 28, 1818.

Citation. Original manuscript translated by Basil Dmytryshyn, E. A. P. Crownhart-Vaughan, and Thomas Vaughan in *The Russian American Colonies: Three Centuries of Russian Eastward Expansion 1798-1867*, Vol. 3 (Portland: Oregon Historical Society Press, 1989).

Location. Most of Lutke's descriptions are of the Indian village at Port Rumiantsev.

Subsistence Practices.

"When it was completely dark we had a very interesting spectacle: a certain extent of land near the settlement was all afire. The Indians who live in this area (around the Ross settlement) eat a wild plant which resembles rye, for which reason our settlers call it *rozhnitsa* [*rozh*, rye]. When the kernels of the rozhnitsa have been harvested, the straw which remains is generally burned. This procedure makes the next year's crop bigger and more flavorful" (Dmytryshyn et al. 1989b:257).

"Their food consists only of acorns and rozhnitsa, and in the summer, whatever the sea provides. They grind acorns as we do coffee, beat it up and mix it with water and heat it. This sweet porridge comprises their main food. In place of saucepans they use reed or grass baskets, into which they put heated stones. There is no intermediary between these baskets and their mouths except their fingers, which they dip into the porridge and lick, and thus satisfy their hunger. Although this form of eating does not arouse an appetite in others, I decided to try it and found that this provision is a bitter, rather unpleasant tasting blend. We did not have an opportunity to observe how they prepare rozhnitsa. It is probably not available at this time of year, because we did not see anyone who had any. However, the fields in many places were burned, probably for the same reason mentioned earlier.

Aside from this they eat all sorts of shellfish and some fish, but not much of the latter because they have no means of catching them. However, we did see one family eating small broadfish about two inches long, which can probably be taken along the coast. The only preparation was to bury them in hot ashes for a while; they were eaten whole, including the skin and ash clinging to it" (Dmytryshyn et al. 1989b:276).

Material Culture.

"Their living quarters are more like beehives or anthills than human habitations. They are made of sticks stuck in the ground in a semicircle about one and one-half arshins high; these are fastened together and then covered with dry grass or tree branches. These dwellings do not give them shelter from rain or foul weather, which, fortunately for them, is quite rare in the area where they live" (Dmytryshyn et al. 1989b:275).

"Industry among these Indians is still in a state of complete infancy, or to state it better, it is nonexistent. They walk around stark naked. Some of them make a kind of shirt for themselves from blankets the Spanish or the Russians give them, which garments, however, do not cover their private parts. But there is very little of this kind of clothing, because the Spanish do not like to give them anything for free, the Indians have nothing to give in exchange, and there are few Russians here. We saw some Indians who had a kind of cloak made out of sea gull skins, but this covered no more than half the back. Considering the type of clothing with which they attempt to cover the back, rather than any other part of the anatomy, one can conclude that they have no conception of modesty. This refers only to the men. The women wear the pelts of wild sheep which they fasten around the waist and allow to hang down below the knees. We saw very few objects of their own handiwork. I have already mentioned the baskets made of grass. Of all the items they make, these deserve special attention because they are so tightly woven that water does not seep through.

Their only weapons are the bow and arrow, which are rather crudely made. Although they live for most of the time near the sea, they have no boats whatsoever. On the shore near the settlement there was something resembling a raft, which consisted of a few bundles of thin reeds fastened together. This contraption, which cannot possibly hold more than two persons at a time, and which in all fairness one can term seaworthy, they use if they have to cross a stream, or in some other such circumstance. Small nets, crudely plaited of grass, conclude this list of handicrafts" (Dmytryshyn et al. 1989b:277).

"Some of the promyshlenniks and Aleuts have married these Indian women. Our interpreter, whose wife is one of these people, told us that she had learned his language very quickly and well, and that she had also learned Aleut handicrafts, such as sewing the whale gut kamleika [waterproof outer garment] and other things. In one hut I saw a rather comely young woman preparing food, and when I approached her I was surprised that she spoke easily and in clear Russian. She invited me to eat her acorn porridge, and then complained about the rain. When I inquired I found that she had lived for some time in the Ross settlement with a promyshlennik, and then had returned to her people" (Dmytryshyn et al. 1989b:278).

"These Indians use a special kind of bathhouse which is really just an underground iurt. An opening is made on one side, through which one must crawl. There is a smoke hole in the top" (Dmytryshyn et al. 1989b:278).

Sociopolitical Organization.

"Such people obviously can have no laws. Nevertheless there was one among them who called himself their leader, and whom our people by custom refer to as a toion. But we could not determine how extensive his power is over all the others. We did not even see any exterior indications of respect shown him by the others, and he would not have looked any different from the others if some of our people had not given him two shirts the day before, both of which he wasted no time in putting on. It appears that this position is hereditary, because his father was also a toion" (Dymtryshyn et al. 1989b:275-76).

Recreation.

"Their play is similar to that of the Kolosh and the Kodiak Aleuts. There are several marked sticks which one person mixes up, concealing the marks; the other person must guess which is which. Idleness has created a situation where persons who have almost nothing to lose have a passion for the game. It is quite remarkable and amazing that among peoples who inhabit the entire Northwest Coast of America, from Kodiak to the 38th parallel, this game of chance is one and the same, even though they have no other relationship, nor the slightest similarity, nor do they have any communication with one another at all" (Dymtryshyn et al. 1989b:278).

Gender Relations.

"Women have no rights which would attract them to return to their previous status. An Indian takes as a wife an Indian woman whom he likes; he keeps her as long as he wishes and discards her whenever he chooses. Women do all the work. In the entire settlement we saw only one man at work–he was weaving a net–and perhaps he was doing that out of boredom. All the rest either play or do nothing. It was a rare woman who was not occupied with some work" (Dymtryshyn et al. 1989b:278).

Vasilii M. Golovnin

Dates of Observation. September and October 1818.

Citation. The original manuscript has been translated by Ella L. Wiswell in the book *Around the World on the Kamchatka, 1817-1819 by V. M. Golovnin* (Honolulu: The University Press of Hawaii and the Hawaiian Historical Society, 1979).

Location. Described Indian villages at Port Rumiantsev and Fort Ross.

Subsistence Practices.

"They do not bother to till the soil for food, but take advantage of the free gifts of nature. Furthermore, they are not too particular in their choice of food; without the least repugnance they consume the flesh of any animal they come across, any type of shellfish or fish, and even reptiles, except poisonous snakes. The most important plant foods consumed by them are oak acorns, which they even preserve for winter use, and wild rye grain, which grows in great abundance here. To harvest the rye grain they resort to a very simple, although rather curious, method: they set fire to the entire field; the grass and stalks, being very dry, burn very fast, while the grain is not consumed by the fire but only scorched. Then the Indians collect the scorched grain and eat it without any further preparation. They usually set these fires at night, so that when approaching the coast one always knows where the Indians have established their camps. In addition to fish and shellfish, the animal food most frequently consumed is the meat of the wild deer, for they have a very easy and simple method of killing these animals. The Indians cover their bodies with a deer skin and tie on a deer's head; disguised in this manner, they stealthily approach a herd, very cleverly imitating the movements and leaps of the animals. After penetrating the herd, they can easily kill as many as they wish with their arrows" (Wiswell 1979:168).

Material Culture.

"The Indians of New Albion, as well as those of California, when living in freedom wear no clothing except a loincloth; only in winter during the cold period do they throw on some skins of animals such as deer, wolves, etc. Their costume consists of a headgear made of feathers, and loincloths made of grass and flowers. Spears and arrows constitute their armaments" (Wiswell 1979:168).

Sociopolitical Organization.

"Furthermore, the chief of the independent Indians who live at the bay came to see me, with an interpreter, and gave me some very important information concerning the unjust claims made to this country by the Spanish, and requested that the Russians take them under their protection and settle among them" (Wiswell 1979:160).

"In the preceding section I have already mentioned that the chief of the people living next to Port Rumiantsev came to see me when my sloop was anchored there. He brought gifts consisting of various parts of their regalia, arrows, and household items, and asked to be taken under Russian protection. An Aleut who had lived over a year among these people acted as interpreter. This chief, called Valenila, definitely wanted more Russians to settle among them in order to protect them from Spanish oppression. He begged me for a Russian flag, explaining that he wanted to raise it as a sign of friendship and peace whenever Russian ships would appear near the shore" (Wiswell 1979:165).

Recreation.

"To pass the time, that hangs so heavily on their hands that they do not know what to do with it, they have invented a game: one player kneels in front of the other, rapidly twirls a bunch of short, specially prepared sticks in his hands, and at the same time emits noises, sings and grimaces trying to be funny and divert the attention of his opponent from his hands. At an opportune moment he quickly thrusts his hands into the grass, hides several of the sticks there, and immediately puts his hands behind his back. His opponent must guess how many sticks were left in the grass; if he fails, he loses, otherwise he wins. They are so addicted to this game, that in Port Rumiantsev, where we gave them tobacco and various trifles in exchange for some of their curios, they immediately settled down to play and right then and there started losing to each other the gifts they had just received. They have some other games similar to this one, but I did not have an opportunity to observe them" (Wiswell 1979:168-69).

Religious Activities.

"I cannot comment on their religion, but do know that they believe in the supernatural power of their witch doctors, or shamans, as the Siberian natives call them. In the above-mentioned port, I witnessed one of these shamans curing a sick man. Sitting over the sick man in the tent, he kept repeating incantations and singing, while waving around a stick with feathers attached to it. The patient's family, who were in the same tent, responded and joined in the singing at certain prescribed times. This went on for over an hour in our presence, and when we left the shaman was still continuing his cure" (Wiswell 1979:169).

Otto Von Kotzebue

Dates of Observation. September 1824.

Citation. The English translation of Otto Von Kotzebue's journal, *A New Voyage Round the World in the Years 1823, 24, 25, and 26*, was first published in 1830 (London: Henry Colburn and Richard Bentley).

Subsistence Practices.

"We sometimes also, but less frequently, saw another species of stag, as large as a horse, with branching antlers; these generally graze on hills, from whence they can see round them on all sides, and appear much more cautious than the small ones. The Indians, however, have their contrivances to take them. They fasten a pair of the stag's antlers on their heads, and cover their bodies with skin; then crawling on all-fours among the high grass, they imitate the movements of the creature while grazing; the herd mistaking them for their fellows, suffer them to approach without suspicion, and are not aware of the treachery till the arrows of the disguised foes have thinned their number" (Kotzebue 1830:116).

"They have no permanent residence, but wander about naked, and, when not employed by the Russians as day-labourers, follow no occupation but the chase. They are not difficult in the choice of their food, but consume the most disgusting things, not excepting all kinds of worms and insects, with good appetite, only avoiding poisonous snakes. For the winter they lay up a provision of acorns and wild rye: the latter grows here very abundantly. When it is ripe, they burn the straw away from it, and thus roast the corn, which is then raked together, mixed with acorns and eaten without any further preparation" (Kotzebue 1830:126-27).

Recreation.

"The Indians here have invented several games of chance: they are passionately fond of gaming, and often play away everything they possess" (Kotzebue 1830:127).

Ferdinand Petrovich von Wrangell

Dates of Observation. September 1833.

Citations. The original manuscript was published by the Imperial Academy of Sciences in 1839. It was translated by Stross and Heizer in 1974 (Berkeley: Archaeological Research Facility, University of California).

Location. Many of Wrangell's observations were made on a trip up the Russian River some distance from the Fort Ross settlement.

Subsistence Practices.

"Their provisions of dough from ground acorns, and a kind of gruel prepared from wild rye and other seeds, were stored in a small number of baskets; also fish, which they catch in the brook by casting on top of the water a powder prepared from a root, there called soap root, which causes the fish to be stunned and float to the surface" (Stross and Heizer 1974:4).

"Since they derive their nourishment mainly from acorns, wild chestnuts and seeds of diverse plants, they cannot form populous groups and must, in order to find adequate sustenance, abandon settlements that have become too populous, and lead a nomadic life" (Stross and Heizer 1974:5).

Material Culture.

"We found the Indian village on sandy soil, entrenched behind shrubbery and dry ditches. It was inhabited by five or six inter-related families. The women had furnished these temporary dwellings, made of flexible shafts of sand-willow and other willows, which can be pushed into the ground quite easily, in such an extraordinarily tasteful manner, that I was most pleasantly surprised by the sight. The colorful shading and the variety of sizes of the willow-leaves (a tree which grows there in great abundance) lent a quite special, rustic aspect to the open huts; the side opening, which serves as a door, is decorated with foliage with special care; several of the huts also communicate with each others by means of internal openings.

The foliage still retained its full freshness; but before it could wither, the inhabitants would have left their pleasant huts; the women load their babies and meager possessions on their backs, on which they carry their burden by means of a strap placed over the forehead; the men decide on a new encampment, and rapidly there rises a new little village, which is again left behind in a few days" (Stross and Heizer 1974:3-4).

"Their headdress, belts, earrings, etc., mostly made of feathers, betray not only their inventiveness, but also a certain penchant for beauty" (Stross and Heizer 1974:5).

Sociopolitical Organization.

"They love their children with great tenderness, but they demand patriarchal obedience, and all the younger members of a tribe offer reverence to age, experience, and skill in drawing the bow. The respect shown for the father is often transmitted to the son; however, the power of the headman in general is very tenuous; for anyone is free to leave his birthplace and to choose a different residence" (Stross and Heizer 1974:5-6).

Recreation.

"After having received tobacco, zwieback [rusk], glass beads, and other trifles from us, they sat down in a circle with their countrymen, our interpreters and vaqueros, and started on their favorite occupation, one may even say the only one engaged in by the men,

if circumstances permit, i.e. the game, even or odd. Two players are seated opposite each other, while on both sides of the players singing choirs are placed; their melodious songs are interrupted only by the abrupt, loud exclamations of the guessing player. His opponent attempts to conceal a number of short sticks, which he holds in one hand behind his back, while he makes diverse and rapid movements with his arms, and beats his chest with his other, free hand in time with the music. The game lasts until one of the players has lost all his possessions. It occupied our guests and the vaqueros all through the night and until well into the morning" (Stross and Heizer 1974:3).

Gender Relations.

"The hunt is the business of men, while the women carry all the heavy burdens, and, quite generally, they are burdened with the onerous tasks. This unusual distribution of the workload is probably the reason for the fact that the women here in general have a much stronger physique then the men who, although tall and well-proportioned, yet seem to be weaker than the women" (Stross and Heizer 1974:4).

Peter Kostromitinov

Dates of Observation. 1830-1838.

Citation. Translated from the original 1839 publication of the Imperial Academy of Sciences by Stross and Heizer (1974).

Note. Kostromitinov provides some information on several tribal groups and their different languages in the vicinity of the Ross Colony (Stross and Heizer 1974:7).

Subsistence Practices.

"The season dictates the place where they have to find their sustenance. In spring they live in the vicinity of the rivers and in locations that abound in water, so that they may catch fish and collect roots and herbs, while they spend the summer in woods and plains, where they collect berries and seeds of wild plants; in autumn they lay in stores of acorns, wild chestnuts, and sometimes nuts, hunt bison and goat [deer] with their arrows. The menu of the Indians encompasses anything they can acquire, large and small land and marine animals, fish, crayfish, roots, herbs, berries, and other products of the soil, even insects and worms. Meat and fish are eaten slightly roasted on coals, all the rest mostly raw. Acorns, collected in large quantity, constitute their main staple food. They prepare them as follows: after the acorns have been picked from the tree, they are dried in the sun, then cleaned and pounded in baskets with stones trimmed for the purpose; then a pit is dug in the sand or some in loose earth, the acorns are put into it, and covered with water, which is constantly absorbed by the soil. This flushing is repeated until the acorns have lost all their characteristic bitterness; having been removed from the pit, they are then boiled in pots, into which glowing hot stones are thrown. If, however, it is desired to make pancakes or a kind of bread from them, the acorns are pounded a little more coarsely, and after their bitterness has been removed, they are allowed to remain in the pit for a while. A kind of dough is produced in this manner, which is then made into flat cakes or cut into pieces, wrapped in broad leaves, and baked on coals. This bread always looks black. Wild chestnuts are prepared in the same manner, but no bread is made from them, and they are eaten as a pulp. The beginning July is convenient for collecting acorns and seeds of wild plants.

When this is finished, they lose no time before they start collecting the seeds of a plant that grows in great quantity on the plain. Its appearance is as follows: it reaches a height of 1 1/2 to 2 feet, several sprouts start from the roots, the leaves are narrow-oblong and covered with a delicate down, have a peculiar aroma, and stick to the fingers, the flowers are yellow and grow in pointed tufts, and the small black seeds resemble Latuk [?]. These seeds are also collected by the Indians in great quantity by shaking them off the plant by means of a spade especially made for the purpose; thereupon they are dried, ground to meal and eaten dry. Their taste has some resemblance to toasted, dried oat meal. Wild rye, wild oats and other grains are collected and, having been suitably prepared, are eaten dry or as a slightly sour mash" (Stross and Heizer 1974:8-9).

Material Culture.

"These true children of nature have no idea of clothing. The men go completely naked, but the women cover the middle part of their bodies in front and in back with the hides of wild goats [deer]; the men bind their hair in a tuft on top of their heads, the women at the nape of the neck; sometimes they let it fall freely; the men fasten the bunches of hair by means of little pieces of wood rather artfully carved from a red palm [redwood?]. Both sexes decorate themselves with pearls from mussels; they wear little bones made from eagles' feet in their ears, and they always go barefoot. This is the entire dress of those that are yet unacquainted with our customs. The Indians that reside closer to Ross and who on occasion work there, possess jackets, trousers, blankets and other objects, which, however, they regard with complete indifference. If they obtain something of this sort, they immediately gamble it away or exchange it for a trifle; the differences in our articles of clothing is unknown to them, and it is a comical sight to sometimes see a savage dressed in women's clothes, with a woman's chemise on top, or with all the shirts

that he owns, so that he can hardly move. Without attachment to any material thing, and being ignorant of the value of things, they sometimes demand a great deal for work performed by them, sometimes, on the other hand, very little; their only purpose is to acquire something so that they can gamble it away again" (Stross and Heizer 1974:7-8).

"Their residences can be classified into summer and winter quarters. During the summer they find shelter in bushes, which are thinned below, and tied together above; in winter, however, they construct barabaras. A pit is dug, some vertical fixed poles are driven into the ground with their pointed ends first, and covered with wood bark, twigs, and grass; an opening is left on top and on the side, the former to let the smoke escape, the latter to serve as entrance into the barabara. Grass and a few goat hides serve as clothing and as bedding. A bow, arrows, a large pot, and sometimes fishing nets constitute the only household goods. The bathhouses are constructed almost the same as the barabaras. A pit is dug, a few poles are placed around it and the whole is covered first with bark, then with earth; on the side a small air vent is made to allow the smoke to escape, and at the bottom of the wall an opening is made to allow entrance, but it is so small that it can be entered only by crawling" (Stross and Heizer 1974:8).

"Their weapons consist in bow and arrow and a spear; all this is made mainly of young fir. The points of arrows and spears consist of sharp, artfully shaped stones, and their bow strings come from sinews of wild goats [deer]; in times of war they use, in addition, a kind of sling, by means of which they throw stones for long distances" (Stross and Heizer 1974:10).

Sociopolitical Organization.

"Under such rude conditions one would not presume that these people would have any idea of a social life or culture. As they live together at times in great numbers, but usually in small compounds, they do not know any kind of submissiveness. He who is endowed with the most relatives is recognized as chieftain or toyon; in larger settlements there are several such toyons, but their authority is negligible. They have neither the right to command nor to punish disobedience. Therefore any respect for the senior members of the family is insignificant; sometimes the experience of old age is consulted on the occasion of some undertaking and that is all. According to their view the bulk of the work is the duty of older men and women; the younger people are saved for emergencies; in other words, the toyons or elders in the tribe do not enjoy the authority as for example with the Kolosh, Aleuts, and similar peoples" (Stross and Heizer 1974:9).

Recreation.

"They do, however, enjoy smoking tobacco very

much, as do all savages; they smoke it by means of specially drilled wooden tubes having a pipe-bowl carved from the same piece. At the thick end or in the pipe bowl an opening is hollowed out, into which they stuff the tobacco; but since the pipe stem as well as the pipe bowl is made in a straight line, they smoke with their heads tilted back in order not to spill the tobacco. They also have a special herb resembling tobacco, which largely grows near the rivers in sandy locations, but the smoke of this herb has a most offensive smell. The Indians that dwell near the settlement are beginning to abandon use of this herb, since they do not lack the opportunity to obtain tobacco by working; those living further away, however, still remain faithful to their own tobacco" (Stross and Heizer 1974:9).

"Both sexes are extraordinarily devoted to gambling, and that may be the reason that their dances are not particularly varied, or much practiced. Once their hunger is stilled, the remaining time is devoted to the game. The most highly regarded and most popular is the guessing game. The individuals that wish to play with each other divide into two groups, sitting opposite each other. Between them they spread a goat [deer] hide, on which each of the parties has deposited little sticks. One among the party takes some grass or something similar into his hand. While holding both hands behind his back, he places the object from one hand into the other, while executing all kinds of gestures. His opponent now must note in which hand the grass is located. When he thinks he knows where it is, he taps the hand in which he believes it to be. If his guess is correct, he receives a few sticks, if not, he has to forfeit some of his. The next pair then continues the game in a similar manner. Once all sticks have passed to one side, that party has won the game, and the objects what were lying about are distributed among the community. The onlookers of whom there usually are many, pass the time by singing all the while, and spur the players on with all kinds of teasing and joking. It can be considered a sign of their gentleness that disputes never arise among the players. The Indians are so given to the game that those among them who work in Ross, sometimes, in spite of being tired after the day's work, enjoy the games until four o'clock in the morning, and then go back to work without having had sufficient sleep" (Stross and Heizer 1974:12).

Religious Activities.

"The deceased are cremated; all the relatives gather around the pyre and show their grief by lamentations and wailing; the nearest relatives cut off their hair and throw it into the fire, and strike their breasts with stones, throw themselves on the ground, and even, out of special attachment to the deceased, pound themselves bloody, or even to death; but such cases are rare. The most valuable of his possessions are cremated with the corpse of the deceased. There are annual commemorative ceremonies; it has been noticed that they almost always are held in the month of February. These rituals consist in the following: ten or more men are selected for presentation, according to the size of the settlement; they first must undergo purification by fasting, and for several days they really consume very little, and above all no meat. After such preparation the chosen persons dress up on the eve of the designated day, in a barabara especially reserved for them, they smear themselves with soot and various colors, ornament themselves with feathers and grasses, and then they sing and dance until darkness settles on them. Then they go into the woods and run around, with firebrands in their hands, singing all the while; then they return to the barabara and spend the night singing, dancing and with contortions. The following day is spent similarly into the morning; on the third day, however, they betake themselves to the relatives of the deceased, who await them in their barabaras and, after a suitable welcome, commence lamentations all together; the old women scratch their faces and strike their chests with stones. The relatives of the deceased positively believe that they are seeing their deceased friends in these actors. During this presentation the entire settlement exercises great abstinence in matters of nourishment, and meat is not eaten, sometimes for a long time.

They only grudgingly answered questions we asked them concerning these rites, and for this reason it was impossible to learn further details" (Stross and Heizer 1974:10).

"The recovery of a sick person usually gives rise to festivities. The recovered person notifies all those living in the vicinity, inviting them as his guests, and the rich people and the toyons even invite Indians living at a greater distance, as long as they are not engaged in dispute with them. Upon arrival of the guests the host presents them with everything he possesses. Supplies acquired with difficulty, sufficient to nourish the family of the host for several months, are consumed within a few hours. When they are all satisfied, they start giving each other good advice, to live in peace and harmony and not to quarrel with each other, and this is followed by song and dance; some sing, some dance, some play tricks; sometimes a woman stands up in the center and sings, while the men take one another by the hands, turn about, or hop around her; some of the men have eagle's bones in their mouths and whistle a gay tune. When a song is over, they all call out 'hoi' and then continue their song. The entire song usually consists of some few words as, for instance, "you love me, and so I love you too"; this is repeated again and again during the dance, the tune is pleasant, but almost always melancholy" (Stross and Heizer 1974:11-12).

"The wizards of shamans of these Indians do not excel in their adroitness and cleverness, as in the case of other savages. When they are about to practice their magic, they go deep into the forest and, after their return do their soothsaying to those that had come to obtain their advice. In order to appease the evil spirit if it is desired to prevent a misfortune, the shaman takes into the forest with him some glass beads or some other thing, which he maintains he gave the demon. After some lapse of time he brings those things back, passes them off as his own, and loses them by gambling. The main art of the shamans consists in healing the sick" (Stross and Heizer 1974:12-13).

Gender Relations.

"The men live in complete idleness; their greatest gratification is to eat their fill and to do nothing. It is up to the women to prepare the food and to do the other housework; as they are almost continually following their nomadic pursuits, the women, on their travels, carry the children as well as the remaining baggage, while the men lead the way with their bows and arrows and only very rarely carry any burden" (Stross and Heizer 1974:8).

Cyrille LaPlace

Dates of Observation. August 1839.

Citations. LaPlace's description of his visit to the Indian village near the Fort Ross stockade is translated from the original French version published in 1855 by Farris (1986b; *News from Native California* 2:22-23, 1988).

Description of Village.

"I accepted therefore with enthusiasm the proposition made by my host [Rotchev, the last manager of Fort Ross from 1838 to 1841] to visit one afternoon before sunset an example of a hamlet which the natives and their families, employed in agricultural work, had established in the vicinity of the fort. Its population was rather considerable and was composed of several hundred individuals" (Farris 1986b:65).

General Observations.

"Mr Rotchev, seeing my astonishment that the contact with the compatriots [Russians] had not modified more the ways and habits of the natives assured me that these people, just like their counterparts in New Archangel [Sitka], obstinately refused to exchange their customs for ours. 'However,' he added, 'thanks to a lot of perseverance and enticements, I have succeeded in diminishing a little this adverse sentiment to whites, among the natives of the tribes which frequent Bodega Bay; several chiefs and a good number of young people, encouraged by the bounty and generosity with which they were treated by the Russian agents, and finding, with reason, horribly miserable the life which they led during the winter in the woods where they had no other protection against the cold and snow than the caves or the shelter of trees, and no other means of subsistence than the unreliable products of the hunt, remain near the fort during the bad season, working with our colonists and are nourished like them. Also one sees their tastes change more each day to the varied articles of adornment, dress and other things with which are paid the services which they provide to the colony. Thus one could hope that if the company retains this establishment for long enough, the natives will be led little by little to submit to the yoke of civilization. Seeing their labors generously paid for, their freedom and religious beliefs, absurd as they are, respected; the most indulgent principle of justice to the point that deportation to one of our other establishments is the most severe punishment which I may inflict on those among them who have committed the worst derelictions against our properties. Seeing, I say, the interest that the public functionaries take in their well-being, they return each spring in greater number than the year before, to cultivate our fields, and attach themselves to us, to the degree that in their desire to remain always in good stead with the colonists, they are generally the first to denounce the trouble-makers who, for vengeance or by love of disorder, kill the beasts in the fields or even destroy our crops.'

'But,' continued my helpful guide [Rotchev], 'I have not yet been able to make these children of nature understand the value of foresight and the charm of property. They are all, men and women, passionate for self-adornment. They seek with eagerness that which satisfies this taste and ask for it in preference to all else. Hardly have they obtained it, than they cover themselves with necklaces, pants, shirts, vests, and consider themselves in this ridiculous attire as being very attractive, the happiest people on earth. But the next day one encounters them as bereft of the ornaments and clothing as they were the day before. It is even common that the tribe to which they belong, and to which each member has been not less generously paid, are found, when they return to Ross toward the end of the bad season, as poor, as denuded of everything with which they were well provided a few months before.

What has become of these often considerable quantities of varied merchandise which they had in their possession? We don't know yet. Were they sold, given to their compatriots who live in the forest all year? This is not likely. One is struck with the realization that giving in to the passion for play, which among these miserable savages is pushed to a point unknown, perhaps, to the peoples of the old world, they have seen their riches pass to the hands of players more clever or more lucky than they'" (Farris 1986b:68-70).

Subsistence Practices.

"The majority [of the women] were busy with housekeeping, preparing meals for their husbands and children. Some were spreading out on the embers some pieces of beef given as rations, or shell-fish, or even fish which these unhappy creatures came to catch either at the nearby river [Gualala River ?] or from the sea; while the others heated the grain [wheat ?] in a willow basket before grinding it between two stones. In the middle of this basket they shook constantly some live coals on which each grain passed rapidly by an ever more accelerated rotating movement until they were soon parched, otherwise the inner side of the basket would be burned by the fire" (Farris 1986b:67).

"This superstition is especially odd since they use these feathered darts [arrows] with a marvelous skill, and can hit the smallest four-footed animals at enormous distances" (Farris 1986b:78).

"To catch the timid creatures of the woods who, ever on the watch, fled with the speed of lightning at the least appearance of danger, these same hunters utilize a subterfuge, thanks to which they nearly always succeed.

One among them, disguised in the skin of a deer, horns on the head and the hide on his back, moves toward the poor beasts grazing peacefully on the plain, until he finds himself near enough, thanks to his disguise, to that which he wishes to make his first prey, to be able to shoot it with a killing arrow. A second was taken the same way, then a third, and the massacre continued thus here and there until the rest of the herd, finally taking alarm, dispersed afar in the high grass or nearby woods" (Farris 1986b:79).

Material Culture.

"Also, from this moment I could move freely in the huts and admit myself thus to the secrets of their interior.

This interior was hardly hidden, it is true, because the habitations of these poor people consisted without exception of miserable huts formed of branches through which the rain and wind passed without difficulty. It was there that all the family, father, mother, and children spent the nights lying pell-mell around the fire, some on cattle hides, the majority on the bare ground, and each one enveloped in a coverlet of wool which served him equally as a mantle during the day, when the weather was cold or wet.

Such was the costume of the men who surrounded me, that it seemed to me all of them were nearly nude, except the chief and several young men, that without doubt the presence of the governor, for whom they showed a profound respect, had decided to

wear European shirt and pants" (Farris 1986b:66).

"Some of these baskets (*paniers*), or more accurately these deep baskets (*vases*) seemed true models of basketmaking, not only by their decoration but by the finished touches of the work. They are made of shoots of straw [?] or compact gorse so solidly held together by the threads, that the fabric was water-resistant, as efficiently as baked clay and earthenware. But, more behind in material civilization that the Kaloches [natives of the Northwest, probably Tlingit], my savages [at Fort Ross] did not know how to construct wooden bowls in which the Indians housekeepers of the northwest came to boil liquids by immersing some stones red-hot from the fire" (Farris 1986b:67-68).

"Down in a circular hole, dug into the soil, and having about five meters of diameter and a quarter of this measure in depth, is placed a roof of a flattened, conical form, constructed of branches covered with sod, such that air could not pass through. In this type of sweating-room, into the interior of which one can only arrive by a very narrow opening, of which the entry is severely forbidden to women, are assembled, sitting on rocks ranged around an enormous brazier, the bathers, among whom the last arriving has the duty of closing with a flat rock or plank, the single entrance so that in a moment the air rises to a very high temperature" (Farris 1986b:72).

Sociopolitical Organization.

"I had a number of reflections of this sort, in contemplating the chief of the village who I had seen the evening before and who had come to pay me a formal visit. I found him seated on a rock in the courtyard of the fort, surrounded by several of his men, all warriors like him. Such was made sufficiently clear by the tattoos which ornamented their faces, also by irregular scars of various wounds, of which the healing had been abandoned, by all appearances, to the Care of Nature.

I was really struck by the dignified air of my new acquaintance in his grand costume. A large mantle of tree bark decorated with brilliantly colored feathers, little shells or mother-of-pearl [abalone?] ingeniously interspersed, was draped majestically on his shoulders, and showed the bizarre but regular designs which covered his large chest and muscular arms. Around his neck were several necklaces of small glass red or black beads; and in his hair, done up and attached on top of his head, were placed some carefully carved wooden pins, crowned by a cluster of black feathers similar to those which adorned his temples, and blended nicely with a mass of copper ear pendants, colored pebbles [magnesite?], and even of animal teeth. There was in the commanding appearance, the attitude of this chief, something noble and imposing. The large proportions of his body, one would have said a statue since he held himself immobile, his proud air, the impassive look of his physiognomy reminded me of the picturesque descriptions that [James Fenimore] Cooper gave his prairie Indians" (Farris 1986b:77-78).

Recreation.

"At every moment of the day, when they have something to lose, one sees them grouped four by four, squatting down on the ground, surrounded by numerous spectators awaiting, nearly always with impatience, the moment when it is their turn to take part. They play a sort of game which is hardly more complicated than double or nothing, so common among our school-children; but to which they have come to give a wholly greater importance by the singularly animated pantomimes to which the action is accompanied among them. In his hands, the playing partner holds two sticks, and while in the presence of his two adversaries whose carefully watching eyes follow with anxiety his least movements, he separates the two sticks, or even rejoins them in one single hand; his associate, sitting beside him, seeks to distract by his cries, gambits, leaps and contortions, the attention of the party hoping to know the truth. If two times in three this person succeeds in saying, at a given moment, how many sticks the player has in the right hand, the stakes belong to him; in the contrary case, it is entirely lost.

So that this description would have some interest for the reader, it would be necessary for me to render all the vivid and lively (sudden) emotions which, on the mobile features of these children of nature; the cries, the gesticulations, the laughter of those who won; the cold impassive air of those who, losing often in a single stroke the fruit of many months of work, became again poorer than they had been before. In every case they suffer the bad fortune with a philosophy, or to be more accurate, a dignified indifference like the ancient stoics; and this savage who came to the game bedecked with glass trinkets, or other ornaments, from head to foot, who had found means in order to make himself more attractive to cover himself with four or five shirts, as well as pants and vests superimposed one over the other, returned to his hut gay as a finch and naked as a worm" (Farris 1986b:70-71).

Gender Relations.

"In vain I sought to discover among the other sex some analogous advantages. I found all the women horribly ugly, having a stupid air, glum, their health broken by misery, by the hard work; and if some young woman showed in her figure, in the features of her face, some vestiges of the charms which in the bosom of civilized societies the women are so generously endowed by nature, they were so dirty, the hide or wool skirt which composed nearly their only garment was so filthy, their hair was so disheveled, that they could only inspire pity and disgust" (Farris 1986b:67).

Stephen Powers

Dates of Observation. 1871-1872.

Citation. Powers (original 1877, reprinted in 1976; *Tribes of California*, [Berkeley: University of California Press]).

Subsistence Practices.

"These Indians make considerable account of the wild oats growing so abundantly in California, which they gather and prepare in the following manner: The harvester swings a large, deep, conical basket under his left arm, and holds in his right hand a smaller one furnished with a suitable handle. When the oats are dead ripe they shatter out easily, and he has only to sweep the small basket through the heads in a semi-circle, bringing it around to the larger one, into which he discharges the contents at every stroke. When the hamper is full he empties it in a convenient place, and the squaws proceed to hull the grain. They place a quantity in a basket, moisten it slightly, then churn and stir the mass with sticks which cause the chaff to accumulate on the surface, when they burn it off by passing firebrands over it. This process is repeated until the grain is tolerably clean.

They then beat it into flour with stones, and roast it for pinole or manufacture it into bread; and the latter article is said by those who have eaten it to be quite palatable and nutritious.

Like all their brethren they are also very fond of acorns, and the old Indians still cling tenaciously to them in preference to the finest wheaten bread. To prepare them for consumption they first strip off the shells one by one, then place a large basket without a bottom on a broad, flat stone, pour into it the hulled acorns, and pound them up fine with long, slender, stone pestles. I had often noticed these bottomless baskets before, and wondered how the bottoms were worn out while the sides remained so good; but here I learned that they were so made for a good reason. The flour thus obtained is bitter, puckery, and unfit to be eaten, but they now take it to the creek for the purpose of sweetening it. In the clean, white sand they scoop out capacious hollows, and with the palms of their hands pat them down smooth and tight. The acorn flour is poured in and covered with water. In the course of two or three hours the water percolates through the sand, carrying with it a portion of the bitterness; and by repeating this process they render the flour perfectly sweet. The bread made from it is deliciously rich and oily, but they contrive somehow to make it as black as a pot, not only on the crust but throughout. Generally it is nothing but a kind of panada or mush, cooked with hot stones in baskets.

In a time of scarcity they cut down the smaller trees in which the woodpeckers have stored away acorns, or climb up and pluck them out of the holes" (Powers 1976:187-88).

"The Gualala also eat a considerable quantity of wild potato, probably cammas, which they call *hi-po*, and which is said to be quite good eating when cooked and peeled. There is a certain locality on the Gualala Creek, called by them *Hi-po-wi*, which signifies "potato place." Unlike the Atlantic tribes, those on this coast seldom consume anything raw, except dried smelt and salmon.

Clams and mussels are great dainties in the season. They also trap ground-squirrels 'and such small deer' by means of a noose attached to a pole bent over, which springs up and hoists the animal into the air" (Powers 1976:188-89).

Material Culture.

"They construct their conical wigwams principally with slabs of redwood bark. I saw in the possession of a Gualala squaw a fancy work-basket, which evinced in its fabric and ornamentation quite an elegant taste and an incredible patience. It was of the shape common for this species of basket–that of a flat, round squash, to use a homely comparison–woven watertight of fine willow twigs. All over the outside of it the down of woodpeckers' scalps was woven in, forming a crimson nap which was variegated with a great number of hanging loops of strung beads and rude outlines of pine trees, webbed with black sprigs into the general texture. Around the edge of the rim was an upright row of little black quail's plumes gayly nodding. There were eighty of these plumes, which would have required the capture of that number of quails, and it must have taken at least one hundred and fifty woodpeckers to furnish the nap on the outside. The squaw was engaged three years in making it, working at intervals, and valued it at $25. No American would collect the materials and make it for four times the money.

Charles Hopps [Haupts], a veteran pioneer, told me that such richly-ornamented baskets were quite frequent among the California Indians, but the Americans were seldom permitted to see them" (Powers 1976:186-87).

"But among these southern tribes the rudest kind of a pipe answers all purposes. The Indian takes any straight stick he happens to find and whittles out of it a stem a foot long and as large as one's little finger, with a rough lump of wood at the end, which is burned or bored out of little to serve for a bowl, the whole pipe being straight, so that the smoker must cant it up a good deal or lie on his back" (Stephens 1976:189).

"They reckon their beads "by the two hundred", as one explained to me, up to a thousand, the word for which is *tush-op-te* (literally 'five two-hundreds')" (Powers 1976:192).

"Man and wife do not sleep apart, as in some Algonkin tribes, but lie down snugly together in a kind of nest, and draw a hare-skin rug over them" (Powers 1976:193).

Sociopolitical Organization.

"The chieftainship is hereditary unless the heir is incompetent, though its functions are very nebulous, and their social system nowadays is patriarchal. But as on Russian River the remnant of them is so shrunken and narrowed down that it saddens their hearts, and they dwell all in one wigwam together for the comforting of their souls, though some who thus abide in common are nowise related" (Powers 1976:193).

Recreation.

"While among the Gualala I had an excellent opportunity of witnessing the gambling game of *wi* and *tep*, and a description of the same, with slight variations, will answer for nearly all the tribes in Central and Southern California.

After playing tennis all the afternoon they assembled in the evening in a large frame-house of one room, made by themselves with tolerable skill, and squatted on the ground around a fire, which it was the children's task constantly to replenish with shavings. There were about forty men, women and youngsters. They first divided off in two equal parties, and then proceeded to make up the grand sweepstakes. One Indian would lay down a half dollar, and another of the opposite section would cover the same. Another would deposit a blanket or a pair of trousers, and one of the other side would match it with an article agreed to be of equal value. A squaw would contribute a dress, or a chemise, or a string of beads, which would be covered as above, and so on until they deemed the stake large enough to be worth their while. It consisted of $8 in silver coin, a large hatful of strings of shell-money, and an immense heap of clothing and blankets, some of then new and very good, and it was worth at least $150.

They gamble with four cylinders of bone about two inches long, two of which are plain and two marked with rings and strings tied around the middle. The game is conducted by four old and experienced men, frequently gray-heads, two for each party, squatting on their knees on opposite sides of the fire. They have before them a quantity of fine dry grass, and with their hands in rapid and juggling motion before and behind them, they roll up each piece of bone in a little bale, and the opposite party presently guess in which hand is the marked bone. Generally only one guesses at a time, which he does with the word '*tep*' (marked one), '*wi*' (plain one). If he guesses right for both the players, they simply toss the bones over to him and his partner, and nothing is scored on either side. If he guesses right for one and wrong for the other, the one for whom he guessed right is 'out', but his partner rolls up the bones for another trial, and the guesser forfeits to them one of the twelve counters. If he guesses wrong for both, they still keep on, and he forfeits two counters.

There are only twelve counters, and when they have been all won over to one side or the other the game is ended. Each Indian then takes out of the stake the article which he or she deposited, together with that placed on it, so that every one of the winning party comes out with double the amount he staked" (Powers 1976:189-90).

"This singular game was protracted until midnight, when we came away, and we learned next morning that it was not concluded til two o'clock. One thing is praiseworthy in the Indian gamblers, and that is the good nature with which they accept all their losses. They very seldom quarrel over a game, and never fight unless inflamed with the white man's *a-ka bish-i-tu* (bad water).

But for all kinds of gambling both sexes and all ages have a positive passion. The Gualala wife of Hopps, although the mother of two little children, abandoned them utterly to her husband's care, watching the game until the 'wee sma hours', when it closed; and, in consequence, Hopps was obliged to get breakfast next morning, a task to which he seemed to be accustomed, and which he accepted with becoming resignation" (Powers 1976:191-92).

Religious Activities.

"Every year brings around the great autumnal games, which continue a matter of two weeks. Besides the spear dance, tennis, gambling, and the like, they amuse themselves with divers[e] other entertainments. One of them is the devil dance, which is gotten up to terrify the women and children, like the *haberfeldtreiben* of the Bavarian peasants. In the midst of the ordinary dances there comes rushing upon the scene an ugly apparition in the shape of a man, wearing a feather mantle on his back reaching from the arm-pits down to the mid-thighs, zebra-painted on his breast and legs with black stripes, bear-skin shako on his head, and his arms stretched out at full length along a staff passing behind his neck. Accoutered in this harlequin rig he dashes at the squaws, capering, dancing, whooping; and they and the children flee for life, keeping several hundred yards between him and themselves. If they are so unfortunate as to touch even his stick all their children will perish out of hand.

The object of this piece of gratuitous foolery seems to be, as among most of the Pomo tribes, merely

to exhibit to the squaws the power of their lords over the infernal regions and its denizens, and thereby remind them forcibly of the necessity of obedience.

Their fashion of the spear dance is different from the Gallinomero (a Pomo group south of Healdsburg on the Russian River). The man who is to be slain stands behind a screen of hazel boughs with his face visible through an aperture; and the spearman, after the usual protracted dashing about and making of feints, strikes him in the face through the hole in the screen. He is then carried off, revives, etc.

The Gualala say the world was made by the Great Man above assisted by the Old Owl; here we doubtless have a Russian graft of their aboriginal belief. The lower animals were created first; man and woman after" (Powers 1976:193-94).

ETHNOGRAPHIC ACCOUNTS

Samuel Barrett

Dates of Fieldwork. Primary fieldwork in 1903, 1904, 1906; museum research in 1914-1915.

Citations. Barrett (1908, 1916, 1952 [volumes 1 and 2], 1975).

Subsistence Practices. Barrett (1952) presents the most detailed description of Pomo subsistence practices and related material culture yet written. The majority of the subsistence activities are very similar to those described in earlier ethnohistorical accounts, especially by Kostromitinov. These include deer hunts in which men stalked their prey dressed in deer masks, antlers, and hides (1952:123); the preparation of many foods as gruels or soups by heating the liquids in tightly woven baskets using fired hot rocks (1952:60); the grinding of acorns in hopper mortars with pestles, and their subsequent leaching in sand-lined pits where water is percolated through the acorn flour (1952:62, 71); the cooking of black acorn bread (1952:71-75); the broiling of many meats on hot coals (1952:97); the preparation of seeds (1952:85); and the use of fish poisons (1952:149-50). Some subsistence practices not mentioned in earlier accounts include the use of brush fences to snare rabbits and quails (1952:129-35).

Material Culture. Much of the material culture described in detail by Barrett is mentioned in earlier accounts. These include hopper mortars, stone pestles, hammerstones (1952:173-79); cooking stones the size of fists used in water tight baskets and underground ovens (1952:175); projectile points made from obsidian (1952:176); clam shell disk beads (1952:289); bows (1952:183); baskets (1952:276); and straight wooden pipes with bulbous bowls (1952:116).

Some of the architectural forms exhibit considerable coherence over time. In general concordance with Lutke, Wrangell, Kostromitinov, and LaPlace, Barrett describes temporary brush shelters used by hunter-gatherer parties during the summer months (1975:40), and small semi-subterranean structures (4.5 to 9 m in diameter, 1.2 m deep) used as sudatory and men's houses (1975:44). However, at least two types of structures described by Barrett were not recorded during the Russian occupation.

One is the classic coastal Pomo house type, which Powers also mentions at Haupt's Ranch, consisting of redwood bark leaned together on a central pole to form an interior space of about 2.4 to 3.6 m in diameter (Barrett 1908:24; 1975:37). In contrast, Kostromitinov, Corney, and Sandels describe houses that were oval, semi-subterranean structures. Kostromitinov describes these "winter" houses as underground "barabaras" that consisted of an understructure of poles placed in the ground covered with bark, twigs, and grass. Barrett (1975:42) does note that "men of means" did build semi-subterranean earth covered lodges.

The other type of structure is the large semi-subterranean dance houses that are a central focus of the ceremonial cycle of later Pomo rancherias. Barrett (1975:45-51) defines these as very imposing structures constructed with eight major posts that are set about 1 to 1.8 m underground to hold up a roof that covers a 12 to 18 m diameter space. That subterranean dance houses were not described by early Russian administrators and visitors to Fort Ross or by Powers at Haupt's Ranch is rather interesting. It may suggest that these structures were relatively late innovations among Kashaya Pomo, dating possibly to the late nineteenth century.

Sociopolitical Organization. Barrett (1908:16) suggests that the village composed the only political division of Pomo peoples, and that each village claimed the nearby land as part of its territory. Each village unit consisted of a "big" captain or chief and several lesser captains or chiefs. The captains or chiefs formed a village council that represented the various families in the community (1908:14-16).

Religious Activities. Barrett (1952:51-60, 64) depicts a variety of ceremonies and feasts that relate to hunting and gathering activities.

Gender Relations. Barrett (1952:64,85,118) notes that men are primarily responsible for hunting and fishing, and that women usually gather vegetable foods.

Alfred Kroeber

Dates of Fieldwork. Not specified.

Citation. Kroeber 1925.

Subsistence Practices. Kroeber's (1925) synthesis relies extensively on Barrett's data.

Material Culture. Kroeber's (1925) discussion relies extensively on Barrett's (1908) data.

Sociopolitical Organization. Similar to Barrett, Kroeber (1925:228-29) defines the village community or tribelet as a political unit. However, he suggests that a community may be composed of one principal settlement and several minor settlements of related kinspeople. The village community is defined as a tract of land that may measure 16 km along the coast and extend a greater distance into the interior hinterland (1925:234). Employing Barrett's locational information on ancient villages and campsites (figure 4.1), Kroeber (1925:233-34) speculates that the Southwestern Pomo were divided into nine tribelets, five on the coast and four in the interior. A head chief who lived in the principal village would represent each tribelet, as well as lesser chiefs who resided in nearby hamlets. The lesser chiefs would have cooperated with the head chief and formed an informal community council (1925:250).

Religious Activities. Kroeber describes three major ceremonies of the Pomo:

1) the Kuksu or Guksu impersonation rituals in which participants wore big-head ornaments and thrust spears at subjects behind a screen of bushes (1925:261-63). This ceremony appears to be the "spear dance" as described by Powers.

2) the "Old Ghost" ceremony in which dancers impersonate deceased individuals from the community (1925:263). This may be the ceremony described by Kostromitinov at Fort Ross in the 1830s.

3) the "Modern Ghost" dance which diffused out of Nevada in 1870 and probably reached the Pomo in 1872 (1925:269). This later ceremony is under the leadership of the "maru" (dreamer or prophet) who communicates with the spirit world through trances and dreams. Kroeber (1925:270) notes that the ceremony represents an Indian revivalistic movement that stresses traditional native lifeways as a reaction against the encroaching Euro-American society.

Edwin Loeb

Dates of Fieldwork. 1921 (graduate seminar), 1924-1925.

Citation. Loeb 1926.

Subsistence Practices. Loeb's (1926:163-76) discussion of hunting game, gathering vegetable resources, and preparing and cooking foodstuffs is very similar to Barrett. Many of the practices described by Loeb are mentioned in ethnohistoric accounts. Loeb does provide greater detail on sea mammal hunting and coastal fishing than Barrett. He describes the use of crude rafts to paddle to offshore rocks where seals and sea lions were bludgeoned with a heavy wooden club (1926:169). Coastal fishing was done from onshore rocks using lines of kelp and wooden hooks (1926:168).

Material Culture. Again, Loeb describes similar kinds of material culture as outlined in Barrett. He also describes conical redwood slab houses, summer brush houses, sudatory or men's houses, and large semi-subterranean "ghost houses" (1926:158-61). He suggests that the large ghost or dance houses were constructed every seven years in a community exclusively for Old Ghost ceremonies (1926:161). He suggests that the Old Ghost ceremonies may have been rotated among nearby communities. Loeb notes that contemporary Pomo people now use the ghost houses to perform the modern ghost cult.

Sociopolitical Organization. Loeb (1926:236-37) recognizes "big chiefs" who served as peacemakers and preachers and "boy chiefs" who assisted the big chiefs in coastal Pomo communities. The positions of leadership tended to be hereditary in so far as the candidate possessed the proper skills for the job. The territory around a village was regarded as the property of the community (1926:234).

Recreation. Loeb (1926:212) describes gambling games recorded by earlier observers, but indicates that these games are played less frequently now and always in the sweat house. At the end of modern ghost dance ceremonies, feasting and gambling take place.

Religious Activities. Loeb (1926:338) describes the death and resurrection ceremony of the Old Ghost ceremony that used to be held in semi-subterranean ghost houses. The Kuksu ceremony that involved secret societies of shamans was held in a brush house or open enclosure in the springtime (1926:354-56). The modern ghost dance started with the Northern Paiute of Nevada in 1870 and diffused west. The Pomo learned of the religious cult from the Patwin in 1872. Loeb (1926:394) notes that the modern ghost dance replaced both the Old Ghost ceremony and the Kuksu secret society. Maru priests or dreamers, of which two or three may practice in one town, borrowed some regalia for their dances, such as the bigheads, from older Patwin Kuksu ceremonies (1926:395-96). Loeb (1926:396) suggests that the contemporary, semi-subterranean, earth-covered, dance houses are similar to those found among tribes to the east. He outlines several architectural innovations, including an interior gallery, painted interior poles, and a tunnel entrance, that have been adopted by Pomo peoples in recent years (1926:395-96).

Gender Relations. Among the coastal Pomo, men reportedly did all the fishing, while women gathered abalone, other seafoods, and most vegetable products. At low tide both men and women went to the shore to gather food (1926:164-65). Women did all the cooking, while men carved up the meat. Men also gathered firewood, obtained salt, made shell money, and tanned hides for clothing. On trips, women served as burden carriers, hauling infants and household utensils on their backs while the men stalked ahead with only their bows and arrows (1926:176, 192).

Edward Gifford

Dates of Fieldwork. 1915-1918, 1934, 1950.

Citations. Gifford and Kroeber 1937, Gifford 1967.

Subsistence Practices. Gifford (1967:1-4) uses Kostromitinov's account to describe the seasonal round and economic activities of the Kashaya Pomo. However, his detailed outline on the ethnobotany and ethnozoology (1967:10-21) of the Kashaya is based primarily on interviews with native informants, especially Herman James. These accounts of hunting deer, preparing various meat and plant foods, and cooking soups, gruels, breads, and meats correspond very closely to early European and American observations. Gifford (1967:17, 19) emphasizes that the Kashaya Pomo did not hunt seals or sea lions, and that no deep-sea fishing took place because they lacked seaworthy boats. He suggests that deep water fish, such as flounder and cod, were not used as sources of food until the coming of the Russians and native Alaskans.

Material Culture. Gifford (1967:21-45) presents a culture element list for the Kashaya Pomo that includes many materials described by earlier observers.

Sociopolitical Organization. Initially, Gifford and Kroeber (1937:117-19) argued that the Pomo were divided into a number of small, autonomous tribelets. Each tribelet or village community consisted of a central village containing an earth-covered assembly or dance house where one or more chiefs resided. Other families were dispersed away from the central village due to quarreling, fear of witchcraft, or for convenience in obtaining food. No tribelet supposedly contained more than one assembly house. In his latter publication, Gifford (1967:7, 43) maintains that the Kashaya Pomo were integrated into one political unit from the Russian River north. The chief, known as Toyon, was the recognized leader of all the Kashaya Pomo between the mouths of the Russian and Gualala rivers. He was replaced by his son Tihana who was chief and preacher for the entire group (1967:45). Herman James's grandmother never mentioned a place that had more than one chief. Gifford believes that no multiple lineage villages existed in the past (1967:43).

Recreation. The odd-even guessing game, described in almost all early European and American accounts, was checked off in Gifford's 1934 culture element list survey; however it was not checked off in the survey he conducted in 1950 (see 1967:29).

Religious Activities. The Old Ghost society is not checked off for either his 1934 or 1950 culture element survey (1967:35). The Kusksu society was remembered by informants and believed to be very ancient. None of Gifford's informants ever saw the Kuksu impersonation ceremony, but their parents told them about it. Some dances associated with the Kuksu society were performed at Haupt's Ranch, and at least one informant (Rosie Smith) remembered the Lole dance (1967:45).

Fred B. Kniffen

Dates of Fieldwork. Late 1930s.

Citation. Kniffen 1939.

Subsistence Practices. Kniffen (1939:385-88) reconstructs the seasonal round for the Kashaya Pomo that is very similar to the one observed by Kostromitinov. Again, many of the subsistence practices described (e.g., boiling water using hot stones, cooking meat and shellfish on embers, hunting with a deer head mask) are similar to earlier observations.

Material Culture. Kniffen (1939:386) defines Kashaya houses as slabs of redwood bark leaned against a central post.

Sociopolitical Culture. Kniffen (1939:384-85) believes the Kashaya Pomo were united as one tribe under a single chief at Fort Ross subsequent to the coming of the Russians. He believes that most of the Kashaya people aggregated at Fort Ross under the chief Toiyon, and that the flat vicinity near the stockade was "covered with the houses of Indians." Toiyon was succeeded by Tahana, who was chief when the Kashaya relocated to Haupt's Ranch. Tahana is reported to have died at the Haupt's rancheria. He was succeeded by Sam Ross who died in 1908 at Haupt's Ranch. Kniffen notes that Robert Smith is the present chief of the Kashaya.

Kniffen (1939:385) disagrees with Kroeber's extension of tribelet units into Kashaya territory. He notes that contemporary Kashaya people have no tradition of dividing the region into village communities or tribelets. There is a "unity" expressed that suggests the Kashaya territory has always been a single political unit.

Omer Stewart

Dates of Fieldwork. 1935.

Citations. Stewart 1935b and 1943.

Subsistence Practices. Stewart (1943:60-61) presents detailed information on native exploitation of coastal plants and animals that largely corroborate observations made in the early nineteenth century.

Much of his information was provided by Rosa Sherd, who was the mother of Robert Smith (Stewart 1935b). She noted that the Kashaya Pomo went to Lake County for obsidian.

Sociopolitical Organization. Stewart (1943:49) notes that all of his informants agreed that in prehistoric times there "was only one tribe and one chief for the whole area of the dialect." Metini was recognized as a major pre-Russian town and Toyon was the recognized leader of the Kashaya Pomo. However, upon closer questioning of his native informants, especially Rosa Sherd, Stewart (1943:50) adds that there appears to be evidence of more than one principal village and multiple chiefs. He believes that separate village communities probably existed in the past, although they may have periodically assembled as a larger group for initiation ceremonies and other festivals.

Mary Jean Kennedy

Dates of Fieldwork. 1953-1954.

Citation. Kennedy 1955.

Subsistence Practices. Kennedy's (1955:106) research indicates that an increasing reliance on Euro-American foods took place among the Kashaya sometime between 1910 and 1950. Essie Parrish, a well-known Kashaya maru and healer, noted that aboriginal foods were more commonly used in her youth (about 1910). Kennedy reports in 1952-1953 that the bulk of the peoples' diet consisted of groceries purchased from stores in Stewart's Point, Healdsburg, or Santa Rosa. The mainstays of their diet were potatoes, beans, bread, tortillas, beef, and pork. Acorn was still used but primarily by the older generation. Middle aged or older women drove miles to favorite tan oak groves to collect acorns. The acorns were ground into flour using grinders and then leached by pouring water through dish towels placed over evergreen branches. The acorns were still cooked as a mush or baked as bread. Various seafoods, such as seaweed, were still held in high esteem (1955: 106-107).

Material Culture. Houses in 1952-1953 were clapboard frame structures of one or two bedrooms. Some houses were surrounded by fences. The majority contained modern butane gas stoves, and a few had gas-burning refrigerators. Since no electricity existed in this area of Sonoma County, oil-burning lamps were used. The houses were heated primarily by wood-burning stoves. Chairs, tables, and couches furnished the houses. Most households had washing machines, and some had sewing machines (Kennedy 1955:92-95).

Kennedy (1955:11-12) observes that no Russian accounts describe dance houses among the Kashaya. Marie James, a Kashaya elder, told Kennedy that she was eight years old (ca. 1857) when the dance house at Fort Ross was constructed. Prior to this, only open brush shelters were built for dances. Two earth-covered dance houses and later an above-ground, board dance house were built at Haupt's Ranch. An above-ground, board dance house existed at the Kashia Rancheria at the time of Kennedy's fieldwork.

Sociopolitical Organization. Kennedy (1955:18) states that the Kashaya today have a tradition of having only one chief over all the tribe. However, she argues that this may be a consequence of Russian colonization. She believes that prior to and during early contact with the Russians each village had a chief defined on the basis of kinship. "The adoption of a single chief gives evidence of the effect of the Russian centralization of authority" (1955:19). She points out that the earliest recognized chief of the Kashaya, Toyon, is a Russian derived word. It is the name given to a native administrator by the Russians (1955:18-19). Kennedy (1955:101-102) lists the Kashaya chiefs since Russian times as Toyon, Tehana, Sam Ross (who died in 1908), Robert Smith, Robert Smith's son, and then Sidney Parrish. She notes that Sam Ross was the last hereditary chief, and that subsequent to his death the chiefs have served in the capacity of chairman of the tribal council. According to Kennedy, the chairmen of the tribal council serve as spokespeople to the outside world. They are accorded little power in internal community affairs. Since the rise of the Bole-Maru cult (modern Ghost cult), the dreamers have become both the religious and secular leaders of the group (1955:102).

Religious Activities. Kennedy (1955:125) provides a detailed picture of the development of the Bole-Maru cult among the Kashaya based largely on the work of Cora Du Bois (1939). The 1870 Ghost Dance movement stimulated a secondary religion, known as the Earth Lodge Cult, among the Hill Patwin and Wintun in 1871/1872 which heralded the end of the world. Subterranean earth lodges were built to protect the faithful from the impending cataclysm. The Kashaya Pomo were invited to attend an Earth Lodge cult ceremony in Lake County or Ukiah around 1872. The Bole-Maru cult was an outgrowth of the Earth Lodge Cult sometime during the spring of 1872. This cult employed dreamers to reveal the "afterlife and supreme being." The first prophets of the Bole-Maru cult arrived at Haupt's Ranch in 1874 (1955:128).

In the late nineteenth and early twentieth centuries, several dreamers appear to have preached in the rancheria at Haupt's Ranch. The dreamers were all males (Kaokbad, Cristoval, Humbolt Jack, Big Jose, Pete Antone) until about 1908-1910, when Annie Jarvis began to experience her first visions (Kennedy 1955:129). From 1912 to 1943, when she died, Annie Jarvis was the maru, healer, and leader of the Kashaya

Pomo. Kennedy feels that the Bole Maru cult had run its course until Annie Jarvis revitalized the movement about 1912. The first female maru stressed traditional Kashaya lifeways over the encroaching Euro-American culture. She banned gambling, alcoholic consumption, fraternization with white people, and sending native children to white boarding schools. She revitalized traditional taboos, native dances, and marriage within the group. People were encouraged to speak the Kashaya Pomo language on the rancheria (1955:132-33,159).

Kennedy (1955:138) argues that World War II was an important watershed for the Kashaya people. Annie Jarvis died in 1943; local employment became very scarce; and the reservation was closed. The families looked for work elsewhere in the region. Essie Parrish, who had assisted Annie Jarvis in Bole-Maru ceremonies, became the maru and leader of the Kashaya after the death of Jarvis. When the reservation was opened after the war, it appears that some people were no longer willing to remain segregated from the white world (see also Oswalt 1964:5-6). Both Pentecostal and Mormon missionaries began visiting the reservation and converting people to the Christian faith. Eventually Essie Parrish joined the Mormon church, while still continuing to serve as the spiritual leader of the Bole-Maru ceremonies. The Mormon church allowed the Kashaya to continue their native dances and feasts, and many of the taboos recognized by Mormons (i.e., no alcohol) were similar to the strictures laid down by Annie Jarvis (1955:146-48). Kennedy (1955:149) suggests that the acceptance of the Latter Day Saints' teachings "ended the spiritual supremacy of the leader of the Bole-Maru." Certainly, the social interaction with white missionaries on the reservations and white Mormons in nearby towns and cities broke down the segregated nature of reservation life after World War II.

Gender Relations. A very significant development among the Kashaya people was the acceptance of women as both preachers and tribal leaders after about 1912. Since that time women have continued to play leading roles in the religious and political activities of the group. Prior to 1912, all the ethnohistoric and ethnographic sources corroborate that men were the political leaders and preachers going back to the initial Russian colonization of Fort Ross.

KASHAYA ORAL TRADITION

The following analysis is based on Kashaya stories transcribed and translated by Robert Oswalt at the Kashia Rancheria. Each story is numbered as a separate text.

Dates of Fieldwork. 1957, 1958, 1959, 1961.

Citation. Oswalt 1964.

Subsistence Practices. Oral tradition strongly suggests that Euro-American foods were not widely accepted by Kashaya people during the early period of contact. In Text 55, Essie Parrish recounts that when white men first came to Fort Ross, they served the Kashaya white man's food. The Kashaya believed the food to be poisonous and threw it in a ditch. In Text 56, Essie Parrish recounts from her father's oldest sister that the white men gave the Kashaya coffee and a grinder. The people did not know how to use the grinder so the coffee beans were leached and cooked using the traditional methods employed for processing acorns. The Kashaya found the coffee beans too harsh and poured them out. In Text 60, Herman James recounts that the Undersea people (Russians) grew wheat that blanketed the land and stored the flour at Fort Ross. He notes that the Kashaya Pomo were used to harvest and grind the wheat into flour. As Herman James relates, at first, the Kashaya did not know about flour, but eventually they ate the food. They still ate pinole, however, in their traditional manner. In Text 67, Herman James notes that the white man's food was not plentiful on the rancheria when he was a child. Traditional methods of hunting and fishing were still employed to harvest food to eat. Fishing spears, composed of three sharpened nails attached to a wooden pole, were used to spear salmon migrating upstream after the first winter rains. In Text 70, Essie Parrish tells about the old days when people gathered mussels and turban snails from coastal rocks before the winter storms. These were packed up the coastal cliffs, probably to village locations. Here holes were dug, lined with gravel, and sea water poured over the shellfish. This method was employed to keep the shellfish fresh for some time. In Text 71, Essie Parrish recounts how deer, rabbits, and squirrels were pounded lightly with a pestle on a mortar stone and baked on the coals. In some cases the meats were barbecued by skewering them with a stick and placing them over the fire. Abalone was pounded hard and then cooked under the ashes. It was especially good with acorn mush. In Text 72, Essie Parrish tells how the old people used to prepare buckeyes by boiling them in a pot, then mashing them on a mortar stone, followed by leaching them in freshwater.

Material Culture. Many of the above texts describe mortars, pestles, harpoons, bows, and arrows presumably still in use in the latter part of the nineteenth century.

Sociopolitical Organization. In Text 57, Essie Parrish describes how leaders of the group would rise in the morning and extol the Kashaya to be industrious. Men should go hunt game and fish so that food could be stored for the upcoming winter. Women should gather acorns and buckeyes.

Religious Activities. In Text 66, Kashaya tradition recounts the trip to Clear Lake in 1872 to participate in the Earth Lodge Cult. People from both Metini and Abaloneville (Haupt's Ranch) travelled to Clear Lake to await the world to end. The Kashaya were given fish from Clear Lake when they arrived, but they did not like the food. They stayed about one month before returning home. In Text 69, Essie Parrish recounts as a child that discipline in the group was better and that people participated in traditional dances and spiritual things. The Kashaya did not know much about white man ways, and people did not wear white man's clothes or eat his food.

SUMMARY OF THE ETHNOHISTORICAL ANALYSIS

The examination of ethnohistorical texts, ethnographic studies, and native oral tradition suggests a complicated process of acculturation has taken place among the Kashaya Pomo since their initial contact with Europeans, Creoles, and native Alaskans. The timing, character, and magnitude of cultural change varied greatly with respect to foods, subsistence practices, material culture, architectural styles, sociopolitical organization, recreational activities, religious ceremonies, and gender relations. As summarized below, the sociopolitical organization of Kashaya society appears to have undergone rapid transformations with the early colonization of Fort Ross, exhibiting evidence of greater centralization in leadership positions. Religious activities seem to have remained relatively unchanged until the 1870s, while many aspects of Kashaya material culture and subsistence practices were commonly employed into the late nineteenth and early twentieth century.

Subsistence Practices. While some kinds of European and Mexican foods were adopted from the Russians by the 1830s (beef, wheat) and from Mexican cowboys by the 1850s (tortillas), aboriginal foods were commonly used by Kashaya people until the late nineteenth and early twentieth centuries as observed by Stephen Powers and recorded in the childhood reminiscences of Essie Parrish and Herman James. Common themes in early ethnohistoric observations and later ethnographic interviews with native peoples are the traditional methods of stalking deer in deer costumes, cooking meats over open embers, cooking stews using the stone boiling method, grinding and leaching acorns, fishing with plant poisons, and collecting and cooking shellfish over hot embers. Interestingly, a number of descriptions detail the collection and preparation of wild oats (*Avena fatua*), a plant that is not indigenous to the region (see Gifford 1967:11).

Wild oats were brought over to California by Europeans, although it is unclear whether the plants dispersed northward from Spanish settlements or came from the initial Russian agricultural fields at Fort Ross. In any event, wild oats are an excellent example of how traditional native harvest practices and food preparation methods were employed to exploit a new plant food. The harvesting of wild oats appears to have changed over time from 1818-1824, when wild oat plants were burned in the field (Golovnin, Kotzebue) to the 1830s (Kostromitinov) and 1870s (Powers) when baskets were used to harvest the grains. We suspect that agricultural intensification by the Russians in the 1830s put a stop to the widespread burning of fields in the vicinity, although it appears to have been revived briefly after the Russians left.

Kennedy (1955:161-62) suggests that aboriginal foods were used long after contact with the first Europeans given their availability, preferred taste, and relatively low costs of harvesting. The changing cultural geography of the Fort Ross region in the late nineteenth century, however, greatly curtailed the efficiency of regional based hunter-gatherer practices. Partitioning of the region into plots of private property bounded by fence lines denied native people access to critical plant and animal resources. At the same time, the greater availability of wage labor provided Kashaya families with an alternative to native foods–the means to purchase potatoes, flour, and beef in stores (Kennedy 1955:161-62). By the 1940s, the younger generation of Kashaya people was apparently developing an acquired taste for the white man's foods. With the decline of the Bole-Maru cult, in which native foods were treated as prestige items, Kennedy (1955:162) notes that store-bought foods composed the bulk of the diet by the early 1950s.

Material Culture. Both archaeological and documentary evidence point to cultural continuity in the production and use of many native artifacts from late prehistoric times through much of the Historic period. These materials include the hopper mortar, pestle, cooking rocks (groundstone fragments), clam shell disk beads, projectile points, millingstones, handstones, wooden pipes, and baskets.

While European raw materials (glass, metal) and European products (glass beads, clothes) sometimes supplemented native materials, there is little evidence that native peoples expended much effort in acquiring or accumulating European goods based on the observations of Kostromitinov and LaPlace in the 1830s. Although some glass tools and projectile points were recovered in the surface assemblages of historic Pomo sites, artifacts manufactured from Napa Valley obsidians were still common (see chapter 5). While the Russians traded glass beads to the native Californians at Fort Ross, these did not take the place of clam shell disk beads as currency among the Kashaya Pomo. The following quotation by John M. Hudson (1897), who studied Pomo bead production near Ukiah, succinctly makes this point.

> Counterfeits appeared as early as 1816, when the Russian explorer Kuskoff ordered made and sent him a certain pattern of glass beads to trade with wild tribes in New Albion. A number of these beads were exhumed from a very old grave not long ago, and prove to be good imitations, both in form and color, but lacking in luster. It is recorded that wild tribes soon detected the cheat and cast them out with abhorrence. Tradition confirms the record with added details of how three Russian traders of charlil kol (devil's beads) were taken unaware and their heads burnt with the beads (Hudson 1897, reprinted in 1975:17-18).

Later ethnohistoric observations (Stephen Powers) and ethnographers describe the continued use of clam disk beads into the late nineteenth and early twentieth century as mortuary offerings and as a means of financing feasts and for obtaining foods and goods within and between tribelet units (see especially Loeb 1926:194-95; Vayda 1967).

The timing of the most significant changes in Kashaya Pomo material culture appears to have taken place after the Russian occupation of Fort Ross, especially during the period of Powers's visit to Haupt's ranch in 1871-1872 and Kennedy's description of the Kashia Rancheria in 1952-53. This argument is best exemplified by the timing of architectural innovations, especially in the construction of winter residential structures and large dance or assembly houses.

Residential Structures. By the 1870s the Kashaya Pomo were adopting architectural innovations of Euro-American ranchers, such as large frame or log houses. Powers (1976:189) described one such house at Haupt's ranch, and Barrett (1916) photographed them among the coastal Pomo in 1901 and 1902. The Euro-American frame houses were supposedly replacing the more traditional coastal Pomo conical redwood houses. However, the conical redwood houses described in great detail by Barrett (1916) and by most subsequent ethnographers were not observed among the Kashaya Pomo until the 1870s by Powers. Prior to the observation by Powers, winter houses are described as semi-subterranean structures that resemble native Alaskan *barabaras* (see Corney, Kostromitinov, and Sandels observations above). Unfortunately, the accounts of these semi-subterranean structures are brief and lack specific details on building materials, layout, and construction methods.

Interestingly, Layton's (1990) excavations of protohistoric house structures at Nightbirds' Retreat and Three Chop Village in Mendocino County indicate that above-ground, conical redwood houses may have some antiquity among the Northern Pomo. Few house structures have yet to be excavated and described by archaeologists in the Fort Ross region.

The discrepancy between the ethnographic observations and later ethnographic studies suggests that innovations in the construction of residential structures took place either during or shortly after the Russian occupation of Fort Ross. It is possible that the conical redwood house is a traditional architectural form of the Kashaya Pomo, and that during the colonization of Fort Ross the Indian workers began to build their winter houses in the fashion of native Alaskan *barabaras*. After the departure of the native Alaskans, they may have switched back to their traditional architectural form. On the other hand, the semi-subterranean structures described by Corney and Kostromitinov may characterize the traditional native winter houses prior to the settlement of Fort Ross.

While this question will not be resolved until detailed excavations of late prehistoric, protohistoric, and historic native "housepits" are undertaken in the Fort Ross region, we believe there is evidence, at least among the neighboring Coast Miwok, that semi-subterranean houses have some antiquity in the region. The description of native houses, somewhere along the Marin County coast, by members of Sir Francis Drake's crew in 1579 resemble later Russian observation of native houses at Fort Ross (see Quinn 1979a:465, 471)

> Having thus had their fill of this times visiting and beholding of us, they departed with joy to their houses, which houses are digged round within the earth, and have from the uppermost brimmes of the circle clefts of wood set up, and joyned close together at the toppe, like our spires on the Steeples of a Church: which being covered with earth, suffer no water to enter, and very warme, the doore in the most part of them, performes the office also of a chimney, to let out the smoake: it is made in bignesse and fashion, like to an ordinary scuttle in a shippe, and standing slopewise: their beds are the hard ground, onely with rushes strewed upon it, lying round about the house, have their fire in the middest, which by reason that the house is but low vaulted, round, and close, giveth a marvellous reflection to their bodies to heate the same (Quinn 1979a:471 [original 1628]).

A similar, but very brief, observation was made by Sebastian Rodriquez Cermeno in his visit to the Marin County coast (probably Drake's Bay see Wagner 1924:6, 8) in 1595.

> Accompanying him were Captain Francisco de Chaves and his ensign, the sergeant and the corporal and three men with shields. These went ashore with the Indians and landed on the beach of the port near some of their underground habitations, in which they live, resembling caves and like those of the Chichimecos Indians of New Spain (Quinn 1979b:410 [original 1596]).

Dance or Assembly House. Kennedy (1955:11) notes that it is odd that no Russian observer mentioned a large dance house at Metini. She reports that the first one may have been constructed at Fort Ross about 1857. It also seems strange to us that Powers did not describe such a structure at Haupt's Ranch. The communal house he describes, where much of the village assembled for gambling, was a large, one-room frame structure (1976:189). Perhaps he was not permitted in or near the semi-subterranean dance house, although he was allowed to view native ceremonies such as the "devil dance" and "spear dance." We suggest that the semi-subterranean, earth-covered dance houses described by Barrett (1916) may have been a later innovation that the Kashaya Pomo adopted from prophets of the Earth Lodge Cult in the early 1870s (after Power's visit to Haupt's Ranch). Kennedy (1955:11) reports that two such structures were eventually built at Haupt's Ranch. By the early twentieth century, the earth-covered dance houses were replaced by above-ground, redwood-planked structures used in the later Bole-Maru ceremonies of Annie Jarvis and Essie Parrish at Haupt's Ranch and the Kashia Rancheria. Maru leaders inspired innovations in the design of the dance houses that included a gallery and tunnel entrance.

Sociopolitical Organization. There is considerable debate about Kashaya sociopolitical organization among ethnographers. We suggest that this debate reflects significant changes that took place in the decision-making structure of the Kashaya peoples at the time of early Russian colonization. While later ethnographers criticized Kroeber's (1925) interpretation of multiple, relatively autonomous tribelets or village communities based largely on Barrett's settlement information (figure 4.1), our preliminary investigation of the archaeological remains of the study area in chapter 5 largely concurs with Kroeber's model.

Russian colonialism apparently accelerated the rise of one recognized tribal leader or "big chief," now remembered as Toyon, among the entire Kashaya linguistic group (see Kennedy 1955:18-19). We believe this shift in the regional structure of the sociopolitical organization coincided with population aggregation north of the stockade after A.D. 1812. We speculate that a number of local chiefs from different village communities would have been represented in the historic community of "Metini." A common practice of the Russian-American Company was to work closely with a recognized leader of the native group in contracting for labor and for local supplies and goods. In the Russian friendship pact with the Kashaya Pomo that was signed in an official gathering on September 22, 1817, the Russian-American Company clearly favored one chief over the others represented at the ceremony. This chief, Chu-gu-an, may have become the Toyon of the Kashaya. The brief transcript of the pact, as translated in Dmytryshyn, Crownhart-Vaughan, and Vaughan (1989c:296-98), follows.

"On September 22, 1817, the Indian Chiefs Chu-gu-an, Amat-tan, Gem-le-le and others, appeared at Fort Ross by invitation. Their greetings, as translated, extended their thanks for the invitation.

Captain Lieutenant Hagemeister expressed gratitude to them in the name of the Russian American Company for ceding to the Company land for a fort, buildings and enterprises, in regions belonging to Chu-gu-an, [land] which the inhabitants call Medeny-ny. [Hagemeister] said he hoped they would not have reason to regret having the Russians as neighbors.

Having heard [what was] translated for him, Chu-gu-an and a second, Amat-tan, whose dwelling was also not far off, replied, 'We are very satisfied with the occupation of this place by the Russians, because we now live in safety from other Indians, who formerly would attack us and this security began only from the time of [the Russian] settlement.'

After this friendly response, gifts were presented to the toion and the others; and to the Chief, Chu-gu-an, a silver medal was entrusted, ornamented with the Imperial Russian seal and the inscription 'Allies [soiuznye] of Russia' and it was stated that this [medal] entitles him to receive respect from the Russians, and for that reason he should not come to them without the medal. It also imposes on him the obligation of loyalty and assistance, incase this is needed. In response to that he and the others declared their readiness and expressed their gratitude for the reception.

After the hospitality, when [the Indians] departed from the fort, a one-gun salute was fired in honor of the chief toion.

We, the undersigned, hereby testify that in our presence the chief toions responded in exactly this way."

In the early twentieth century, further changes took place in the sociopolitical organization of the Kashaya. Sam Ross, who died in 1908, was the last hereditary chief of the Kashaya who provided secular and possibly religious leadership for the group. After his death, the Kashaya elected tribal leaders who served as chairs of the tribal council. In this new capacity, tribal chairs functioned primarily as spokespeople to the outside community. Secular and religious leadership within the group was now inspired by the maru dreamers. While earlier leaders were all males, the rise of the Bole-Maru Cult provided women with access to positions of leadership. Since 1912, women have been increasingly influential in the decisionmaking of the Kashaya group.

Recreation. Various gambling games were described by almost every early visitor to Fort Ross. These gambling games continued to be an important activity of the Kashaya Pomo until sometime after 1912, when Annie Jarvis forbade gambling and drinking. It is noteworthy that in the Cultural Element List compiled by Gifford (1967:29), the "Odd-even guessing game" is remembered by informants in his 1934 survey, but is not checked off in his 1950 survey.

Religious Practices. Kostromitinov and Powers describe native ceremonies that may have been part of the Old Ghost ceremony and Kusku ceremony. Most Pomo ethnographers argue that these rituals have considerable antiquity. Crew members of Sir Francis Drake's 1579 sojourn along the Marin coast reported similar ceremonies involving women scratching and beating themselves until they bled as described by Kostromitinov (see Quinn 1979a:471-72). Significant changes took place in the early 1870s with the advent of the Earth Lodge Cult and the Bole-Maru Cult. The Bole-Maru Cult incorporated some aspects of traditional religious practices with innovations inspired by dreamers. This revivalistic crusade inspired pride in traditional Indian lifeways and preached segregation from whites. Kennedy (1955:158-60) stresses that the cult was really an anti-acculturation movement that motivated Kashaya people to continue to speak their own language, to seek mates among the Kashaya Pomo, and to employ traditional material culture, foods, dances, costumes, subsistence practices, and taboo observances. Kennedy argues persuasively that the isolation of the Kashia Rancheria in combination with the Bole-Maru Cult were responsible for the late adoption of Euro-American foods and material culture, and for the number of fluent native speakers prior to World War II.

Gender Relations. Early ethnohistoric observations suggest that many domestic and subsistence related activities were segregated by gender. Women tended to gather plant foods, to collect shellfish and seafoods, to carry burdens, to undertake most domestic chores, and to tend children. Men were inclined to hunt and fish, carry on in the sudatory, and lead the group on trips carrying no more than their bows and arrows. Men served as both the secular and spiritual leaders of the Kashaya Pomo until the early twentieth century, when women openly began to exert their considerable influence in the decision-making organization of the local group.

Conlcusion

The analysis of ethnohistorical texts, ethnographic studies, and native oral traditions tends to corroborate the general findings of our archaeological survey. Native responses to Russian colonial practices were manifested in the organizational structure of the local Indian community. Population aggregation north of the Fort Ross stockade appears to have coincided with the centralization of native leadership positions. Whereas the sociopolitical organization of late prehistoric and protohistoric times was probably characterized by many small polities who maintained their own leaders, the Russians recognized and apparently facilitated the emergence of a single leader for the amalgamated Kashaya Pomo community there. An analysis of the archaeological, ethnohistorical, and ethnographic data indicates that significant changes took place in the material culture, subsistence practices, and religious ceremonies of the Kashaya Pomo. The timing of the most significant changes, however, did not occur during the Russian occupation of Fort Ross, but during the late nineteenth and early twentieth centuries. The initial native to responses to the Ross Colony were much more subtle; no significant or dramatic upheavals in the material culture, subsistence practices, and religious ceremonies of the local population appear to have taken place.

CHAPTER SEVEN

CONCLUSION

I N THIS FIRST VOLUME of the Archaeology and Ethnohistory of Fort Ross, California series, we outlined the research agenda that directs our investigation of the historic Ross Colony in northern California. We are examining how Pacific Coast hunter-gatherers responded to the mercantile practices of the Russian-American Company which administered Fort Ross from 1812 to 1841. The company recruited Europeans, Creoles, and native laborers from Siberia, the Aleutian Islands, Kodiak Island, coastal Alaska, and northern California to work there. The close interaction of ethnic groups from many different homelands represents a fertile ground for stimulating cultural exchange of architectural styles, material goods, methods of craft production, subsistence practices, diet, dress, and ceremonies. Furthermore, the company's payment of commodities or scrip to its work force provided them with access to various European, American, and Asian goods in the company store. The research issues we are addressing concern the effects that mercantile labor and inter-ethnic relationships had on the acculturation process of native workers at Fort Ross. We are especially interested in examining the long-term effects of cohabitation and marriage between Pomo/ Miwok women and native Alaskan men.

The present study is a preliminary investigation of the native Californian population at Ross. Using the direct historical approach—an approach that incorporates information from archaeological investigations, ethnohistorical observations, ethnographic studies, and native oral traditions—we developed a diachronic framework for evaluating cultural change from prehistoric times to about A.D. 1953. In the future we will collaborate with Kashaya tribal scholars to push the diachronic framework to the present.

PREHISTORIC AND
PROTOHISTORIC DEVELOPMENTS

Current archaeological research suggests the study area was used by native peoples as early as 6000-8000 years ago. These early sites are broad, diffuse lithic scatters that extend across the coastal terrace. We speculate that these sites were produced by repeated foraging and hunting ventures over an extensive resource zone in which various tools were lost or discarded. Other early sites may have once been situated along former coastlines to the west of the study area, but subsequent sea level rise, tectonic activity, and coastal erosion would have destroyed or inundated them.

Current data suggest that the intensive occupation of this area did not begin until about 1000 years ago in the Lower Emergent period. The number and diversity of site types increased greatly in the following Upper Emergent or Protohistoric period (A.D. 1500-1812). We have identified a settlement pattern composed of large sites with diverse lithic and faunal assemblages distributed along the ridge tops and ridge slopes, and lithic scatters, shell-bearing deposits, and petroglyphs along the coastal terrace, the lower slopes of the first ridge and the interior hinterland.

We interpret this settlement pattern as the remains of central-based village communities that once flourished across the region in protohistoric times. We argue that villages were once dispersed along the ridge tops and ridge slopes, probably about .5 to 2.5 km apart. These residential bases would have been ideally located to take advantage of both coastal and interior hinterland resources. The settlements on the first ridge system would have been situated no more than five km from rocky intertidal habitats, the coastal terrace, the South Fork of the Gualala River, or the second ridge system. From these residential bases, foraging parties or specialized task groups could have exploited, within a few hours walk, a variety of seafoods, terrestrial seeds, nuts, tubers, and terrestrial game.

Our interpretation of the archaeological data suggests that native peoples established small hamlets and food processing stations along the coastal terrace and lower slopes of the first ridge. Cupule rocks were also produced in locations with good vistas of the ocean. The interior hinterland of the Gualala River contains sites that may have functioned as chert quarries, hunting camps, and plant processing locations. Cupule rocks and other kinds of petroglyphs were also produced in the interior recesses of rugged mountain valleys.

The central-based village communities probably maintained territorial boundaries in an east/west orientation that crosscut the coastal, ridge top and slope, valley, and riverine habitats, as proposed earlier by Omer Stewart (1943). We also support Stewart's (1943) and Kroeber's (1925) interpretations that each village community was a relatively autonomous polity and under the influence of its own chiefs or leaders. It is significant that these models derived from analyses of regional settlement patterns: Kroeber relied on Barrett's (1908) spatial information of ancestral villages and campsites, while Stewart undertook his own reconnaissance work in the study area. Stewart (1943) suggested that a settlement hierarchy may have functioned in the region comprised of large villages with assembly houses and smaller hamlets lacking such structures. It is not yet possible to evaluate critically whether such a settlement hierarchy existed in the study area. Furthermore, our analysis of ethnohistoric texts raises questions about the existence of large, semi-subterranean assembly or dance houses in the

region prior to the late nineteenth century. In light of this problem, it is important to recognize that in Stewart's (1935b) original field notes some of his Kashaya consultants (e.g., Rosa Sherd, Marie James) described "important" villages as those associated with "sweat houses." They did not mention the existence of assembly or dance houses at early Kashaya villages.

Future archaeological research will be directed towards addressing many unresolved questions concerning the proposed central-based village model. We are contemplating field research that will provide more refined information on the overall spatial layout of the settlements; the size, floorplans, and construction methods of architectural features; the occupation histories of the sites (use-durations, seasonal use patterns), and intra-site spatial patterning of artifacts, floral remains, and faunal specimens. We are especially interested in documenting the residential architecture associated with late prehistoric and protohistoric settlements, as well as evaluating whether public architecture, such as sweat houses, dance houses, or assembly houses, are found at large villages.

A provocative finding of our investigation to date is the evidence of population increase during the Protohistoric period. This finding contradicts Dobyn's (1983) prediction of substantial depopulation as a consequence of "pandemics" that may have swept across North America in the first half of the sixteenth century. Evidently, early Spanish explorations along the coast of California, and Sir Francis Drake's visit among the native peoples of nearby Marin County in 1579 did not unleash a lethal "virgin soil epidemic" on a regional scale. Strong evidence of measles, small pox, whooping cough, chicken pox, and other diseases was not documented among the Kashaya Pomo until about 1815 to 1839. However, we recognize that the evaluation of Dobyn's hypothesis may be complicated by additional factors that we have yet to consider. Fort Ross may represent a relatively isolated region in the rugged mountain terrain of coastal northern California that was comparatively immune from sixteenth or seventeenth century epidemics. It is even possible that the demographic increase in protohistoric times at the Ross Colony may reflect refugee populations fleeing northward from inflicted populated areas, such as coastal Marin County or the San Francisco Bay Area.

THE COLONIZATION OF FORT ROSS

The establishment of the Fort Ross Counter as the southernmost counter of the Russian-American Company initiated a very complex acculturation process for the Kashaya Pomo. Our analyses of archaeological remains, ethnohistorical texts, ethnographic studies, and native oral traditions indicate that the colonization of Fort Ross did not trigger a sudden or catastrophic transformation in the traditional lifeways of the Kashaya Pomo. Rather the timing, rates, and magnitude of cultural change fluctuated widely among the different dimensions of Kashaya society that we examined. Furthermore, different causal factors appear to have kicked off changes in some aspects of Kashaya society and not in others.

The most significant initial response to Russian colonial practices was the reorganization of the sociopolitical structure of the Kashaya communities. According to our interpretation of the archaeological data, individual families and small groups from ridge top village communities aggregated north of the stockade in a number of residential compounds. Some of these sites appear to date to the Russian occupation, while others may date to later ranch times. We believe the archaeological evidence of population aggregation coincides with ethnohistorical evidence of sociopolitical changes taking place among the Kashaya Pomo. We speculate that former, autonomous village communities were each represented by their own leaders drawn largely from influential families in the local population. The breakup of the ridge top village communities near Fort Ross and the movement of some individuals and families to the Russian colony (with others probably resettling in the outlying hinterland) would have significant implications for Kashaya Pomo sociopolitical organization. Multiple chiefs from the remnants of traditionally autonomous village communities were now residing in residential compounds that comprised the Indian neighborhood at Fort Ross, as evidenced in both the 1817 Kashaya/Russian friendship pact and the later 1848 Ross census. A single "big chief," known as Toyon, emerged among the Kashaya Pomo to represent the entire group to the Russian administrators. It appears that the other chiefs were eventually ranked in a loosely defined hierarchy that delineated different roles in the political, ceremonial, and economic cycle of the group (see Bean and Theodoratus 1978:295).

The rise of a more centralized political system probably stemmed, in large part, from Russian colonial practices of working with a recognized leader of a native group. As Kennedy (1955:19) notes, "the adoption of a single chief gives evidence of the effect of the Russian centralization of authority." Other factors, however, may have also influenced this change. The greater size of the historic Kashaya community at Fort Ross may have stimulated a more hierarchical organization in order to control more effectively and to monitor information from a greater number of family units (e.g., Johnson 1973).

Russian colonization appears to have had less of an initial impact on other aspects of Kashaya culture. Our archaeological survey data suggest that protohistoric and historic residential sites are very comparable, containing similar kinds of lithic artifacts and faunal remains. Similar activities involving the production, use, and discard of lithics, the exploitation of mollusks, and the hunting of terrestrial game such as deer and elk transcend both Upper Emergent and historic times. Ethnohistorical accounts, ethnographic studies, and Kashaya oral tradition support these archaeological findings. Many Kashaya material items and subsistence practices continued to be employed into the late nineteenth and early twentieth centuries.

Some changes, of course, did take place during the initial period of European colonization. These changes include: a shift in the location of seafood processing activities; a decrease in the overall quantity of fire-cracked rocks that may indicate new methods of food preparation; and the presence of cow and sheep bones in surface assemblages indicating that new foods were being cooked and consumed. While obsidian continued to be obtained from the Napa Valley source, moldblown glass from alcoholic beverage bottles were being used as an alternative raw material source for manufacturing traditional native tool forms such as projectile points. Ceramics are present on the historic sites, but it is still unclear whether they were used as containers or as new sources of raw materials for manufacturing traditional native artifacts (such as ornaments).

The timing of the most significant changes in Kashaya Pomo material culture and subsistence practices appears to have taken place after the Russian occupation of Fort Ross. Some Mexican foods were adopted in the mid-nineteenth century, and changes in residential architecture were taking place at this time. It appears that earlier semi-subterranean house structures were modified or replaced by above ground, conical redwood houses. By the late nineteenth century, Euro-American frame houses and semi-subterranean dance houses were being incorporated into the Kashaya community. The tempo of cultural change increased greatly in the early to mid-twentieth century when a number of innovations were adopted as outlined in Kennedy (1955). Some of these innovations include: above ground dance houses; Euro-American household furnishings, appliances, and tools; and Euro-American store-bought foods.

According to ethnohistorical accounts, "ancient" religious rites including the "Old Ghost" ceremony and Kusku ceremony were practiced up until the early 1870s. Subsequently, with the advent of the Bole-Maru cult, the religious ceremonies of the Kashaya Pomo appear to have been transformed by maru dreamers. The development of the Bole-Maru Cult had implications for traditional gender roles in Kashaya culture. Beginning about 1912 women openly served as religious and political leaders of the group. Popular recreational activities, such as gambling, were banned at this time.

Changes in traditional Kashaya ceremonies in the nineteenth century were not stimulated by Euro-American religions, such as the Russian Orthodox Church. While a Russian Orthodox chapel was built at Fort Ross, and occasional services were held in the structure, there is little evidence that the church had any long-term influence on the Kashaya Pomo. Rather, innovations in Kashaya religion were adopted from fellow Native American prophets who were preaching an anti-white, anti-acculturation, revivalistic movement in the late nineteenth century. In the twentieth century, Euro-American religions, such as the Mormon church, began to have an impact on Kashaya religious practices.

NATIVE ACCULTURATION AT FORT ROSS

The preliminary results of our research, in contrast to recent studies of Spanish missions in California (e.g., Hoover 1989; Hornbeck 1989), suggest that the mercantile colony of Fort Ross can not be characterized as an institution of "directed historical change" in which one of its primary goals was to enculturate native workers in European ways. While the Russians were sometimes brutal in "recruiting" local natives as agricultural workers, the general policy of the Russian-American Company was not to produce Russian-Orthodox neophytes. Rather they allowed the native workers to live in their own communities and to observe their own customs, taboos, ceremonies, and subsistence practices. There is little evidence that the Russian administrators at Fort Ross attempted to regulate the native Californians' material culture or religious practices. In fact, Kostromitinov, LaPlace, and other Russian-American Company employees and visitors were amazed at how conservative the native Californian workers were in adopting European customs. Kostromitinov (1976:13[1830-38]) succinctly summarizes the apparent ambivalence the local natives exhibited towards European technology:

> Their inattention and indifference to everything goes to extremes. They look at our watches, burning-glasses, and mirrors, or listen to our music without attention and do not ask to know how and why all this is produced. Only such objects as might frighten them make some impression, but that probably more because of their timidity than thirst for knowledge.

However, while the native Californian workers

may have exhibited little outward interest in European technology, the European observers were amazed at the fluid movement of European/Asian goods within the native community. As agrarian laborers at Fort Ross, the Kashaya Pomo were paid "in kind" with tobacco, food, clothes, and other commodities. Almost every European who made observations about the native workers described their propensity to gamble away the goods exchanged to them by the Russians. The European observers did not directly identify any person or family who was accumulating a surplus of Euro/Asian goods in the community. The questions remains as to what happened to the nonlocal goods. Were they simply recirculated among the native workers at Fort Ross, or did some individuals, such as Chief Toyon, accumulate these goods in secret? Were the goods circulated to Pomo communities who resided in "the woods" some distance from Fort Ross?

The inter-ethnic community at Fort Ross served as a conduit of cultural exchange between the Kashaya Pomo, native Alaskans, Creoles, and Russians. Ethnohistorical texts demonstrate that marriages between Kashaya Pomo women and native Alaskan men were common in the Russian colony. Furthermore, Lutke (1989:278[1818]) observed that some native California women had learned to make Aleut handicrafts such as sewing the whale gut *kamleika* (waterproof outer garment). Yet our study suggests that the *long-term* impact of these inter-ethnic interactions was relatively ambiguous. Current data indicate that either the transfer of Aleut/Koniag technology, material culture, or maritime-oriented lifeways to the Kashaya Pomo happened rarely, or that this information was not transmitted to successive generations of Kashaya Pomo after the Russians and native Alaskans withdrew from Fort Ross in 1841.

The native Alaskans stationed at Fort Ross brought with them a highly sophisticated technology for exploiting a diverse range of maritime resources. Employing their *baidarkas*, harpoon arrows, darts, throwing sticks, and fishing equipment they hunted sea mammals in open waters and harvested deep-water ocean fishes. The adoption of this technology by the Kashaya Pomo would have allowed them to expand the breadth of marine resources that they harvested beyond the inter-tidal waters that they traditionally exploited. Yet ethnohistoric and ethnographic observations all concur that the Kashaya Pomo never adopted any kind of ocean-going vessels, and that their maritime subsistence practices remained relatively unchanged through much of the nineteenth and early twentieth centuries. The Kashaya Pomo continued to fish from rocks near the shore and to collect mollusks and plant foods in inter-tidal waters.

In fact, Gifford (1967) claims the Kashaya Pomo

did not hunt seals, sea lions, and sea otters. Loeb (1926) suggests that the coastal Pomo did hunt sea mammals, but that they relied on crude rafts of redwood driftwood and clubs as weapons. This technology contrasted dramatically with the hunting methods employed by the native Alaskans in open water. As Edwin Loeb (1926:169) observed:

> The frail rafts of the coast people were not strong enough to make the trip of a mile to a mile and a half in the open sea to the farthest sea rocks, so seals (piun, C) and sea lions (Ka pduka, water bear, C) were obtained after a long swim. Seal hunting was done at low tide during a certain month in the summer time. The hunters chosen were all good swimmers, and each took the precaution of abstaining from meat and women for a day before the enterprise, furthermore each man prayed to sharks before entering the water. The shark would be addressed after this manner: yal kanea nigum capeduia, C (You-two bite no O shark). The swimmers carried a special club (piun catco kale hai, C, seal hit for stick) for hitting seals, a straight club made of half green hard oak. When they landed at the rock they killed three, four or five seals by hitting them over the head while they slept; each swimmer then dragged back a seal or two attached to a rope.

In conclusion, the mercantile colonial system at Fort Ross allowed the Kashaya Pomo considerable latitude in choosing whether to adopt European and native Alaskans innovations. Evidently the Kashaya Pomo maintained a very conservative world view, selectively adopting only a relatively few traits (e.g., glass for making projectile points) that were integrated into Kashaya material culture. The fact that at least some native Californian women and their children reportedly went north to Alaska with their mates (although some returned home, see Jackson 1983), probably negated the influence of the most acculturated segment of the Kashaya population. The conservative, tenacious, pro-Indian ethos of the Kashaya Pomo continued to characterize the group during the late nineteenth and early twentieth centuries, and it is still very much in evidence among the Kashaya Pomo people today.

APPENDICES

APPENDIX 3.1

SELECTED PLANTS OCCURRING IN THE FORT ROSS REGION AND THEIR USES BY INDIGENOUS PEOPLE

Information compiled from: Barrett 1952, Baumhoff 1963, Chestnut 1902, DeLapp, Smith and Powell 1978, DeLapp and Powell 1979a, DeLapp and Powell 1979b, Gifford 1967, Goodrich et al. 1980, Kniffen 1939, Loeb 1926, Munz and Keck 1973

Scientific Name	Common Name	Use
Protista		
Phaeophyta	Algae	
	Brown Algae	
Postelsia palmiformis	Sea Palm (n)	Food (Barrett 1952:95, Gifford 1967:10, Stewart 1943:61)
Porphyra perforata	Nori (n)	Food (Barrett 1952:94, Chestnut 1902:299, Gifford 1967:10)
Nereocystis leutkeana	Bull Kelp (n)	Fishing Line (Loeb 1926), Food (Barrett 1952:94)
Plantae	Plants	
Sphenophyta	Horsetails	
Equisetaceae	Scouring Rushes	
Equisetum variegatum	Horsetail (n)	Abrasive (Chestnut 1902:304)
Equisetum telemateia	Giant Horsetail (n)	Abrasive, Cordage, Medicine (Goodrich et al. 1980)
Pterophyta	Ferns	
Ficiales	Broad-Leaved Ferns	
Pteridaceae	Bracken Ferns	
Pteridium aquilinum	Bracken Fern (n)	Basketry (Chestnut 1902:304, Gifford 1967:11)
Adiantum jordani	Maidenhair Fern (n)	Ear Piercing (Chestnut 1902:303, Loeb 1926)
Adiantum pedatum	Five-Finger Fern (n)	Basketry (Chestnut 1902:303), Ear Piercing (Gifford 1967:11)
Asplplaceae	Wood Ferns	
Polystichum munitum	Sword Fern (n)	Food Preparation (Gifford 1967:11)
Blechnaceae	Creeping Ferns	
Woodwardia radicans	Chain Fern (n)	Food Preparation (Gifford 1967:11)

Coniferophyta	Cone Bearers	
Coniferales	Conifers	
Pinaceae	Pine Family	
Abies grandis	Grand Fir (n)	
Pinus lambertiana	Sugar Pine (n)	Food (Barrett 1952:79, Chestnut 1902:307, Gifford 1967:11)
Pinus muricata	Bishop Pine (n)	Basketry (Gifford 1967:11), Medicine (Barrett 1952:80)
Pinus radiata	Monterey Pine (i)	
Pseudotsuga menziesii	Douglas Fir (n)	Basketry, Food (Chestnut 1902:309), Firewood (Gifford 1967:11)
Taxodiaceae	Redwood Family	
Sequoia sempervirens	Coast Redwood (n)	Construction, Medicine (Gifford 1967:11), Bowls (Loeb 1926), Clothing (Barrett 1952:292)
Cupressaceae	Cypress Family	
Cupressus pygmaea	Pigmy Cypress (n)	
Cupressus sargentii	Sargent Cypress (n)	
Taxales	Yew Family	
Taxaceae	Yews	
Taxus brevifolia	Western Yew (n)	Food (Barrett 1952:184, Chestnut 1902:305), Basketry, Bows (Gifford 1967:11, Loeb 1926)
Torreya californica	California Nutmeg (n)	Food (Barrett 1952:81), Medicine (Gifford 1967:11), Basketry (Kniffen 1939)
Anthophyta	Flowering Plants	
Dicotoledoneae	Dicots	
Lauraceae	Laurel Family	
Umbellaria californica	California Laurel (n)	Food, Medicine (Barrett 1952:78, Chestnut 1902:349, Gifford 1967:13, Loeb 1926)
Ranunculaceae	Crowsfoot Family	
Delphinium decorum	Larkspur (n)	
Delphinium luteum	Coast Larkspur (n)	
Ranunculus californicus	California Buttercup (n)	

Scientific Name	Common Name	Use
Geraniaceae	Geranium Family	
Geranium dissectum	Common Wild Geranium (i)	
Erodium botrys	Broad-Leaf Filaree (i)	
Erodium cicutarium	Red-Stem Filaree (i)	
Oxalidaceae	Wood-Sorrel Family	
Oxalis oregana	Redwood Sorrel (n)	Medicine (Gifford 1967:13)
Euphorbiaceae	Spurge Family	
Eremocarpus setigeris	Turkey Mullein (n)	Fish Poison (Barrett 1952:150, Chestnut 1902:321, Loeb 1926), Medicine (Chestnut 1902:363)
Violaceae	Violet Family	
Viola sempervirens	Evergreen Violet (n)	Pigment (Loeb 1926)
Papaveraceae	Poppy Family	
Eschscholtzia californica	California Poppy (n)	Medicine (Chestnut 1902:351)
Cruciferae	Mustard Family	
Brassica campestris	Field Mustard (i)	Food (Chestnut 1902:352)
Caryophyllaceae	Pink Family	
Cerastium viscosum	Mouse-Ear Chickweed (i)	
Silene gallica	Windmill Pink (i)	
Portulaceae	Purslane Family	
Lewisia nevadensis	Bitterroot (n)	
Polygonaceae	Buckwheat Family	
Eriogonum vimineum	Wild Buckwheat (n)	

Primulaceae — Primrose Family

Trientalis latifolia — Star Flower (n)

Anagallis arvensis — Pimpernel (i)

Plantaginaceae — Plantain Family

Plantago lanceolata — Buckhorn (i)

Plantago hookeriana — Hooker's Plantain (n)

Ericaceae — Heath Family

Ledum glandulosum — Coast Labrador Tea (n) — Beverage (Goodrich et al. 1980)

Rhododendron macrophyllum — Coast Rhododendron (n) — Decoration (cf. Gifford 1967:14)

Gaultheria shallon — Salal (n) — Food (Barrett 1952:84, Gifford 1967:14)

Arbutus menziesii — Madrone (n) — Medicine (Gifford 1967:14), Food (Barrett 1952, Chestnut 1902:374)

Arctostaphylos columbiana — Hairy Manzanita (n) — Medicine (Gifford 1967)

Arctostaphylos glandulosa — Eastwood Manzanita (n) — Food, Medicine (Gifford 1967:14, Kniffen 1939)

Arctostaphylos manzanita — Common Manzanita (n) — Food, Beverage, Medicine (Barrett 1952:81, Chestnut 1902:375), Bows (Loeb 1926)

Arctostaphylos nummularia — Fort Bragg Manzanita (n)

Arctostaphylos viscida — Whiteleaf Manzanita (n) — Food (Kniffen 1939)

Vaccinium ovatum — California Huckleberry (n) — Food (Chestnut 1902ZZ:377, Gifford 1967:15, Kniffen 1939, Loeb 1926)

Vaccinium parvifolium — Red Huckleberry (n) — Food (Barrett 1952:84, Kniffen 1939, Loeb 1926)

Asclepladaceae — Milkweed Family

Asclepias eriocarpa — Milkweed (n) — Cordage, Dye (Barrett 1952:446, Chestnut 1902:379, Loeb 1926), Clothing (Kniffen 1939)

Convolvulaceae — Morning-Glory Family

Convolvulus arvensis — Bindweed (i)

Polemoniaceae — Phlox Family

Navarretia pubescens — Downy Navaretia (n) — Medicine (Gifford 1967:15)

Linanthus bicolor — Phlox (n)

Scientific Name	Common Name	Use
Hydrophyllaceae	**Waterleaf Family**	
Eriodictyon californicum	Yerba Santa (n)	Medicine (Chestnut 1902:381)
Boraginaceae	**Borage Family**	
Myosotis versicolor	Forget-Me-Not (n)	
Plagiobothrys fulvus	Popcorn-Flower (n)	Food, Dye (Chestnut 1902:382)
Solanaceae	**Nightshade Family**	
Nicotiana bigelovii	Tobacco (n)	Smoking (Barrett 1952:116, Chestnut 1902:332, Gifford 1967))
Scrophulariaceae	**Figwort Family**	
Mimulus aurantiacus	N. Bush Monkeyflower (n)	Medicine (Goodrich et al. 1980)
Scrophularia californica	California Figwort (n)	Medicine (Gifford 1967:15)
Collinsia heterophylla	Chinese Houses (n)	
Digitalis purpurea	Foxglove (i)	
Orthocarpus faucibarbatus	Owl's Clover (n)	Decoration (Goodrich et al. 1980)
Synthyris reniformis	Snow Queen (n)	
Labiatidae	**Mint Family**	
Trichostema lanceolatum	Vinegarweed (n)	Fish Poison, Medicine (Chestnut 1902:385)
Satureja douglassii	Yerba Buena (n)	Medicine (Chestnut 1902:383, Gifford 1967:15)
Crassulaceae	**Stonecrop Family**	
Dudleya farinosa	Coast Live-Forever (n)	
Saxifragaceae	**Saxifrage Family**	
Whipplea modesta	Yerba De Selva (n)	
Ribes californicum	Hillside Gooseberry (n)	Food (Barrett 1952:83, Chestnut 1902:353)
Ribes sanguineum	Pink Flowering Currant (n)	Fire Drill (Loeb 1926), Food (Barrett 1952:84)
Rosaceae	**Rose Family**	

Scientific Name	Common Name	Uses (References)
Holodiscus discolor	Creambush (n)	Arrows (Gifford 1967:13)
Fragaria vesca	Wood Strawberry (n)	Food (Gifford 1967:13, Kniffen 1939, Loeb 1926)
Adenostema fasciculatum	Chamise (n)	
Cercocarpus betuloides	Mountain Mahogany (n)	Spears, Arrows, Tools (Barrett 1952, Chestnut 1902:354, Loeb 1926)
Rubus leucodermis	Western Black Raspberry (n)	Food (Barrett 1952:83, Chestnut 1902:355, Gifford 1967:13, Kniffen 1939, Loeb 1926)
Rubus parvifloris	Western Thimbleberry (n)	Food (Barrett 1952:83, Chestnut 1902:354, Gifford 1967:13, Kniffen 1939, Loeb 1926)
Rubus spectabilis	Salmonberry (n)	Food (Barrett 1952:84, Gifford 1967:13, Loeb 1926)
Rubus ursinus	California Blackberry (n)	Food (Barrett 1952:83, Chestnut 1902, Gifford 1967:13, Kniffen 1939, Loeb 1926)
Rosa gymnocarpa	Wood Rose (n)	Food (Barrett 1952)
Amelanchier alnifolia	Western Service Berry (n)	Arrows (Chestnut 1902:355, Loeb 1926), Medicine (Gifford 1967:13), Food (Barrett 1952:84)
Heteromeles arbutifolia	Toyon (n)	Food (Barrett 1952:84, Chestnut 1902:355, Gifford 1967:13, Loeb 1926)
Leguminosae	Pea Family	
Cercis occidentalis	Redbud (n)	Basketry (Chestnut 1902:356)
Lupinus arboreus	Beach Lupine (n)	Cordage (Gifford 1967:13)
Trifolium depauperatum	Dwarf Sack Clover (n)	Food (Kniffen 1939)
Trifolium microcephalum	Maiden Clover (n)	Food (Kniffen 1939)
Trifolium wormskioldii	Clover (n)	Medicine, Brushes (Gifford 1967:13, Loeb 1926), Food (Chestnut 1902:362, Kniffen 1939)
Lotus formosissimus	Trefoil (n)	
Lotus micranthus	Small-Flower Trefoil (n)	
Lathyrus sulphureus	Sulfur Pea (n)	
Betulaceae	Birch Family	
Corylus cornuta	Hazelnut (n)	Food (Barrett 1952:81, Chestnut 1902:333, Gifford 1967:12), Fish Traps (Kniffen 1939)
Alnus oregona	Red Alder (n)	Medicine (Goodrich et al. 1980)
Alnus rhombifolia	White Alder (n)	Medicine (Chestnut 1902:332, Gifford 1967:12)
Fagaceae	Beech Family	
Castanopsis chrysophylla	Giant Chinquapin (n)	Food (Barrett 1952:81, Gifford 1967:12)
Castanopsis c. Var. minor	Golden Chinquapin (n)	Food (Barrett 1952:81, Chestnut 1902:333, Gifford 1967:12))
Lithocarpus densiflora	Tan Oak (n)	Food (Barrett 1952:67, Chestnut 1902, Gifford 1967:12), Kniffen 1939)

Scientific Name	Common Name	Use
Quercus agrifolia	Coast Live Oak (n)	Food (Chestnut 1902, Gifford 1967:12)
Quercus chrysolepis	Canyon Live Oak (n)	Food (Barrett 1952:68, Baumhoff 1963, Chestnut 1902:342, Kniffen 1939)
Quercus douglasi	Blue Oak (n)	Food (Barrett 1952:68, Baumhoff 1963)
Quercus dumosa	Scrub Oak (n)	Food (Barrett 1952:68, Baumhoff 1963, Chestnut 1902:343)
Quercus durata	Leather Oak (n)	
Quercus garryana	Oregon Oak (n)	Food (Barrett 1952:68, Chestnut 1902:343, Gifford 1967, Kniffen 1939)
Quercus kellogii	California Black Oak (n)	Food (Barrett 1952:67, Chestnut 1902:342, Gifford 1967, Kniffen 1939)
Quercus lobata	Valley Oak (n)	Food (Barrett 1952:67, Baumhoff 1963, Chestnut 1902:343, Kniffen 1939)
Quercus wislizenii	Interior Live Oak (n)	Food (Baumhoff 1963)
Myrlcaceae	**Wax-Myrtle Family**	
Myrica californica	Pacific Wax-Myrtle (n)	
Salicaceae	**Willow Family**	
Salix scouleriana	Willow (n)	Basketry, Firewood (Gifford 1967:12), Arrows, Clothing (Barrett 1952:293)
Urtlcaceae	**Nettle Family**	
Urtica holosericea	Nettle (n)	Cordage (Loeb 1926), Medicine (Gifford 1967:13)
Onagraceae	**Evening-Primrose Family**	
Boisduvalia stricta	Primrose (n)	Food (Barrett 1952:86, Chestnut 1902:370)
Clarkia amoena	Farewell-To-Spring (n)	
Oenothera ovata	Evening-Primrose (n)	
Arlstolochlaceae	**Birthwort Family**	
Asarum caudatum	Wild-Ginger (n)	Medicine (Chestnut 1902:345, Gifford 1967:13)
Myrtaceae	**Myrtle Family**	
Eucalyptus globulus	Blue Gum (i)	
Vitaceae	**Grape Family**	
Vitis californica	California Grape (n)	Food, Cordage (Barrett 1952:82, Chestnut 1902:369, Gifford 1967:14, Loeb 1926)

Rhamnaceae — Buckthorn Family

Species	Common Name	Uses
Rhamnus californica	California Coffeeberry (n)	Medicine (Chestnut 1902:368, Gifford 1967:14)
Ceanothus foliosus	Wavyleaf Ceanothus (n)	
Ceanothus gloriosus	Navarro Ceanothus (n)	
Ceanothus incanus	Coast Whitethorn (n)	
Ceanothus integerrimus	Deerbrush (n)	Food, Basketry (Chestnut 1902:368)
Ceanothus jepsonii	Jepson Ceanothus (n)	
Ceanothus parryi	Parry Ceanothus (n)	
Ceanothus thyrsiflorus	Blueblossom (n)	Soap, Decoration (Goodrich et al. 1980)
Ceanothus velutinus	Varnishleaf Ceanothus (n)	

Loranthaceae — Mistletoe Family

Species	Common Name	Uses
Phoradendron flavescens	Mistletoe (n)	Medicine (Barrett 1952:69, Gifford 1967:13)

Hippocastanaceae — Buckeye Family

Species	Common Name	Uses
Aesculus californica	Buckeye (n)	Food, Fire (Barrett 1952:76), Fish Poison (Gifford 1967:14), Medicine (Chestnut 1902:366)

Aceraceae — Maple Family

Species	Common Name	Uses
Acer macrophyllum	Bigleaf Maple (n)	Gambling Staves (Gifford 1967:14), Basketry (Chestnut 1902:365)

Anacardiaceae — Sumac Family

Species	Common Name	Uses
Rhus diversiloba	Poison Oak (n)	Tattoo Pigment (Gifford 1967:14), Medicine (Chestnut 1902:364)

Araliaceae — Ginseng Family

Species	Common Name	Uses
Aralia californica	Elk Clover (n)	Medicine (Chestnut 1902:371, Gifford 1967:14)

Umbelliferae — Carrot Family

Species	Common Name	Uses
Sanicula bipinnatifida	Purple Sanicle (n)	
Sanicula crassicaulis	Gamble Weed (n)	
Torilis arvensis	Hedge Parsley (i)	
Osmorhiza chilensis	Mountain Sweet-Cicely (n)	
Daucus pusillus	Rattlesnake Weed (n)	
Heracleum lanatum	Cow Parsnip (n)	Food (Chestnut 1902:373), Medicine (Gifford 1967)
Angelica lucida	Angelica (n)	Medicine (Chestnut 1902:371, Gifford 1967, Loeb 1926)

Scientific Name	Common Name	Use
Eryngium armatum	Coyote Thistle (n)	Medicine (Goodrich et al. 1980)
Foeniculum vulgare	Sweet Fennel (i)	
Cornaceae	Dogwood Family	
Cornus nuttallii	Mountain Dogwood (n)	Arrows, Basketry (Kniffen 1939)
Garryaceae	Silktassel Family	
Garrya elliptica	Coast Silktassel (n)	Medicine (Goodrich et al. 1980)
Rubiaceae	Madder Family	
Galium californicum	California Bedstraw (n)	
Galium nuttallii	Climbing Bedstraw (n)	
Galium triflorum	Fragrant Bedstraw (n)	
Caprifoliaceae	Honeysuckle Family	
Sambucus callicarpa	Elderberry (n)	Medicine (Gifford 1967:15), Musical Instruments (Loeb 1926), Food (Barrett 1952:319)
Lonicera hispidula	California Honeysuckle (n)	Pipe Stems (Gifford 1967:15)
Lonicera involucrata	Twinberry (n)	
Dipsacaceae	Teasle Family	
Dipsacus fullonum	Fuller's Teasle (i)	
Cucurbitaceae	Gourd Family	
Marah fabaceus	Common Man-Root (n)	Fish Poison, Medicine (Gifford 1967:14, Loeb 1926)
Compositae	Sunflower Family	
Madia madioides	Tarweed (n)	Food (cf. Barrett 1952:87, Gifford 1967:15)
Eriophyllum lanatum	Eriophyllum (n)	
Baccharis pilularis	Coyote Brush (n)	
Achillea millefoleum	Common Yarrow (i)	
Artemisia californica	Coast Sagebrush (n)	
Artemisia vulgaris	Mugwort (n)	Medicine (Chestnut 1902:391)
Adenocaulon bicolor	Trail Plant (n)	Medicine (Gifford 1967:15)
Senecio sylvaticus	Ragwort (i)	

Species	Common Name	Use (References)
Gnaphalium pupureum	Cudweed (n)	
Cirsium vulgare	Bull Thistle (i)	
Carduus tenuifloris	Italian Thistle (i)	
Hypochoeris glabra	Smooth Cat's Ear (i)	
Hypochoeris radicata	Hairy Cat's Ear (i)	
Sonchus asper	Sow Thistle (i)	
Hieracium albiflorum	White-Flower Hawkweed (n)	
Monocotyledoneae	Monocots	
Liliaceae	Lily Family	
Xerophyllum tenax	Bear Grass (n)	Medicine (Goodrich et al. 1980)
Chlorogalum pomeridianum	Soap Plant (n)	Soap, Fish Poison (Gifford 1967:12, Loeb 1926), Adhesive (Barrett 1952:284)
Smilacena racemosa	Fat Solomon (n)	
Zigadenus fremontii	Star Lily (n)	
Lilium columbianum	Columbia Lily (n)	Food (Barrett 1952:89, Chestnut 1902:323, Goodrich et al. 1980)
Calochortus amabilis	Mariposa Lily (n)	
Trillium ovatum	Western Trillium (n)	Medicine (Chestnut 1902:329)
Typhaceae	Cat-Tail Family	
Typha latifolia	Soft Flag (n)	Food (Barrett 1952:92, Chestnut 1902:310)
Amaryllidaceae	Amaryllis Family	
Allium falcifolium	Wild Onion (n)	Food (Barrett 1952:89, Chestnut 1902:323, Kniffen 1939, Loeb 1926)
Brodiaea coronaria	Brodiaea Lily (n)	Food (Barrett 1952:90, Chestnut 1902:326)
Brodiaea laxa	Grass Nut (n)	Food (Barrett 1952:90, Gifford 1967:12, Kniffen 1939)
Iridaceae	Iris Family	
Iris douglasiana	Wild Iris (n)	Cordage (Chestnut 1902:330, Kniffen 1939)
Sisyrinchium bellum	Blue-Eyed Grass (n)	Medicine (Goodrich et al. 1980)
Orchidaceae	Orchid Family	
Corallorhiza maculata	Spotted Coral-Root (n)	Medicine (Chestnut 1902)

Scientific Name	Common Name	Use
Juncaceae	Rush Family	
Juncus balticus	Wire Rush (n)	Basketry (Gifford 1967)
Juncus bufonius	Toad Rush (n)	
Juncus effusus	Rush (n)	Basketry, Fish Traps (Chestnut 1902:318)
Cyperaceae	Sedge Family	
Carex sp.	Sedge (n)	Basketry (Barrett 1952, Gifford 1967:12)
Carex tumulicola	Sedge (n)	Basketry (cf. Gifford 1967:11)
Gramineae	Grasses	
Bromus diandrus	Ripgut (i)	
Bromus marginatus	Mountain Brome (n)	Food (Chestnut 1902:312)
Bromus orcuttianus	Orcutt Brome (n)	
Bromus mollis	Soft Chess (i)	
Bromus racemosus	Smooth Soft Chess (i)	
Bromus vulgaris	Bromegrass (n)	
Festuca californica	California Fescue (n)	
Festuca dertonensis	European Foxtail Fescue (i)	
Festuca myuros	False Foxtail Fescue (i)	
Festuca occidentalis	Western Fescue (n)	
Poa pratensis	Kentucky Bluegrass (n)	
Briza minor	Little Quakinggrass (i)	
Cynosurus echinatus	Annual Dogtail (i)	
Melica bulbosa	Oniongrass (n)	Food (Gifford 1967:11)
Melica Geyerii	Geyer's Oniongrass (n)	
Elymus triticoides	Rye Grass (n)	Food (Chestnut 1902:314)
Hordeum stebbinsi	Foxtail (n)	Food (Chestnut 1902:313)
Hordeum californicum	California Barley (n)	
Trisetum cernuum	Tall Trisetum (n)	
Deschampsia caespitosa	Pacific Hairgrass (n)	
Aira caryophyllea	Silver Hairgrass (i)	
Avena barbata	Slender Wild Oat (i)	
Avena fatua	Wild Oat (i)	Food (Chestnut 1902:311, Gifford 1967:11, Kniffen 1939)

Food (Gifford 1967:11)

Avena sativa	Cultivated Oat (i)
Holcus lanatus	Velvetgrass (i)
Danothia californica	California Oatgrass (n)
Calamagrostis bolanderii	Bolander's Reedgrass (n)
Calamagrostis nutkaensis	Pacific Reedgrass (n)
Agrostis exarata	Spike Redtop (n)
Gastridium ventricosum	Nitgrass (i)
Stipa pulchra	Purple Stipe (n)
Hierochloe occidentalis	California Sweetgrass (n)

Notes: Classification follows Munz and Keck (1973).

(n) = Native species   (i) = Introduced species

APPENDIX 3.2

SELECTED INVERTEBRATES OCCURRING IN THE FORT ROSS REGION AND
THEIR USES BY INDIGENOUS PEOPLE

Information compiled from: Barrett 1952; Garth and Tilden 1986; Gifford 1967; Loeb 1926; Pogue and Howell 1979; Ricketts et al. 1985; Smith and Carlton 1975; Stewart 1943.

SCIENTIFIC NAME	COMMON NAME	USE
Cnidaria	Coelenterates	
Anthozoa	Sea Anemones, Corals	
Actiniria	Sea Anemones	
Actiniidae	Sea Anemones	
Anthopleura elegantissima	Aggregated Anemone	Food (Gifford 1967:20; Loeb 1926:164; Stewart 1943:60)
Anthopleura xanthogrammica	Giant Green Anemone	Food (Gifford 1967:20; Loeb 1926:164; Stewart 1943:60)
Madreporaia	Stony Corals	
Balanophyllia elegans	Orange Cup Coral	
Annelida	Segmented Worms	
Oligochaeta	Earthworms	
Lumbrichus sp.	Angleworm	Food (cf. Barrett 1952:110; Loeb 1926:164)
Arthropoda	Arthropods	
Crustacea	Crustaceans	
Cirripedia	Barnacles	
Thoracica	Barnacles	
Balanus nubilis	Acorn Barnacle	Food (Loeb 1926:164)
Pollicipes polymerus	Goose Barnacle	Food (Gifford 1967:20; Stewart 1943:60)
Semibalanus cariossus	Barnacle	Food (Stewart 1943:60)
Decapoda	Shrimp, Lobster, and Crabs	
Caridea	Shrimps	Food (cf. Barrett 1952:107)
Palinura	Spiny Lobsters	Food (Loeb 1926:165)
Brachyura	True Crabs	Food (Gifford 1967:20; Loeb 1926:165; Stewart 1943:60)
Hemigraspus oregonensis	Oregon Shore Crab	
Hemigraspus nudus	Purple Shore Crab	
Cancer productus	Red Crab	
Pachygraspus crassipes	Striped Shore Crab	
Insecta	Insects	
Pterygota	Winged Insects	
Orthoptera	Grasshoppers	
Melanoplus devastator	Devastating Grasshopper	Food (cf. Barrett 1952:108; Loeb 1926:164)

SCIENTIFIC NAME	COMMON NAME	USE
Lepidoptera	Butterflies and Moths	
Dioptidae	Oak Moths	
Phryganidia californica	California Oak Moth	
Noctuidae	Millers and Cutworms	
Pseudaletia unipuncta	Armyworm	Food (Barrett 1952:108)
Lycaenidae	Blues, Coppers, and Hairstreaks	
Brephidium exilis	Pygmy Blue	
Plebejus acmon	Acmon Blue	
Strymon melinus	Common Hairstreak	
Danaidae	Milkweed Butterflies	
Danaus plexippus	Monarch	
Numphalidae	Brush-Footed Butterflies	
Nymphalis californica	California Tortoise-Shell	
Nymphalis antiopa	Mourning Cloak	
Polygonia faunus	Rustic Anglewing	
Vanessa atalanta	Red Admiral	
Vanessa cardui	Painted Lady	
Adelpha bredowi	California Sister	
Junonia coenia	Buckeye	
Pieridae	Whites and Sulphurs	
Anthocharis sara	Sara Orange-Tip	
Zerene eurydice	California Dogface	
Papilionidae	Swallowtails	
Papilio rutulus	Western Tiger Swallowtail	
Batthus philenor	Pipevine Swallowtail	
Coleoptera	Beetles	
Cicindelidae	Tiger Beetles	
Omus californicus	California Black Tiger Beetle	
Cicindela oregona	Oregon Tiger Beetle	
Elateridae	Click Beetles	
Alaus melanops	Eyed Elater	
Limonius sp.	Common Click Beetle	
Tenebrionidae	Darkling Ground Beetles	
Eleodes sp.	Stink Beetle	

SCIENTIFIC NAME	COMMON NAME	USE
Coccinellidae	Ladybird Beetles	
Hippodamia convergens	Convergent Ladybird	
Chilocorus orbis	Two-Stabbed Ladybeetle	
Cerambycidae	Longhorn beetles	
Rosalia funebris	Banded Alder Borer	
Chrysomelidae	Leaf beetles	
Diabrotica undecimpunctata	Western Spotted Cucumber Beetle	
Hymenoptera	Ants, Wasps, and Bees	
Cynipidae	Gall Wasps	
Andricus californicus	California Oak Gall Wasp	
Torymidae	Chalcid Wasps	
Torymus californicus	Oak Gall Chalcid	
Formicidae	Ants	
Camponotus laevigatus	Giant Carpenter Ant	
Vespidae	Yellowjackets	
Vespula pensylvanica	Yellowjacket	Food (Barrett 1952:109; Gifford 1967:20)
Vespula maculata	White Hornet	Food (Barrett 1952:109; Gifford 1967:20)
Arachnida	Spiders and Mites	
Aphonopelma	Tarantula	
Lycosa gulosa	Forest Wolf Spider	
Latrodectus mactans	Black Widow	
Dermacentor sp.	Tick	
Mollusca	Molluscs	
Cephalopoda	Octopi, Squids, and Cuttlefish	
Octopoda	Octopi	
Octopus dofleini	Pacific Giant Octopus	Food (Stewart 1943:61)
Polyplacophora	Chitons	
Acanthochitonidae	Giant Chitons	
Cryptochiton stelleri	Gumboot Chiton	Food (Gifford 1967:21; Stewart 1943:61)
Mopaliidae	Mossy Chitons	
Katharina tunicata	Black Katy	Food (Gifford 1967:21; Loeb 1926:61)
Gastropoda	Snails	
Archaeogastropoda	Limpets, Abalones, and Turbans	

Scientific Name	Common Name	Use
Haliotidae	Abalones	Decoration (Loeb 1926:155)
Haliotis cracherodoii	Black Abalone	Food (Gifford 1967:21; Stewart 1943:61)
Haliotis rufescens	Red Abalone	Food (Gifford 1967:21; Stewart 1943:61)
Haliotis kamtschatkana	Little Abalone	
Fissurellidae	Keyhole Limpets	
Diadora aspera	Rough Keyhole Limpet	Food (Stewart 1943:61)
Acmaeidae	True Limpets	
Acmaea mitra	White-Cap Limpet	Food (Gifford 1967:20)
Collisella pelta	Shield Limpet	Food (Gifford 1967:20)
Notoacmaea scutum	Pacific Plate Limpet	Food (Gifford 1967:20)
Collisella digitalis	Fingered Limpet	
Colisella scabra	Rough Limpet	
Trochidae	Top Shells	
Tegula funebrale	Black Tegula	Food (Gifford 1967:20)
Tegula brunnea	Brown Tegula	Food (Gifford 1967:20)
Calliostoma annulatum	Ringed Top Shell	
Turbinidae	Turban Shells	
Astrea undosa	Wavy Turban	
Astrea gibberosa	Red Turban	
Mesogastropoda	Snails	
Littorinidae	Periwinkles	
Littorina scutulata	Periwinkle	Food (Stewart 1943:61)
Neogasrtopoda	Whelks, Rock Snails, etc.	
Thaididae		
Thais canaliculata	Purple Dogwinkle	Food (Gifford 1967:20)
Thais emarginata	Emarginate Dogwinkle	
Thais lima	Pale Dogwinkle	
Olivella biplicata	Purple Olive Shell	Beads (Gifford 1967:20)
Bivalvia	Bivalves	
Mytiloida	Mussels et al.	
Mytilidae	Mussels	
Mytilus californianus	California Mussel	Food (Gifford 1967:21; Stewart 1943:60)
Pterioda	Scallops and Oysters	
Ostreidae	Oysters	
Ostrea lurida	Olympia Oyster	
Veneroida	Clams	

SCIENTIFIC NAME	COMMON NAME	USE
Veneridae	Hard-Shelled Clams	
Saxidomus nuttali	Common Washington Clam	Beads (Gifford 1967:21; Loeb 1926:176; Stewart 1943:61)
Saxidomus giganteus	Giant Washington Clam	
Cardiidae	Cockles	
Clinocardium nuttali	Heart Cockle	Food, Beads (Loeb 1926:176; Stewart 1943:61)
Echinodermata	Starfish, Sea Urchins, and Sea Cucumbers	
Echinoidea	Sea Urchins	
Strongylocentrotus purpuratus	Purple Urchin	Food (Gifford 1967:20; Stewart 1943:61)
Asterioda	Sea Stars	
Patiria miniata	Bat Star	
Pisaster ocreaceus	Ochre Sea Star	
Pychnopodia helianthoides	Sunflower Star	
Holothuroidea	Sea Cucumbers	Food (Stewart 1943:61)

Notes: Taxonomy follows Powell and Hogue (1979) for insects, and Smith and Carlton (1975) for marine invertebrates.

APPENDIX 3.3

SELECTED FISH OCCURRING IN THE FORT ROSS REGION AND
THEIR USES BY INDIGENOUS PEOPLE

Information compiled from: Barrett 1952; Baumhoff 1963; Gifford 1967; Kniffen 1939; Loeb 1926; Moyle 1976; Roedel 1953.

SCIENTIFIC NAME	COMMON NAME	USE
Agnatha	Jawless Fishes	
Petromyzontes	Lampreys	
Petromyzontidae	Lamprey Family	
Lampetra tridentata	Pacific Lamprey (a)	Food (Gifford 1967:20)
Chondrichthyes	Cartilagenous Fishes	
Lamniformes	Sharks	All sharks were considered sacred (Loeb 1926:169).
Hexanchidae	Cowsharks	
Notorynchus maculatum	Sevengill Cowshark (s)	
Lamnidae	Mackerel Sharks	
Isurus Glaucus	Bonito Shark (s)	
Carcharodon carcharias	White Shark (s)	
Lamna ditropis	Salmon Shark (s)	
Cetorhinidae	Basking Sharks	
Cetorhinus maximus	Basking Shark (s)	
Triakidae	Smoothhound Sharks	
Triakis semifasciata	Leopard Shark (s)	
Rhinotriakis henlei	Brown Smoothhound (s)	
Carcharhinidae	Requiem Sharks	
Galeorhinus zyopterus	Soupfin Shark (s)	
Squalidae	Dogfish	
Squalus acanthias	Dogfish (es)	
Rajiformes	Rays	
Rajidae	Skates	
Raja binoculata	Big Skate (s)	
Raja inornata	California Skate (s)	
Raja rhina	Longnose Skate (s)	
Myliobatidae	Eagle Rays	
Holorhinus californicus	Bat Ray (s)	
Osteichthys	Bony Fishes	

SCIENTIFIC NAME	COMMON NAME	USE
Acipenseridae	Sturgeon	
Acipenser transmontanus	White Sturgeon (a)	
Acipenser medirostris	Green Sturgeon (a)	
Clupeidae	Herring	
Clupea pallasi	Pacific Herring (s)	
Engraulidae	Anchovies	
Engraulis mordax	Northern Anchovy (s)	
Salmonidae	Salmon	
Oncorhyncus tshawytscha	Chinook Salmon (a)	Food (Barrett 1952:104; Loeb 1926:168)
Oncorhyncus kisutch	Coho Salmon (a)	Food (Barrett 1952:104; Loeb 1926:168)
Oncorhyncus gorbuscha	Humpback Salmon (a)	Food (Barrett 1952:104; Loeb 1926:168)
Salmo gairdneri	Steelhead/Rainbow Trout (a,f)	Food (Loeb 1926:168)
Osmeridae	Smelt	
Hypomesus pretiosus	Surf Smelt (s)	Food (Gifford 1967:19-20; Loeb 1926:168)
Spirinchus starksi	Night Smelt (s)	Food (Gifford 1967:19-20; Loeb 1926:168)
Cyprinidae	Minnows	Food (Kniffen 1939:363)
Lavinia exilicauda	Hitch (f)	
Hesperoleucus symmetricus	California Roach (f)	
Mylopharodon conocephalus	Hardhead (f)	
Ptychocheilus grandis	Sacramento Squawfish (f)	
Rhinichthys osculus	Speckled Dace (f)	
Catostomidae	Suckers	
Catostomus occidentalis	Sacramento Sucker (f)	Food (Kniffen 1939:363)
Gasterosteidae	Sticklebacks	
Gasterosteus aculeatus	Threespine Stickleback (f,a)	
Pleuronectidae	Righteyed Flounders	Food (Gifford 1967:19)
Hippoglossus stenolepis	Pacific Halibut (s)	
Eopsetta jordani	Petrale Sole (s)	
Parophrys vetulus	English Sole (s)	
Glyptocephalus zachirus	Rex Sole (s)	
Atherinidae	Silversides	
Atherinopsis californiensis	Jacksmelt (s)	Food (Gifford 1967:19-20; Loeb 1926:168)
Atherinops affinis	Topsmelt (s)	Food (Gifford 1967:19-20; Loeb 1926:168)
Carangidae	Jack	
Trachurus symmetricus	Pacific Jack Mackerel (s)	

SCIENTIFIC NAME	COMMON NAME	USE
Cyblidae	Spanish Mackerel	
Sarda lineolata	California Bonito (s)	
Sciaenidae	Croaker	
Seriphus politus	Queenfish/Sea Trout (s)	Food (Gifford 1967:19; Loeb 1926:168)
Cynoscion nobilis	White Seabass/Sea Trout (s)	Food (Gifford 1967:19; Loeb 1926:168)
Genyonemus lineatus	White Croaker (s)	
Embiotocidae	Surfperch	Food (Gifford 1967:19)
Hyperprosopon argenteum	Walleye Surfperch (s)	
Hypsurus caryi	Rainbow Surfperch (s)	
Rhacochilus vacca	Pile Perch (s)	
Embiotoca lateralis	Striped Seaperch (s)	
Brachyistius frenatus	Kelp Perch (s)	
Hysterocarpus traski	Tule Perch (f)	
Cymatogaster aggregata	Shiner Perch (s)	
Scorpaenidae	Rockfish	
Sebastodes flavidus	Yellowtail Rockfish (s)	
Sebastodes melanops	Black Rockfish (s)	
Sebastodes mystinus	Blue Rockfish (s)	
Sebastodes pinniger	Orange Rockfish (s)	
Sebastodes rosaceus	Rosy Rockfish (s)	
Anoplopomatidae	Sablefish	
Anoplopoma fimbria	Sablefish/Coalfish (s)	Food (Gifford 1967:19)
Ophiodontidae	Lingcod	
Ophiodon elongatus	Lingcod/Blue Cod (s)	Food (Gifford 1967:19)
Cottidae	Sculpins	
Leptocottus armatus	Staghorn Sculpin (s,f)	
Scorpaenichthys marmoratus	Cabezon/Bullhead (s)	Food (Gifford 1967:19; Loeb 1926:168)
Cottus asper	Prickly Sculpin (f,s)	
Cottus aleuticus	Coastrange Sculpin (f)	
Cottus gulosus	Riffle Sculpin (f)	
Hexagrammidae	Greenling	
Hexagrammos decagrammus	Kelp Greenling (s)	
Cebidichthyidae	Monkeyfaces	Food (Gifford 1967:19)
Cebidichthys violaceus	Monkeyface-Eel (s)	
Stichaeidae	Pricklebacks	Food (Gifford 1967:19)
Xiphister mucosus	Rock-Eel (s)	

Notes: Classifcation follows Moyle (1976) and Roedel (1953).

(s) = Salt water   (f) = Fresh water   (a) = Anadromous

A COMPLETE LIST OF REPTILES AND AMPHIBIANS OCCURRING IN THE FORT ROSS REGION

AND THEIR USES BY INDIGENOUS PEOPLE

Information Compiled From: Barrett 1952; Gifford 1967; Kniffen 1939; Loeb 1926; Stebbins 1985.

SCIENTIFIC NAME	COMMON NAME	USE
Amphibia	Amphibians	
Urodela	Salamanders & Newts	Medicine (Loeb 1926:327-8)
Ambystomatidae	Mole Salamanders	
Ambystoma gracile	Northwestern Salamander	
Dicamptodontidae	Giant Salamanders et al.	
Dicamptodon ensatus	Pacific Giant Salamander	
Rhyacotritonidae	Olympic Salamanders	
Rhyacotriton variegatus	Southern Olympic Salamander	
Salamandridae	Newts	
Taricha granulosa	Rough-Skinned Newt	
Taricha rivularis	Red-Bellied Newt	
Taricha torosa	Coast Range Newt	
Plethodontidae	Lungless Salamanders	
Ensatina eschscholtzi	Ensatina	
Batrachoseps attenuatus	California Slender Salamander	
Aneides flavipunctatus	Speckled Black Salamander	
Aneides lugubris	Arboreal Salamander	
Salientia	Frogs & Toads	Poisoning (Barrett 1952:105)
Bufonidae	Toads	
Bufo boreas	Western Toad	
Hylidae	Treefrogs	
Hyla regilla	Pacific Treefrog	
Ranidae	True Frogs	
Rana aurora	Red-Legged Frog	
Rana boylei	Foothill Yellow-Legged Frog	
Rana catesbiana	Bullfrog (i)	
Reptilia	Reptiles	
Testudines	Turtles	
Emydidae	Water Turtles	
Clemmys marmorata	Western Pond Turtle	Food (Barrett 1952:105; Gifford 1967:19; Loeb 1926:170)

Clemmys marmorata	Western Pond Turtle	Food (Barrett 1952:105; Gifford 1967:19; Loeb 1926:170)

SCIENTIFIC NAME	COMMON NAME	USE
Cheloniidae	Sea Turtles	
Lepidochelys olivacea	Pacific Ridley	
Dermochelidae	Leatherback Sea Turtles	
Dermochelys coriacea	Leatherback	
Squamata	Squamates	
Sauria	Lizards	Medicine (Loeb 1926;328)
		Poisoning (Ibid. p. 331)
Iguanidae	Iguanas et al.	
Sceloporus occidentalis	Western Fence Lizard	
Sceloporus graciosus	Sagebrush Lizard	
Scincidae	Skinks	
Eumeces skiltonianus	Western Skink	Charms (cf. Loeb 1926:310)
Anguidae	Alligator Lizards	
Elgaria multicarinata	Southern Alligator Lizard	
Elgaria coerulea	Northern Alligator Lizard	
Ophidia	Snakes	
Boidae	Boas	
Charina bottae	Rubber Boa	
Colubridae	Colubrids	
Diadophis punctatus	Ringneck Snake	
Contia tenuis	Sharp-Tailed Snake	
Coluber constictor	Yellow-Bellied Racer	
Masticophis lateralis	Striped Racer	
Pituophis melanoleucus	Gopher Snake	Charms (Loeb 1926:310), Medicine (Ibid. p. 325)
Lampropeltis getulus	Common Kingsnake	
Lampropeltis zonata	Mountain Kingsnake	
Thamnophis sirtalis	Common Garter Snake	
Thamnophis elegans	Western Terrestrial Garter Snake	
Thamnophis couchi	Western Aquatic Garter Snake	
Hypsiglena torquata	Night Snake	
Crotalidae	Rattlesnakes	
Crotalus viridis	Western Rattlesnake	Medicine (Loeb 1926:328)

Note: Classification follows Stebbins (1985).

    (i) = Introduced

APPENDIX 3.5

SELECTED BIRDS IN THE FORT ROSS REGION AND THEIR USES BY INDIGENOUS PEOPLES

Information compiled from: Barrett 1952; Gifford 1967; Grinnell and Miller 1944;
Kniffen 1939; Loeb 1926; Scott 1983.

SCIENTIFIC NAME	COMMON NAME	USE
Aves	Birds	
Gaviidae	Loons	
Gavia inmer	Common Loon	
Podicipedidae	Grebes	Food (Barrett 1952:101)
Aechmophorus occidentalis	Western Grebe	
Podiceps nigricolis	Eared Grebe	
Podylimbus podiceps	Pied-Billed Grebe	
Diomedeidae	Albatrosses	
Diomedea nigripes	Black-Footed Albatross	
Procellariidae	Shearwaters and Petrels	
Puffinus griseus	Sooty Shearwater	
Hydrobatidae	Storm-Petrels	
Oceanodroma leucorhoa	Leach's Storm-Petrel	
Oceanodroma homochroa	Ashy Storm-Petrel	
Pelecanidae	Pelicans	
Pelecanus occidentalis	Brown Pelican	Not Eaten, Medicine (Gifford 1967:18)
Phalacrocoracidae	Cormorants	
Phalacrocorax auritus	Double-Crested Cormorant	Not Eaten (Gifford 1967:18,19), Food (Loeb 1926:167)
Ardeidae	Herons	Food (Barrett 1952:101)
Botaurus lentiginosus	American Bittern	
Nycticorax nycticorax	Black-Crowned Night Heron	
Egretta thula	Snowy Egret	
Casmerodius albus	Great Egret	
Ardea herodias	Great Blue Heron	Bone Whistles (Gifford 1967:18)
Anatidae	Swans, Geese, and Ducks	Food (Barrett 1952:100)
Cygnus columbianus	Tundra Swan	
Branta Canadensis	Canada Goose	
Anas platyrhynchos	Mallard	Food, Feathers (Gifford 1967:18; Loeb 1926:156)
Anas streptera	Gadwall	
Anas crecca	Green-Winged Teal	
Anas americana	American Widgeon	

SCIENTIFIC NAME	COMMON NAME	USE
Anas acuta	Northern Pintail	
Anas clypeata	Northern Shoveler	
Anas cyanoptera	Cinnamon Teal	
Oxyura jamaicensis	Ruddy Duck	
Aix spinosa	Wood Duck	
Aythya valisineria	Canvasback	
Aythya americana	Redhead	
Aythya collaris	Ring-Necked Duck	
Aythya affinis	Lesser Scaup	
Melanitta nigra	Black Scoter	Not Eaten (Gifford 1967:19)
Melanitta perspicillata	Surf Scoter	Not Eaten (Gifford 1967:19)
Bucephala clangula	Common Goldeneye	
Bucephala albeola	Bufflehead	
Mergus merganser	Common Merganser	

Rallidae — Rails and Coots

Rallus limicola	Virginia Rail	
Porzana carolina	Sora	
Fulica americana	American Coot	Food (Gifford 1967:18)

Recurvirostridae — Stilts and Avocets

Recurvirostra americana	American Avocet	

Charadriidae — Plovers

Charadrius alexandrinus	Snowy plover	
Charadrius vociferus	Killdeer	Not Eaten (Barrett 1952:101)
Pluvialis squatarola	Black-Bellied Plover	

Scolopacidae — Sandpipers — Food (Barrett 1952:101)

Limosa fedoa	Marbled Godwit	
Numenius americanus	Long-Billed Curlew	
Numenius phaeopus	Whimbrel	
Catoptrophorus semipalmatus	Willet	Not Eaten (Gifford 1967:19)
Tringa melanoleuca	Greater Yellowlegs	
Actitis macularia	Spotted Sandpiper	
Limnodromus griseus	Short-Billed Dowitcher	
Limnodromus scolopaceus	Long-Billed Dowitcher	
Gallinago gallinago	Common Snipe	Poison (Loeb 1926:167)
Aphriza virgata	Surfbird	
Calidris alpina	Dunlin	
Calidris alba	Sanderling	
Calidris mauri	Western Sandpiper	
Calidris minutilla	Least Sandpiper	

Laridae — Gulls and Terns

Larus argentatus	Herring Gull	Food (Gifford 1967:18; Loeb 1926:167)

SCIENTIFIC NAME	COMMON NAME	USE
Larus occidentalis	Western Gull	Food (Giffrod 1967:18; Loeb 1926:167)
Larus glaucescens	Glaucous-Winged Gull	Food (Gifford 1967:18; Loeb 1926:167)
Sterna forsteri	Forster's Tern	
Alcidae	Auks and Puffins	
Uria aalge	Common Murre	
Cepphus columba	Pidgeon Guillemot	
Brachyramphus marmoratus	Marbled Murrelet	
Ptychoramphus aleuticus	Cassin's Auklet	
Cerorhinca monocerata	Rhinoceros Auklet	
Fratercula cirrhata	Tufted Puffin	
Cathartidae	Vultures	
Cathartes aura	Turkey Vulture	Feathers (Gifford 1967:18; Loeb 1926:154)
Accipitridae	Hawks and Eagles	Not Eaten (Barrett 1952:102)
Aquila chrysaetos	Golden Eagle	Feathers, Whistles (Barrett 1952:102; Loeb 1926:167)
Circus cyaneus	Northern Harrier	
Accipiter striatus	Sharp-Shinned Hawk	
Accipiter cooperi	Cooper's Hawk	Not Eaten (Gifford 1967:19)
Buteo jamaicensis	Red-Tailed Hawk	Feathers (Gifford 1967:18)
Buteo lagopus	Rough-Legged Hawk	
Pandion haliaetus	Osprey	Feathers (Gifford 1967:18)
Falconidae	Falcons	
Falco sparverius	American Kestrel	Not Eaten (Gifford 1967:19)
Falco peregrinus	Peregrine Falcon	
Phasianidae	Grouse	
Dendragapus obscurus	Blue Grouse	Food (Gifford 1967:18; Loeb 1926:167)
Callipepla californica	California Quail	Food, Plumes (Gifford 1967:18; Loeb 1926:155,165)
Meleagris gallopavo	Wild Turkey	
Columbidae	Pigeons and Doves	
Columba fasciata	Band-Tailed Pigeon	Food (Gifford 1967:17; Loeb 1926:166)
Zenaida macroura	Mourning Dove	Food (Gifford 1967:18)
Tytonidae	Barn Owls	
Tyto alba	Common Barn-Owl	
Strigidae	Owls	
Asio flammeus	Short-Eared Owl	
Asio otus	Long-Eared Owl	
Bubo virginianus	Great Horned Owl	Bad Omen, Medicine (Gifford 1967:18; Loeb 1926:167)
Strix occidentalis	Spotted Owl	
Otus kennicottii	Western Screech Owl	Bad Omen (Gifford 1967:18)
Glaucidium gnoma	Northern Pygmy-Owl	

SCIENTIFIC NAME	COMMON NAME	USE
Aegolius acadicus	Northern Saw-Whet Owl	
Athene cunicularia	Burrowing Owl	
Caprimulgidae	Nightjars	
Phalaenoptilus nuttalii	Common Poorwill	
Chordeiles minor	Common Nighthawk	
Apodidae	Swifts	
Chaetura vauxi	Vaux's Swift	
Trochilidae	Hummingbirds	Protected (Loeb 1926:167)
Calypte anna	Anna's Hummingbird	
Selasphorus rufus	Rufous Hummingbird	
Selasphorus sasin	Allen's Hummingbird	
Alcedinidae	Kingfishers	
Ceryle alcyon	Belted Kingfisher	Not Killed (Gifford 1967:19)
Picidae	Woodepeckers	
Colaptes auratus	Northern Flicker	Food, Feathers (Gifford 1967:19; Loeb 1926:155)
Melanerpes formicivorus	Acorn Woodpecker	
Picoides albolarvatus	White-Headed Woodpecker	
Melanerpes lewis	Lewis' Woodpecker	
Sphyrapicus ruber	Red-Breasted Sapsucker	Feathers (Barrett 1952:99; Loeb 1926:155)
Picoides pubescens	Downy Woodpecker	
Picoides villosus	Hairy Woodpecker	
Drycopus pileatus	Pileated Woodpecker	Bad Luck (Gifford 1967:19)
Tyrannidae	Tyrant Flycatchers	
Tyrannus verticalis	Western Kingbird	
Myiarchus cinerascens	Ash-Throated Flycatcher	
Contopus borealis	Olive-Sided Flycatcher	
Contopus sordidulus	Western Wood-Peewee	
Sayornis nigricans	Black Phoebe	
Sayornis saya	Say's Phoebe	
Empidonax difficilis	Western Flycatcher	
Alaudidae	Larks	
Eremophila alpestris	Horned Lark	Food (Loeb 1926:166)
Hirundinidae	Swallows	
Tachycineta thalassina	Violet-Green Swallow	
Progne subis	Purple Martin	
Stelgidopteryx serripennis	Rough-Winged Swallow	
Hirundo pyrrhonota	Cliff Swallow	
Hirundo rustica	Barn Swallow	Not Eaten (Gifford 1967:19)

SCIENTIFIC NAME	COMMON NAME	USE
Corvidae	Jays, Crows, and Magpies	
Aphelocoma coerulescens	Scrub Jay	Not Eaten (Barrett 1952:99; Gifford 1967:19)
Cyanocitta stelleri	Steller's Jay	Food (Barrett 1952:99; Gifford 1967:19; Loeb 1926:166)
Corvus brachyrhyncos	American Crow	Feathers (Loeb 1926:167) Not Eaten (Gifford 1967:19)
Corvus Corax	Common Raven	Feathers (Barrett 1952:102)
Muscicapidae	Wrentits	
Chamea fasciata	Wrentit	
Paridae	Titmice and Chickadees	
Parus inornatus	Plain Titmouse	
Parus rufescens	Chestnut-Backed Chickadee	
Aegithalidae	Bushtits	
Psaltriparus minimus	Bushtit	
Certhiidae	Creepers	
Certhia americana	Brown Creeper	
Sittidae	Nuthatches	
Sitta carolinensis	White-breasted Nuthatch	
Sitta canadensis	Red-Breasted Nuthatch	
Troglodytidae	Wrens	
Troglodytes aedon	House Wren	
Troglodytes troglodytes	Winter Wren	
Thryomanes bewickii	Bewick's Wren	
Cistothorus palustris	Marsh Wren	
Salpinctes obsoletus	Rock Wren	
Muscicapidae	Thrushes	
Regulus satrapa	Golden-Crowned Kinglet	
Regulus calendula	Ruby-Crowned Kinglet	
Polioptila caerulea	Blue-Gray Gnatcatcher	
Sialia mexicana	Western Bluebird	Not Eaten (Gifford 1967:19)
Myadestes townsendii	Townsend's Solitaire	
Catharus ustulatus	Swainson's Thrush	
Catharus guttatus	Hermit Thrush	
Ixoreus naevius	Varied Thrush	Food (Gifford 1967:19)
Turdus migratorius	American Robin	Food (Gifford 1967:19; Loeb 1926:166)
Laniidae	Shrikes	
Lanius ludovicianus	Loggerhead Shrike	
Mimidae	Mimic Thrushes	
Mimus polyglottos	Northern Mockingbird	
Toxostoma redivivum	California Thrasher	

Scientific Name	Common Name	Use
Motacillidae	Pipits	
Anthus spinoletta	Water Pipit	
Cinclidae	Dippers	
Cinclus mexicanus	American Dipper	
Bombycillidae	Waxwings	
Bombycilla garrulus	Bohemian Waxwing	
Bombycilla cedrorum	Cedar Waxwing	
Vireonidae	Vireos	
Vireo huttoni	Hutton's Vireo	
Vireo gilvus	Warbling Vireo	
Emberizidae	Warblers and Sparrows	
Parulinae	Sparrows	
Vermivora celate	Orange-Crowned Warbler	
Dendroica coronata	Yellow-Rumped Warbler	
Dendroica townsendi	Townsend's Warbler	
Wilsonia pusilla	Wilson's Warbler	
Geothlypis trichas	Common Yellowthroat	
Cardinalinae	Grosbeaks and Buntings	
Pheucticus melanocephalus	Black-Headed Grosbeak	
Passerina amoena	Lazuli Bunting	
Pipilo erythrophthalmus	Rufous-Sided Towhee	
Pipilo fuscus	Brown Towhee	
Emberizinae	Sparrows	Food (Loeb 1926:166)
Passerculus sandwichensis	Savannah Sparrow	
Melospiza melodia	Song Sparrow	
Chondestes grammacus	Lark Sparrow	
Junco hyemalis	Dark-Eyed Junco	
Zonotrichia leucophrys	White-Crowned Sparrow	
Zonotrichia atricapilla	Golden-Crowned Sparrow	
Passerella iliaca	Fox Sparrow	
Icterinae	Blackbirds and Orioles	
Sturnella neglecta	Western Meadowlark	Food, Feathers (Gifford 1967:19; Loeb 1926:166)
Agelaius phoeniceus	Red-Winged Blackbird	
Agelaius tricolor	Tricolored Blackbird	
Euphagus cyanocephalus	Brewer's Blackbird	Not Eaten (Gifford 1967:19) Food (Barrett 1952:103)
Molothrus ater	Brown-Headed Cowbird	
Icterus galbula	Northern Oriole	Feathers (Loeb 1926:156)
Icterus cucullatus	Hooded Oriole	Feathers (Loeb 1926:156)
Piranga ludoviciana	Western Tanager	

SCIENTIFIC NAME	COMMON NAME	USE
Fringillidae	Finches	
Carduelis pinus	Pine Siskin	
Carduelis tristis	American Goldfinch	
Carduelis psaltria	Lesser Goldfinch	
Caprodacus purpureus	Purple Finch	
Caprodacus mexicanus	House Finch	

Note: Taxonomy follows Scott 1983.

APPENDIX 3.6

A COMPLETE LIST OF MAMMALS OCCURRING IN THE FORT ROSS REGION AND
THEIR USES BY INDIGENOUS PEOPLE

Information Compiled From: Barrett 1952; Gifford 1967; Hall 1981; Jameson and Peeters 1988; Kniffen 1939; Loeb 1926.

SCIENTIFIC NAME	COMMON NAME	USE
Mammalia	Mammals	
Marsupalia	Marsupials	
Didelphidae	Opossums	
Didelphis virginianus	Opossum (i)	
Insectivora	Insectivores	
Soricidae	Shrews	
Sorex bendirii	Marsh Shrew	
Sorex pacificus	Pacific Shrew	
Sorex trowbridgii	Trowbridge's Shrew	
Sorex vagrans	Vagrant Shrew	
Talpidae	Moles	
Neurotrichus gibbsii	Shrew Mole	
Scapanus orarius	Coast Mole	Skin (Gifford 1967:17)
Scapanus latimanus	Broad-Footed Mole	Skin (Gifford 1967:17)
Chiroptera	Bats	
Vespertilionidae	Vesper Bats	
Antrozous pallidus	Pallid Bat	
Eptesicus fuscus	Big Brown Bat	
Lasionycteris noctivagans	Silver-Haired Bat	
Lasiurus borealis	Red Bat	
Lasiurus cinereus	Hoary Bat	
Myotis californicus	California Bat	
Myotis evotis	Long-Eared Bat	
Myotis lucifugus	Little Brown Bat	
Myotis thysanodes	Fringed Bat	
Myotis volans	Long-Legged Bat	
Myotis Yumanensis	Yuma Bat	
Pipistrellus hesperus	Western Pipistrelle	
Plecotus townsendii	Townsend's Long-Eared Bat	
Molossidae	Free-Tailed Bats	
Tadarida brasiliensis	Guano Bat	
Lagomorpha	Rabbits et al.	
Leporidae	Rabbits	
Lepus californicus	Jackrabbit	Food, Skin (Gifford 1967:17; Loeb 1926:170)
Sylvilagus bachmani	Brush Rabbit	Food, Skin (Gifford 1967:17; Loeb 1926:154,171)

SCIENTIFIC NAME	COMMON NAME	USE
Rodentia	Rodents	
Aplodontidae	Mountain Beavers	
Aplodontia rufa	Mountain Beaver	
Sciuridae	Squirrels	
Spermophilus beecheyi	California Ground Squirrel	Food (Gifford 1967:17; Loeb 1926:170)
Sciurus griseus	Western Gray Squirrel	Food, Skin, Bone (Gifford 1967:17; Loeb 1926:170)
Sciurus niger	Fox Squirrel (i)	Food (Gifford 1967:17)
Tamiasciurus douglasii	Chickaree	
Tamias sonomae	Sonoma Chipmunk	
Tamias ochrogenys	Redwood Chipmunk	
Geomyidae	Pocket Gophers	
Thomomys bottae	Botta's Pocket Gopher	Food (Gifford 1967:17; Loeb 1926:170)
Heteromyidae	Kangaroo Rats	
Dipodomys californicus	California Kangaroo Rat	
Muridae	Mice & Rats	
Cricetinae	Deer Mice & Wood Rats	
Neotoma fuscipes	Dusky-Footed Wood Rat	Food (Gifford 1967:17; Loeb 1926:170)
Peromyscus boylii	Brush Mouse	
Peromyscus truei	Pinyon Mouse	
Peromyscus maniculatus	Deer Mouse	
Reithrodontomys megalotis	Harvest Mouse	
Microtinae	Voles	
Arborimus longicaudus	Red Tree Vole	
Clethrionomys californicus	California Red-Backed Vole	
Microtus californicus	California Meadow Vole	Food (Gifford 1967:17; Loeb 1926:170)
Murinae	Old World Rats & Mice	
Rattus rattus	Roof Rat (i)	
Zapodidae	Jumping Mice	
Zapus trinotatus	Pacific Jumping Mouse	
Erithizontidae	Porcupines	
Erethizon dorsatum	Porcupine	
Cetacea	Cetaceans	
Odontoceti	Toothed Whales	
Delphinidae	Dolphins	
Lagenorhynchus obliquidens	White-Sided Dolphin	
Orcinus orca	Killer Whale	
Stenella coeruleoalba	Blue and White Dolphin	
Tursiops truncatus	Bottlenosed Dolphin	

SCIENTIFIC NAME	COMMON NAME	USE
Phocoenidae	Porpoises	
Phocoena phocoena	Harbor Porpoise	
Phocoenoides dalli	Dall's Porpoise	
Physeteridae	Sperm Whales	
Kogia breviceps	Pigmy Sperm Whale	
Kogia simus	Dwarf sperm Whale	
Physeter macrocephalus	Sperm Whale	
Ziphiidae	Beaked Whales	
Berardius bairdii	Baird's Beaked Whale	
Mesoplodon stejnegeri	Stejneger's Beaked Whale	
Ziphius cavirostris	Cuvier's Beaked Whale	
Mysticeti	Baleen Whales	
Eschrichtidae	Gray Whales	
Eschrichtus robustus	Gray Whale	Medicine (cf. Gifford 1967:17)
Balaenopteridae	Rorquals	
Balaenoptera acutorostrata	Minke Whale	
Balaenoptera borealis	Sei Whale	
Balaenoptera musculus	Blue Whale	
Balaenoptera physalus	Fin Whale	
Megaptera noveangliae	Humpback Whale	
Balaenidae	Right Whales	
Balaena glacialis	Northern Right Whale	
Carnivora	Carnivores	
Canidae	Dogs et al.	
Canis familiaris	Domestic Dog (i)	
Canis latrans	Coyote	Taboo (Barrett 1952:112)
Canis lupus	Wolf (e)	Taboo (Barrett 1952:112)
Urocyon cinereoargentus	Gray Fox	Killed when rabid (Gifford 1967:16), Taboo (Barrett 1952:112)
Ursidae	Bears	
Ursus arctos	Grizzly Bear (e)	Food, Hides (Gifford 1967:16; Loeb 1926:171)
Ursus americanus	Black Bear	Food, Hides (Gifford 1967:16; Loeb 1926:171)
Procyonidae	Raccoons and Ringtails	
Bassariscus astutus	Ringtail	Skin (Gifford 1967:16)
Procyon lotor	Raccoon	Food (Gifford 1967:16; Loeb 1926:171), Taboo (Barrett 1952:112)
Mustelidae	Skunks and Weasels	
Enhydra lutris	Sea Otter (e)	Skin (Loeb 1926:154), Food (Loeb 1926:170)
Lutra canadensis	River Otter	Food (Loeb 1926:170)

SCIENTIFIC NAME	COMMON NAME	USE
Martes americana	Marten	
Martes pennanti	Fisher	Skin (Gifford 1967:16)
Mephitis mephitis	Striped Skunk	Medicine (Gifford 1967:16), Food (Loeb 1926:170)
Spilogale putorius	Spotted Skunk	Both Skunks Taboo (Barrett 1952:112)
Mustela erminea	Ermine	
Mustela frenata	Long-Tailed Weasel	
Mustela vison	Mink	Skin (Gifford 1967:16), Food (Loeb 1926:170), Taboo (Barrett 1952)
Taxidea taxus	Badger	
Felidae	Cats	
Felis catus	Domestic Cat (i)	
Felis concolor	Mountain Lion	Food, Hides (Gifford 1967:17; Loeb 1926:171), Taboo (Barrett 1952)
Lynx rufus	Bobcat	Hides (Gifford 1967:17; Loeb 1926:154), Food (Loeb 1926:170)
Pinnipedia	Seals	
Otariidae	Eared Seals	
Arctocephalus townsendi	Guadelupe Fur Seal	
Callhorinus ursinus	Northern Fur Seal	
Eumetopias jubatus	Steller's Sea Lion	
Zalophus californanus	California Sea Lion	Food (Loeb 1926:169)
Phocidae	Seals	
Mirounga angustirostris	Northern Elephant Seal	
Phoca vitulina	Harbor Seal	Food (Gifford 1967:17), Skin (Loeb 1926:169)
Perissodactyla	Horses et al.	
Equidae	Horses	
Equus caballus	Horse (i)	
Artiodactyla	Pigs, Cattle, Sheep & Deer	
Suidae	Pigs	
Sus scrofa	Pig (i)	
Cervidae	Deer	
Cervus elaphus	Roosevelt Elk (e)	Food, Hides, Antlers (Gifford 1967:16; Loeb 1926:170)
Odocoileus hemionus	Mule Deer	Food, Hides, Sinew, (Gifford 1967:16) Bone (Loeb 1926:156-7)
Bovidae	Cattle, Sheep & Goats	
Bos taurus	Cow (i)	
Ovis aries	Sheep (i)	
Capra hircus	Goat (i)	

Notes: Classification follows Hall and Kelson (1959) and Jameson and Peeters (1988).

(i): Introduced   (e): Locally extirpated

APPENDIX 4.1

FORT ROSS REGION DATA BASE

Site	SM	RS	Hab	LS	O	C	MF-O	S	G	Sc	Area-m2	Loc
C-283				x			x					h
C-284				x			x					h
C-285				x			x					h
C-286				x					x			h
C-287				x				x				h
C-288				x				x				h
C-403					x		x					h
C-404					x		x					h
C-405					x		x					h
C-406					x		x					h
C-407					x		x					h
C-408					x		x					h
C-409					x		x					h
C-410					x		x					h
C-411					x		x					h
C-412					x		x					h
C-413					x		x					h
C-414					x		x					h
C-415					x		x					h
C-416					x		x					h
C-417					x			x				h
C-418					x			x				h
C-419					x			x				h
C-420					x			x				h
C-421					x		x					h
C-444					x		x					h
C-460					x			x				h
C-796									x			r
C-797									x			r

KEY

SITE TYPES

  SM = shell middens   RS = rock shelters   Hab = habitation sites
  LS = lithic scatters   O = other site types

ENVIRONMENTAL ZONES

  C = conifers   MF-O = mixed forest-with oak   S = savannah
  G = grassland   Sc = scrub

SITE LOCATIONS (LOC)

  c = coast   r = ridge   h = hinterland

Site	SM	RS	Hab	LS	O	C	MF-O	S	G	Sc	Area-m2	Loc
C-903			x						x			c
C-905			x						x			h
MEN-789	x		x						x		2600	c
MEN-1628	x								x		200	c
MEN-2019				x			x				225	h
MEN-2135		x		x			x				4000	h
MEN-2136		x							x		16000	h
MEN-2203			x				x				400	h
MEN-2233			x				x				50000	h
MEN-2270				x	x		x				13500	h
MEN-2303	x						x				1750	h
MEN-2304				x			x				900	h
SON-162	x								x		139	c
SON-163	x								x		139	c
SON-164	x								x		254	c
SON-165	x							x			372	c
SON-166	x								x			c
SON-167	x							x			116	c
SON-168	x								x		139	c
SON-169	x								x		117	c
SON-170	x								x		254	c
SON-171	x									x	74	c
SON-172	x									x	70	c
SON-173	x								x		1400	c
SON-174	x		x						x		346	c
SON-175	x		x						x		18241	c
SON-176			x						x			r
SON-177	x		x						x			r
SON-178	x		x					x				r
SON-179	x		x				x					r
SON-180			x						x			r
SON-181	x		x						x		1393	r
SON-182	x		x				x				3716	h
SON-183	x		x						x		929	h
SON-184			x						x			h
SON-185			x					x			292	h
SON-186	x		x				x				50	h
SON-187/H				x				x				h
SON-188	x								x			c
SON-189	x		x									h
SON-191	x					x					182	c
SON-192	x		x					x			502	c
SON-193	x						x				348	c
SON-194	x	x				x					56	c
SON-195	x	x				x					37	c
SON-196							x					c

Site	SM	RS	Hab	LS	Q	C	MF-Q	S	G	Sc	Area-m2	Loc
SON-197	x	x				x					348	c
SON-228				x					x		4536	c
SON-229				x					x		58	c
SON-230	x								x		46	c
SON-231	x		x						x		21	c
SON-232	x						x				46	c
SON-233	x								x		89	c
SON-234									x			c
SON-235	x						x				46	c
SON-236	x								x		583	c
SON-237									x		46	c
SON-238	x								x		279	c
SON-239	x						x				465	c
SON-240	x						x				182	c
SON-241	x		x				x				1760	c
SON-242	x						x				174	c
SON-243	x						x				182	c
SON-244							x				232	c
SON-245							x				244	c
SON-246	x						x				46	c
SON-247	x								x		410	c
SON-248	x								x		89	c
SON-249	x								x		174	c
SON-250	x								x		348	c
SON-251	x								x		114	c
SON-252	x								x		180	c
SON-253	x								x		3	c
SON-254	x		x				x				900	c
SON-255	x								x		81	c
SON-256	x								x		697	c
SON-257	x						x				81	c
SON-258	x								x		66	c
SON-259	x					x					29	c
SON-260	x						x				697	c
SON-261									x			c
SON-262	x								x		29	c
SON-263	x		x						x		29	c
SON-264	x					x					465	c
SON-271			x				x				2090	c
SON-342	x								x		5900	c
SON-343	x								x		182	c
SON-344								x				c
SON-345	x	x	x						x		46	c
SON-346	x								x		23	c
SON-347	x								x		150	c
SON-348/H	x	x	x						x		68000	c

Site	SM	RS	Hab	LS	O	C	MF-O	S	G	Sc	Area-m2	Loc
SON-350	x		x						x		748	c
SON-352	x								x		56	c
SON-353	x								x		1350	c
SON-354	x								x		690	c
SON-355	x								x		2240	c
SON-356	x								x		1950	c
SON-357					x			x				c
SON-360	x								x			c
SON-361	x							x				c
SON-365/H	x				x				x		3200	c
SON-366	x								x			c
SON-368	x								x		105	r
SON-369	x		x						x		75	r
SON-373					x				x			h
SON-384			x						x			h
SON-385			x				x					r
SON-386									x			r
SON-403	x	x							x		33	c
SON-453	x								x		690	c
SON-458	x	x							x		35	c
SON-459				x					x		348	c
SON-460	x								x		232	c
SON-462	x							x			261	c
SON-463	x		x					x			650	c
SON-464	x		x					x			400	c
SON-465	x		x						x		160	c
SON-467	x								x		465	c
SON-471				x					x		1394	c
SON-472				x					x			c
SON-473				x					x		279	c
SON-474				x					x			c
SON-475	x		x						x		111	c
SON-476				x					x			c
SON-477	x								x		182	c
SON-478				x					x		1452	c
SON-479				x					x		182	c
SON-480	x		x						x		7	c
SON-481	x								x		30	c
SON-482	x		x						x		186	c
SON-483				x					x		348	c
SON-484				x			x					c
SON-485				x	x				x		929	c
SON-486				x					x		523	c
SON-489	x		x						x		1024	c
SON-490			x						x		6070	h

Site	SM	RS	Hab	LS	O	C	MF-O	S	G	Sc	Area-m2	Loc
SON-491	x								x		232	c
SON-492	x								x		84	c
SON-493	x		x						x		465	c
SON-494	x		x						x		66	c
SON-495	x		x						x		1394	c
SON-496	x		x						x		46	c
SON-497	x								x		465	c
SON-498	x		x						x		9	c
SON-499				x					x			c
SON-500			x						x		372	c
SON-501	x		x						x		111	c
SON-502	x								x		58	c
SON-503	x		x						x		74	c
SON-504			x	x					x		1045	c
SON-505	x		x				x				697	c
SON-506	x		x						x		130	c
SON-507				x					x		1394	c
SON-508	x								x		595	c
SON-509				x			x					c
SON-511	x		x						x		209	c
SON-512	x		x				x				1338	c
SON-513	x		x						x		523	c
SON-514					x		x				2	c
SON-520/H	x								x		900	c
SON-526/H				x	x		x				4375	h
SON-527/H			x	x			x				750	h
SON-528				x				x			1250	h
SON-529				x				x			1250	h
SON-530				x			x				37500	h
SON-537				x				x			182	h
SON-538				x				x			410	h
SON-539	x		x			x					8100	h
SON-540	x					x					5400	h
SON-541	x								x		90	c
SON-659	x								x		1875	r
SON-663				x			x				120	h
SON-664				x			x				100	h
SON-670	x			x	x	x					3750	c
SON-687	x								x		450	c
SON-688	x								x		1536	c
SON-689	x								x			c
SON-690	x								x		900	c
SON-691	x								x			c
SON-697	x								x		1000	c
SON-698	x								x		100	c
SON-732	x							x			1741	c

Site	SM	RS	Hab	LS	O	C	MF-O	S	G	Sc	Area-m2	Loc
SON-733	x								x		66	c
SON-734	x								x		279	c
SON-735	x								x		18	c
SON-736	x		x						x		4645	c
SON-737	x		x						x		2787	c
SON-738	x		x					x			7330	c
SON-739	x		x					x			730	c
SON-742	x						x				450	c
SON-743	x						x				161	c
SON-862	x					x					375	c
SON-863	x					x					875	c
SON-865				x					x		460	c
SON-867				x					x		30500	c
SON-868	x								x		85	c
SON-869	x								x		160	c
SON-870		x					x				3	c
SON-876				x					x			c
SON-877				x					x			c
SON-923	x								x		192	c
SON-924	x								x		48	c
SON-925	x		x						x		12500	c
SON-996				x			x				500	r
SON-997				x			x					r
SON-998	x		x						x		962	r
SON-999	x		x					x			36	h
SON-1000			x					x			10000	h
SON-1001					x			x				h
SON-1002				x					x		5000	h
SON-1003				x					x			h
SON-1004					x		x				8	h
SON-1005				x				x				h
SON-1006					x			x			4	h
SON-1007				x			x				100	h
SON-1008				x			x				45000	h
SON-1009				x			x				100	h
SON-1010					x		x				1	h
SON-1011				x			x				4000	h
SON-1012				x			x					h
SON-1013				x				x				h
SON-1043	x						x				12	h
SON-1057				x					x		1500	c
SON-1091	x										220	c
SON-1175	x									x	2028	c
SON-1183	x								x		130	c
SON-1184	x								x		448	c
SON-1185	x								x		2500	c

Site	SM	RS	Hab	LS	O	C	MF-O	S	G	Sc	Area-m2	Loc
SON-1204	x								x		145600	c
SON-1205	x								x		292800	c
SON-1206	x								x		3135	c
SON-1207	x								x		232	c
SON-1309/H			x						x		6050	r
SON-1325				x					x		100	h
SON-1327				x				x			150	h
SON-1335/H			x	x					x			h
SON-1346	x								x		3780	c
SON-1350	x							x			750	c
SON-1392				x				x			350	r
SON-1393				x			x				4292	r
SON-1423					x			x			8	h
SON-1424				x			x				2500	h
SON-1425			x						x		6000	h
SON-1426				x				x			800	h
SON-1451				x					x		75	c
SON-1452					x				x		300	c
SON-1453				x					x		10000	c
SON-1454/H				x	x				x		15000	c
SON-1455	x						x				500	c
SON-1481	x								x		756	c
SON-1512/H			x	x			x				20000	c
SON-1513				x				x			4400	r
SON-1514					x				x		4	r
SON-1516	x		x						x		30000	r
SON-1517	x								x		4810	h
SON-1518				x					x		660	r
SON-1519	x								x		4000	r
SON-1520	x								x		30000	r
SON-1521	x								x		900	r
SON-1522				x					x		20000	r
SON-1523			x						x		10000	r
SON-1524	x								x		40000	r
SON-1525				x		x					2000	h
SON-1549	x								x		100	c
SON-1566	x								x		3600	c
SON-1586	x								x		250	c
SON-1603/H			x				x				40599	h
SON-1604				x			x				7800	h
SON-1605				x					x		2000	h
SON-1606				x					x		1320	h
SON-1609				x					x		512	h
SON-1610			x				x				8263	h
SON-1618	x					x					136	c
SON-1619	x					x					625	c

Site	SM	RS	Hab	LS	O	C	MF-O	S	G	Sc	Area-m2	Loc
SON-1620	x								x		160	c
SON-1621	x								x		136	c
SON-1622	x								x		476	c
SON-1623	x	x							x		90	c
SON-1624	x								x		345	c
SON-1625	x								x		900	c
SON-1626				x					x		900	c
SON-1627				x					x		330	c
SON-1628				x					x		3800	c
SON-1629	x								x		50	c
SON-1630/H				x	x				x		11700	c
SON-1631	x								x		486	c
SON-1632	x						x				725	c
SON-1633		x					x				48	c
SON-1634	x					x					90	c
SON-1635	x					x					378	c
SON-1636				x					x		629	c
SON-1637	x					x					300	c
SON-1638	x					x					4000	c
SON-1639	x					x					247	c
SON-1640	x					x					50	c
SON-1641	x					x					2992	c
SON-1642	x					x					204	c
SON-1643	x					x					1350	c
SON-1644	x					x					1664	c
SON-1645				x					x		8550	c
SON-1646	x								x		99	c
SON-1649	x								x		940	c
SON-1650/H	x								x		3192	c
SON-1651	x						x				135	c
SON-1652	x								x		60	c
SON-1653	x								x		70	c
SON-1654	x								x		180	c
SON-1655	x								x		100	c
SON-1656	x								x		100	c
SON-1657	x								x		100	c
SON-1659				x			x				3000	r
SON-1660	x						x				90	c
SON-1661				x					x			c
SON-1672/H	x		x				x				25200	c
SON-1675	x					x					4000	c
SON-1676	x								x		900	r
SON-1677	x					x					13750	r
SON-1682				x					x		1280	c
SON-1686				x					x		300	c
SON-1688	x						x				300	c
SON-1710	x								x		390	c
SON-1712				x					x		4200	c
SON-1713	x								x		484	c
SON-1714	x								x		63	c

Site	SM	RS	Hab	LS	Q	C	MF-Q	S	G	Sc	Area-m2	Loc
SON-1715	x								x		1260	c
SON-1716				x					x		3750	c
SON-1717				x					x		260	c
SON-1718	x								x		1976	c
SON-1719	x								x		2640	c
SON-1720				x					x		3650	c
SON-1721	x								x			c
SON-1727	x								x		180	c
SON-1728	x								x		140	c
SON-1729	x								x		252	c
SON-1730	x							x			1290	c
SON-1731	x								x		129	c
SON-1740	x						x				24500	h
SON-1741	x						x				80	h
SON-1742				x			x				252	h
SON-1774				x					x		128	h
SON-1793			x					x			400	r
SON-1808	x					x					500	r
SON-1809				x			x				31250	r
SON-1814	x					x					1400	h
SON-1815				x		x					150	h
SON-1816				x		x					100	h
SON-1817				x			x				50	h
SON-1825	x						x				3750	r
SON-1829				x			x				3780	h
SON-1878	x		x						x		2107	c
SON-1879					x				x		2	c
SON-1880	x		x						x		2024	c
SON-1881	x					x					471	c
SON-1882	x							x			54	c
SON-1883			x					x			8247	r
SON-1884	x			x				x			3044	r
SON-1885	x							x			919	c
SON-1886/H	x					x					94	c
SON-1887					x				x		0	c
SON-1888	x		x						x		85	c
SON-1889	x								x		189	c
SON-1890	x					x					871	c
SON-1892	x								x		4	c
SON-1894				x				x			156	c
SON-1895/H	x							x			203	c
SON-1896	x							x			166	c
SON-1897/H			x						x		2800	c
SON-1898/H	x				x				x			c

APPENDIX 5.1

LITHIC ARTIFACTS FROM FORT ROSS SITES

Location	Collection-date	Field-Spec-no	Site	Unit	Artifact-sequence	Count	Artifact-category	Raw-material
a	6/07/88	4	Son 670	2s 0e	1	2	go	sa
a	6/07/88	4	Son 670	2s 0e	2	1	mf	sa
a	6/07/88	6	Son 670	6s 0e	1	8	fc	ba
a	6/07/88	7	Son 670	6s 0e	1	1	go	sa
a	6/07/88	10	Son 670	0n 6w	1	2	fc	ba
a	6/07/88	10	Son 670	0n 6w	2	1	fc	ba
a	6/07/88	11	Son 670	0n 1e	1	1	mf	sa
a	6/07/88	13	Son 670	nw quad	1	1	mf	sa
a	6/07/88	14	Son 670	se quad	1	1	go	sa
a	6/07/88	14	Son 670	se quad	2	1	go	sa
a	6/07/88	15	Son 670	ne quad	1	1	bt	ob
a	6/09/88	1	Son 1878	0n 0e	1	1	bf	ch
a	6/09/88	1	Son 1878	0n 0e	2	1	sc	ch
a	6/09/88	2	Son 1878	22n 0e	1	1	em	ch
a	6/09/88	2	Son 1878	22n 0e	2	1	sh	ch
a	6/09/88	2	Son 1878	22n 0e	3	1	em	ch

continued

KEY   ARTIFACT CATEGORY

bc	=	battered cobble	ma	=	mano (handstone)
bcf	=	battered cobble fragment	mf	=	mano (handstone) fragment
bf	=	biface fragment	nt	=	net weight
bi	=	biface	oo	=	other
bm	=	basin millingstone	pc	=	primary cortical flake
bmf	=	basin millingstone fragment	pe	=	pestle
bt	=	biface thinning flake	pp	=	projectile point
cf	=	core fragment	ppf	=	projectile point fragment
co	=	core	sc	=	secondary cortical flake
em	=	edged-modified flake	sh	=	shatter
fc	=	fire-cracked rock	sm	=	slab millingstone
go	=	ground stone fragment	smf	=	slab millingstone fragment
ha	=	hammerstone	uf	=	uniface fragment
hm	=	hopper mortar	un	=	uniface
if	=	interior flake			

RAW MATERIAL					
ba	=	basalt	ob	=	obsidian
ch	=	chert	qu	=	quartz
gw	=	graywacke	sa	=	sandstone
o	=	other	sc	=	schist

NOTE

All point provenience coordinates listed under the column "Unit" in appendices 5.1, 5.2, 5.4, and 5.5 are measured from the site datum unless otherwise indicated. The point provenience coordinate, 90 @ 11m is 90 degrees from site datum at a distance of 11 meters. The point provenience coordinate, Sub B 6 @ 28 m, is 6 degrees from subdatum B at a distance of 28 meters.

Location	Collection-date	Field-Spec-no	Site	Unit	Artifact-sequence	Count	Artifact-category	Raw-material
a	6/10/88	1	Son 1878	6s 0e	1	1	em	ch
a	6/10/88	1	Son 1878	6s 0e	2	1	sh	o
a	6/10/88	2	Son 1878	14s 0e	1	1	bt	ch
a	6/10/88	3	Son 1878	12s 0e	1	2	pc	ch
a	6/10/88	3	Son 1878	12s 0e	2	1	em	ch
a	6/10/88	4	Son 1878	8s 0e	1	1	pc	ch
a	6/10/88	4	Son 1878	8s 0e	2	2	sh	ch
a	6/10/88	9	Son 1878	0n 13e	1	1	bf	ch
a	6/10/88	10	Son 1878	0n 17e	1	1	if	ch
a	6/10/88	11	Son 1878	0n 23e	1	1	co	ch
a	6/10/88	13	Son 1878	90 @ 11m	1	1	ma	ba
a	6/10/88	14	Son 1878	ne quad	1	1	ma	sa
a	6/10/88	14	Son 1878	ne quad	2	1	ha	sa
a	6/10/88	14	Son 1878	ne quad	3	1	cf	ch
a	6/10/88	14	Son 1878	ne quad	4	1	go	sa
a	6/10/88	15	Son 1878	ne quad	1	1	em	ch
a	6/10/88	16	Son 1878	se nonrandom	1	1	em	ch
a	6/10/88	16	Son 1878	se nonrandom	2	1	ppf	ch
a	6/10/88	16	Son 1878	se nonrandom	3	1	em	ch
a	6/10/88	16	Son 1878	se nonrandom	4	1	bt	ch
a	6/10/88	16	Son 1878	se nonrandom	5	1	bt	ch
a	6/10/88	16	Son 1878	se nonrandom	6	1	ppf	ch
a	6/10/88	16	Son 1878	se nonrandom	7	1	em	ch
a	6/10/88	16	Son 1878	se nonrandom	8	1	if	ch
a	6/10/88	16	Son 1878	se nonrandom	9	1	if	ba
a	6/10/88	16	Son 1878	se nonrandom	10	1	em	ch
a	6/10/88	16	Son 1878	se nonrandom	11	1	bf	ch
a	6/10/88	16	Son 1878	se nonrandom	12	1	pc	qu
a	6/10/88	16	Son 1878	se nonrandom	13	1	cf	ch
a	6/10/88	16	Son 1878	se nonrandom	14	1	if	ch
a	6/10/88	18	Son 1878	sw quad	1	1	go	sa
a	6/10/88	19	Son 1878	sw quad	1	1	sm	sa
a	6/16/88	1	Son 1879	nonrandom	1	1	mf	sa
a	6/16/88	2	Son 1879	nonrandom	1	1	go	sa
b	6/08/88	1	Son 1880	0n 0e	1	1	if	ob
b	6/08/88	1	Son 1880	0n 0e	2	1	bt	ob
b	6/08/88	2	Son 1880	0n 1e	1	1	em	ch
b	6/08/88	2	Son 1880	0n 1e	2	1	bf	ch
b	6/08/88	2	Son 1880	0n 1e	3	1	co	ch
b	6/08/88	2	Son 1880	0n 1e	4	1	em	ob
b	6/08/88	2	Son 1880	0n 1e	5	1	bt	ob
b	6/08/88	2	Son 1880	0n 1e	6	1	bt	ob
b	6/08/88	2	Son 1880	0n 1e	7	2	if	ob
b	6/08/88	2	Son 1880	0n 1e	8	1	sh	ch
b	6/08/88	3	Son 1880	2s 0e	1	1	bt	ob
b	6/08/88	5	Son 1880	0n 2w	1	1	sh	ch
b	6/08/88	6	Son 1880	0n 2w	1	1	sm	sa
b	6/08/88	6	Son 1880	0n 2w	2	2	go	sa
b	6/08/88	7	Son 1880	2s 0e	1	1	go	sa

Location	Collection-date	Field-Spec-no	Site	Unit	Artifact-sequence	Count	Artifact-category	Raw-material
b	6/08/88	11	Son 1880	Sub A 2n 0e	1	1	bt	ob
b	6/08/88	15	Son 1880	Sub A 2s 0e	1	1	sc	ob
b	6/08/88	15	Son 1880	Sub A 2s 0e	2	1	sc	ob
b	6/08/88	17	Son 1880	Sub A 6s 0e	1	1	ma	sa
b	6/08/88	19	Son 1880	Sub A 0n 2w	1	1	cf	ch
b	6/08/88	20	Son 1880	Sub A 0n 4w	1	1	cf	ch
b	6/08/88	24	Son 1880	Sub B 0n 2w	1	1	if	ob
b	6/08/88	25	Son 1880	Sub B 2s 0e	1	1	pc	ch
b	6/08/88	26	Son 1880	Sub A 0n 1e	1	1	em	ob
b	6/08/88	27	Son 1880	138 @ 10m	1	2	em	ch
b	6/09/88	2	Son 1881	Sub A 2s 0e	1	1	sh	ob
b	6/09/88	4	Son 1881	Sub A 0n 2w	1	1	sm	sa
b	6/09/88	5	Son 1881	268 @ 15.2m	1	1	sh	qu
b	6/09/88	6	Son 1881	Sub A 292 @ 4m	1	1	sc	ch
b	6/09/88	9	Son 1881	166 @ 7.3m	1	1	sh	ob
b	6/09/88	10	Son 1881	0n 0e	1	1	cf	ch
b	6/09/88	10	Son 1881	0n 0e	2	1	go	sa
b	6/09/88	10	Son 1881	0n 0e	3	1	go	sa
b	6/09/88	11	Son 1881	2s 0e	1	1	smf	sa
b	6/09/88	12	Son 1881	0n 1e	1	1	sh	ch
b	6/09/88	14	Son 1880	Sub C 0nw 0sw	1	1	go	sa
b	6/09/88	15	Son 1880	Sub C 0nw 4sw	1	1	ma	ba
b	6/09/88	16	Son 1880	Sub C 0nw 2sw	1	1	ma	sa
b	6/09/88	16	Son 1880	Sub C 0nw 2sw	2	1	fc	sa
b	6/09/88	18	Son 1880	Sub C 140 @ 2.4m	1	1	go	sa
b	6/09/88	19	Son 1880	Sub C 301 @ 7.5m	1	1	go	sa
c	6/06/88	9	Son 1895	0n 4w	1	1	go	sa
c	6/06/88	15	Son 1895	6s 0e	1	1	cf	ch
c	6/06/88	17	Son 1895	ne quad	1	1	go	sa
c	6/06/88	18	Son 1895	ne quad	1	1	sc	ob
c	6/06/88	18	Son 1895	ne quad	2	1	go	sa
c	6/06/88	18	Son 1895	ne quad	3	1	if	ob
c	6/06/88	19	Son 1895	sw quad	1	1	go	sa
c	6/06/88	33	Son 1885	12s 0e	1	1	if	ch
c	6/06/88	35	Son 1885	sw quad	1	1	cf	ch
c	6/06/88	35	Son 1885	sw quad	2	1	sc	ch
c	6/06/88	35	Son 1885	sw quad	3	1	sc	ch
c	6/06/88	35	Son 1885	sw quad	4	1	sc	ch
c	6/06/88	35	Son 1885	sw quad	5	1	if	ch
c	6/06/88	35	Son 1885	sw quad	6	1	bt	ob
c	6/06/88	35	Son 1885	sw quad	7	1	em	ob
c	6/06/88	35	Son 1885	sw quad	8	1	bt	ob
c	6/06/88	40	Son 1885	0n 4w	1	1	sh	ch
c	6/06/88	47	Son 1885	se quad/nw quad	1	1	sh	ch
c	6/06/88	47	Son 1885	se quad/nw quad	2	1	go	sa
c	6/06/88	48	Son 1885	nw quad	1	1	un	ob
c	6/06/88	48	Son 1885	nw quad	2	1	ppf	ob
c	6/06/88	48	Son 1885	nw quad	3	1	em	ch
c	6/06/88	48	Son 1885	nw quad	4	1	em	ch

Location	Collection-date	Field-Spec-no	Site	Unit	Artifact-sequence	Count	Artifact-category	Raw-material
c	6/06/88	48	Son 1885	nw quad	5	1	if	ch
c	6/06/88	48	Son 1885	nw quad	6	5	go	sa
c	6/06/88	49	Son 1885	0n 6w	1	1	sc	ch
c	6/08/88	1	Son 1896	0n 1e	1	1	fc	sc
c	6/08/88	2	Son 1896	0n 3e	1	1	go	sa
c	6/08/88	3	Son 1896	0n 5e	1	3	go	sa
c	6/08/88	4	Son 1896	0n 7e	1	1	go	sa
c	6/08/88	12	Son 1896	4n 0e	1	1	go	ba
c	6/08/88	22	isolate		1	1	sm	sa
c	6/09/88	1	Son 1895	110 @ 61m	1	1	bcf	sa
c	6/10/88	2	Son 1895	edge of nos	1	1	bc	sa
c	6/10/88	9	Son 1882	2n 0e	1	1	go	sa
c	6/13/88	1	isolate		1	1	sm	sa
c	6/14/88	1	Son 1894	roadcut	1	1	hm	sa
c	6/14/88	2	Son 1894	roadcut	1	3	if	ob
c	6/14/88	2	Son 1894	roadcut	2	1	sh	ob
c	6/14/88	2	Son 1894	roadcut	3	1	bt	ob
c	6/14/88	2	Son 1894	roadcut	4	1	bf	ob
c	6/14/88	2	Son 1894	roadcut	5	1	bt	ob
c	6/14/88	2	Son 1894	roadcut	6	2	if	ob
c	6/14/88	2	Son 1894	roadcut	7	2	cf	ch
c	6/14/88	2	Son 1894	roadcut	8	1	sc	ch
c	6/14/88	2	Son 1894	roadcut	9	2	sh	ch
c	6/14/88	2	Son 1894	roadcut	10	1	go	sa
c	6/14/88	2	Son 1894	roadcut	11	1	em	ch
c	6/14/88	2	Son 1894	roadcut	12	3	sh	sc
c	6/14/88	3	Son 1894	roadcut	1	1	sc	ob
c	6/14/88	4	Son 1894	roadcut	1	1	em	ch
d	6/07/88	1	Son 1883	nonrandom	1	1	pp	ob
d	6/07/88	1	Son 1883	nonrandom	2	1	nt	sa
d	6/07/88	2	Son 1883	nonrandom	1	1	bf	ob
d	6/08/88	2	Son 1883	4s 0e	1	5	go	sa
d	6/08/88	2	Son 1883	4s 0e	2	1	bt	ob
d	6/08/88	2	Son 1883	4s 0e	3	1	if	ch
d	6/08/88	2	Son 1883	4s 0e	4	1	if	ch
d	6/08/88	2	Son 1883	4s 0e	5	1	em	ch
d	6/08/88	3	Son 1883	6s 03	1	3	go	sa
d	6/08/88	6	Son 1883	12s 0e	1	1	em	ch
d	6/08/88	6	Son 1883	12s 0e	2	1	em	ch
d	6/08/88	7	Son 1883	0n 0e	1	1	go	sa
d	6/08/88	9	Son 1883	2n 0e	1	1	if	ch
d	6/08/88	9	Son 1883	2n 0e	3	4	go	sa
d	6/08/88	10	Son 1883	4n 0e	1	1	sh	ch
d	6/08/88	11	Son 1883	6n 0e	1	3	go	sa
d	6/08/88	11	Son 1883	6n 0e	3	1	if	ob
d	6/08/88	11	Son 1883	6n 0e	4	1	sh	ch
d	6/08/88	15	Son 1883	10n 0e	1	1	go	sa
d	6/08/88	16	Son 1883	20s 0e	1	1	sh	ch
d	6/08/88	19	Son 1883	14n 0e	1	1	bf	ob

Location	Collection-date	Field-Spec-no	Site	Unit	Artifact-sequence	Count	Artifact-category	Raw-material
d	6/08/88	19	Son 1883	14n 0e	2	1	bt	ob
d	6/08/88	19	Son 1883	14n 0e	3	1	cf	ch
d	6/08/88	19	Son 1883	14n 0e	4	1	nf	ch
d	6/09/88	1	Son 1883	16n 0e	1	1	if	ch
d	6/09/88	1	Son 1883	16n 0e	2	1	bf	ob
d	6/09/88	2	Son 1883	18n 0e	1	2	go	sa
d	6/09/88	2	Son 1883	18n 0e	2	1	co	ch
d	6/09/88	2	Son 1883	18n 0e	3	1	fc	sa
d	6/09/88	2	Son 1883	18n 0e	4	1	pc	ch
d	6/09/88	2	Son 1883	18n 0e	5	1	sh	ch
d	6/09/88	2	Son 1883	18n 0e	6	1	bt	ob
d	6/09/88	2	Son 1883	18n 0e	7	1	bt	ob
d	6/09/88	4	Son 1883	20n 0e	1	1	pp	ch
d	6/09/88	4	Son 1883	20n 0e	2	1	sh	ch
d	6/09/88	4	Son 1883	20n 0e	3	1	bt	ob
d	6/09/88	4	Son 1883	20n 0e	4	1	bt	ob
d	6/09/88	5	Son 1883	22n 0e	1	1	fc	sa
d	6/09/88	5	Son 1883	22n 0e	2	1	if	ch
d	6/09/88	6	Son 1883	26n 0e	1	1	if	ob
d	6/09/88	6	Son 1883	26n 0e	2	1	bt	ob
d	6/09/88	6	Son 1883	26n 0e	3	1	if	ch
d	6/09/88	6	Son 1883	26n 0e	4	1	if	ch
d	6/09/88	7	Son 1883	24n 0e	1	1	bf	ob
d	6/09/88	8	Son 1883	30s 0e	1	1	pc	ch
d	6/09/88	8	Son 1883	30s 0e	2	1	cf	qu
d	6/09/88	8	Son 1883	30s 0e	3	1	go	sa
d	6/09/88	8	Son 1883	30s 0e	4	1	go	sa
d	6/09/88	9	Son 1883	28n 0e	1	1	bt	ob
d	6/09/88	9	Son 1883	28n 0e	2	1	em	ch
d	6/09/88	9	Son 1883	28n 0e	3	1	bt	ch
d	6/09/88	9	Son 1883	28n 0e	4	1	go	sa
d	6/09/88	9	Son 1883	28n 0e	5	1	cf	ch
d	6/09/88	10	Son 1883	34s 0e	1	5	go	sa
d	6/09/88	10	Son 1883	34s 0e	2	1	sh	ch
d	6/09/88	11	Son 1883	30n 0e	1	1	em	ch
d	6/09/88	11	Son 1883	30n 0e	2	1	if	ch
d	6/09/88	11	Son 1883	30n 0e	3	1	go	sa
d	6/09/88	11	Son 1883	30n 0e	4	3	bt	ob
d	6/09/88	11	Son 1883	30n 0e	5	1	sh	ch
d	6/09/88	11	Son 1883	30n 0e	6	2	go	sa
d	6/09/88	11	Son 1883	30n 0e	7	1	pc	ch
d	6/09/88	13	Son 1883	0n 5e	1	2	go	sa
d	6/09/88	14	Son 1883	0n 3e	1	1	sh	ob
d	6/09/88	15	Son 1883	0n 1e	1	1	cf	ch
d	6/09/88	15	Son 1883	0n 1e	2	1	mf	sa
d	6/09/88	16	Son 1883	0n 7e	1	1	cf	ch
d	6/09/88	16	Son 1883	0n 7e	2	1	mf	sa
d	6/09/88	16	Son 1883	0n 7e	3	1	em	ch
d	6/09/88	17	Son 1883	0n 9e	1	1	go	sa

Location	Collection-date	Field-Spec-no	Site	Unit	Artifact-sequence	Count	Artifact-category	Raw-material
d	6/09/88	18	Son 1883	0n 19e	1	1	go	sa
d	6/09/88	19	Son 1883	0n 21e	1	1	sh	ch
d	6/09/88	20	Son 1883	13n 2e	1	1	sh	ch
d	6/09/88	21	Son 1883	8n 4e	1	1	if	ch
d	6/09/88	22	Son 1883	5e 97n	1	1	go	sa
d	6/09/88	23	Son 1883	27n 0e	1	1	cf	ch
d	6/09/88	24	Son 1883	29n 03	1	2	sh	ch
d	6/09/88	25	Son 1883	26n 2e	1	1	if	ch
d	6/09/88	26	Son 1883	22n 8e	1	1	sm	sa
d	6/09/88	27	Son 1883	23n 10e	1	1	em	ch
d	6/09/88	27	Son 1883	23n 10e	2	1	ma	sa
d	6/09/88	27	Son 1883	23n 10e	3	2	go	gw
d	6/09/88	27	Son 1883	23n 10e	4	2	go	sa
d	6/09/88	30	Son 1883	6e 17.30n	1	1	co	ch
d	6/09/88	31	Son 1883	35n 2e	1	1	go	sa
d	6/09/88	33	Son 1883	32n 4e	1	1	ha	sa
d	6/09/88	36	Son 1883	2e 33n	1	1	sc	ch
d	6/09/88	36	Son 1883	2e 33n	2	1	em	ch
d	6/09/88	36	Son 1883	2e 33n	3	1	sc	ob
d	6/09/88	36	Son 1883	2e 33n	4	1	if	ch
d	6/09/88	36	Son 1883	2e 33n	5	1	go	sa
d	6/09/88	37	Son 1883	31n 4e	1	1	go	sa
d	6/09/88	38	Son 1883	23n 8e	1	1	go	sa
d	6/09/88	38	Son 1883	23n 8e	3	4	mf	sa
d	6/09/88	38	Son 1883	23n 8e	4	1	go	sa
d	6/09/88	38	Son 1883	23n 8e	5	1	if	ch
d	6/09/88	39	Son 1883	33n 8e	1	1	mf	sa
d	6/09/88	41	Son 1883	31n 0e	1	1	cf	ch
d	6/09/88	41	Son 1883	31n 0e	2	1	go	sa
d	6/09/88	42	Son 1883	22n 10e	1	1	sh	ch
d	6/09/88	42	Son 1883	22n 10e	2	4	go	sa
d	6/09/88	43	Son 1883	21n 10e	1	1	go	sa
d	6/09/88	44	Son 1883	19n 8e	1	1	go	sa
d	6/09/88	45	Son 1883	4.2n 12e	1	1	ma	sa
d	6/09/88	45	Son 1883	4.2n 12e	2	1	go	sa
d	6/09/88	46	Son 1883	18n 12e	1	1	mf	sa
d	6/09/88	47	Son 1883	27n 8e	1	1	go	sa
d	6/09/88	48	Son 1883	18n 12e	1	1	go	sa
d	6/09/88	49	Son 1883	12n 12e	1	1	mf	sa
d	6/09/88	50	Son 1883	13n 12e	1	2	ma	sa
d	6/09/88	51	Son 1883	12n 8e	1	1	sc	ch
d	6/09/88	51	Son 1883	12n 8e	2	1	go	sa
d	6/09/88	51	Son 1883	12n 8e	3	1	pc	ob
d	6/09/88	52	Son 1883	25n 14e	1	1	pe	sa
d	6/09/88	52	Son 1883	25n 14e	2	2	go	sa
d	6/09/88	53	Son 1883	30n 14e	1	1	if	ch
d	6/09/88	53	Son 1883	30n 14e	2	1	if	ch
d	6/09/88	53	Son 1883	30n 14e	3	1	if	ch
d	6/09/88	53	Son 1883	30n 14e	4	1	if	ch

Location	Collection-date	Field-Spec-no	Site	Unit	Artifact-sequence	Count	Artifact-category	Raw-material
d	6/09/88	53	Son 1883	30n 14e	5	2	go	sa
d	6/09/88	54	Son 1883	20n 10e	1	2	go	sa
d	6/09/88	54	Son 1883	20n 10e	2	1	sh	ba
d	6/09/88	56	Son 1883	20n 2e	1	1	sc	ch
d	6/09/88	57	Son 1883	31n 12e	1	1	cf	ch
d	6/09/88	58	Son 1883	23n 10e	1	3	go	sa
d	6/09/88	59	Son 1883	4n 8e	1	1	go	sa
d	6/09/88	61	Son 1883	25.5n 12e	1	1	cf	ch
d	6/09/88	63	Son 1883	32n 12e	1	1	fc	sa
d	6/09/88	64	Son 1883	21.5n 12e	1	1	go	sa
d	6/09/88	65	Son 1883	9n 10e	1	1	co	ch
d	6/09/88	65	Son 1883	9n 10e	2	2	mf	sa
d	6/09/88	66	Son 1883	14n 10e	1	1	go	sa
d	6/09/88	68	Son 1883	5n 10e	1	4	go	sa
d	6/10/88	1	Son 1883	4n 32e	1	1	if	ch
d	6/10/88	1	Son 1883	4n 32e	2	2	go	sa
d	6/10/88	1	Son 1883	4n 32e	3	2	go	sa
d	6/10/88	2	Son 1883	0n 24e	1	1	go	sa
d	6/10/88	4	Son 1883	12n 32e	1	1	go	sa
d	6/10/88	5	Son 1883	16n 24e	1	1	em	ch
d	6/10/88	5	Son 1883	16n 24e	2	1	fc	sa
d	6/10/88	5	Son 1883	16n 24e	3	1	pf	sa
d	6/10/88	6	Son 1883	8n 40e	1	1	go	ba
d	6/10/88	7	Son 1883	10n 36e	1	2	go	sa
d	6/10/88	7	Son 1883	10n 36e	2	1	co	ch
d	6/10/88	8	Son 1883	24n 24e	1	1	go	sa
d	6/10/88	8	Son 1883	24n 24e	2	1	fc	sa
d	6/10/88	10	Son 1883	32n 24e	1	1	sh	qu
d	6/10/88	10	Son 1883	32n 24e	2	1	sc	ch
d	6/10/88	10	Son 1883	32n 24e	3	1	if	ch
d	6/10/88	10	Son 1883	32n 24e	4	1	if	ob
d	6/10/88	10	Son 1883	32n 24e	5	2	go	sa
d	6/10/88	10	Son 1883	32n 24e	6	1	ha	sa
d	6/10/88	11	Son 1883	4n 16e	1	1	sh	ch
d	6/10/88	11	Son 1883	4n 16e	2	1	em	ob
d	6/10/88	12	Son 1883	12n 16e	1	1	bf	ch
d	6/10/88	13	Son 1883	20n 16e	1	3	pc	ch
d	6/10/88	13	Son 1883	20n 16e	2	3	go	sa
d	6/10/88	13	Son 1883	20n 16e	3	1	em	ch
d	6/10/88	13	Son 1883	20n 16e	4	1	sh	sc
d	6/10/88	13	Son 1883	20n 16e	5	3	if	ch
d	6/10/88	13	Son 1883	20n 16e	6	2	cf	ch
d	6/10/88	14	Son 1883	32n 16e	1	4	go	sa
d	6/10/88	14	Son 1883	32n 16e	2	1	pp	ob
d	6/10/88	14	Son 1883	32n 16e	3	1	if	ch
d	6/10/88	14	Son 1883	32n 16e	4	1	sh	ch
d	6/10/88	14	Son 1883	32n 16e	5	1	sh	qu
d	6/10/88	14	Son 1883	32n 16e	6	1	sc	ch
d	6/10/88	14	Son 1883	32n 16e	7	1	fc	sa

Location	Collection-date	Field-Spec-no	Site	Unit	Artifact-sequence	Count	Artifact-category	Raw-material
d	6/10/88	16	Son 1883	32n 38e	1	1	em	ch
d	6/10/88	16	Son 1883	32n 38e	2	1	sc	ch
d	6/10/88	16	Son 1883	32n 38e	3	1	em	ob
d	6/10/88	16	Son 1883	32n 38e	5	1	bf	ob
d	6/10/88	16	Son 1883	32n 38e	6	1	if	ch
d	6/10/88	16	Son 1883	32n 38e	7	1	pe	ba
d	6/10/88	16	Son 1883	32n 38e	8	1	go	sa
d	6/10/88	16	Son 1883	32n 38e	9	1	go	ba
d	6/10/88	16	Son 1883	32n 38e	10	2	go	gw
d	6/10/88	16	Son 1883	32n 38e	16	6	go	ba
d	6/10/88	16	Son 1883	32n 38e	17	15	go	sa
d	6/10/88	16	Son 1883	32n 38e	18	1	mf	sa
d	6/10/88	16	Son 1883	32n 38e	19	3	go	ba
d	6/10/88	16	Son 1883	32n 38e	20	1	bt	ob
d	6/10/88	17	Son 1883	36n 32e	1	1	em	ob
d	6/10/88	17	Son 1883	36n 32e	2	1	bt	ob
d	6/10/88	17	Son 1883	36n 32e	3	1	sm	sa
d	6/10/88	17	Son 1883	36n 32e	4	1	co	ch
d	6/10/88	17	Son 1883	36n 32e	5	1	cf	ch
d	6/10/88	17	Son 1883	36n 32e	6	1	mf	sa
d	6/10/88	17	Son 1883	36n 32e	7	1	sh	ch
d	6/10/88	17	Son 1883	36n 32e	8	9	go	sa
d	6/10/88	18	Son 1883	40n 24e	1	1	bf	ob
d	6/10/88	18	Son 1883	40n 24e	2	1	sh	ch
d	6/10/88	18	Son 1883	40n 24e	3	1	if	ch
d	6/10/88	18	Son 1883	40n 24e	4	1	bc	sa
d	6/10/88	18	Son 1883	40n 24e	5	2	go	sa
d	6/10/88	19	Son 1883	48n 24e	1	1	go	sa
d	6/10/88	20	Son 1883	40n 22e	1	1	em	ob
d	6/10/88	20	Son 1883	40n 22e	2	1	bt	ob
d	6/10/88	20	Son 1883	40n 22e	3	1	em	ch
d	6/10/88	20	Son 1883	40n 22e	4	1	if	ch
d	6/10/88	21	Son 1883	36n 16e	1	2	go	sa
d	6/10/88	21	Son 1883	36n 16e	2	2	go	ba
d	6/13/88	1	Son 1883	0n 2w	1	2	sh	ch
d	6/13/88	2	Son 1883	0n 6w	1	1	pp	ob
d	6/13/88	2	Son 1883	0n 6w	2	1	mf	sa
d	6/13/88	2	Son 1883	0n 6w	3	1	go	sa
d	6/13/88	4	Son 1883	0n 4w	1	1	sc	ch
d	6/13/88	4	Son 1883	0n 4w	2	1	go	sa
d	6/13/88	5	Son 1883	0n 8w	1	1	sc	ch
d	6/13/88	6	Son 1883	0n 20w	1	1	sh	ch
d	6/13/88	6	Son 1883	0n 20w	2	1	sh	ob
d	6/13/88	8	Son 1883	8s 12w	1	1	bf	ob
d	6/13/88	8	Son 1883	8s 12w	2	1	cf	ch
d	6/13/88	8	Son 1883	8s 12w	3	1	pc	ch
d	6/13/88	8	Son 1883	8s 12w	4	1	sc	ch
d	6/13/88	8	Son 1883	8s 12w	5	1	bt	ch
d	6/13/88	8	Son 1883	8s 12w	6	1	bt	ob

Location	Collection-date	Field-Spec-no	Site	Unit	Artifact-sequence	Count	Artifact-category	Raw-material
d	6/13/88	8	Son 1883	8s 12w	7	1	go	sa
d	6/13/88	9	Son 1883	12s 20w	1	2	em	ch
d	6/13/88	9	Son 1883	12s 20w	2	1	sh	ch
d	6/13/88	9	Son 1883	12s 20w	3	4	go	sa
d	6/13/88	10	Son 1883	16s 28w	1	5	go	sa
d	6/13/88	11	Son 1883	0s 12w	1	2	em	ch
d	6/13/88	11	Son 1883	0s 12w	3	4	go	sa
d	6/13/88	12	Son 1883	28s 20w	1	1	sh	ch
d	6/13/88	12	Son 1883	28s 20w	2	2	sh	ch
d	6/13/88	14	Son 1883	32s 12w	1	2	go	sa
d	6/13/88	15	Son 1883	36s 20w	1	1	go	sa
d	6/13/88	16	Son 1883	16s 12w	1	1	sc	ch
d	6/13/88	16	Son 1883	16s 12w	2	1	pc	ch
d	6/13/88	16	Son 1883	16s 12w	3	2	go	sa
d	6/13/88	16	Son 1883	16s 12w	4	1	em	sc
d	6/13/88	17	Son 1883	188 @ 31m	1	1	sm	sa
d	6/13/88	18	Son 1883	245 @ 67m	1	1	co	ch
d	6/13/88	19	Son 1883	24s 12w	1	1	em	ch
d	6/13/88	19	Son 1883	24s 12w	2	1	sh	ch
d	6/13/88	19	Son 1883	24s 12w	3	1	sh	ch
d	6/13/88	19	Son 1883	24s 12w	4	1	fc	sa
d	6/13/88	19	Son 1883	24s 12w	5	1	go	sa
d	6/13/88	20	Son 1883	268 @ 51.8m	1	1	cf	ch
d	6/13/88	20	Son 1883	268 @ 51.8m	2	1	sc	ch
d	6/13/88	20	Son 1883	268 @ 51.8m	3	1	cf	ch
d	6/13/88	20	Son 1883	268 @ 51.8m	4	1	sc	ob
d	6/13/88	22	Son 1883	28s 4e	1	1	sc	ch
d	6/13/88	22	Son 1883	28s 4e	2	1	pc	ch
d	6/13/88	22	Son 1883	28s 4e	3	5	go	sa
d	6/13/88	23	Son 1883	36s 4e	1	8	go	sa
d	6/13/88	23	Son 1883	36s 4e	2	1	if	ch
d	6/13/88	23	Son 1883	36s 4e	3	1	go	gw
d	6/13/88	24	Son 1883	4s 4e	1	3	sh	ch
d	6/13/88	24	Son 1883	4s 4e	2	1	sh	qu
d	6/13/88	24	Son 1883	4s 4e	3	3	go	sa
d	6/13/88	24	Son 1883	4s 4e	4	9	go	sa
d	6/13/88	25	Son 1883	12s 4e	1	1	em	ch
d	6/13/88	25	Son 1883	12s 4e	2	1	sh	ch
d	6/13/88	25	Son 1883	12s 4e	3	1	go	sa
d	6/13/88	25	Son 1883	12s 4e	4	1	go	ba
d	6/13/88	26	Son 1883	20s 4e	1	1	if	ob
d	6/13/88	26	Son 1883	20s 4e	2	1	pp	ch
d	6/13/88	26	Son 1883	20s 4e	3	2	em	ch
d	6/13/88	26	Son 1883	20s 4e	4	2	cf	ch
d	6/13/88	26	Son 1883	20s 4e	5	3	sh	ch
d	6/13/88	26	Son 1883	20s 4e	6	2	if	ch
d	6/13/88	26	Son 1883	20s 4e	7	2	if	ch
d	6/13/88	26	Son 1883	20s 4e	8	1	mf	sa
d	6/13/88	26	Son 1883	20s 4e	9	3	go	sa

Location	Collection-date	Field-Spec-no	Site	Unit	Artifact-sequence	Count	Artifact-category	Raw-material
d	6/13/88	26	Son 1883	20s 4e	10	1	go	ba
d	6/13/88	26	Son 1883	20s 4e	11	1	go	ba
d	6/14/88	2	Son 1883	8s 12e	1	1	go	sa
d	6/14/88	4	Son 1883	4s 20e	1	3	go	sa
d	6/14/88	5	Son 1883	12s 20e	1	1	cf	ch
d	6/14/88	7	Son 1883	20s 20e	1	24	go	s
d	6/14/88	7	Son 1883	20s 20e	2	1	ma	sa
d	6/14/88	7	Son 1883	20s 20e	3	1	bc	sa
d	6/14/88	7	Son 1883	20s 20e	4	1	sc	ch
d	6/14/88	7	Son 1883	20s 20e	5	1	bf	ch
d	6/14/88	7	Son 1883	20s 20e	6	1	sh	ch
d	6/14/88	7	Son 1883	20s 20e	7	3	if	ob
d	6/14/88	7	Son 1883	20s 20e	8	2	bf	ob
d	6/14/88	7	Son 1883	20s 20e	9	2	bt	ob
d	6/14/88	8	Son 1883	170 @ 20m	1	1	em	ob
d	6/14/88	8	Son 1883	170 @ 20m	2	1	if	ob
d	6/14/88	9	Son 1883	23s 2e	1	1	go	sa
d	6/14/88	9	Son 1883	23s 2e	2	1	if	ch
d	6/14/88	9	Son 1883	23s 2e	3	2	go	sa
d	6/14/88	9	Son 1883	23s 2e	4	1	pc	ch
d	6/14/88	11	Son 1883	19s 2e	1	1	if	ch
d	6/14/88	11	Son 1883	19s 2e	2	1	bf	ob
d	6/14/88	12	Son 1883	135 @ 25m	1	1	pc	ob
d	6/14/88	13	Son 1883	28s 4e	1	1	sh	ch
d	6/14/88	13	Son 1883	28s 4e	2	2	go	sa
d	6/14/88	14	Son 1883	28s 2e	1	1	go	sa
d	6/14/88	14	Son 1883	28s 2e	2	2	go	sa
d	6/14/88	15	Son 1883	174 @ 40m	1	3	go	sa
d	6/14/88	15	Son 1883	174 @ 40m	2	1	if	ob
d	6/14/88	15	Son 1883	174 @ 40m	3	1	nf	ob
d	6/14/88	16	Son 1883	9.5s 2e	1	1	cf	ch
d	6/14/88	17	Son 1883	25s 1.4e	1	1	go	sa
d	6/14/88	19	Son 1883	192 @ 39m	1	1	ha	sa
d	6/14/88	19	Son 1883	192 @ 39m	2	1	go	sa
d	6/14/88	20	Son 1883	184 @ 47m	1	1	co	ch
d	6/14/88	21	Son 1883	25s 1.5e	1	1	co	ch
d	6/14/88	22	Son 1883	6s 8.4e	1	1	sh	ch
d	6/14/88	23	Son 1883	0n 24e, 164 @ 20m	1	2	go	sa
d	6/14/88	24	Son 1883	0n 24e, 324 @ 21m	1	1	bf	ch
d	6/14/88	24	Son 1883	0n 24e, 324 @ 21m	2	3	go	sa
d	6/14/88	24	Son 1883	0n 24e, 324 @ 21m	3	1	go	gw
d	6/14/88	25	Son 1883	0n 24e, 320 @ 26m	1	1	em	ch
d	6/14/88	25	Son 1883	0n 24e, 320 @ 26m	2	3	go	sa
d	6/14/88	26	Son 1883	0n 24e, 68 @ 28m	1	2	if	ob
d	6/14/88	26	Son 1883	0n 24e, 68 @ 28m	2	1	em	ch
d	6/14/88	26	Son 1883	0n 24e, 68 @ 28m	3	1	fc	sa
d	6/14/88	26	Son 1883	0n 24e, 68 @ 28m	4	1	go	sa
d	6/14/88	27	Son 1883	0n 24e, 9 @ 37m	1	1	bt	ob
d	6/14/88	27	Son 1883	0n 24e, 9 @ 37m	2	1	nf	ob

Location	Collection-date	Field-Spec-no	Site	Unit	Artifact-sequence	Count	Artifact-category	Raw-material
d	6/14/88	27	Son 1883	0n 24e, 9 @ 37m	3	1	if	ob
d	6/14/88	27	Son 1883	0n 24e, 9 @ 37m	4	1	cf	ch
d	6/14/88	27	Son 1883	0n 24e, 9 @ 37m	5	2	go	sa
d	6/14/88	27	Son 1883	0n 24e, 9 @ 37m	6	1	cf	ch
d	6/14/88	28	Son 1883	0n 24e, 17 @ 40m	1	3	go	sa
d	6/14/88	28	Son 1883	0n 24e, 17 @ 40m	2	1	ha	sa
d	6/14/88	29	Son 1883	0n 24e, 354 @ 34m	1	1	if	ch
d	6/14/88	29	Son 1883	0n 24e, 354 @ 34m	2	1	cf	ch
d	6/14/88	30	Son 1883	0n 24e, 348 @ 34m	1	1	co	ch
d	6/14/88	31	Son 1883	0n 50e, 347 @ 40m	1	1	bf	ch
d	6/14/88	31	Son 1883	0n 50e, 347 @ 40m	2	1	bf	ch
d	6/14/88	31	Son 1883	0n 50e, 347 @ 40m	3	1	cf	ch
d	6/14/88	31	Son 1883	0n 50e, 347 @ 40m	4	1	go	sc
d	6/14/88	31	Son 1883	0n 50e, 347 @ 40m	5	3	mf	sa
d	6/14/88	31	Son 1883	0n 50e, 347 @ 40m	6	4	go	sa
d	6/14/88	32	Son 1883	0n 50e, 347 @ 44m	1	2	if	ob
d	6/14/88	32	Son 1883	0n 50e, 347 @ 44m	2	1	ha	sa
d	6/14/88	33	Son 1883	0n 50e, 4 @ 26m	1	1	mf	sa
d	6/14/88	33	Son 1883	0n 50e, 4 @ 26m	2	5	go	sa
d	6/14/88	34	Son 1883	0n 50e, 323 @ 21m	1	2	go	sa
d	6/14/88	34	Son 1883	0n 50e, 323 @ 21m	2	1	em	ch
d	6/14/88	34	Son 1883	0n 50e, 323 @ 21m	3	1	go	ba
d	6/14/88	34	Son 1883	0n 50e, 323 @ 21m	5	3	go	sa
d	6/14/88	35	Son 1883	0n 50e, 395 @ 27m	1	4	go	sa
d	6/14/88	35	Son 1883	0n 50e, 395 @ 27m	2	2	mf	sa
d	6/14/88	36	Son 1883	0n 50e, 354 @ 20m	1	2	go	sa
d	6/14/88	37	Son 1883	0n 50e, 352 @ 30m	1	1	bf	ob
d	6/14/88	38	Son 1883	0n 50e, 352 @ 30m	1	2	go	sa
d	6/14/88	38	Son 1883	0n 50e	2	1	mf	sa
d	6/14/88	39	Son 1883	0n 50e, 359 @ 34m	1	1	pp	ch
d	6/14/88	39	Son 1883	0n 50e, 359 @ 34m	2	1	go	gw
d	6/14/88	39	Son 1883	0n 50e, 359 @ 34m	3	1	smf	sa
d	6/14/88	40	Son 1883	0n 50e, 349 @ 46m	1	1	pc	ob
d	6/14/88	40	Son 1883	0n 50e, 349 @ 46m	2	1	go	sa
d	6/14/88	41	Son 1883	0n 50e, 349 @ 42m	1	1	bf	ob
d	6/14/88	42	Son 1883	0n 50e, 8 @ 37m	1	1	mf	sa
d	6/14/88	42	Son 1883	0n 50e, 8 @ 37m	2	15	go	s
d	6/14/88	42	Son 1883	0n 50e, 8 @ 37m	3	1	em	c
d	6/14/88	42	Son 1883	0n 50e, 8 @ 37m	4	3	cf	ch
d	6/14/88	42	Son 1883	0n 50e, 8 @ 37m	5	1	sh	ob
d	6/14/88	42	Son 1883	0n 50e, 8 @ 37m	6	1	if	ob
d	6/14/88	42	Son 1883	0n 50e, 8 @ 37m	7	1	pc	sc
d	6/14/88	43	Son 1883	0n 50e, 7 @ 62m	1	1	sh	ch
d	6/14/88	44	Son 1883	0n 0e, 340 @ 40m	1	1	go	sa
d	6/15/88	1	Son 1883	0n 0e, 274 @ 121m	1	1	go	sc
d	6/15/88	2	Son 1884	sub A 2w 0n	1	2	go	sa
d	6/15/88	3	Son 1884	sub A 2s 0e	1	1	sc	ch
d	6/15/88	4	Son 1884	sub A 0n 6w	1	1	sh	ch
d	6/15/88	4	Son 1884	sub A 0n 6w	2	1	go	sa

Location	Collection-date	Field-Spec-no	Site	Unit	Artifact-sequence	Count	Artifact-category	Raw-material
d	6/15/88	5	Son 1884	sub A 0n 8w	1	1	sh	ch
d	6/15/88	6	Son 1884	sub A 0n 16w	1	1	go	sa
d	6/15/88	6	Son 1884	sub A 0n 16w	2	1	sh	sc
d	6/15/88	7	Son 1884	sub A 0n 16w	1	1	go	sa
d	6/15/88	9	Son 1884	12n 16w	1	1	pp	ch
d	6/15/88	9	Son 1884	12n 16w	2	1	cf	ch
d	6/15/88	9	Son 1884	12n 16w	3	1	bt	ch
d	6/15/88	9	Son 1884	12n 16w	4	1	go	sa
d	6/15/88	10	Son 1884	sub A 14n 16w	1	1	sc	ch
d	6/15/88	12	Son 1884	sub A 0n 16w, 28 @17m	1	1	go	sa
d	6/15/88	13	Son 1884	sub A 13n 10w	1	1	em	ch
d	6/15/88	14	Son 1884	sub A 14n 11w	1	1	ppf	ch
d	6/15/88	15	Son 1884	sub A 11n 10.5w	1	1	pp	ob
d	6/15/88	16	Son 1884	sub A 11n 12w	1	1	un	ob
d	6/15/88	17	Son 1884	sub A 0n 16w, 352 @28m	1	1	if	ch
d	6/15/88	17	Son 1884	sub A 0n 16w,352 @28m	2	1	nt	sa
d	6/15/88	18	Son 1884	sub A 0n 16w, 2 @ 30m	1	1	go	sa
d	6/15/88	18	Son 1884	sub A 0n 16w, 2 @ 30m	2	1	sh	ch
d	6/15/88	19	Son 1884	sub A 0n 16w, 6 8 @11m	1	1	cf	ch
d	6/15/88	20	Son 1884	sub A 0n 16w, 84 @10m	1	1	cf	ch
d	6/15/88	21	Son 1884	sub A 0n 16w, 75 @16m	1	1	go	sa
d	6/15/88	23	Son 1884	sub A 1s 31w	1	1	if	ch
d	6/15/88	24	Son 1884	sub A 0n 16w, 233 @17m	1	1	go	sa
d	6/15/88	26	Son 1884	sub B 0n 1e	1	1	go	sa
d	6/15/88	28	Son 1884	sub B 0n 3e	1	2	go	sa
d	6/15/88	29	Son 1884	sub B 2s 0e	1	1	em	ch
d	6/15/88	30	Son 1884	sub B 6s 0e	1	1	cf	ch
d	6/15/88	31	Son 1884	sub B 10s 0e	1	1	pc	ch
d	6/15/88	31	Son 1884	sub B 10s 0e	2	1	go	sa
d	6/15/88	31	Son 1884	sub B 10s 0e	3	1	sh	ch
d	6/15/88	31	Son 1884	sub B 10s 0e	4	1	pc	sc
d	6/15/88	32	Son 1884	sub B 0n 5e	1	1	em	ch
d	6/15/88	32	Son 1884	sub B 0n 5e	2	1	em	ch
d	6/15/88	32	Son 1884	sub B 0n 5e	3	4	go	sa
d	6/15/88	33	Son 1884	sub B 14s 0e	1	1	go	sa
d	6/15/88	35	Son 1884	sub B 0n 11e	1	4	go	sa
d	6/15/88	36	Son 1884	sub B 0n 9e	1	3	go	sa
d	6/15/88	37	Son 1884	sub B 0n 15e	1	1	go	sa
d	6/15/88	38	Son 1884	sub B 7s 4w	1	1	pc	ch
d	6/15/88	39	Son 1884	sub B 4n 4w	1	1	em	ch
d	6/15/88	39	Son 1884	sub B 4n 4w	2	2	go	sa
d	6/15/88	39	Son 1884	sub B 4n 4w	3	1	ha	ch
d	6/15/88	39	Son 1884	sub B 4n 4w	4	1	if	ob
d	6/15/88	39	Son 1884	sub B 4n 4w	5	1	sh	ch
d	6/15/88	39	Son 1884	sub B 4n 4w	6	3	go	sa
d	6/15/88	40	Son 1884	sub B 4n 0e	1	5	go	sa
d	6/15/88	40	Son 1884	sub B 4n 0e	2	1	em	ch
d	6/15/88	41	Son 1884	sub B 24s 22.5 w	1	1	pp	ob
d	6/15/88	43	Son 1884	sub B 165 @ 14m	1	1	sh	qu

Location	Collection-date	Field-Spec-no	Site	Unit	Artifact-sequence	Count	Artifact-category	Raw-material

Location	Collection-date	Field-Spec-no	Site	Unit	Artifact-sequence	Count	Artifact-category	Raw-material
d	6/15/88	43	Son 1884	sub B 165 @ 14m	2	2	sh	ch
d	6/15/88	44	Son 1884	sub B 6 @ 28m	1	1	cf	qu
d	6/15/88	44	Son 1884	sub B 6 @ 28m	2	1	bt	ch
d	6/15/88	45	Son 1884	sub B 4s 0e	1	21	go	sa
d	6/15/88	45	Son 1884	sub B 4s 0e	2	1	bf	ob
d	6/15/88	45	Son 1884	sub B 4s 0e	3	4	sh	ch
d	6/15/88	45	Son 1884	sub B 4s 0e	4	3	if	ch
d	6/16/88	1	d-7	isolate	1	2	cf	ch
d	6/16/88	2	d-7	isolate	1	2	ma	sa
e	6/07/89	1	Son 1888	0n 0e	1	1	if	ch
e	6/07/89	3	Son 1888	4n 0e	1	1	go	sa
e	6/07/89	3	Son 1888	4n 0e	2	1	if	ch
e	6/07/89	6	Son 1888	0n 6w	1	1	bt	ob
e	6/07/89	6	Son 1888	0n 6w	2	1	em	ch
e	6/07/89	7	Son 1888	2s 0e	1	2	if	ch
e	6/07/89	7	Son 1888	2s 0e	2	1	go	sa
e	6/07/89	8	Son 1888	4s 0e	1	1	bt	ob
e	6/07/89	9	Son 1888	6s 0e	1	1	if	ch
e	6/07/89	10	Son 1888	0n 1e	1	1	em	ob
e	6/07/89	10	Son 1888	0n 1e	2	3	bt	ob
e	6/07/89	10	Son 1888	0n 1e	3	1	sc	ch
e	6/07/89	11	Son 1888	1n 2w	1	3	em	ch
e	6/07/89	11	Son 1888	1n 2w	2	3	if	ch
e	6/07/89	11	Son 1888	1n 2w	3	2	sc	ch
f	6/02/89	4	Son 174	0n 0e	1	1	bt	ob
f	6/02/89	5	Son 174	8n 0e	1	1	bt	ob
f	6/05/89	15	Son 174	327 @ 9m	1	1	bc	ch
f	6/05/89	17	Son 174	57 @24.9m	1	1	em	ob
h	6/07/89	1	Son 228	198 @ 3.47m	1	2	bt	ob
h	6/07/89	2	Son 228	220 @ 3.13m	1	1	em	ch
h	6/07/89	3	Son 228	219 @ 3.62m	1	1	bt	ob
h	6/07/89	4	Son 228	203 @ 11.26m	1	1	bt	ob
h	6/07/89	5	Son 228	205 @ 13.12m	1	1	bt	ob
h	6/07/89	6	Son 228	208 @ 14.78	1	1	em	ch
h	6/07/89	7	Son 228	209 @ 16.08m	1	1	sh	ch
h	6/07/89	8	Son 228	214 @ 11.89m	1	1	if	ob
h	6/07/89	9	Son 228	235 @ 8.6m	1	1	if	ob
h	6/07/89	10	Son 228	267 @ 4.39m	1	1	cf	sa
h	6/07/89	11	Son 228	267 @ 3.46m	1	1	cf	sa
h	6/07/89	12	Son 228	282 @ 10.85m	1	1	if	ob
h	6/07/89	13	Son 228	310 @ 31.23m	1	1	if	ob
h	6/07/89	14	Son 228	316 @ 34.27m	1	1	if	ob
h	6/07/89	15	Son 228	316 @ 34.02m	1	1	if	ob
h	6/07/89	16	Son 228	330 @ 17.31m	1	1	if	ch
h	6/07/89	17	Son 228	342 @ 21m	1	1	if	ob
h	6/07/89	18	Son 228	344 @ 14.92m	1	1	if	ch
h	6/07/89	18	Son 228	344 @ 14.92m	2	2	em	ch
h	6/07/89	18	Son 228	344 @ 14.92m	3	1	mf	sa
h	6/08/89	19	Son 228	346 @ 13.97m	1	1	if	ch

Location	Collection-date	Field-Spec-no	Site	Unit	Artifact-sequence	Count	Artifact-category	Raw-material
h	6/08/89	20	Son 228	347 @ 16.48m	1	1	if	ob
h	6/08/89	21	Son 228	6 @ 19.26m	1	1	bf	ob
h	6/08/89	22	Son 228	2 @ 21.26m	1	1	if	ch
h	6/08/89	23	Son 228	21 @ 31.94m	1	1	if	ch
h	6/08/89	24	Son 228	31 @ 24.90m	1	1	if	ob
h	6/08/89	25	Son 228	39 @ 26.45m	1	1	if	ch
h	6/08/89	26	Son 228	118 @ 11.05m	1	1	bc	sa
h	6/08/89	28	Son 228	139 @ 18.10m	1	1	if	ch
h	6/08/89	29	Son 228	149 @ 30.30m	1	1	nf	ob
h	6/08/89	29	Son 228	149 @ 30.30m	2	1	if	ob
h	6/08/89	30	Son 228	158 @ 31.78m	1	1	if	ob
h	6/08/89	31	Son 228	159 @ 39.60m	1	1	if	ch
h	6/08/89	32	Son 228	164 @ 11.63m	1	1	if	ob
h	6/08/89	33	Son 228	165 @ 30.66m	1	1	if	ob
h	6/08/89	34	Son 228	189 @ 46.60m	1	1	if	ob
h	6/08/89	35	Son 228	198 @ 53.00m	1	1	bcf	sa
i	6/08/89	1	Son 1889	0n 0e	1	1	bt	ob
i	6/08/89	3	Son 1889	0n 2w	1	1	uf	ob
i	6/08/89	4	Son 1889	2s 0e	1	1	go	sa
i	6/08/89	5	Son 1889	356 @ 5.1m	1	1	go	sa
i	6/08/89	8	Son 1889	96 @ 5.1m	1	1	em	ob
i	6/08/89	8	Son 1889	96 @ 5.1m	2	1	if	ob
i	6/08/89	11	Son 1889	200 @ 2.8m	1	1	fc	sa
i	6/08/89	11	Son 1889	200 @ 2.8m	2	1	if	ob
i	6/08/89	12	Son 1889	33 @ 5.3m	1	1	em	ch
i	6/08/89	12	Son 1889	33 @ 5.3m	2	1	bf	ch
i	6/08/89	16	Son 1889	0 @ 6.2m	1	1	mf	sa
i	6/08/89	16	Son 1889	0 @ 6.2m	2	1	em	ch
i	6/08/89	17	Son 1889	322 @ 6.2m	1	1	co	ch
i	6/08/89	18	Son 1889	337 @ 3.9m	1	1	em	ch
i	6/08/89	20	Son 1889	352 @ 4.1m	1	1	go	sa
i	6/08/89	21	Son 1889	38 @ 6.5m	1	1	em	ch
i	6/08/89	22	Son 1889	120 @ 1.3m	1	1	pe	sa
i	6/08/89	23	Son 1889	348 @ 7.2m	1	1	go	sa
k	6/14/89	1	Son 1890	0n 0e	1	1	if	ob
k	6/15/89	1	Son 1890	0n 0e	1	3	sh	ch
k	6/15/89	1	Son 1890	0n 0e	2	1	bi	ch
k	6/15/89	1	Son 1890	0n 0e	3	1	sc	ch
k	6/15/89	2	Son 1890	16 @ 15.2m	1	2	bt	ob
k	6/15/89	5	Son 1890	313 @ 32.5m	1	1	em	ch
l	6/02/89	1	Son 1886	0n 0e	1	1	em	qu
l	6/02/89	2	Son 1886	0n 0e	1	20	fc	sa
l	6/02/89	2	Son 1886	0n 0e	2	1	em	ch
l	6/02/89	2	Son 1886	0n 0e	3	2	em	ch
l	6/02/89	2	Son 1886	0n 0e	4	1	pe	gw
l	6/02/89	2	Son 1886	0n 0e	5	1	mf	ba
l	6/02/89	2	Son 1886	0n 0e	6	4	go	ba
l	6/02/89	2	Son 1886	0n 0e	7	1	bc	ba
l	6/02/89	2	Son 1886	0n 0e	8	1	fc	sa

Location	Collection-date	Field-Spec-no	Site	Unit	Artifact-sequence	Count	Artifact-category	Raw-material
1	6/02/89	2	Son 1886	0n 0e	9	3	go	gw
1	6/02/89	3	Son 1886	2n 0e	1	7	go	sa
1	6/02/89	3	Son 1886	2n 0e	2	3	em	ch
1	6/02/89	3	Son 1886	2n 0e	3	1	ma	sa
1	6/02/89	3	Son 1886	2n 0e	4	5	fc	sa
1	6/02/89	3	Son 1886	2n 0e	5	1	sc	ch
1	6/02/89	3	Son 1886	2n 0e	6	3	if	ch
1	6/02/89	3	Son 1886	2n 0e	7	1	sc	ch
1	6/02/89	3	Son 1886	2n 0e	8	1	bf	ch
1	6/02/89	3	Son 1886	2n 0e	9	1	if	ob
1	6/02/89	6	Son 1886	0n 4w	1	2	sc	ch
1	6/02/89	6	Son 1886	0n 4w	2	1	if	ch
1	6/02/89	6	Son 1886	0n 4w	3	1	go	ba
1	6/02/89	6	Son 1886	0n 4w	4	2	go	sa
1	6/02/89	6	Son 1886	0n 4w	5	3	go	sa
1	6/05/89	1	Son 1886	0n 2w	1	1	em	ch
1	6/05/89	2	Son 1886	0n 2w	1	1	pp	ch
1	6/05/89	2	Son 1886	0n 2w	2	1	pp	ch
1	6/05/89	2	Son 1886	0n 2w	3	3	em	ch
1	6/05/89	2	Son 1886	0n 2w	4	1	co	ch
1	6/05/89	2	Son 1886	0n 2w	5	2	em	ch
1	6/05/89	2	Son 1886	0n 2w	6	1	cf	ch
1	6/05/89	2	Son 1886	0n 2w	7	1	if	ch
1	6/05/89	2	Son 1886	0n 2w	8	1	if	qu
1	6/05/89	2	Son 1886	0n 2w	9	1	em	ch
1	6/05/89	2	Son 1886	0n 2w	10	1	if	ch
1	6/05/89	2	Son 1886	0n 2w	11	1	pc	ch
1	6/05/89	2	Son 1886	0n 2w	12	1	em	ch
1	6/05/89	2	Son 1886	0n 2w	13	1	em	ch
1	6/05/89	2	Son 1886	0n 2w	14	2	pc	ch
1	6/05/89	2	Son 1886	0n 2w	15	2	go	gw
1	6/05/89	2	Son 1886	0n 2w	16	1	go	ba
1	6/05/89	2	Son 1886	0n 2w	17	1	mf	sa
1	6/05/89	2	Son 1886	0n 2w	18	25	fc	sa
1	6/05/89	3	Son 1886	2s 0e	1	1	em	ch
1	6/05/89	3	Son 1886	2s 0e	2	1	go	ba
1	6/05/89	3	Son 1886	2s 0e	3	1	mf	sa
1	6/05/89	3	Son 1886	2s 0e	4	2	go	sa
1	6/05/89	3	Son 1886	2s 0e	5	27	fc	sa
1	6/05/89	3	Son 1886	2s 0e	6	4	bc	ba
1	6/05/89	3	Son 1886	2s 0e	7	1	em	ch
1	6/05/89	3	Son 1886	2s 0e	8	1	sc	ch
1	6/05/89	3	Son 1886	2s 0e	9	1	pc	ch
1	6/05/89	3	Son 1886	2s 0e	10	1	em	ch
1	6/05/89	3	Son 1886	2s 0e	11	1	em	sc
1	6/05/89	6	Son 1886	0n 1e	1	0	if	ch
1	6/05/89	6	Son 1886	0n 1e	2	1	em	ob
1	6/05/89	6	Son 1886	0n 1e	3	2	if	ob
1	6/05/89	6	Son 1886	0n 1e	4	1	go	sa

Location	Collection-date	Field-Spec-no	Site	Unit	Artifact-sequence	Count	Artifact-category	Raw-material
1	6/05/89	6	Son 1886	0n 1e	5	5	fc	sa
1	6/05/89	6	Son 1886	0n 1e	6	3	mf	sa
1	6/05/89	8	Son 1886	0n 6w	1	1	sc	ch
1	6/05/89	8	Son 1886	0n 6w	2	1	go	sa
1	6/05/89	10	Son 1886	6s 0e	1	2	if	ch
1	6/05/89	10	Son 1886	6s 0e	2	2	sc	ch
1	6/05/89	10	Son 1886	6s 0e	3	3	mf	sa
1	6/05/89	10	Son 1886	6s 0e	4	1	co	ch
1	6/05/89	11	Son 1886	4s 0e	1	6	go	sa
1	6/05/89	11	Son 1886	4s 0e	2	3	fc	sa
1	6/05/89	11	Son 1886	4s 0e	3	1	cf	ch
1	6/05/89	11	Son 1886	4s 0e	4	1	sh	ch
1	6/05/89	11	Son 1886	4s 0e	5	1	em	ch
1	6/05/89	13	Son 1886	4n 0e	1	2	if	ob
1	6/05/89	13	Son 1886	4n 0e	2	1	em	ob
1	6/05/89	13	Son 1886	4n 0e	3	1	sc	ch
1	6/05/89	13	Son 1886	4n 0e	4	6	if	ch
1	6/05/89	13	Son 1886	4n 0e	5	1	em	ch
1	6/05/89	13	Son 1886	4n 0e	6	4	mf	sa
1	6/05/89	13	Son 1886	4n 0e	7	2	fc	sa
1	6/08/89	1	Son 1891	random	1	1	em	ch
1	6/28/89	1	Son 1892	309 @ 83m	1	2	go	sa
1	6/28/89	2	Son 1892	320 @ 86m	1	1	sh	ch
1	6/28/89	3	Son 1892	349 @ 71m	1	1	sh	ch
1	6/28/89	4	Son 1892	e	1	1	ha	sa
1	6/28/89	6	Son 1892	f	1	1	go	sa
1	6/28/89	6	Son 1892	f	2	1	em	ob
1	6/28/89	8	Son 1892	d	1	1	go	sa
1	6/28/89	10	Son 1892	c	1	1	if	ch
1	6/28/89	10	Son 1892	c	2	1	bt	ob
1	6/28/89	10	Son 1892	c	3	1	sc	ch
1	6/28/89	10	Son 1892	c	4	1	bc	gw
1	6/28/89	10	Son 1892	c	5	1	go	sa
1	6/28/89	14	Son 1892	l	1	1	go	sa
1	6/28/89	15	Son 1892	b	1	1	em	ch

APPENDIX 5.2

MOLLUSK REMAINS FROM FORT ROSS SITES

Location	Collection-Date	Field-Spec-No	Site	Unit	Artifact-Sequence	Count	Element	Taxon
a	6/07/88	1	Son 670	0n 0e	1	4	fragment	ui
a	6/07/88	1	Son 670	0n 0e	2	1	plate	chiton
a	6/07/88	2	Son 670	2n 03	1	8	fragment	ui, barnacle
a	6/07/88	3	Son 670	4n 0e	1	2	fragment	ui
a	6/07/88	4	Son 670a	2s 0e	1	1	fragment	ui
a	6/07/88	5	Son 670	4s 0e	1	1	cap	. plate limpet
a	6/07/88	8	Son 670	0n 2w	1	4	fragment	ui
a	6/07/88	11	Son 670	0n 1e	1	1	fragment	ui
a	6/07/88	13	Son 670	nw quad	1	10	fragment	ui
a	6/07/88	13	Son 670	nw quad	2	2	fragment	abalone
a	6/07/88	13	Son 670	nw quad	3	1	cap	plate limpet
a	6/07/88	13	Son 670	nw quad	4	1	aperture	black turban snail
a	6/07/88	14	Son 670	se quad	1	1	whorl	abalone
a	6/10/88	7	Son 1878	0n 12w	1	2	fragment	ui
a	6/10/88	13	Son 1878	90 @ 11m	1	4	fragment	abalone
a	6/10/88	15	Son 1878	ne quad	1	20	fragment	ui
a	6/10/88	15	Son 1878	ne quad	2	2	cap	plate limpets
a	6/10/88	15	Son 1878	ne quad	3	2	umbo	mussel
a	6/10/88	15	Son 1878	ne quad	4	1	fragment	abalone
a	6/10/88	17	Son 1878	350 @ 20m	1	1	fragment	abalone
b	6/08/88	1	Son 1880	0n 0e	1	20	fragment	ui, abalone
b	6/08/88	2	Son 1880	0n 1e	1	10	fragment	ui
b	6/08/88	2	Son 1880	0n 1e	2	2	fragment	abalone
b	6/08/88	2	Son 1880	0n 1e	3	1	fragment	limpet
b	6/08/88	2	Son 1880	0n 1e	4	1	plate	chiton
b	6/08/88	3	Son 1880	2s 0e	1	1	fragment	ui
b	6/08/88	5	Son 1880	0n 2w	1	1	fragment	ui
b	6/08/88	10	Son 1880	Sub A 0n 0e	1	39	fragment	ui
b	6/08/88	10	Son 1880	Sub A 0n 0e	2	1	umbo	mussel, also 2 fragments
b	6/08/88	10	Son 1880	Sub A 0n 0e	3	1	fragment	abalone
b	6/08/88	10	Son 1880	Sub A 0n 0e	4	2	plate	chiton
b	6/08/88	10	Son 1880	Sub A 0n 0e	5	1	body whorl	black turban snail
b	6/08/88	11	Son 1880	Sub A 2n 0e	1	6	fragment	ui
b	6/08/88	11	Son 1880	Sub A 2n 0e	2	2	cap	plate limpet, dunce cap limpet
b	6/08/88	11	Son 1880	Sub A 2n 0e	3	2	umbo	mussel
b	6/08/88	11	Son 1880	Sub A 2n 0e	4	1	body whorl	black turban snail
b	6/08/88	12	Son 1880	Sub A 4n 0e	1	3	fragment	ui, abalone, mussel
b	6/08/88	13	Son 1880	Sub A 0n 1e	1	17	fragment	ui
b	6/08/88	13	Son 1880	Sub A 0n 1e	2	1	aperture	black turban snail
b	6/08/88	13	Son 1880	Sub A 0n 1e	3	1	fragment	abalone
b	6/08/88	14	Son 1880	Sub A 0n 3e	1	4	fragment	ui
b	6/08/88	14	Son 1880	Sub A 0n 3e	2	1	fragment	barnacle
b	6/08/88	15	Son 1880	Sub A 2s 0e	1	15	fragment	ui
b	6/08/88	15	Son 1880	Sub A 2s 0e	2	3	whole	black turban snail

Note: Under "Taxon" 'ui' = unidentifiable shell.

Location	Collection-Date	Field-Spec-No	Site	Unit	Artifact-Sequence	Count	Element	Taxon
b	6/08/88	15	Son 1880	Sub A 2s 0e	3	1	cap	plate limpet
b	6/08/88	15	Son 1880	Sub A 2s 0e	4	3	umbo	mussel
b	6/08/88	15	Son 1880	Sub A 2s 0e	5	1	fragment	barnacle
b	6/08/88	16	Son 1880	Sub A 4s 0e	1	20	fragment	ui
b	6/08/88	16	Son 1880	Sub A 4s 0e	2	8	whole	black turban snail
b	6/08/88	16	Son 1880	Sub A 4s 0e	3	4	fragment	barnacle
b	6/08/88	16	Son 1880	Sub A 4s 0e	4	1	umbo	mussel
b	6/08/88	17	Son 1880	Sub A 6s 0e	1	1	body whorl	black turban snail
b	6/08/88	18	Son 1880	Sub A 8s 0e	1	2	fragment	ui
b	6/08/88	19	Son 1880	Sub A 0n 2w	1	10	fragment	ui
b	6/08/88	20	Son 1880	Sub A 0n 4w	1	6	fragment	ui
b	6/08/88	22	Son 1880	Sub B 0n 0e	1	14	fragment	ui, abalone, turban snail
b	6/08/88	22	Son 1880	Sub B 0n 0e	2	1	umbo	mussel
b	6/08/88	23	Son 1880	Sub B 2n 0e	1	2	fragment	ui
b	6/08/88	24	Son 1880	Sub B 0n 2w	1	20	fragment	ui, mussel, barnacle
b	6/08/88	24	Son 1880	Sub B 0n 2w	2	1	fragment	abalone
b	6/08/88	24	Son 1880	Sub B 0n 2w	3	1	cap	plate limpet
b	6/08/88	25	Son 1880	Sub B 2s 0e	1	13	fragment	ui, abalone
b	6/08/88	26	Son 1880	Sub A 0n 1e	1	8	fragment	ui
b	6/08/88	26	Son 1880	Sub A 0n 1e	2	1	umbo	mussel
b	6/08/88	26	Son 1880	Sub A 0n 1e	3	1	plate	chiton
b	6/09/88	1	Son 1881	Sub A 0n 0e	1	16	fragment	ui, abalone
b	6/09/88	1	Son 1881	Sub A 0n 0e	2	1	umbo	mussel
b	6/09/88	2	Son 1881	Sub A 2s 0e	1	14	fragment	ui
b	6/09/88	3	Son 1881	Sub A 0n 1e	1	7	fragment	ui
b	6/09/88	3	Son 1881	Sub A 0n 1e	2	1	cap	plate limpet
b	6/09/88	3	Son 1881	Sub A 0n 1e	3	1	plate	chiton
b	6/09/88	4	Son 1881	Sub A 0n 2w	1	4	fragment	ui
b	6/09/88	4	Son 1881	Sub A 0n 2w	2	1	umbo	mussel
b	6/09/88	4	Son 1881	Sub A 0n 2w	3	2	plate	chiton
b	6/09/88	4	Son 1881	Sub A 0n 2w	4	1	fragment	sea urchin
b	6/09/88	4	Son 1881	Sub A 0n 2w	5	3	fragment	barnacle
b	6/09/88	4	Son 1881	Sub A 0n 2w	6	1	cap	plate limpet
b	6/09/88	4	Son 1881	Sub A 0n 2w	7	2	fragment	abalone
b	6/09/88	5	Son 1881	268 @ 15.2m	1	1	cap	plate limpet
b	6/09/88	8	Son 1881	Sub A 204 @ 1.4m	1	1	fragment	abalone
b	6/09/88	8	Son 1881	Sub A 204 @ 1.4m	2	1	cap	plate limpet
b	6/09/88	10	Son 1881	0n 0e	1	7	fragment	ui
b	6/09/88	10	Son 1881	0n 0e	2	7	cap	1 owl limpet, 5 plate limpets
b	6/09/88	10	Son 1881	0n 0e	3	7	fragment	barnacle
b	6/09/88	10	Son 1881	0n 0e	4	1	umbo	mussel
b	6/09/88	10	Son 1881	0n 0e	5	1	whole	black turban snail
b	6/09/88	11	Son 1881	2s 0e	1	5	fragment	ui, mussel
b	6/09/88	11	Son 1881	2s 0e	2	1	plate	chiton
b	6/09/88	11	Son 1881	2s 0e	3	1	cap	dunce cap limpet
b	6/09/88	11	Son 1881	2s 0e	4	1	fragment	sea urchin
b	6/09/88	11	Son 1881	2s 0e	5	6	fragment	barnacle
b	6/09/88	12	Son 1881	0n 1e	1	6	fragment	ui
b	6/09/88	12	Son 1881	0n 1e	2	1	cap	plate limpet
b	6/09/88	12	Son 1881	0n 1e	3	1	plate	chiton

Location	Collection-Date	Field-Spec-No	Site	Unit	Artifact-Sequence	Count	Element	Taxon
b	6/09/88	12	Son 1881	0n 1e	4	2	fragment	barnacle
b	6/09/88	13	Son 1881	0n 2w	1	12	fragment	ui
b	6/09/88	13	Son 1881	0n 2w	2	2	umbo	mussel
b	6/09/88	13	Son 1881	0n 2w	3	2	cap	plate limpet
b	6/09/88	13	Son 1881	0n 2w	4	2	fragment	abalone
b	6/09/88	13	Son 1881	0n 2w	5	1	body whorl	black turban snail
b	6/09/88	13	Son 1881	0n 2w	6	4	fragment	barnacle
b	6/09/88	13	Son 1881	0n 2w	7	1	plate	chiton
b	6/09/88	13	Son 1881	0n 2w	8	1	fragment	sea urchin
b	6/09/88	14	Son 1880	Sub C 0nw 0sw	1	1	fragment	ui
b	6/09/88	14	Son 1880	Sub C 0nw 0sw	2	1	fragment	abalone
b	6/09/88	14	Son 1880	Sub C 0nw 0sw	3	3	plate	chiton
b	6/09/88	14	Son 1880	Sub C 0nw 0sw	4	1	umbo	mussel
b	6/09/88	15	Son 1880	Sub C 0nw 4sw	1	14	fragment	ui
b	6/09/88	15	Son 1880	Sub C 0nw 4sw	2	1	fragment	abalone
b	6/09/88	15	Son 1880	Sub C 0nw 4sw	3	1	umbo	mussel
b	6/09/88	15	Son 1880	Sub C 0nw 4sw	4	2	fragment	barnacle
b	6/09/88	15	Son 1880	Sub C 0nw 4sw	5	1	cap	ribbed limpet
b	6/09/88	16	Son 1880	Sub C 0nw 2sw	1	1	whorl	abalone, also 2 fragments
b	6/09/88	16	Son 1880	Sub C 0nw 2sw	2	1	cap	horned slipper 1
c	6/06/88	1	Son 1895	0n 0e	1	27	fragment	ui, chiton, mussel, abalone
c	6/06/88	1	Son 1895	0n 0e	2	1	body whorl	black turban snail
c	6/06/88	1	Son 1895	0n 0e	3	2	plate	chiton
c	6/06/88	1	Son 1895	0n 0e	4	1	umbo	mussel
c	6/06/88	1	Son 1895	0n 0e	5	2	fragment	barnacle
c	6/06/88	2	Son 1895	0n 1e	1	20	fragment	ui, mussel
c	6/06/88	2	Son 1895	0n 1e	2	3	plate	chiton
c	6/06/88	2	Son 1895	0n 1e	3	5	fragment	barnacle
c	6/06/88	3	Son 1895	0n 3e	1	20	fragment	ui, mussel, abalone
c	6/06/88	3	Son 1895	0n 3e	2	5	fragment	barnacle
c	6/06/88	3	Son 1895	0n 3e	3	2	plate	chiton
c	6/06/88	3	Son 1895	0n 3e	4	1	body whorl	black turban snail
c	6/06/88	4	Son 1895	2n 0e	1	15	fragment	ui, chiton, mussel
c	6/06/88	4	Son 1895	2n 0e	2	2	fragment	barnacle
c	6/06/88	4	Son 1895	2n 0e	3	1	cap	plate limpet
c	6/06/88	4	Son 1895	2n 0e	4	1	umbo	mussel
c	6/06/88	4	Son 1895	2n 0e	5	1	plate	chiton
c	6/06/88	5	Son 1895	4n 0e	1	10	fragment	ui, mussel
c	6/06/88	5	Son 1895	4n 0e	2	1	fragment	barnacle
c	6/06/88	5	Son 1895	4n 0e	3	2	plate	black chiton
c	6/06/88	6	Son 1895	6n 0e	1	2	fragment	ui, chiton
c	6/06/88	7	Son 1895	8n 0e	1	3	fragment	ui, barnacle
c	6/06/88	8	Son 1895	0n 2w	1	6	fragment	ui, mussel
c	6/06/88	9	Son 1895	0n 4w	1	8	fragment	ui, abalone
c	6/06/88	9	Son 1895	0n 4w	2	1	fragment	barnacle
c	6/06/88	9	Son 1895	0n 4w	3	1	umbo	mussel
c	6/06/88	10	Son 1895	0n 6w	1	3	fragment	ui, mussel
c	6/06/88	10	Son 1895	0n 6w	2	2	fragment	barnacle
c	6/06/88	10	Son 1895	0n 6w	3	1	plate	chiton
c	6/06/88	11	Son 1895	0n 8w	1	2	fragment	ui

Location	Collection-Date	Field-Spec-No	Site	Unit	Artifact-Sequence	Count	Element	Taxon
c	6/06/88	11	Son 1895	0n 8w	2	2	fragment	barnacle
c	6/06/88	12	Son 1895	0n 10w	1	5	fragment	ui, barnacle
c	6/06/88	13	Son 1895	2s 0e	1	20	fragment	ui, mussel, abalone
c	6/06/88	13	Son 1895	2s 0e	2	6	fragment	barnacle
c	6/06/88	13	Son 1895	2s 0e	3	1	plate	black chiton
c	6/06/88	13	Son 1895	2s 0e	4	1	cap	plate limpet
c	6/06/88	14	Son 1895	4s 0e	1	10	fragment	ui, mussel, chiton
c	6/06/88	14	Son 1895	4s 0e	2	1	cap	plate limpet
c	6/06/88	14	Son 1895	4s 0e	3	1	fragment	barnacle
c	6/06/88	15	Son 1895	6s 0e	1	3	fragment	ui, barnacle
c	6/06/88	17	Son 1895	ne quad	1	3	fragment	abalone
c	6/06/88	18	Son 1895	ne quad	1	9	fragment	abalone
c	6/06/88	19	Son 1895	sw quad	1	4	fragment	abalone
c	6/06/88	20	Son 1895	se quad	1	10	fragment	ui, mussel, abalone, chiton
c	6/06/88	22	Son 1895	81 @ 18.2m	1	3	fragment	abalone
c	6/06/88	23	Son 1885	0n 0e	1	13	fragment	ui
c	6/06/88	25	Son 1885	8n 0e	1	1	fragment	ui
c	6/06/88	26	Son 1885	10n 0e	1	2	fragment	barnacle
c	6/06/88	28	Son 1885	14n 0e	1	3	fragment	ui, abalone
c	6/06/88	28	Son 1885	14n 0e	2	1	fragment	barnacle
c	6/06/88	35	Son 1885	sw quad	1	5	fragment	abalone
c	6/06/88	35	Son 1885	sw quad	2	1	umbo	mussel
c	6/06/88	40	Son 1885	0n 4w	1	2	fragment	ui
c	6/06/88	41	Son 1885	0n 10w	1	4	fragment	ui, barnacle, turban snail
c	6/06/88	42	Son 1885	0n 8w	1	20	fragment	ui
c	6/06/88	42	Son 1885	0n 8w	2	4	plate	chiton
c	6/06/88	42	Son 1885	0n 8w	3	1	cap	plate limpet
c	6/06/88	42	Son 1885	0n 8w	4	3	whole	1 eroded periwinkle
c	6/06/88	42	Son 1885	0n 8w	5	2	umbo	mussel
c	6/06/88	42	Son 1885	0n 8w	6	4	fragment	barnacle
c	6/06/88	43	Son 1885	0n 12w	1	7	fragment	ui
c	6/06/88	44	Son 1885	14s 0e	1	1	plate	chiton
c	6/06/88	45	Son 1885	0n 11e	1	1	fragment	ui
c	6/06/88	46	Son 1885	0n 7e	1	1	plate	chiton
c	6/06/88	48	Son 1885	nw quad	1	5	fragment	abalone
c	6/06/88	49	Son 1885	0n 6w	1	20	fragment	ui, limpet
c	6/06/88	49	Son 1885	0n 6w	2	2	fragment	barnacle
c	6/06/88	49	Son 1885	0n 6w	3	3	plate	chiton
c	6/06/88	49	Son 1885	0n 6w	4	2	umbo	mussel
c	6/08/88	1	Son 1896	0n 1e	1	4	fragment	ui, chiton
c	6/08/88	1	Son 1896	0n 1e	2	2	fragment	barnacle
c	6/08/88	1	Son 1896	0n 1e	3	3	plate	black chiton
c	6/08/88	2	Son 1896	0n 3e	1	4	fragment	ui, chiton, mussel
c	6/08/88	2	Son 1896	0n 3e	2	2	fragment	barnacle
c	6/08/88	2	Son 1896	0n 3e	3	1	plate	black chiton
c	6/08/88	3	Son 1896	0n 5e	1	1	fragment	ui
c	6/08/88	3	Son 1896	0n 5e	2	1	fragment	barnacle
c	6/08/88	3	Son 1896	0n 5e	3	2	plate	black chiton
c	6/08/88	4	Son 1896	0n 7e	1	20	fragment	ui, abalone, mussel, chiton
c	6/08/88	4	Son 1896	0n 7e	2	1	body whorl	black turban snail

Location	Collection-Date	Field-Spec-No	Site	Unit	Artifact-Sequence	Count	Element	Taxon
c	6/08/88	4	Son 1896	0n 7e	3	1	fragment	barnacle
c	6/08/88	4	Son 1896	0n 7e	4	1	plate	black chiton
c	6/08/88	8	Son 1896	0s 0e	1	2	fragment	ui
c	6/08/88	8	Son 1896	0s 0e	2	2	plate	black chiton
c	6/08/88	8	Son 1896	0s 0e	3	1	umbo	mussel
c	6/08/88	8	Son 1896	0s 0e	4	1	fragment	barnacle
c	6/08/88	9	Son 1896	2s 0e	1	2	fragment	ui
c	6/08/88	10	Son 1896	0n 0e	1	20	fragment	ui, chiton, abalone
c	6/08/88	10	Son 1896	0n 0e	2	1	body whorl	black turban snail
c	6/08/88	10	Son 1896	0n 0e	3	3	fragment	barnacle
c	6/08/88	10	Son 1896	0n 0e	4	2	umbo	mussel
c	6/08/88	10	Son 1896	0n 0e	5	5	plate	black chiton
c	6/08/88	10	Son 1896	0n 0e	6	1	cap	plate limpet
c	6/08/88	11	Son 1896	2n 0e	1	20	fragment	ui, mussel, abalone, chiton
c	6/08/88	11	Son 1896	2n 0e	2	1	cap	keyhole limpet
c	6/08/88	11	Son 1896	2n 0e	3	9	fragment	barnacle
c	6/08/88	11	Son 1896	2n 0e	4	4	umbo	mussel
c	6/08/88	11	Son 1896	2n 0e	5	7	plate	black chiton
c	6/08/88	11	Son 1896	2n 0e	6	1	body whorl	black turban snail
c	6/08/88	12	Son 1896	4n 0e	1	1	fragment	barnacle
c	6/08/88	12	Son 1896	4n 0e	2	3	plate	black chiton
c	6/08/88	13	Son 1896	6n 0e	1	2	fragment	ui, barnacle
c	6/08/88	14	Son 1896	0n 0w	1	20	fragment	ui, chiton, limpet
c	6/08/88	14	Son 1896	0n 0w	2	4	cap	limpet
c	6/08/88	14	Son 1896	0n 0w	3	6	fragment	barnacle
c	6/08/88	14	Son 1896	0n 0w	4	6	umbo	mussel
c	6/08/88	14	Son 1896	0n 0w	5	8	plate	black chiton
c	6/08/88	14	Son 1896	0n 0w	6	2	body whorl	black turban snail
c	6/08/88	15	Son 1896	2w 0e	1	10	fragment	ui, abalone, chiton
c	6/08/88	15	Son 1896	2w 0e	2	5	plate	black chiton
c	6/08/88	16	Son 1896	4w 0n	1	8	fragment	ui, chiton, mussel
c	6/08/88	16	Son 1896	4w 0n	2	1	cap	plate limpet
c	6/08/88	16	Son 1896	4w 0n	3	2	fragment	barnacle
c	6/08/88	16	Son 1896	4w 0n	4	2	umbo	mussel
c	6/08/88	16	Son 1896	4w 0n	5	2	plate	black chiton
c	6/08/88	17	Son 1896	6w 0n	1	20	fragment	ui, mussel, abalone
c	6/08/88	17	Son 1896	6w 0n	2	1	whole	Olivella
c	6/08/88	17	Son 1896	6w 0n	3	1	cap	plate limpet
c	6/08/88	17	Son 1896	6w 0n	4	4	plate	chiton
c	6/08/88	17	Son 1896	6w 0n	5	6	umbo	mussel
c	6/08/88	17	Son 1896	6w 0n	6	7	fragment	barnacle
c	6/08/88	18	Son 1896	8w 0n	1	10	fragment	ui, mussel, chiton, snail
c	6/08/88	18	Son 1896	8w 0n	2	1	cap	plate limpet
c	6/08/88	18	Son 1896	8w 0n	3	1	fragment	barnacle
c	6/08/88	18	Son 1896	8w 0n	4	2	plate	black chiton
c	6/08/88	18	Son 1896	8w 0n	5	1	umbo	mussel
c	6/08/88	19	Son 1896	10w 0n	1	1	fragment	ui
c	6/08/88	19	Son 1896	10w 0n	2	2	fragment	barnacle
c	6/08/88	20	Son 1896	ne quad	1	6	fragment	ui, abalone
c	6/08/88	21	Son 1896	sw quad	1	20	fragment	abalone

Location	Collection-Date	Field-Spec-No	Site	Unit	Artifact-Sequence	Count	Element	Taxon
c	6/10/88	6	Son 1882	ne quad	1	5	fragment	ui, abalone
c	6/10/88	7	Son 1882	nw quad	1	1	fragment	abalone
c	6/10/88	8	Son 1882	0n 0e	1	8	fragment	ui
c	6/10/88	8	Son 1882	0n 0e	2	1	plate	chiton
c	6/10/88	8	Son 1882	0n 0e	3	1	aperture	black turban snail
c	6/10/88	8	Son 1882	0n 0e	4	1	fragment	barnacle
c	6/10/88	9	Son 1882	2n 0e	1	10	fragment	ui, barnacle
c	6/10/88	9	Son 1882	2n 0e	2	1	body whorl	black turban snail
c	6/10/88	10	Son 1882	4n 0e	1	30	fragment	ui, barnacle, chiton
c	6/10/88	11	Son 1882	0n 1e	1	2	fragment	ui
c	6/10/88	12	Son 1882	0n 3e	1	1	plate	chiton
c	6/10/88	13	Son 1882	0n 0w	1	4	fragment	ui
c	6/10/88	13	Son 1882	0n 0w	2	1	umbo	mussel
c	6/10/88	14	Son 1882	0n 2w	1	1	fragment	barnacle
c	6/10/88	15	Son 1882	0s 0e	1	15	fragment	ui
c	6/10/88	15	Son 1882	0s 0e	2	2	umbo	mussel
c	6/10/88	15	Son 1882	0s 0e	3	3	plate	chiton
c	6/10/88	15	Son 1882	0s 0e	4	3	fragment	barnacle
c	6/10/88	16	Son 1882	2s 0e	1	6	fragment	ui
c	6/10/88	16	Son 1882	2s 0e	2	2	plate	chiton
d	6/08/88	1	Son 1883	2s 0e	1	6	fragment	ui, barnacle, mussel
d	6/08/88	2	Son 1883	4s 0e	1	11	fragment	ui
d	6/08/88	2	Son 1883	4s 0e	2	1	fragment	abalone
d	6/08/88	2	Son 1883	4s 0e	3	2	umbo	mussel
d	6/08/88	2	Son 1883	4s 0e	4	1	cap	plate limpet
d	6/08/88	2	Son 1883	4s 0e	5	2	fragment	barnacle
d	6/08/88	3	Son 1883	6s 03	1	3	fragment	ui, chiton
d	6/08/88	4	Son 1883	8s 0e	1	6	fragment	ui
d	6/08/88	5	Son 1883	10s 0e	1	10	fragment	ui
d	6/08/88	6	Son 1883	12s 0e	1	5	fragment	ui
d	6/08/88	6	Son 1883	12s 0e	2	1	cap	dunce cap limpet
d	6/08/88	7	Son 1883	0n 0e	1	10	fragment	ui, abalone
d	6/08/88	8	Son 1883	14s 0e	1	5	fragment	ui
d	6/08/88	9	Son 1883	2n 0e	1	5	fragment	ui, abalone
d	6/08/88	10	Son 1883	4n 0e	1	20	fragment	ui, abalone, mussel
d	6/08/88	10	Son 1883	4n 0e	2	1	cap	plate limpet
d	6/08/88	10	Son 1883	4n 0e	3	2	fragment	barnacle
d	6/08/88	11	Son 1883	6n 0e	1	6	fragment	ui
d	6/08/88	11	Son 1883	6n 0e	2	1	fragment	barnacle
d	6/08/88	11	Son 1883	6n 0e	3	1	umbo	mussel
d	6/08/88	11	Son 1883	6n 0e	4	1	plate	chiton
d	6/08/88	12	Son 1883	8n 0e	1	1	cap	plate chiton
d	6/08/88	12	Son 1883	8n 0e	2	1	fragment	sea urchin
d	6/08/88	13	Son 1883	16s 0e	1	30	fragment	ui
d	6/08/88	13	Son 1883	16s 0e	2	2	cap	plate limpet
d	6/08/88	13	Son 1883	16s 0e	3	2	plate	chiton
d	6/08/88	13	Son 1883	16s 0e	4	2	fragment	barnacle
d	6/08/88	14	Son 1883	22s 0e	1	7	fragment	ui, barnacle
d	6/08/88	15	Son 1883	10n 0e	1	10	fragment	ui, abalone, barnacle, limpet
d	6/08/88	15	Son 1883	10n 0e	2	2	plate	chiton

Location	Collection-Date	Field-Spec-No	Site	Unit	Artifact-Sequence	Count	Element	Taxon
d	6/08/88	16	Son 1883	20s 0e	1	5	fragment	ui
d	6/08/88	16	Son 1883	20s 0e	2	1	body whorl	black turban snail
d	6/08/88	16	Son 1883	20s 0e	3	1	cap	plate limpet
d	6/08/88	17	Son 1883	24s 0e	1	5	fragment	ui, barnacle, abalone
d	6/08/88	17	Son 1883	24s 0e	2	1	cap	horned slipper limpet
d	6/08/88	18	Son 1883	12n 0e	1	3	cap	plate chiton
d	6/09/88	3	Son 1883	26s 0e	1	2	fragment	ui, abalone
d	6/09/88	4	Son 1883	20n 0e	1	1	fragment	ui
d	6/09/88	8	Son 1883	30s 0e	1	5	fragment	ui
d	6/09/88	9	Son 1883	28n 0e	1	3	fragment	ui, abalone
d	6/09/88	9	Son 1883	28n 0e	2	1	umbo	mussel
d	6/09/88	11	Son 1883	30n 0e	1	10	fragment	ui, mussel, abalone, limpet
d	6/09/88	15	Son 1883	0n 1e	1	1	cap	shield limpet
d	6/09/88	21	Son 1883	8n 4e	1	5	fragment	ui, abalone, turban snail
d	6/09/88	28	Son 1883	33n 10e	1	1	umbo	mussel
d	6/09/88	32	Son 1883	9n 6e	1	99	fragment	ui
d	6/09/88	35	Son 1883	35n 0e	1	10	fragment	ui, abalone
d	6/09/88	36	Son 1883	2e 33n	1	1	umbo	mussel
d	6/09/88	36	Son 1883	2e 33n	2	2	cap	dunce cap, plate limpet
d	6/09/88	36	Son 1883	2e 33n	3	1	fragment	barnacle
d	6/09/88	37	Son 1883	31n 4e	1	2	fragment	ui, abalone
d	6/09/88	40	Son 1883	34n 03	1	1	whorl	abalone
d	6/09/88	44	Son 1883	19n 8e	1	1	fragment	abalone
d	6/09/88	51	Son 1883	12n 8e	1	5	fragment	abalone
d	6/09/88	55	Son 1883	10.2n 12e	1	2	fragment	ui
d	6/09/88	65	Son 1883	9n 10e	1	1	fragment	abalone
d	6/13/88	1	Son 1883	0n 2w	1	5	fragment	ui
d	6/13/88	1	Son 1883	0n 2w	2	1	fragment	barnacle
d	6/13/88	2	Son 1883	0n 6w	1	3	fragment	ui, abalone
d	6/13/88	2	Son 1883	0n 6w	2	1	plate	chiton
d	6/13/88	2	Son 1883	0n 6w	3	2	fragment	barnacle
d	6/13/88	3	Son 1883	0n 10w	1	2	fragment	ui
d	6/13/88	4	Son 1883	0n 4w	1	2	fragment	abalone
d	6/13/88	4	Son 1883	0n 4w	2	1	umbo	mussel
d	6/13/88	4	Son 1883	0n 4w	3	1	plate	chiton
d	6/13/88	5	Son 1883	0n 8w	1	30	fragment	ui
d	6/13/88	5	Son 1883	0n 8w	2	2	umbo	mussel
d	6/13/88	5	Son 1883	0n 8w	3	1	fragment	barnacle
d	6/13/88	7	Son 1883	0n 22w	1	2	cap	plate chiton
d	6/13/88	8	Son 1883	8s 12w	1	2	fragment	abalone
d	6/13/88	10	Son 1883	16s 28w	1	1	fragment	abalone
d	6/13/88	11	Son 1883	0s 12w	1	2	fragment	abalone
d	6/13/88	11	Son 1883	0s 12w	2	1	umbo	mussel
d	6/13/88	16	Son 1883	16s 12w	1	5	fragment	ui, abalone
d	6/13/88	16	Son 1883	16s 12w	2	1	umbo	mussel
d	6/13/88	24	Son 1883	4s 4e	1	1	fragment	abalone
d	6/14/88	3	Son 1883	24s 12e	1	1	fragment	abalone
d	6/14/88	5	Son 1883	12s 20e	1	1	fragment	abalone
d	6/14/88	7	Son 1883	20s 20e	1	5	fragment	ui, abalone
d	6/14/88	7	Son 1883	20s 20e	2	2	whole	black turban snail

Location	Collection-Date	Field-Spec-No	Site	Unit	Artifact-Sequence	Count	Element	Taxon
d	6/14/88	10	Son 1883	11s 3e	1	1	fragment	abalone
d	6/14/88	11	Son 1883	19s 2e	1	1	cap	plate limpet
d	6/14/88	23	Son 1883	0n 24e, 164 @ 20m	1	3	fragment	abalone
d	6/14/88	28	Son 1883	0n 24e, 164 @20m	1	5	fragment	abalone
d	6/14/88	38	Son 1883	0n 50e, 352 @30m	1	1	fragment	abalone
d	6/14/88	39	Son 1883	0n 50e, 359 @ 34m	1	1	fragment	abalone
d	6/15/88	27	Son 1884	sub B 4s 0e	1	1	fragment	barnacle
d	6/15/88	32	Son 1884	sub B 0n 5e	1	2	fragment	ui, barnacle
d	6/15/88	34	Son 1884	sub B 0n 7e	1	8	fragment	mussel, abalone
d	6/15/88	34	Son 1884	sub B 0n 7e	2	2	plate	chiton
d	6/15/88	35	Son 1884	sub B 0n 11e	1	1	fragment	ui
d	6/15/88	35	Son 1884	sub B 0n 11e	2	2	plate	chiton
d	6/15/88	35	Son 1884	sub B 0n 11e	3	1	fragment	barnacle
d	6/15/88	35	Son 1884	sub B 0n 11e	4	1	cap	plate limpet
d	6/15/88	36	Son 1884	sub B 0n 9e	1	10	fragment	ui
d	6/15/88	36	Son 1884	sub B 0n 9e	2	2	umbo	mussel
d	6/15/88	36	Son 1884	sub B 0n 9e	3	1	fragment	barnacle
d	6/15/88	39	Son 1884	sub B 4n 4w	1	1	fragment	abalone
e	6/07/89	1	Son 1888	0n 0e	1	20	fragment	ui, mussel
e	6/07/89	1	Son 1888	0n 0e	2	3	cap	limpet
e	6/07/89	1	Son 1888	0n 0e	3	3	fragment	abalone
e	6/07/89	1	Son 1888	0n 0e	4	1	fragment	barnacle
e	6/07/89	1	Son 1888	0n 0e	5	8	plate	chiton
e	6/07/89	2	Son 1888	2n 0e	1	10	fragment	ui, abalone, mussel
e	6/07/89	2	Son 1888	2n 0e	2	4	plates	chiton
e	6/07/89	2	Son 1888	2n 0e	3	1	fragment	barnacle
e	6/07/89	3	Son 1888	4n 0e	1	15	fragment	ui, mussel, clam, snail
e	6/07/89	3	Son 1888	4n 0e	2	2	umbo	mussel
e	6/07/89	3	Son 1888	4n 0e	3	5	plate	chiton
e	6/07/89	3	Son 1888	4n 0e	4	1	aperture	black turban snail
e	6/07/89	3	Son 1888	4n 0e	5	1	fragment	barnacle
e	6/07/89	3	Son 1888	4n 0e	6	3	cap	plate limpet
e	6/07/89	4	Son 1888	0n 2w	1	30	fragment	ui, sea urchin, mussel, limpet
e	6/07/89	4	Son 1888	0n 2w	2	1	cap	plate limpet
e	6/07/89	4	Son 1888	0n 2w	3	3	fragment	barnacle
e	6/07/89	4	Son 1888	0n 2w	4	1	body whorl	black turban snail
e	6/07/89	4	Son 1888	0n 2w	5	3	umbo	mussel
e	6/07/89	4	Son 1888	0n 2w	6	11	plate	chiton
e	6/07/89	6	Son 1888	0n 6w	1	20	fragment	ui, mussel, abalone
e	6/07/89	6	Son 1888	0n 6w	2	2	plate	chiton
e	6/07/89	6	Son 1888	0n 6w	3	3	fragment	barnacle
e	6/07/89	6	Son 1888	0n 6w	4	1	umbo	mussel
e	6/07/89	6	Son 1888	0n 6w	5	1	whole	eroded perwinkle
e	6/07/89	7	Son 1888	2s 0e	1	20	fragment	ui, abalone, chiton
e	6/07/89	7	Son 1888	2s 0e	2	1	fragment	barnacle
e	6/07/89	7	Son 1888	2s 0e	3	1	fragment	horned slipper limpet
e	6/07/89	7	Son 1888	2s 0e	4	2	umbo	mussel
e	6/07/89	7	Son 1888	2s 0e	5	4	plate	chiton
e	6/07/89	7	Son 1888	2s 0e	6	2	whole	black turban snail
e	6/07/89	8	Son 1888	4s 0e	1	30	fragment	ui, mussel, abalone

Location	Collection-Date	Field-Spec-No	Site	Unit	Artifact-Sequence	Count	Element	Taxon
e	6/07/89	8	Son 1888	4s 0e	2	7	fragment	barnacle
e	6/07/89	8	Son 1888	4s 0e	3	6	cap	plate limpet
e	6/07/89	8	Son 1888	4s 0e	4	6	whole	black turban snail
e	6/07/89	8	Son 1888	4s 0e	5	3	umbo	mussel
e	6/07/89	8	Son 1888	4s 0e	6	17	plate	chiton
e	6/07/89	9	Son 1888	6s 0e	1	2	fragment	ui, barnacle, limpet
e	6/07/89	10	Son 1888	0n 1e	1	20	fragment	ui, abalone
e	6/07/89	10	Son 1888	0n 1e	2	1	fragment	barnacle
e	6/07/89	10	Son 1888	0n 1e	3	4	umbo	mussel
e	6/07/89	10	Son 1888	0n 1e	4	2	whole	black turban snail
e	6/07/89	10	Son 1888	0n 1e	5	3	cap	limpet
e	6/07/89	10	Son 1888	0n 1e	6	3	plate	chiton
e	6/07/89	11	Son 1888	1n 2w	1	5	fragment	ui, chiton
e	6/07/89	11	Son 1888	1n 2w	2	1	cap	keyhole limpet
e	6/07/89	11	Son 1888	1n 2w	3	1	plate	chiton
f	6/02/89	1	Son 174	6n 0e	1	16	fragment	ui
f	6/02/89	1	Son 174	6n 0e	2	10	fragment	abalone
f	6/02/89	1	Son 174	6n 0e	3	1	umbo	mussel
f	6/02/89	1	Son 174	6n 0e	4	5	plate	chiton
f	6/02/89	2	Son 174	2n 0e	1	16	fragment	ui
f	6/02/89	2	Son 174	2n 0e	2	2	fragment	abalone
f	6/02/89	2	Son 174	2n 0e	3	1	umbo	mussel
f	6/02/89	2	Son 174	2n 0e	4	4	plate	chiton
f	6/02/89	2	Son 174	2n 0e	5	1	fragment	mussel
f	6/02/89	3	Son 174	4n 0e	1	2	fragment	mussel
f	6/02/89	3	Son 174	4n 0e	2	1	fragment	barnacle
f	6/02/89	3	Son 174	4n 0e	3	3	plates	chiton
f	6/02/89	4	Son 174	0n 0e	1	1	fragment	mussel
f	6/02/89	4	Son 174	0n 0e	2	1	fragment	clam
f	6/02/89	5	Son 174	8n 0e	1	40	fragment	ui
f	6/02/89	5	Son 174	8n 0e	2	7	plates	chiton
f	6/02/89	5	Son 174	8n 0e	3	3	fragment	abalone
f	6/02/89	5	Son 174	8n 0e	4	1	umbo	mussel
f	6/02/89	6	Son 174	Sub A 0n 0e	1	3	fragments	ui
f	6/02/89	6	Son 174	Sub A 0n 0e	2	7	fragments	abalone
f	6/02/89	7	Son 174	Sub A 0n 1e	1	3	fragment	ui
f	6/02/89	7	Son 174	Sub A 0n 1e	2	1	fragment	abalone
f	6/02/89	7	Son 174	Sub A 0n 1e	3	1	fragment	barnacle
f	6/02/89	9	Son 174	Sub A 310@2.54m	1	1	plate	chiton
f	6/02/89	9	Son 174	Sub A 310@2.54m	2	1	umbo	mussel
f	6/05/89	1	Son 174	149 @ 1.45 m	1	1	fragment	abalone
f	6/05/89	3	Son 174	217 @ 13.6 m	1	1	plate	chiton
f	6/05/89	5	Son 174	174 @ 17.2 m	1	2	fragment	barnacle
f	6/05/89	9	Son 174	180 @ 13.5m	1	2	fragment	abalone
f	6/05/89	10	Son 174	175 @ 19.3m	1	1	fragment	abalone
f	6/05/89	11	Son 174	245 @ 34.0 m	1	2	fragment	abalone
f	6/05/89	14	Son 174	316 @ 10 m	1	2	fragments	abalone
f	6/05/89	14	Son 174	316 @ 10 m	2	3	plates	chiton
f	6/05/89	16	Son 174	327 @ 12.3 m	1	1	fragment	abalone
i	6/08/89	1	Son 1889	0n 0e	1	3	fragment	ui, mussel, chiton

Location	Collection-Date	Field-Spec-No	Site	Unit	Artifact-Sequence	Count	Element	Taxon
i	6/08/89	1	Son 1889	0n 0e	2	3	whole	black turban snail
i	6/08/89	1	Son 1889	0n 0e	3	1	plate	chiton
i	6/08/89	1	Son 1889	0n 0e	4	1	fragment	barnacle
i	6/08/89	1	Son 1889	0n 0e	5	2	cap	plate limpet
i	6/08/89	2	Son 1889	0n 1e	1	3	fragment	ui, mussel
i	6/08/89	2	Son 1889	0n 1e	2	2	cap	ribbed limpet
i	6/08/89	3	Son 1889	0n 2w	1	10	fragment	ui, clam, chiton, mussel
i	6/08/89	3	Son 1889	0n 2w	2	4	fragment	barnacle
i	6/08/89	3	Son 1889	0n 2w	3	2	cap	ribbed, horned slipper
i	6/08/89	3	Son 1889	0n 2w	4	2	umbo	mussel
i	6/08/89	3	Son 1889	0n 2w	5	3	whole	black turban snail
i	6/08/89	4	Son 1889	2s 0e	1	10	fragment	ui, mussel, abalone, chiton
i	6/08/89	4	Son 1889	2s 0e	2	1	plate	chiton
i	6/08/89	4	Son 1889	2s 0e	3	3	cap	plate limpet
i	6/08/89	4	Son 1889	2s 0e	4	1	umbo	mussel
i	6/08/89	4	Son 1889	2s 0e	5	2	fragment	barnacle
i	6/08/89	6	Son 1889	302 @ 3.2m	1	1	fragment	abalone
i	6/08/89	6	Son 1889	302 @ 3.2m	2	2	cap	plate limpet
i	6/08/89	7	Son 1889	140 @ 2.9m	1	1	fragment	barnacle
i	6/08/89	8	Son 1889	96 @ 5.1m	1	10	fragment	ui, black turban snail
i	6/08/89	9	Son 1889	41 @ 8.6m	1	2	cap	ribbed limpet
i	6/08/89	10	Son 1889	50 @ 4.7m	1	1	cap	plate limpet
i	6/08/89	11	Son 1889	200 @ 2.8m	1	1	umbo	mussel
i	6/08/89	12	Son 1889	33 @ 5.3 m	1	1	cap	plate limpet
i	6/08/89	13	Son 1889	22 @ 9.1m	1	2	cap	plate limpet
i	6/08/89	13	Son 1889	22 @ 9.1m	2	1	fragment	barnacle
i	6/08/89	14	Son 1889	14 @ 5.4 m	1	1	cap	plate limpet
i	6/08/89	15	Son 1889	8 @ 6.8m	1	1	umbo	mussel
i	6/08/89	20	Son 1889	352 @ 4.1 m	1	3	cap	plate limpet
k	6/15/89	1	Son 1890	0n 0e	1	30	fragment	ui, abalone, snail, sea urchin
k	6/15/89	1	Son 1890	0n 0e	2	5	fragment	barnacle
k	6/15/89	1	Son 1890	0n 0e	3	5	umbo	mussel
k	6/15/89	1	Son 1890	0n 0e	4	1	body whorl	black turban snail
k	6/15/89	1	Son 1890	0n 0e	5	3	plate	chiton
k	6/15/89	2	Son 1890	16 @ 15.2m	1	5	fragment	ui, mussel
k	6/15/89	4	Son 1890	334 @ 3.13m	1	5	fragment	ui, abalone
k	6/15/89	4	Son 1890	334 @ 3.13m	2	1	fragment	barnacle
k	6/15/89	4	Son 1890	334 @ 3.13m	3	3	plate	chiton
l	6/02/89	1	Son 1886	0n 0e	1	39	cap	limpet
l	6/02/89	1	Son 1886	0n 0e	2	13	fragment	chiton
l	6/02/89	1	Son 1886	0n 0e	3	4	plate	chiton
l	6/02/89	1	Son 1886	0n 0e	4	13	whole	turban snail
l	6/02/89	1	Son 1886	0n 0e	5	22	fragment	barnacle
l	6/02/89	1	Son 1886	0n 0e	6	20	fragment	ui, mussel, abalone
l	6/02/89	1	Son 1886	0n 0e	7	5	umbo	mussel
l	6/02/89	1	Son 1886	0n 0e	8	2	whole	dogwinkle
l	6/02/89	2	Son 1886	0n 0e	1	1	fragment	black chiton
l	6/02/89	4	Son 1886	2n 0e	1	99	fragment	ui, mussel, abalone, chiton
l	6/02/89	4	Son 1886	2n 0e	2	5	umbo	mussel
l	6/02/89	4	Son 1886	2n 0e	3	3	plate	gumbo chiton

Location	Collection-Date	Field-Spec-No	Site	Unit	Artifact-Sequence	Count	Element	Taxon
1	6/02/89	4	Son 1886	2n 0e	5	9	fragment	barnacle
1	6/02/89	4	Son 1886	2n 0e	6	4	whole	dogwinkle
1	6/02/89	4	Son 1886	2n 0e	7	22	cap	plate limpet
1	6/02/89	4	Son 1886	2n 0e	8	11	cap	ribbed limpet
1	6/02/89	4	Son 1886	2n 0e	9	10	whole	black turban snail
1	6/02/89	5	Son 1886	0n 4w	1	30	fragment	ui, abalone, mussel, chiton
1	6/02/89	5	Son 1886	0n 4w	2	9	umbo	mussel
1	6/02/89	5	Son 1886	0n 4w	3	36	cap	plate limpet
1	6/02/89	5	Son 1886	0n 4w	4	37	cap	ribbed limpet
1	6/02/89	5	Son 1886	0n 4w	5	2	whole	Olivella
1	6/02/89	5	Son 1886	0n 4w	6	11	fragment	barnacle
1	6/02/89	5	Son 1886	0n 4w	7	3	plate	black chiton
1	6/02/89	5	Son 1886	0n 4w	8	1	plate	gumbo chiton
1	6/02/89	5	Son 1886	0n 4w	9	4	whole	black turban snail
1	6/02/89	5	Son 1886	0n 4w	10	3	whole	land snail
1	6/02/89	5	Son 1886	0n 4w	11	1	whole	dogwinkle
1	6/05/89	1	Son 1886	0n 2w	1	50	fragment	ui, abalone, mussel, limpet
1	6/05/89	1	Son 1886	0n 2w	2	1	whorl	abalone
1	6/05/89	1	Son 1886	0n 2w	3	1	plate	gumbo chiton
1	6/05/89	1	Son 1886	0n 2w	4	17	plate	black chiton
1	6/05/89	1	Son 1886	0n 2w	5	58	cap	plate limpet
1	6/05/89	1	Son 1886	0n 2w	6	1	cap	horned slipper limpet
1	6/05/89	1	Son 1886	0n 2w	7	28	cap	ribbed limpet
1	6/05/89	1	Son 1886	0n 2w	8	10	umbo	mussel
1	6/05/89	1	Son 1886	0n 2w	9	27	fragment	barnacle
1	6/05/89	1	Son 1886	0n 2w	10	21	whole	black turban snail
1	6/05/89	1	Son 1886	0n 2w	11	4	whole	land snail
1	6/05/89	1	Son 1886	0n 2w	12	1	whole	Olivella
1	6/05/89	1	Son 1886	0n 2w	13	2	whole	dogwinkle
1	6/05/89	2	Son 1886	0n 2w	2	1	fragment	mussel
1	6/05/89	3	Son 1886	2s 0e	1	1	fragment	mussel
1	6/05/89	4	Son 1886	2s 0e	1	50	fragment	ui, abalone, chiton, mussel
1	6/05/89	4	Son 1886	2s 0e	2	1	plate	gumbo chiton
1	6/05/89	4	Son 1886	2s 0e	3	21	plate	black chiton
1	6/05/89	4	Son 1886	2s 0e	4	39	cap	plate limpet
1	6/05/89	4	Son 1886	2s 0e	5	18	cap	ribbed limpet
1	6/05/89	4	Son 1886	2s 0e	6	7	umbo	mussel
1	6/05/89	4	Son 1886	2s 0e	7	27	fragment	barnacle
1	6/05/89	4	Son 1886	2s 0e	8	1	cap	horned slipper limpet
1	6/05/89	4	Son 1886	2s 0e	9	13	whole	black turban snail
1	6/05/89	4	Son 1886	2s 0e	10	1	whole	dogwinkle
1	6/05/89	5	Son 1886	0n 1e	1	50	fragment	ui, abalone, mussel, whelk
1	6/05/89	5	Son 1886	0n 1e	2	7	umbo	mussel
1	6/05/89	5	Son 1886	0n 1e	3	41	cap	plate limpet
1	6/05/89	5	Son 1886	0n 1e	4	1	cap	horned slipper limpet
1	6/05/89	5	Son 1886	0n 1e	5	24	cap	ribbed limpet
1	6/05/89	5	Son 1886	0n 1e	6	1	plate	gumbo chiton
1	6/05/89	5	Son 1886	0n 1e	7	1	plate	ui chiton
1	6/05/89	5	Son 1886	0n 1e	8	14	plate	black chiton
1	6/05/89	5	Son 1886	0n 1e	9	14	fragment	barnacle

Location	Collection-Date	Field-Spec-No	Site	Unit	Artifact-Sequence	Count	Element	Taxon
1	6/05/89	5	Son 1886	0n 1e	10	1	fragment	crab
1	6/05/89	5	Son 1886	0n 1e	11	1	whole	Olivella
1	6/05/89	5	Son 1886	0n 1e	12	1	whole	dogwinkle
1	6/05/89	5	Son 1886	0n 1e	13	11	whole	black turban snail
1	6/05/89	7	Son 1886	0n 6w	1	30	fragment	ui, chiton, black turban snail
1	6/05/89	7	Son 1886	0n 6w	2	6	fragment	barnacle
1	6/05/89	7	Son 1886	0n 6w	3	1	whole	Olivella
1	6/05/89	7	Son 1886	0n 6w	4	2	plate	black chiton
1	6/05/89	7	Son 1886	0n 6w	5	11	cap	plate limpet
1	6/05/89	7	Son 1886	0n 6w	6	7	cap	ribbed limpet
1	6/05/89	7	Son 1886	0n 6w	7	1	cap	rough limpet
1	6/05/89	7	Son 1886	0n 6w	8	1	whole	black turban snail
1	6/05/89	9	Son 1886	6s 0e	1	50	fragment	ui, mussel, abalone, snail
1	6/05/89	9	Son 1886	6s 0e	2	1	whorl	abalone
1	6/05/89	9	Son 1886	6s 0e	3	6	umbo	mussel
1	6/05/89	9	Son 1886	6s 0e	4	27	cap	plate limpet
1	6/05/89	9	Son 1886	6s 0e	5	15	cap	ribbed limpet
1	6/05/89	9	Son 1886	6s 0e	6	15	fragment	barnacle
1	6/05/89	9	Son 1886	6s 0e	7	1	whole	snail (ui)
1	6/05/89	9	Son 1886	6s 0e	8	1	whole	dogwinkle
1	6/05/89	9	Son 1886	6s 0e	9	1	whole	land snail
1	6/05/89	9	Son 1886	6s 0e	10	8	whole	black turban snail
1	6/05/89	9	Son 1886	6s 0e	11	1	whole	Olivella
1	6/05/89	9	Son 1886	6s 0e	12	1	plate	chiton (ui)
1	6/05/89	9	Son 1886	6s 0e	13	2	plate	gumbo chiton
1	6/05/89	9	Son 1886	6s 0e	14	2	plate	black chiton
1	6/05/89	12	Son 1886	4s 0e	1	30	fragment	ui, mussel, chiton, limpet
1	6/05/89	12	Son 1886	4s 0e	2	17	fragment	barnacle
1	6/05/89	12	Son 1886	4s 0e	3	41	cap	plate limpet
1	6/05/89	12	Son 1886	4s 0e	4	13	cap	ribbed limpet
1	6/05/89	12	Son 1886	4s 0e	5	11	plate	black chiton
1	6/05/89	12	Son 1886	4s 0e	6	5	whole	black turban snail
1	6/05/89	12	Son 1886	4s 0e	7	4	umbo	mussel
1	6/05/89	12	Son 1886	4s 0e	8	1	whole	land snail
1	6/05/89	12	Son 1886	4s 0e	9	2	cap	rough limpet
1	6/05/89	14	Son 1886	4n 0e	1	50	fragment	ui, mussel, abalone, snail
1	6/05/89	14	Son 1886	4n 0e	2	13	plate	black chiton
1	6/05/89	14	Son 1886	4n 0e	3	1	plate	chiton (ui)
1	6/05/89	14	Son 1886	4n 0e	4	1	plate	gumbo chiton
1	6/05/89	14	Son 1886	4n 0e	5	10	umbo	mussel
1	6/05/89	14	Son 1886	4n 0e	6	23	fragment	barnacle
1	6/05/89	14	Son 1886	4n 0e	7	51	cap	plate limpet
1	6/05/89	14	Son 1886	4n 0e	8	1	cap	keyhole limpet
1	6/05/89	14	Son 1886	4n 0e	9	2	cap	rough limpet
1	6/05/89	14	Son 1886	4n 0e	10	11	cap	ribbed limpet
1	6/05/89	14	Son 1886	4n 0e	11	2	cap	horned slipper limpet
1	6/05/89	14	Son 1886	4n 0e	12	2	cap	dunce cap limpet
1	6/05/89	14	Son 1886	4n 0e	13	1	whole	land snail
1	6/05/89	14	Son 1886	4n 0e	14	9	whole	black turban snail
1	6/28/89	5	Son 1892	e	1	99	fragment	ui, abalone, limpet, chiton

Location	Collection-Date	Field-Spec-No	Site	Unit	Artifact-Sequence	Count	Element	Taxon
1	6/28/89	5	Son 1892	e	2	4	fragment	barnacle
1	6/28/89	5	Son 1892	e	3	5	fragment	snail
1	6/28/89	5	Son 1892	e	4	26	cap	horned slipper, ribbed, plate
1	6/28/89	5	Son 1892	e	5	6	whole	black turban snail
1	6/28/89	5	Son 1892	e	6	24	umbo	mussel
1	6/28/89	5	Son 1892	e	7	11	plate	chiton
1	6/28/89	7	Son 1892	f	1	99	fragment	ui, mussel, abalone, limpet
1	6/28/89	7	Son 1892	f	2	7	fragment	barnacle
1	6/28/89	7	Son 1892	f	3	5	plate	chiton
1	6/28/89	7	Son 1892	f	4	10	cap	plate limpet
1	6/28/89	7	Son 1892	f	5	12	umbo	mussel
1	6/28/89	9	Son 1892	d	1	99	fragment	ui, abalone, mussel, snail
1	6/28/89	9	Son 1892	d	2	2	fragment	barnacle
1	6/28/89	9	Son 1892	d	3	6	whole	black turban snail
1	6/28/89	9	Son 1892	d	4	7	plate	chiton
1	6/28/89	9	Son 1892	d	5	6	umbo	mussel
1	6/28/89	9	Son 1892	d	6	8	cap	keyhole, horned slipper, plate
1	6/28/89	11	Son 1892	c	1	99	fragment	ui, abalone, snail (ridged)
1	6/28/89	11	Son 1892	c	2	1	plate	chiton
1	6/28/89	11	Son 1892	c	3	1	umbo	mussel
1	6/28/89	11	Son 1892	c	4	1	cap	plate limpet
1	6/28/89	13	Son 1892	a	1	1	fragment	abalone
1	6/28/89	15	Son 1892	b	1	1	umbo	mussel
1	6/28/89	15	Son 1892	b	2	1	fragment	ui, barnacle

APPENDIX 5.3

VERTEBRATE FAUNAL REMAINS FROM FORT ROSS SURVEY SITES

Site	Taxon	Side	Element	NISP	Frag's.	Cut	Burned	Catalog #
Son-174	*Bos taurus*	r	Tibia	1	1	1	0	6-2-89-8-f
Son-174	*Bos taurus*	r	Scapula	1	1	1	0	6-5-89-11-f
Son-174	*C. elaphus r.*	l	Mandible	1	1	0	0	6-5-89-8-f-1
Son-174	*C. elaphus r.*	r	L Pm 2	1	0	0	0	6-5-89-9-f-1
Son-174	*C. elaphus r.*	l	Mandible	1	1	0	0	6-5-89-7-f-1
Son-174	L. Mammal	-	Long Bone	1	1	0	0	6-5-89-6-f-1
Son-174	L. Mammal	-	Long Bone	1	1	0	0	6-5-89-9-f-1
Son-174	L. Mammal	-	Long Bone	2	2	0	0	6-2-89-6-f
Son-174	L. Mammal	-	Bone	2	2	0	0	6-2-89-5-f
Son-174	L. Mammal	-	Long Bone	1	1	0	0	6-5-89-3-f
Son-174	*O. hemionus*	l	Tibia	1	1	0	0	6-5-98-8-f-1
Son-1880	*C. elaphus r.*	r	L Pm 2	1	1	0	0	B-6-8-88-24-f
Son-1880	L. Mammal	-	Long Bone	1	1	0	0	B-6-8-88-19-f
Son-1880	L. Mammal	-	Long Bone	2	2	0	0	B-6-8-88-24-f
Son-1880	L. Mammal	-	Long Bone	1	1	0	0	B-6-8-88-2-f
Son-1880	L. Mammal	-	Vertebra	1	1	0	0	B-6-8-88-15-f
Son-1880	L. Mammal	-	Vertebra	1	1	0	0	B-6-8-88-25-f
Son-1880	L. Mammal	-	Long Bone	1	1	0	0	B-6-8-88-25-f
Son-1880	L. Mammal	-	Long Bone	1	1	0	0	B-6-8-88-3-f
Son-1880	L. Mammal	-	Bone	1	1	0	0	B-6-8-88-11-f
Son-1880	M. Mammal	r	Scapula	1	1	0	0	B-6-8-88-16-f
Son-1880	*O. hemionus*	r	Naviculo-Cuboid	1	0	0	0	B-6-8-88-20-f
Son-1880	*O. hemionus*	r	Mandible	1	1	0	0	B-6-8-88-2-f
Son-1880	*O. hemionus*	l	Astragalus	1	0	0	0	B-6-8-88-1-f
Son-1881	L. Bird	r	Phalanx 2	1	0	0	0	B-6-9-88-12-f
Son-1881	L. Mammal	-	Long Bone	1	1	1	1	B-6-9-88-12-f
Son-1883	L. Mammal	-	Long Bone	1	1	0	1	D-6-9-89-6-f
Son-1886	*Bos taurus*	l	Phalanx 3	1	0	0	0	L-6-2-89-4-f
Son-1886	*E. lutris*	r	Radius	1	1	0	1	L-6-5-89-1-f-2
Son-1886	L. Mammal	-	Long Bone	1	1	0	0	L-6-5-89-4-f
Son-1886	L. Mammal	-	Long Bone	1	1	0	1	L-6-2-89-1-f
Son-1886	L. Mammal	-	Long Bone	1	1	0	0	L-6-5-89-7-f
Son-1886	L. Mammal	-	Cranium	1	1	0	0	L-6-5-89-9-f
Son-1886	L. Mammal	-	Long Bone	1	1	0	0	L-6-5-89-9-f
Son-1886	L. Mammal	-	Long Bone	1	1	0	1	L-6-5-89-1-f-1
Son-1886	L. Mammal	-	Long Bone	3	3	0	0	L-6-5-89-1-f-2
Son-1886	L. Mammal	-	Long Bone	5	5	0	1	L-6-5-89-5-f
Son-1886	*O. hemionus*	r	L M 3	1	0	0	0	L-6-5-89-4-f

Site	Taxon	Side	Element	NISP	Frag's.	Cut	Burned	Catalog #
Son-1886	*O. hemionus*	l	Astragalus	1	0	0	0	L-6-5-89-4-f
Son-1886	*O. hemionus*	l	Metacarpal	1	1	0	0	L-6-5-89-1-f-2
Son-1886	*O. hemionus*	l	Humerus	2	2	1	0	L-6-2-89-5-f-1
Son-1886	*O. hemionus*	r	Naviculo-Cuboid	1	0	0	0	L-6-2-89-5-f-1
Son-1886	*O. hemionus*	l	Fibula	1	1	0	0	L-6-2-89-5-f-1
Son-1886	*Ovis aries*	l	Metacarpal	1	1	0	0	L-6-5-89-9-f
Son-1886	*P. vitulina*	l	Radius	1	1	0	0	L-6-5-89-14-f
Son-1886	*S. bachmani*	l	Mandible	1	1	0	0	L-6-5-89-4-f
Son-1886	*T. bottae*	r	Ilium	1	0	0	0	L-6-5-89-5-f
Son-1886	*Z. californicus*	r	Tarsal	1	0	0	0	L-6-2-89-5-f-1
Son-1888	L. Mammal	-	Vertebra	1	1	0	0	E-6-7-89-7-f
Son-1888	L. Mammal	-	Long Bone	1	1	0	1	E-6-7-89-8-f
Son-1888	L. Mammal	-	Scapula	1	1	0	0	E-6-7-89-4-f
Son-1888	L. Mammal	-	Rib	1	1	0	0	E-6-7-89-4-f
Son-1890	L. Mammal	-	Long Bone	1	1	0	1	K-6-15-89-2-f
Son-1890	L. Mammal	-	Long Bone	2	2	0	1	K-6-15-89-1-f
Son-1890	*O. hemionus*	r	Scapula	1	1	0	0	K-6-15-89-3-f
Son-1890	*Ovis Aries*	-	Molar	1	1	0	0	K-6-15-89-2-f
Son-1895	*Bos taurus*	-	Vertebra	1	1	0	0	C-6-6-88-4-f
Son-1895	L. Mammal	-	Cranium	1	1	0	0	C-6-6-88-3-f-1
Son-1895	*O. hemionus*	-	Metacarpal	1	1	0	0	C-6-6-88-7-f
Son-1896	L. Mammal	-	Axis	1	1	0	1	C-6-8-88-1-f

APPENDIX 5.4

GLASS, CERAMIC, AND METAL ARTIFACTS FROM FORT ROSS SITES

Loca-tion	Collection-Date	Field-Spec-no	Artifact-Sequence	Site	Unit	Artifact-Category	Count	MNI	Diagnostics	Comments
a	6/10/88	2	1	Son 1878	14s 0e	hc	1	1	base	porcelain, footring sherd, Chinese bowl shape, very white, clear glaze
a	6/10/88	13	1	Son 1878	sw quad	wg	1	1		moldblown glass, colorless, ess, modified, bulb of percussion
a	6/10/88	16	1	Son 1878	se nonrandom	hc	1	1	base	Chinese porcellaneous stoneware, footring sherd from shallow bowl
a	6/10/88	17	1	Son 1878	nw quad	g	1	1		moldblown container glass, light blue-green color
a	6/14/88	20	1	Son 1878	sw quad, 200m	hc	1	1	rim	hollowware form, possibly chamberpot, creamware body and glaze, crazed
a	10/16/90	1	1	Son 1878	nw quad	wg	1	1		moldblown glass, light olive-green alcoholic beverage bottle, worked edge
b	6/08/88	1	1	Son 1880	0n 0e	hc	1	1	rim	white-bodied earthenware cup or bowl cup or bowl, sherd burned
b	6/08/88	11	1	Son 1880	Sub A 2n 0e	g	1	1		moldblown glass, dark olive-green wine bottle, nondiagnostic body sherds
b	6/08/88	11	1	Son 1880	Sub A 2n 0e	be	1	1		white opaque glass bead
b	6/08/88	15	1	Son 1880	Sub A 2s 4w	g	1	1		moldblown glass, dark olive-green wine bottle, same vessel as b/6/8/88-11
b	6/08/88	20	1	Son 1880	Sub A 0n quad	g	1	1		moldblown glass, dark olive-green wine bottle, same vessel as b/6/8/88-11
b	6/08/88	21	1	Son 1880	Sub A se quad	g	2	1		moldblown glass, dark olive-green wine bottle, same vessel as b/6/8/88-11
b	6/08/88	21	1	Son 1880	Sub A se	hc	1	1		porcelain, very white, similar to a/6/10/88-2
b	6/08/88	25	1	Son 1880	Sub B 2s quad	g	1	1		moldblown glass, dark olive-green wine bottle, same vessel as b/6/8/88-11
b	4/08/91	1	1	Son 1880	Sub A se	wg	1	1	base	moldblown glass, light olive-green, worked edge, burned
c	6/06/88	17	1	Son 1895	ne quad	hc	1	1		European-style porcelain, body sherd, white-bodied, hollow form
c	6/06/88	18	1	Son 1895	ne quad	wg	1	1		small glass sherd, work ed edge, maybe moldblown

KEY

ARTIFACT CATEGORY

g = glass
hc = historic ceramic
me = metal
wg = worked glass

Location	Collection-Date	Field-Spec-no	Artifact-Sequence	Site	Unit	Artifact-Category	Count	MNI	Diagnostics	Comments
c	6/06/88	19	1	Son 1895	sw quad	g	1	1		moldblown glass, dark olive-green alcoholic beverage bottle fragment
c	6/06/88	21	1	Son 1895	130 @ 22.6m	g	1	1	mamelon	moldblown glass, dark olive-green wine bottle base
c	6/06/88	47	1	Son 1885	se quad/nw quad	hc	2	1	base	polychrome pearlware cup, footring, white body, green floral motif, glaze
c	6/10/88	1	1	Son 1895	nonrandom	g	2	1		black moldblown glass, neck sherds, alcoholic beverage bottle
d	6/08/88	10	1	Son 1883	4n 0e	g	1	1		moldblown glass, dark olive-green alcoholic beverage bottle fragment
d	6/13/88	21	1	Son 1883	14s 4w	g	1	1		flat glass, blue-green, concoidal wear/impact scarring on edge
d	6/13/88	25	1	Son 1883	12s 4e	g	1	1		moldblown glass, edge of seal or finish, same vessel as d/6/8/88-10
d	6/15/88	22	1	Son 1884	248 @ 44m	hc	1	1	base	fragment of industrial porcelain electical insulator cylinder
f	6/02/89	3	1	Son 174	4n 0e	me	11	2		square iron spike fragments, foliating, rusting; also large nail fragments
f	6/02/89	5	1	Son 174	8n 0e	g	4	3		two are flat glass, two are moldblown container glass of same vessel
f	6/02/89	5	1	Son 174	8n 0e	hc	2	1	handle	white improved earthenware, handle of pitcher, large cup, or serving vessel
f	6/02/89	5	1	Son 174	8n 0e	me	2	1		nails
f	6/02/89	6	1	Son 174	0n 0e	g	1	1		flat glass, colorless
f	6/02/89	7	1	Son 174	0n 1e	g	1	1		moldblown glass, olive-green wine bottle
f	6/05/89	2	1	Son 174	336 @ 8.7 2m	hc	1	1	rim	Chin. porcellaneous stoneware, bowl sherd, blurred cobalt decoration
f	6/05/89	4	1	Son 174	171 @ 19.5m	g	1	1	embossing	body sherd, square "Hostetter's Bitters" bottle (1820s-1910s), black
f	6/05/89	10	1	Son 174	175 @ 19.3m	g	1	1		moldblown colorless container glass
f	6/05/89	11	1	Son 174	245 @ 34.0m	g	1	1		moldblown glass, olive-green wine bottle, same vessel as f/6/2/89-7
f	6/05/89	12	1	Son 174	358 @ 9.27m	me	1	1	whole	iron tongue hinge valve, for padlock type lock
f	6/05/89	13	1	Son 174	355 @ 19.7m	me	1	1	whole	iron tongue hinge valve, same as f/6/5/89-12
h	6/08/89	27	1	Son 228	126 @ 11.03m	g	1	1		colorless container glass, possibly moldblown
l	6/02/89	3	1	Son 1886	2n 0e	hc	1	1		creamware, thin, clear crazed glaze, body chalky, soft, white, form?
l	6/02/89	5	1	Son 1886	0n 4w	hc	1	1		creamware, buff-cream-bodied earthenware with yellowish lead glaze, form?
l	6/02/89	6	1	Son 1886	0n 4w	g	1	1		heated glass, no identification

Loca-tion	Collection-Date	Field-Spec-no	Artifact-Sequence	Site	Unit	Artifact-Category	Count	MNI	Diagnostics	Comments
1	6/05/89	3	1	Son 1886	2s 0e	g	1	1		flat glass, colorless, patinated surface, probably architectural
1	6/05/89	9	1	Son 1886	6s 0e	g	2	1		flat glass, same as 1/6 /5/89-3; also colorless moldblown container, body sherd
1	6/05/89	10	1	Son 1886	6s 0e	hc	1	1		creamware, white earthenware body sherd, form?
1	6/05/89	11	1	Son 1886	4s 0e	g	2	1		moldblown glass, same as 1/6/5/89-9; also olive-green moldblown container
1	6/08/89	1	1	Son 1891	253 @ 23.9m	me	1			unidentified metal fragment
1	6/08/89	1	2	Son 1891	280 @ 20m	me	1			square nail
1	6/08/89	1	4	Son 1891	nonrandom	me	1			wood and nail fragments

APPENDIX 5.5

BEADS FROM FORT ROSS SITES

Location	Collection -Date	Field- Spec-No	Site	Unit	Artifact -Category	Artifact -Sequence	Count
b	6/08/88	11	Son 1880	Sub A 2n 0e	be	1	1
l	6/05/89	4	Son 1886	2s 0e	be	1	1
l	6/28/89	12	Son 1892	e	be	1	1

KEY

ARTIFACT CATEGORY   be = bead

APPENDIX 5.6

LITHICS

a

e

b

f

c

g

d

a. Side-notched projectile point
   A-6/10/88-16-L-2

b. Corner-notched point
   D-6/7/88-1-L-1

c. Corner-notched point
   D-6/9/88-4-L-1

d. Corner-notched point
   L-6/5/89-2-L-1

e. Shouldered-lanceolate point
   D-6/13/88-2-L-1

f. Shouldered-lanceolate point
   D-6/13/88-26-L-2

g. Shouldered-lanceolate point
   D-6/15/88-9-L-1

LITHICS

a

d

b

e

c

f

g

a. Biface/Pojectile point
   L-6/5/89-2-L-2

b. Biface
   A-6/9/88-1-L-1

c. Biface
   A-6/10/88-16-L-11

d. Uniface
   D-6/15/88-16-L-1

e. Core
   D-6/9/88-65-L-1

f. Edge-modified flake
   I-6/8/89-8-L-1

g. Core
   L-6/5/89-10-L-4

GROUND STONE

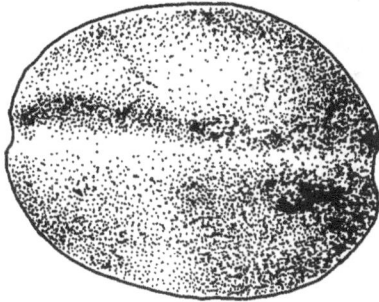

a

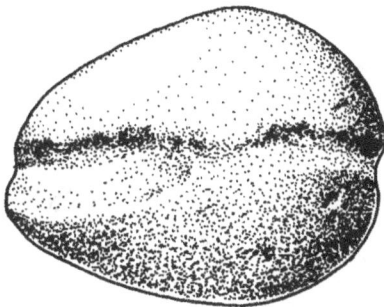

b

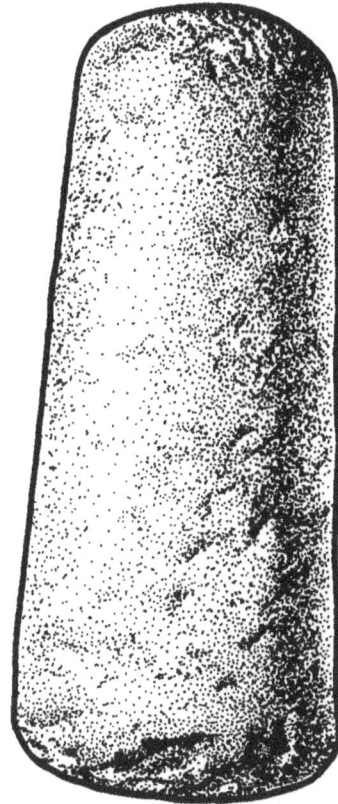

c

a. Net weight
   D-6/7/88-1-L2

b. Net weight
   D-6/15/88-17-L-2

c. Pestle
   D-6/9/88-52-L-1

GROUND STONE

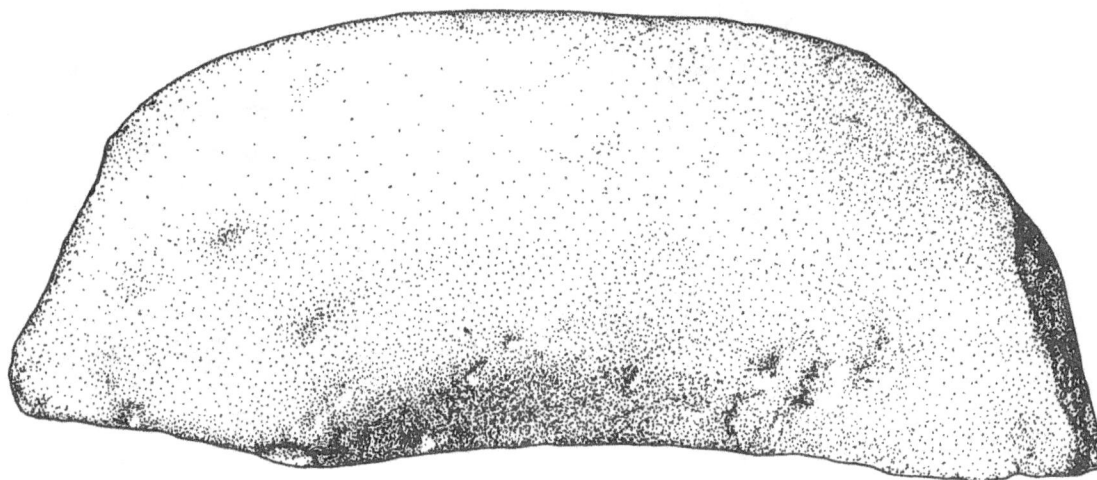

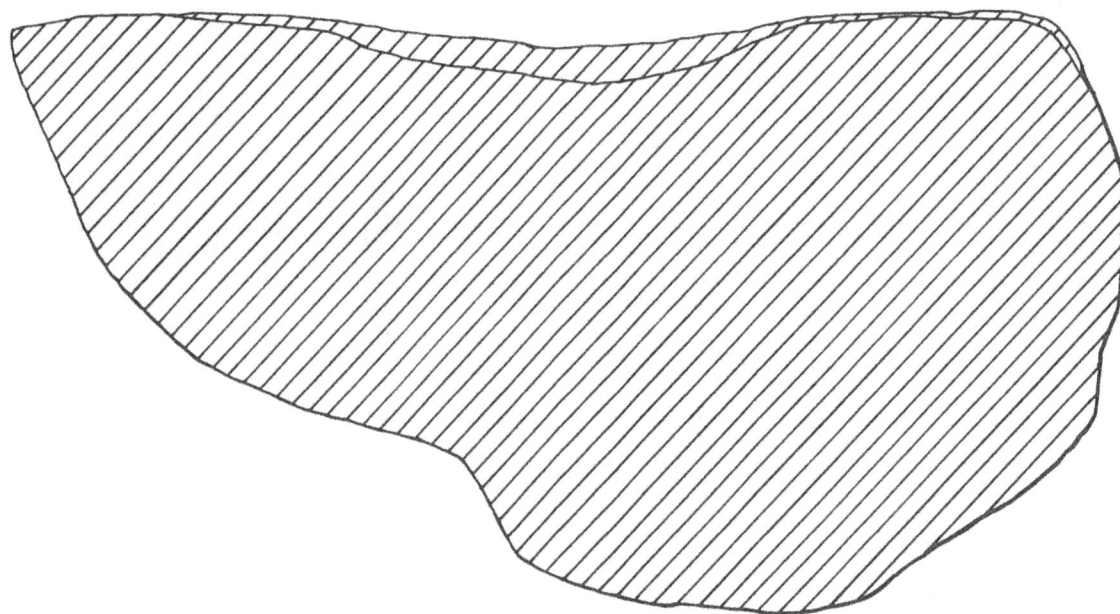

Hopper Mortar
C-6/14/88-1-L-1

GROUND STONE

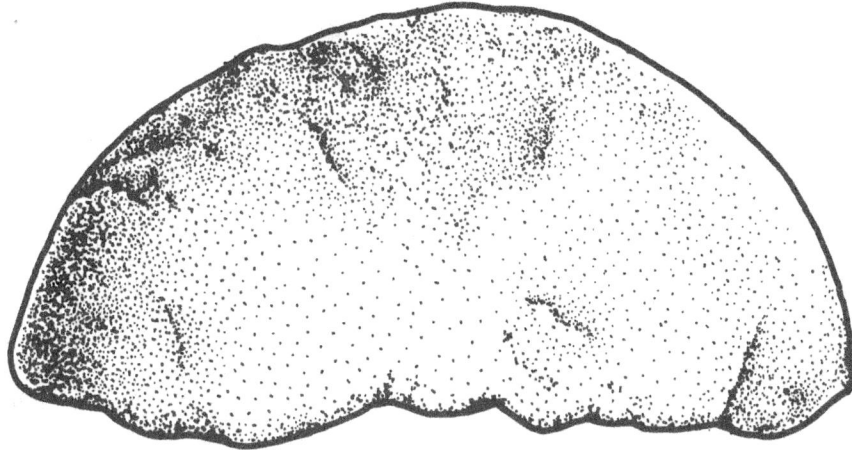

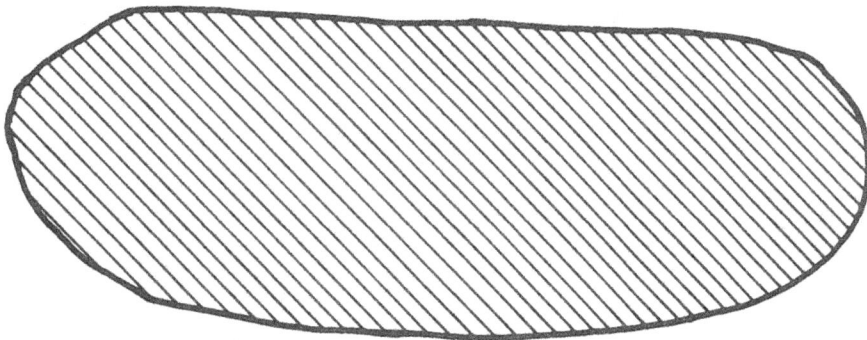

Handstone fragment
L-6/2/89-3-L-3

GLASS, BEADS, CERAMIC

a

c

d

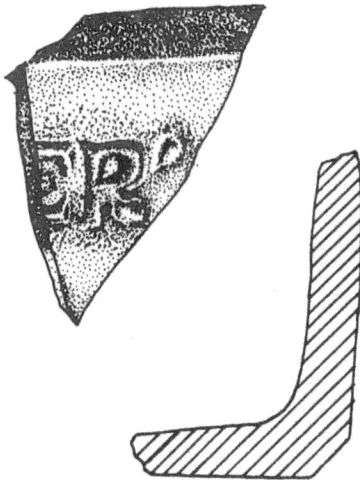

b

e

a Worked glass
   A-10/16/90-1-G

b Glass fragment
   F-6/5/89-4-G

c Glass bead
   B-6/8/89-11-BE-1

d Clam shell disk bead
   L-6/5/89-4-BE-1

e Ceramic
   C-6/6/88-47-HC-1

REFERENCES

Allison, Eric
  1989 Archaeological Site Record, CA-SON-1793. On file, Northwest Information Center, Sonoma State University.

Alt, D. D., and D. W. Hyndman
  1975 *Roadside Geology of Northern California.* Mountain Press Publishing Co., Missoula, Montana.

Alvarez, Susan Harding
  1991 Cultural Resources Inventory of Austin Creek State Recreation Area, A Unit of the California Department of Parks and Recreation, Guerneville, Sonoma County, California. On file, Northern Region Headquarters, California Department of Parks and Recreation, Santa Rosa, California.

Alvarez, Susan Harding and David Fredrickson
  1989 Cultural Resources Inventory, Sonoma Coast State Beach From Goat Rock to Bodega Bay, Sonoma County, California. On file, Anthropological Studies Center, Sonoma State University.

Armstrong, C. F.
  1980a Geologic Map Exclusive of Landslides — Southern Sonoma County. In Geology for Planning in Sonoma County. M. E. Huffman and C. F. Armstrong. Plate 3A. *California Division of Mines and Geology, Special Report* 120.

  1980b Geologic Map Exclusive of Landslides — Southern Sonoma County. In Geology for Planning in Sonoma County. M. E. Huffman and C. F. Armstrong. Plate 3B. *California Division of Mines and Geology, Special Report* 120.

Bailey, E. H., W. P. Irwin, and D. L. Jones
  1964 Franciscan and Related Rocks, and their Significance in the Geology of Western California. *California Division of Mines and Geology Bulletin* 183.

Bancroft, Hubert Howe
  1886 *The Works of Hubert Howe Bancroft, History of California* Vol. 19. The History Company, San Francisco.

Barrett, S. A.
  1908 The Ethno-Geography of the Pomo and Neighboring Indians. *University of California Publications in American Archaeology and Ethnology* Vol. 6.

  1916 Pomo Buildings. In *Holmes Anniversary Volume: Anthropological Essays Presented to William Henry Holmes in Honor of his 70th Birthday.* J. W. Bryan Press, Washington D.C.

  1952 Material Aspects of Pomo Culture. *Bulletin of the Public Museum of the City of Milwaukee* Vol. 20, Parts 1 and 2.

  1975 Pomo Buildings. In *Seven Early Accounts of the Pomo Indians and their Culture,* edited by R. F. Heizer, pp. 37-63. Archaeological Research Facility, University of California, Berkeley.

Batman, Richard
  1985 *The Outer Coast.* Harcourt Brace Jovanovich Publishers, San Diego.

Baumhoff, Martin A.
  1963 Ecological Determinants of Aboriginal California Populations. *University of California Publications in American Archaeology and Ethnology* Vol. 49, no. 2, pp. 155-236.

  1982 North Coast Point Types. In *Cultural Resource Overview for the Mendocino National Forest and East Lake Planning Unit, BLM, California,* edited by H. McCarthy, W. Hildebrandt, and L. Swenson, pp. 1-43, Appendix A. California Archaeological Consultants, Inc.

Bean, Lowell John and Dorothea Theodoratus
  1978 Western Pomo and Northeastern Pomo. In *Handbook of North American Indians, California,* Vol. 8, edited by R. F. Heizer, pp. 289-305. Smithsonian Institution Press, Washington D.C.

Beardsley, Richard K.
  1954 Temporal and Areal Relationships in Central California Archaeology. *University of California Archaeological Survey Report* No. 24, Part 1.

Bedrossian, T. L.
  1974. Geology of the Marin Headlands. *California Geology* 27(4):75-88.

Bickel, P. M.
  1978 Changing Sea Levels Along the California Coast: Anthropological Implications. *Journal of California Anthropology* 5(1):6-20.

Binford, Lewis
  1982 The Archaeology of Place. *Journal of Anthropological Archaeology* 1:5-31.

Black, Lydia T.
  1977 The Konyag (Inhabitants of the island of Kodiak) by Iosaf [Bolotov] (1794-1799) and by Gideon (1804-1807). *Arctic Anthropology* 14(2):79-108.

  1989 Russia's American Adventure. *Natural History* 12:45-57.

Blake, M. C., Jr., J. T. Smith, C. M. Wentworth, and R. H. Wright
  1971. *Preliminary Geologic Map of Western Sonoma County and Northernmost Marin County, California.* United States Geological Survey.

Blomkvist, E. E.
1972 A Russian Scientific Expedition to California
      and Alaska, 1839-1849. *Oregon Historical
      Quarterly* June 1972, pp. 101-170. (Article
      translated by B. Dmytryshyn and E. A. P.
      Crownhart-Vaughan).

Bloom, A. L.
1971 Glacial-Eustatic and Isostatic Controls of Sea
      Level Since the Last Glaciation. In *The
      Late Cenozoic Glacial Changes*, edited by
      K. K. Turekian, pp. 355-79. Yale
      University Press, New Haven.

1983 Sea Level and Coastal Changes. In *Late
      Quaternary Environments of the United
      States*, Vol. 2, edited by H. E. Wright Jr.,
      pp. 42-51. University of Minnesota Press,
      Minneapolis.

Bowen, O. E.
1951 Highways and Byways of Particular Geologic
      Interest. In Geologic Guidebook of the San
      Francisco Bay Counties, edited by O. P.
      Jenkins, pp. 315-80. *California Division
      of Mines Bulletin* 154.

Bower, John
1986 *In Search of the Past*. The Dorsey Press,
      Chicago.

Bramlette, Allan and Katherine M. Dowdall
1989 Differences in Site Constituents at Salt Point:
      Alternative Explanations. In *Proceedings
      of the Society for California Archaeology*
      2: 139-51. Society for California
      Archaeology, San Diego, California.

Bramlette, Allan and David Fredrickson
1990 A Cultural Resource Study for a Burn
      Management Plan at Salt Point State Park,
      Sonoma County, California. On file,
      Anthropological Studies Center, Sonoma
      State University.

Burley, David
1985 Social Organization in Historic Societies: A
      Critical Commentary. In *Status, Structure
      and Stratification: Current Archaeological
      Reconstructions*, edited by M. Thompson,
      M. Garcia, F. Kense, pp. 415-18.
      University of Calgary, Alberta.

Carlson, E. V. (Ed.).
1976 Fort Ross State Historic Park: Resource
      Management Plan and General
      Development Plan. State of California—
      The Resources Agency, Department of
      Parks and Recreation, Sacramento,
      California.

Castillo, Edward D.
1978 The Impact of Euro-American Exploration and
      Settlement. In *Handbook of North
      American Indians, California*, Vol. 8,
      edited by R.F. Heizer, pp. 99-127.
      Smithsonian Institution, Washington D.C.

Charlton, Thomas H.
1981 Archaeology, Ethnohistory, and Ethnology:
      Interpretive Interfaces. In *Advances in
      Archaeological Method and Theory*, Vol.
      4, edited by M. Schiffer, pp. 129-76.
      Academic Press, New York.

Chernykh, Yegor
1967 Agriculture of Upper California. A Long Lost
      Account of Farming in California as
      Recorded by A Russian Observor at Fort
      Ross in 1841. Original 1841 manuscript
      edited and translated by James Gibson. *The
      Pacific Historian* Vol 11, No. 1, pp. 10-
      28.

1968 Two New Chernykh Letters: More Original
      Documentation on the Russian Post
      Relinquished in 1841 to General Sutter.
      Original 1836 letters edited and translated
      by James Gibson. *The Pacific Historian*
      Vol 12, No. 3, pp. 48-56 and Vol 12, No.
      4, pp. 54-60.

Chestnut, V. K.
1902 Plants Used by the Indians of Mendocino
      County, California. *Contributions of the
      National Herbarium* 7:295-422.

Chevigny, Hector
1965 *Russian America The Great Alaskan Venture
      1741-1867*. Binford and Mort Publishing,
      Portland, Oregon.

Clark, Donald W.
1974 *Contributions to the Later Prehistory of
      Kodiak Island, Alaska*. National Museum
      of Man Mercury Series, Archaeological
      Survey of Canada, Paper No. 20. Ottawa.

1985 Archaeological Test at the Russian Three
      Saints Bay Colony, Alaska. *Historical
      Archaeology* 19(2):114-21.

Coleman, R. G., D. E. Lee, L. B. Beatty, and W. W.
      Brannock
1965 Eclogites and Eclogites—Their Differences
      and Similarities. *Geological Society of
      America Bulletin* 76(5):483-508.

Compton, R. R.
1966 Granitic and Metamorphic Rocks of the
      Salinian Block, California Coast Ranges.
      In: Geology of Northern California. E. H.
      Bailey, ed. pp. 277-88. *California
      Division of Mines and Geology Bulletin*
      190.

Corney, Peter
1896 (first published in 1821) *Voyages in the
      Northern Pacific. Narrative of Several
      Trading Voyages from 1813 to 1818,
      Between the Northwest Coast of America,
      the Hawaiian Islands and China, With A
      Description of the Russian Establishments
      on the Northwest Coast*. Thomas G.
      Thrum, Publisher, Honolulu, Hawaii.

Costello, Julia G. and David Hornbeck
1989 Alta California: An Overview. In *Columbian Consequences* Vol. 1, edited by David Hurst Thomas, pp. 303-332. Smithsonian Institution Press, Washington D.C.

Crowell, Aron
1990 Archaeological Investigations at Three Saints Bay, an 18th Century Russian Settlement on Kodiak Island, Alaska. National Science Foundation proposal, Washington D.C.

Deetz, James
1963 Archaeological Investigations at La Purisima Mission. *Archaeological Survey Annual Report* 5:163-208. University of California, Los Angeles.

1988 American Historical Archeology: Methods and Results. *Science* 239:362-67.

1989 Archaeography, Archaeology, or Archeology? *American Journal of Archaeology* 93:429-35.

DeLapp, J. A., and W. R. Powell
1979 *Soil-Vegetation Map for the Fort Ross 7.5 Minute Quadrangle (61D-3). Sonoma County, California.* Pacific Southwest Forest and Range Experiment Station, Forest Service, U.S. Department of Agriculture.

1979 *Soil-Vegetation Map for the Plantation 7.5 Minute Quadrangle (61C-4). Sonoma County, California.* Pacific Southwest Forest and Range Experiment Station, Forest Service, U.S. Department of Agriculture.

DeLapp, J. A., B. F. Smith, and W. R. Powell
1978 *Soil-Vegetation Map for the Arched Rock 7.5 Minute Quadrangle (63A-2). Sonoma County, California.* Pacific Southwest Forest and Range Experiment Station, Forest Service, U.S. Department of Agriculture.

Dmytryshyn, Basil, E. A. P. Crownhart-Vaughan, and Thomas Vaughan
1989a Introduction. In *The Russian American Colonies Three Centuries of Russian Eastward Expansion 1798-1867*, Vol. 3, A Documentary Record, edited by B. Dmytryshyn, E. A. P. Crownhart-Vaughan and T. Vaughan, pp. xxvii-lxxx. Oregon Historical Society Press, Portland.

1989b September 4-28, 1818. From the Diary of Fedor P. Lutke during his Circumnavigation Aboard the Sloop *Kamchatka*, 1817-1819: Observations on California. In *The Russian American Colonies Three Centuries of Russian Eastward Expansion 1798-1867*, Vol. 3, A Documentary Record, edited by B. Dmytryshyn, E. A. P. Crownhart-Vaughan and T. Vaughan, pp. 257-85. Oregon Historical Society Press, Portland.

1989c September 22, 1817. A Treaty Between the Russian American Company and the Kashaya Pomo Indians, Ceding Land for Fort Ross. In *The Russian American Colonies Three Centuries of Russian Eastward Expansion 1798-1867*, Vol. 3, A Documentary Record, edited by B. Dmytryshyn, E. A. P. Crownhart-Vaughan and T. Vaughan, pp. 296-98. Oregon Historical Society Press, Portland.

Dmytryshyn, Basil and E. A. P. Crownhart-Vaughan
1976 *Colonial Russian America: Kyrill T. Khlebnikov's Reports, 1817-1832.* Oregon Historical Society, Portland.

Dobyns, Henry F.
1983 *Their Number Become Thinned: Native American Population Dynamics in Eastern North America.* University of Tennessee Press, Knoxville.

Dowdall, Katherine M.
1988 An Archaeological Collections Analysis of Excavated Materials From CA-SON-473 (Salt Point State Park). On File, Northern Region Headquarters, California Department of Parks and Recreation, Santa Rosa, California.

Dubois, Cora
1939 The 1870 Ghost Dance. *Anthropological Records.* Vol. 3, No. 1.

Duflot de Mofras
1937 *Travels on the Pacific Coast* Vol. 1 and 2. Translation and editing of original 1844 publication by Marguerite E. Wilbur. Fine Arts Press, Santa Ana, California.

Duhaut-Cilly, Auguste Bernard
1946 *An Episode from the Narrative of Auguste Bernard Duhaut-Cilly.* Translation of 1828 account by Charles F. Carter. Silverado Press, Bohemian Grove, California.

Dunnell, Robert C.
1990 Methodological Impacts of Catastrophic Depopulation of American Archaeology and Ethnology. Paper presented at the 55th Annual Meeting of the Society for American Archaeology, Las Vegas, Nevada.

Edwards, Robert
1975 Archaeological Field School at Fort Ross. On file, Cultural Heritage Section, Archaeology Laboratory, Department of Parks and Recreation, Sacramento, California.

Ernst, W. G.
1965 Mineral Paragenesis in Fransiscan Metamorphic Rocks, Panoche Pass, California. *Geological Society of America Bulletin* 76:879-914.

1979 California and Plate Tectonics. *California Geology* 32(9):187-96.

Eschmeyer, W. N., E. S. Herald, and H. Hammann
1983 *A Field Guide to Pacific Coast Fishes of North America*. Houghton Mifflin, Co., Boston.

Farnsworth, Paul
1987 The Economics of Acculturation in the California Missions: A Historical and Archaeological Study of Mission Nuestra Senora de la Soledad. Ph.D. dissertation, University of California, Los Angeles.

Farris, Glenn J.
1981 Preliminary Report of the 1981 Excavations of the Fort Ross Fur Warehouse. On file, Cultural Heritage Section, Archaeology Laboratory, Department of Parks and Recreation, Sacramento, California.

1984 Descriptions of the Russian Orchard at Fort Ross from the Spanish and French Language Inventories. On file, Cultural Heritage Section, Archaeology Laboratory, Department of Parks and Recreation, Sacramento, California.

1986a Cultural Resource Survey at the Fort Ross Campground, Sonoma County, California. On file, Cultural Heritage Section, Archaeology Laboratory, Department of Parks and Recreation, Sacramento, California.

1986b Description of a Visit to an Indian Village Adjacent to Fort Ross by Cyrille LaPlace, 1839. Appendix B in Cultural Resource Survey at the Fort Ross Campground, Sonoma County, California, by Glenn Farris, pp. 65-80. On file, Cultural Heritage Section, Archaeology Laboratory, Department of Parks and Recreation, Sacramento, California.

1988 A French Visitor's Description of the Fort Ross Rancheria in 1839. *News from Native California* 2:22-23.

1989a The Russian Imprint on the Colonization of California. In *Columbian Consequences*, Vol. 1, edited by David Hurst Thomas, pp. 481-97. Smithsonian Institution Press, Washington D.C.

1989b Recognizing Indian Folk History as Real History: A Fort Ross Example. *American Indian Quarterly* 13:471-80.

1990 Fort Ross California: Archaeology of the Old Magazin. In *Russia in North America: Proceedings of the 2nd International Conference on Russian America*, edited by Richard A. Pierce, pp. 475-505. The Limestone Press, Fairbanks, Alaska.

Fedorova, Svetlana G.
1973 *The Russian Population in Alaska and California Late 18th Century — 1867*. Translated and edited by Richard A. Pierce and Alton S. Donnelly. Limestone Press, Kingston, Ontario.

1975 *Ethnic Processes in Russian America*. Occasional Papers No. 1, Anchorage Historical and Fine Arts Museum, Anchorage, Alaska.

Fitzhugh, William W.
1985 Introduction. In *Cultures in Contact: The Impact of European Contacts on Native American Cultural Institutions A.D. 1000-1800*, edited by W. Fitzhugh, pp. 1-15. Smithsonian Institution Press, Washington D.C.

Foster, Dan
1983a Archaeological Site Record, CA-SON-1423. On file, Northwest Information Center, Sonoma State University.

1983b Archaeological Site Record, CA-SON-1424. On file, Northwest Information Center, Sonoma State University.

1987 Archaeological Survey of S-111 Study Area, Fort Ross Quad. On file, Northwest Information Center, Sonoma State University.

Fredrickson, David
1962 Archaeological Investigations Within Construction Site Area of Unit 1 of Pacific Gas and Electric Company's Atomic Park, Sonoma County, California. On file, Manuscript No. 324, Lowie Museum of Anthropology, University of California, Berkeley.

1974a A Preliminary Evaluation of the Archaeological Potential of 2078 Acres of the Navarro Ranch Near Cazadero, Sonoma County, California. On file, Manuscript No. 5-50, Northwest Information Center, Sonoma State University.

1974b A Preliminary Evaluation of the Archaeological Potential of 1600 acres of the Gualala Land Development Corporation Located in the Drainage of the South Fork of the Gualala River, Sonoma County, California. On file, Manuscript No. 5-55, Northwest Information Center, Sonoma State University.

1974c Cultural Diversity in Early Central California: A View From the North Coast Ranges. *Journal of California Anthropology* 1:41-54.

1984a The North Coastal Region. In *California Archaeology* by Michael Moratto, pp. 471-528. Academic Press, Orlando.

1984b The Use of Obsidian Analyses to Establish "Units of Contemporaneity." Paper presented at the Annual Meeting of the Society for American Archaeology, Portland, Oregon.

1987 The Use of Borax Lake Obsidian Through Time and Space. Paper presented at the Annual Meeting of the Society for California Archaeology, Fresno, California.

1989 Spatial and Temporal Patterning of Obsidian Materials in the Geyers Region. In *Current Directions in California Obsidian Studies,* edited by Richard Hughes, pp. 95-110. Contributions of the University of California Archaeological Research Facility 48.

Fritts, H. C.
1965 Tree Ring Evidence for Climatic Changes in Western North America. *Monthly Weather Review* 93(7):421-43.

Garth, J. S. and J. W. Tilden
1986 *California Butterflies.* California Natural History Guide #51. University of California Press, Berkeley.

Gibson, James R.
1969 Russia in California, 1833, Report of Governor Wrangel. *Pacific Northwest Quarterly* 60:205-215.

1976 *Imperial Russia in Frontier America: The Changing Geography of Supply of Russian America, 1784-1867.* Oxford University Press, New York.

1986 *Russian Expansion in Siberia and America: Critical Contrasts.* Kennan Institute for Advanced Russian Studies. Smithsonian Institution Building, Washington D.C.

1987 *Russian Dependence Upon the Natives of Russian America.* Kennan Institute for Advanced Russian Studies Occasional Papers No. 70. Smithsonian Institution Building, Washington D.C.

1988 The Maritime Trade of the North Pacific Coast. In *Handbook of North American Indians, History of Indian-White Relations,* Vol. 4, edited by Wilcomb E. Washburn, pp. 375-90. Smithsonian Institution Press, Washington D.C.

Gifford, E. W.
1922 California Kinship Terminologies. *University of California Publications in American Archaeology and Ethnology* 18:1-285.

1967 Ethnographic Notes on the Southwestern Pomo. *Anthropological Records* 25:1-48.

Gifford, E. W. and A. L. Kroeber
1937 Culture Element Distributions: IV, Pomo. *University of California Publications in American Archaeology and Ethnology* 37:117-254.

Goldman, Irving
1940 The Alkatcho Carrier of British Columbia. In *Acculturation in Seven American Indian Tribes* edited by Ralph Linton, pp. 333-89. Peter Smith, Glouchester, Mass.

Golovnin, Vasilii M.
1979 *Around the World on the Kamchatka 1817-1819.* Translation of the original 1822 edition (Part 1) by Ella L. Wiswell. The Hawaiian Historical Society and The University Press of Hawaii, Honolulu.

Goodrich, Jennie., Claudia Lawson, and Vanna Parrish Lawson
1980 *Kashaya Pomo Plants.* American Indian Monograph Series, No. 2. American Indian Studies Center, University of California at Los Angeles.

Greengo, R. E.
1955 4-SON-299 Shell Analysis Progress Report. On file, Manuscript No. 208, Lowie Museum of Anthropology, University of California, Berkeley.

Griggs, G. B. and R. E. Johnson
1979. Coastline Erosion: Santa Cruz County. *California Geology* 32(4):67-75.

Grinnell, J. and A. H. Miller
1944 The Distribution of the Birds of California, Cooper Ornithological Club. *Pacific Coast Avifauna* 18.

Haase, Ynez D.
1952 The Russian-American Company in California. M.A. Thesis, University of California, Berkeley.

Hamilton, Scott
1985 The Social Organization of the Hudson's Bay Company: The Brandon House Case. In *Status, Structure, and Stratification: Current Archaeological Reconstructions,* edited by M. Thompson, M. Garica, and F. Kense, pp. 379-86. University of Calgary, Alberta.

Hart, E. W.
1978 Limestone, Dolomite, and Shell Resources of the Coast Ranges Province, California. *California Division of Mines and Geology Bulletin* 197.

Heizer, Robert F.
1941 The Direct-Historical Approach in California Archaeology. *American Antiquity* 7:98-122.

1975 *Seven Early Accounts of the Pomo Indians and Their Culture,* edited by R. F. Heizer. Archaeological Research Facility, University of California, Berkeley.

1978 History of Research. In *Handbook of North American Indians, California,* Vol. 8, edited by R. F. Heizer, pp. 6-15. Smithsonian Institution Press, Washington D.C.

Heizer, Robert F. and Albert B. Elsasser
1980 *The Natural World of the California Indians.* University of California Press, Berkeley.

Herskovits, Melville J.
1938 *Acculturation the Study of Culture Contact.* J. J. Augustin Publisher, New York.

Hoover, Robert L.
1989 Spanish-Native Interaction and Acculturation in the Alta California Missions. In *Columbian Consequences* Vol. 1, edited by David Hurst Thomas, pp. 395-406. Smithsonian Institution Press, Washington D.C.

Hombeck, David
1989 Economic Growth and Change at the Missions of Alta California, 1769-1846, In *Columbian Consequences* Vol. 1,. edited by David Hurst Thomas, pp. 423-34. Smithsonian Institution Press, Washington D.C.

Horsman, Reginald
1988 United States Indian Policies, 1776-1815. In *Handbook of North American Indians: History of Indian-White Relations*, Vol. 4, edited by Wilcomb E. Washburn, pp. 29-39. Smithsonian Institution Press, Washington D.C.

Howard, A. D.
1951 Development of the Landscape of the San Francisco Bay Counties. In *Geologic Guidebook of the San Francisco Bay Counties*, edited by O. P. Jenkins, pp. 95-106. *California Division of Mines Bulletin* 154.

Hudson, John W.
1897 Pomo Wampum Makers an Aboriginal Double Standard. *Overland Monthly* 30:101-108. (Reprinted in 1975 in *Seven Accounts of the Pomo Indians and their Culture*, edited by R. Heizer, pp. 9-20.)

Huffman, M. E. and C. F. Armstrong
1980 Geology for Planning in Sonoma County. *California Division of Mines and Geology, Special Report* 120.

Hylkema, Mark
1986 Analysis of Chert Debitage: SON-1455. Appendix C in Cultural Resource Survey at the Fort Ross Campground, Sonoma County, California, by Glenn Farris, pp. 81-91. On file, Cultural Heritage Section, Archaeology Laboratory, California Department of Parks and Recreation, Sacramento, California.

Jackson, Robert
1983 Intermarriage at Fort Ross: Evidence from the San Rafael Mission Baptismal Register. *Journal of California and Great Basin Anthropology* 5:240-41.

Jackson, Robert, Michael Boynton, William Olsen and R. Weaver
1988 California Archaeological Resource Identification and Data Acquisition Program: Sparse Lithic Scatters. Manual prepared by the Office of Historic Preservation, Sacramento, California.

Jackson, Thomas L.
1989 Late Prehistoric Obsidian Production and Exchange in the North Coast Ranges, California. In *Current Directions in California Obsidian Studies*, edited by Richard Hughes, pp. 79-94. Contributions of the University of California Archaeological Research Facility 48.

Jacobs, Wilbur R.
1988 British Indian Policies to 1783. In *Handbook of North American Indians History of Indian-White Relations*, Vol. 4, edited by Wilcomb E. Washburn, pp. 5-12. Smithsonian Institution Press, Washington D.C.

Jameson, E. W. and H. J. Peeters
1988 *California Mammals.* California Natural History Guides #52. University of California Press, Berkeley.

Johnson, Gregory
1973 *Local Exchange and Early State Development in Southwest Iran.* Museum of Anthropology, University of Michigan Anthropological Papers 37.

Johnson, John
1989 The Chumash and the Missions. In *Columbian Consequences*, Vol. 1, edited by David Hurst Thomas, pp. 365-76. Smithsonian Institution Press, Washington D.C.

Jordan, Richard H. and Richard A. Knecht
1988 Archaeological Research on Western Kodiak Island, Alaska: The Development of Koniag Culture. In *Aurora The Late Prehistoric Development of Alaska's Native People*, edited by Robert Shaw, Roger K. Harritt, Don E. Dumond, pp. 225-306. Alaska Anthropological Association Monograph Series No. 4.

Kari, James
1983 Kalifornsky, the Californian from Cook Inlet. *Alaska in Perspective* 5:1-11.

Kennedy, Mary Jean
1955 Culture Contact and Acculturation of the Southwestern Pomo. Ph.d. Dissertation, University of California, Berkeley.

Khlebnikov, Kyrill
1976 *Colonial Russian America: Kyrill T. Khlebnikov's Reports, 1817-1832.* Translation and editing of original 1861 publication by Basil Dmytryshyn and E. A. P. Crownhart-Vaughan. Oregon Historical Society, Portland.

1990 *The Khlebnikov Archive. Unpublished Journal (1800-1837) and Travel Notes (1820, 1822, and 1824).* Edited by Leonid Shur. Translated by John Bisk. University of Alaska Press, Fairbanks.

King, Robert F.
1974a An Archaeological Survey of the Navarro Ranch Land Development in Northwestern Sonoma County, California. On file, Manuscript No. S-111, Northwest Information Center, Sonoma State University.

1974b An Archaeological Survey of 1600 Acres (Gualala Land Development Corporation) in the Drainage of the South Fork of the Gualala River, Sonoma County, California. On file, Manuscript No. S-110, Northwest Information Center, Sonoma State University.

Kintigh, Keith
1984 Measuring Archaeological Diversity by Comparison with Simulated Assemblages. *American Antiquity* 49:44-54.

1988 Diversity Module. In *The Archaeologist's Analytical Toolkit* by Keith Kintigh, pp. 48-66. Computer program manual available from Keith Kintigh, Department of Anthropology, Arizona State University, Tempe.

1989 Sample Size, Significance, and Measures of Diversity. In *Quantifying Diversity in Archaeology*, edited by Robert D. Leonard and George T. Jones, pp. 25-36. Cambridge University Press, Cambridge.

Kirch, Patrick and Roger C. Green
1987 History, Phylogeny, and Evolution in Polynesia. *Current Anthropology* 28:431-56.

Knecht, Richard A.
1985 Nunakaxvak: Koniag Society on the Russian-American Frontier. M.A. Thesis, Bryn Mawr College, Pennsylvania.

Knecht, Richard A. and Richard A. Jordan
1985 Nunakakhnak: An Historic Koniag Village in Karluk, Kodiak Island, Alaska. *Arctic Anthropology* 22:17-35.

Kniffen, Fred
1939 Pomo Geography. *University of California Publications in American Archaeology and Ethnology*. Vol. 36, no. 6, pp. 353-400.

Knudson, S. J.
1985 *Culture in Retrospect.* Waveland Press, Inc., Prospect Heights, Illinois.

Kostromitinov, P.
1974 Notes on the Indians in Upper California. In *Ethnographic Observations on the Coast Miwok and Pomo by Contre-Admiral F. P. Von Wrangell and P. Kostromitinov of the Russian Colony Ross, 1839*, pp. 7-18. Translation and editing of original 1839 publication by Fred Stross and Robert Heizer. Archaeological Research Facility, University of California, Berkeley.

Kotzebue, Otto Von
1830 *A New Voyage Round the World, in the Years 1823, 24, 25, and 26.* Volumes 1 and 2. Henry Colbum and Richard Bentley, London.

Kroeber, A. L.
1925 *Handbook of the Indians of California.* Smithsonian Institution, Bureau of American Ethnology, Bulletin 78. (Reprinted in 1976 by Dover Publications, Inc., New York.)

Kunkel, P. H.
1974 The Pomo Kin Group and the Political Unit in Aboriginal California. *The Journal of California Anthropology* 1:7-18.

LaMarche, V. C., Jr. and R. E. Wallace
1972 Evaluation of Effects on Trees of Past Movements of the San Andreas Fault, Northern California. *Geological Society of America Bulletin* 83:265-76.

LaPlace, Cyrille
1986 Description of a Visit to an Indian Village Adjacent to Fort Ross by Cyrille LaPlace, 1839. Translation and editing of 1854 original French publication by Glenn Farris. Appendix B in Cultural Resource Survey at the Fort Ross Campground, Sonoma County, California, by Glenn Farris, pp. 65-80. On file, Cultural Heritage Section, Archaeology Laboratory, California Department of Parks and Recreation, Sacramento, California.

1988 A French Visitor's Description of the Fort Ross Rancheria in 1839. Translation and editing of 1854 original French publication by Glenn Farris. *News from Native California* 2:22-23.

Lawson, Claudia and Vanna Parrish Lawson
1976 Kashaya Pomo Ethnobotanical Project. *Journal of California Anthropology* 3:132-35.

Layton, Thomas N.
1990 *Western Pomo Prehistory: Excavations at Albion Head, Nightbirds' Retreat, and Three Chop Village, Mendocino County, California.* Monograph 32, Institute of Archaeology, University of California, Los Angeles.

Levulett, Valerie A. and William R. Hildebrandt
  1987 *The King Range Archaeological Project: Results of the 1984 Field Season.* Anthropological Studies Center, Sonoma State University.

Lightfoot, Kent G.
  1985 Shell Midden Diversity: A Case Example from Coastal New York. *North American Archaeologist* 6:289-324.

Lightfoot, Kent G. and Roberta A. Jewett
  1986 The Shift to Sedentary Life: A Consideration of the Occupation Duration of Early Mogollon Pithouse Villages. In *Mogollon Variability*, edited by Charlotte Benson and Steadman Upham, pp. 9-43. New Mexico State University, The University Museum Occasional Papers 15.

Lightfoot, Kent G., Robert Kalin and James Moore
  1987 *Prehistoric Hunter-Gatherers of Shelter Island, New York: An Archaeological Study of the Mashomack Preserve.* Contributions of the University of California Archaeological Research Facility 46.

Loeb, E. M.
  1926 Pomo Folkways. *University of California Publications in American Archaeology and Ethnology* 19(2):149-405.

Louderback, G. D.
  1951 Geologic History of San Francisco Bay. In Geologic Guidebook of the San Francisco Bay Counties, edited by O. P. Jenkins, pp. 75-94. *California Division of Mines Bulletin* 154.

Lutke, Fedor P.
  1989 September 4-28, 1818. From the Diary of Fedor P. Lutke during his Circumnavigation Aboard the Sloop *Kamchatka*, 1817-1819: Observations on California. In *The Russian American Colonies Three Centuries of Russian Eastward Expansion 1798-1867*, Vol. 3, A Documentary Record, edited and translated by Basil Dmytryshyn, E. A. P. Crownhart-Vaughan, and Thomas Vaughan, pp. 257-85. Oregon Historical Society Press, Portland.

Matthewson, R. C.
  1859 Plat Map and Field Notes of the Muniz Rancho Finally Confirmed to Manuel Torres. Copy on file, Cultural Heritage Section, Archaeology Laboratory, California Department of Parks and Recreation, Sacramento, California.

McGinnis, S. M.
  1984 *Freshwater Fishes of California*, Natural History Guides #49. University of California Press, Berkeley.

McKenzie, John
  1963 Historic Resources and Indian Sites at Fort Ross State Historic Park as Identified by John McKenzie, August 20, 1963. Manuscript on file, Cultural Heritage Section, Archaeology Laboratory, California Department of Parks and Recreation, Sacramento.

McLendon, Sally and Robert L. Oswalt
  1978 Pomo: Introduction. In *Handbook of North American Indians, California* Vol. 8, edited by Robert F. Heizer, pp. 274-88. Smithsonian Institution Press, Washington D.C.

Mead, Margaret
  1932 *The Changing Culture of an Indian Tribe.* Columbia University Press, New York.

Meighan, Clement W.
  1967 Appendix: Comparative Notes on Two Historic Village Sites. In Ethnographic Notes on the Southwestern Pomo, by E. W. Gifford, pp. 46-47. *Anthropological Records* Vol. 25. University of California Press, Berkeley.

Merriam, C. Hart
  1938 Indians Visited 1901-1929. Index Cards. On file, Manuscript No. 427, Lowie Museum of Anthropology, University of California, Berkeley.

  1967 *Ethnographic Notes on California Indian Tribes III. Ethnological Notes on Central California Indian Tribes.* Compiled and edited by Robert F. Heizer. Reports of the University of California Archaeological Survey no. 68, part 3.

  1968 *Village Names in Twelve California Mission Records.* Assembled and edited by Robert F. Heizer. Reports of the University of California Archaeological Survey no. 74.

  1977 *Ethnogeographic and Ethnosynonymic Data from Northern California Tribes.* Assembled and edited by Robert F. Heizer. Archaeological Research Facility, University of California, Berkeley.

Milliman, J. D., and K. O. Emery
  1968 Sea Levels During the Past 35,000 Years. *Science* 162:1121-23.

Monks, Gregory
  1985 Status and Fur Trade in the Northern Department, 1821-1870. In *Status, Structure and Stratification: Current Archaeological Reconstructions*, edited by M. Thompson, M. T. Garcia, F. J. Kense, pp. 407-411. University of Calgary, Alberta.

Moratto, Michael
  1984 *California Archaeology.* Academic Press, Orlando, Florida.

Moyle, P. B.
1976 *Inland Fishes of California.* University of California Press, Berkeley.

Munz, P. A. and D. D. Keck.
1973 *A California Flora, With Supplement.* University of California Press, Berkeley.

Nelson, Nels
1909 Russian River to Golden Gate Mounds (General). On file, Manuscript No. 351, Lowie Museum of Anthropology, University of California, Berkeley.

O'Connor, Denise M.
1984 Trade and Tableware: A Historical and Distributional Analysis of the Ceramics from Fort Ross, California. M.A. Thesis, California State University, Sacramento.

Ogden, Adele
1933 Russian Sea-Otter and Seal Hunting on the California Coast, 1803-1841. In *The Russians in California*, edited by E. O. Essig, pp. 29-51. California Historical Society, San Francisco.

1941 *The California Sea Otter Trade, 1784-1848.* University of California Press, Berkeley.

Origer, Thomas M.
1987 *Temporal Control in the Southern North Coast Ranges of California: The Application of Obsidian Hydration Analysis.* Papers in Northern California Anthropology 1. Northern California Anthropological Group, Berkeley.

Origer, Thomas M. and Brian Wickstrom
1982 The Use of Hydration Measurements to Date Obsidian Materials from Sonoma County, California. *Journal of California and Great Basin Anthropology* 4:123-31.

Oswalt, Robert L.
1957 Russian Loanwords in Southwestern Pomo. *International Journal of American Linguistics* 23:245-47.

1964 Kashaya Texts. *University of California Publications in Linguistics* Vol. 36.

1988 History Through the Words Brought to California by the Fort Ross Colony. *News from Native California* Vol. 2, No. 3 pp. 20-22.

Page, B. M.
1966 Geology of the Coast Ranges of California. In Geology of Northern California, edited by E. H. Bailey, pp. 255-76. *California Division of Mines and Geology Bulletin* 190.

Parkman, E. Breck
1984 Archaeological Site Record, CA-SON-1451. On file, Northwest Information Center, Sonoma State University.

1990a Excavation of CA-SON-1446H. On file, Northern Region Headquarters, California Department of Parks and Recreation, Santa Rosa, California.

1990b Toward a Proto-Hokan Ideology. Paper presented at the 23rd Annual Chacmool Archaeological Conference, University of Calgary, Alberta.

Payeras, Mariano
1979 (entry for October 11, 1822) Diary of Mariano Payeras, Travels of the Canon Fernandez de San Vincente To Ross. Translated by Michael S. Tucker and Nicholas Del Cioppo. Submitted for distribution at the Conference on Russian America at Sitka, Alaska in 1979. Copy on file, Fort Ross Interpretive Library, Fort Ross, California.

Peter, J.
1938 Site Survey of the Tomales, Bodega Bay, and Sonoma County Coast. On file, Manuscript # 436, Lowie Museum of Anthropology, University of California, Berkeley.

Phillips, George H.
1981 *The Enduring Struggle: Indians in California History.* Boyd and Fraser Publishing Co., San Francisco.

Pierce, Richard A.
1988 Russian and Soviet Eskimo Indian Policies. In *Handbook of North American Indians History of Indian-White Relations*, Vol. 4, edited by Wilcomb E. Washburn, pp. 119-27. Smithsonian Institution, Washington D.C.

Pilling, A. and C. Meighan
1949 Archaeological Site Survey Record, CA-SON-175. On file, Northwest Information Center, Sonoma State University.

Porter, Cris D.
1985 Archeological Monitoring of a Portion of the West Wall Replacement, Fort Ross State Historic Park, Sonoma County, California. On file, Northern Region Headquarters, California Department of Parks and Recreation, Santa Rosa, California.

Powell, J. A. and C. L. Hogue
1979 *California Insects.* California Natural History Guide #44. University of California Press, Berkeley.

Powers, Stephen
1976 *Tribes of California.* University of California Press, Berkeley (originally published in 1877 in Contributions to North American Ethnology Volume 3, Department of the Interior, U.S. Geographical and Geological Survey of the Rocky Mountain Region, Government Printing Office, Washington D.C.)

Prager, Gabriella
    1985   A Comparison of Social Structure in North
           West Company and the Hudson's Bay
           Company. In *Status, Structure and
           Stratification*, edited by Marc Thompson,
           M. T. Garcia, and F. J. Kense, pp. 387-92.
           University of Calgary, Alberta.

Prentice, C. S.
    1989   Earthquake Geology of the Northern San
           Andreas Fault Near Point Arena, California.
           Unpublished doctoral dissertation,
           California Institute of Technology,
           Pasadena, California.

Pritchard, William E.
    1970   Archeology of Salt Point. In Cooperative
           Planning for Educational Use of Salt Point
           State Park, edited by Eugene E. Morris, pp.
           22-33. On file, Northern Region Headquar-
           ters, California Department of Parks and
           Recreation, Santa Rosa, California.

Purser, Margaret
    1990   Historical Artifacts. Report on Surface Finds
           from Fort Ross Quads A, B, C, D, F, and L.
           On file, Fort Ross Archaeological Project,
           Archaeological Research Facility,
           University of California, Berkeley.

Purser, Margaret, Vicki Beard and Adrian Praetzellis
    1990   Archaeological Investigations for the
           Stockade Wall Replacement Project, Fort
           Ross State Historic Park, Sonoma County,
           California. On file, Anthropological
           Studies Center, Sonoma State University.

Quinn, David B.
    1979a *America from Concept to Discovery: Early
           Explorations of North America*, Vol. 1.
           Arno Press, New York.

    1979b *The Extension of Settlement in Florida,
           Virginia, and the Spanish Southwest*, Vol.
           5. Arno Press, New York.

Ramenofsky, Ann F.
    1987   *Vectors of Death: The Archaeology of
           European Contact*. University of New
           Mexico Press, Albuquerque, New Mexico.

Ray, Arthur J.
    1988   The Hudson's Bay Company and Native
           People. In *Handbook of North American
           Indians History of Indian-White Relations*,
           Vol. 4, edited by Wilcomb E. Washburn,
           pp. 335-50. Smithsonian Institution
           Press, Washington D.C.

Redfield, Robert, Ralph Linton and Melville Herskovits
    1936   Memorandum for the Study of Acculturation.
           American Anthropologist 38:149-52.

Ricketts, E. F., J. Calvin, J. W. Hedgpeth, and D. W.
           Phillips
    1985   *Between Pacific Tides*. Stanford University
           Press.

Riddell, Francis
    1955   *Archaeological Excavation on the Farallon
           Islands, California*. Reports of the
           University of California Archaeological
           Survey 32: 1-18.

Ritter, D. F.
    1978   *Process Geomorphology*. Wm. Brown, Co.
           Dubuque, Iowa.

Ritter, Eric W.
    1972   Preliminary Report on Archaeological
           Investigations at Fort Ross. On file,
           Cultural Heritage Section, Archaeology
           Laboratory, California Department of
           Parks and Recreation, Sacramento,
           California.

Roedel, P. M.
    1953   Common Ocean Fishes of the California
           Coast. California Department of Fish and
           Game. *Fish Bulletin* #91.

Ross Census
    1848   Praesidio Ross. January the 8th 1848. Liste of
           Indians at Present Time. Manuscript on
           file, Vallejo Papers, Vol. 3, No. 326.
           Bancroft Library, University of California,
           Berkeley.

Rousselot, Jean-Loup, William Fitzhugh, and Aron
           Crowell
    1988   Maritime Eonomies of the North Pacific Rim.
           In *Crossroads of Continents*, edited by
           William Fitzhugh and Aron Crowell, pp.
           151-72. Smithsonian Institution Press,
           Washington D.C.

Sahlins, Marshall
    1985   *Islands of History*. University of Chicago
           Press, Chicago.

Schenck, E.
    1926   The Emerville Shellmound: Final Report.
           *University of California Publications in
           American Archaeology and Ethnology*
           23(3):147-282.

Schulz, Jeanette
    1984   Archaeological Site Record, CA-SON-1454/H.
           On file, Northwest Information Center,
           Sonoma State University.

Schwaderer, Rae, Jennifer Ferneau and E. Breck Parkman
    1990   Coyote's Hole: Preliminary Investigations of
           CA-SON-348, the Duncan's Landing Cave
           Site, Sonoma Coast. Paper presented at the
           24th Annual Meeting of the Society for
           California Archaeology, Foster City.

Scott, S. L. (Ed.)
    1983   *Field Guide to the Birds of North America*.
           National Geographic Society. Kingsport
           Press. Kingsport, Tennessee.

Sharer, Robert J. and Wendy Ashmore
    1987   *Archaeology Discovering Our Past*. Mayfield
           Publishing Co., Mountain View,
           California.

Shay, C. Thomas
1985 Aspects of Ethnobotany in the Red River Settlement in the Late Nineteenth Century. In *Status, Structure, and Stratification*, edited by M. Thompson, M. Garcia, and F. Kense, pp. 365-70. University of Calgary, Alberta.

Simmons, William S.
1988 Culture Theory in Contemporary Ethnohistory. *Ethnohistory* 35:1-14.

Simons, Dwight D.
1990 Vertebrate Remains from the Albion Sites. In *Western Pomo Prehistory*, by Thomas N. Layton, pp. 37-51. Monograph 32. Institute of Archaeology, University of California, Los Angeles.

Simons, Dwight D., Thomas N. Layton, and Ruthann Knudson
1985 A Fluted Point from the Mendocino County Coast, California. *Journal of California and Great Basin Anthropology* 7:260-69.

Smith, Janice C.
1974 Pomo and Promyshlenniki: Time and Trade Goods at Fort Ross. M.A. Thesis, University of California, Los Angeles.

Smith, R. I. and J. T. Carlton
1975 *Light's Manual: Intertidal Invertebrates of the Central California Coast*. University of California Press, Berkeley.

Snow, Dean
1980 *The Archaeology of New England*. Academic Press, New York.

Snow, Dean and Kim Lanphear
1988 European Contact and Indian Depopulation in the Northeast: The Timing of the First Epidemics. *Ethnohistory* 35:15-33.

Spencer-Hancock, Diane
1980 *Fort Ross: Indians-Russians-Americans*. Fort Ross Interpretive Association, Jenner, California.

Spencer-Hancock, Diane and William E. Pritchard
1982 The Chapel at Fort Ross. *California History* 61:3-17.

Spencer Pritchard, Diane
1991 The Good, the Bad and the Ugly: Russian-American Company Employees of Fort Ross. *The Californians* 8 (no. 6):42-49.

Stebbins, R. C.
1985 *A Field Guide to Western Reptiles and Amphibians*. Houghton Mifflin Co., Boston.

Steward, Julian
1942 The Direct Historical Approach to Archaeology. *American Antiquity* 7:337-43.

1944 Re Archaeological Tools and Jobs. *American Antiquity* 10:99-100.

Stewart, Omer C.
1935a Archaeological Site Survey Record, CA-SON-175. On file, Northwest Information Center, Sonoma State University.

1935b Omer Stewart's field notes. On file, Dorothea Theodoratus, JCR Research, Fair Oaks, California.

1943 Notes on Pomo Ethnogeography. *University of California Publications in American Archaeology and Ethnology* Vol. 40, No. 2, pp. 29-62.

Stewart, Suzanne B.
1980 Archaeological Overview of Sonoma and Napa Counties. On file, Northwest Information Center, Sonoma State University.

Stillinger, Robert
1975 A Preliminary Analysis of Sonoma S.D.A.-1 (CA-SON-670). On file, Manuscript No. S-6295, Northwest Information Center, Sonoma State University.

Stirton, R. A.
1951 Prehistoric Land Animals of the San Francisco Bay Region. In Geologic Guidebook of the San Francisco Bay Counties, edited by O. P Jenkins, pp. 177-86. *California Division of Mines Bulletin* 154.

Strong, William Duncan
1935 *An Introduction to Nebraska Archaeology*. Smithsonian Miscellaneous Collection 93 (no. 10): 1-315. Smithsonian Institution, Washington D.C.

Stross, Fred and Robert Heizer
1974 *Ethnographic Observations on the Coast Miwok and Pomo by Contre-Admiral F. P. Von Wrangell and P. Kostromitinov of the Russian Colony Ross, 1839*. Archaeological Research Facility, University of California, Berkeley.

Sullivan, R.
1975 Geological Hazards Along the Coast South of San Francisco. *California Geology* 28(2):27-33.

Swagerty, William R.
1988 Indian Trade in Trans-Mississippi West to 1870. In *Handbook of North American Indians History of Indian-White Relations*, Vol. 4, edited by Wilcomb E. Washburn, pp. 351-74. Smithsonian Institution Press, Washington D.C.

Swiden, Christina
1986 Analysis of Shellfish Remains from SON-1455. Appendix A in Cultural Resource Survey at the Fort Ross Campground, Sonoma County, California, by Glenn Farris, pp. 55-64. On file, Cultural Heritage Section, Archaeology Laboratory, California Department of Parks and Recreation, Sacramento, California.

Taliaferro, N. L.
1951 Geology of the San Francisco Bay Counties. In Geologic Guidebook of the San Francisco Bay Counties, edited by O. P. Jenkins, pp. 117-50. *California Division of Mines Bulletin* 154.

Thomas, Bryn
1976a Historic Sites Researches at Fort Ross, California. On file, Cultural Heritage Section, Archaeology Laboratory, California Department of Parks and Recreation, Sacramento, California.

1976b Archaeological Progress Report of the Old Commandants' House Excavation, 1976 Field Season. On file, Cultural Heritage Section, Archaeology Laboratory, California Department of Parks and Recreation, Sacramento, California.

Thomas, David Hurst
1975 Nonsite Sampling in Archaeology: Up the Creek Without a Site? In *Sampling in Archaeology*, edited by James Mueller, pp. 61-81. University of Arizona Press, Tucson.

1989 *Columbian Consequences*, Vol. 1. Smithsonian Institution Press, Washington D.C.

Thompson, Nelson B. and David Fredrickson
1979 An Archaeological Survey of the Stillwater Cove Regional Park, Sonoma County, California. On file, Manuscript No. S-1563, Northwest Information Center, Sonoma State University.

Tikhmenev, P. A.
1978 *A History of the Russian-American Company*. Translation and editing of original 1861-63 publications by Richard A. Pierce and A. S. Donnelly. University of Washington Press, Seattle.

Tomlin, Kaye
1991 Fort Ross State Historic Park Timeline. Manuscript on file with author.

Tomlin, Kaye and Stephen Watrous
1990 *Outpost of an Empire, Fort Ross: The Russian Colony in California*. Fort Ross Interpretive Association, Fort Ross, California.

Treganza, Adan E.
1954 Fort Ross A Study in Historical Archaeology. *Reports of the University of California Archaeological Survey* No. 23:1-26.

Tremaine, Kim
1989 Obsidian as a Time Keeper: An Investigation in Absolute and Relative Dating. M.A. Thesis, Sonoma State University.

Tremaine, Kim and David Fredrickson
1988 Induced Obsidian Hydration Experiments: An Investigation in Relative Dating. *Materials Research Society Symposium Proceedings* 123:271-78.

Trigger, Bruce G.
1981 Archaeology and the Ethnographic Present. *Anthropologica* 23:3-17.

Vayda, Andrew P.
1967 Pomo Trade Feasts. In *Tribal and Peasant Economies*, edited by G. Dalton, pp. 494-500. Natural History Press, New York.

Vallejo, Mariano G.
1979 Confidential Information Concerning the Ross Settlement. Copy of 1833 manuscript translated by Michael S. Tucker and Nicholas Del Cioppo. Submitted for Distribution at the Conference on Russian America at Sitka, Alaska in 1979. On File, Fort Ross Interpretive Association Library, Fort Ross, California.

Von der Porten, Edward
1964 Fort Ross, California Sites Investigated in 1962-64 by the Archaeology class of the Community Service Program of Santa Rosa Junior College. On file, Cultural Heritage Section, Archaeology Laboratory, Department of Parks and Recreation, Sacrametno, California.

Wagner, Henry
1924 The Voyage to California of Sebastian Rodriguez Cermeño in 1595. *California Historical Society Quarterly* 3:3-24.

Wagner, D. L. and E. J. Bortugno
1983 Geology of the Santa Rosa Quadrangle. *California Geology* 36(12):259-63.

Waselkov, Gregory A.
1987 Shellfish Gathering and Shell Midden Archaeology. In *Advances in Archaeological Method and Theory* Vol. 10, edited by Michael Schiffer, pp. 93-210. Academic Press, Orlando, Florida.

Wedel, Waldo R.
1938 *The Direct-Historical Approach in Pawnee Archaeology*. Smithsonian Miscellaneous Collection 97 (no. 7):1-21.

West, G. J.
1988 *Pollen, Sediment and Charcoal Analysis: A Study of Fire and its Relationship to a Coastal Redwood (Sequoia sempervirens (D. Don) Endl.) Forest, Sonoma County, California*. Report prepared for the Anthropological Studies Center, Rohnert Park, California.

White, Greg
1989 A Report of Archaeological Investigations at Eleven Native American Coastal Sites, MacKerricher State Park, Mendocino County, California. On file, Cultural Heritage Section, Archaeology Laboratory, California Department of Parks and Recreation, Sacramento.

1991 The North Coast. Paper presented at the 25th Annual Meeting of the Society for California Archaeology, Sacramento.

White, Greg, Terry Jones, James Roscoe, and Lawrence Weigel
1982 Temporal and Spatial Distribution of Concave Base Projectile Points from the North Coast Ranges, California. *Journal of California and Great Basin Anthropology* 4:67-79.

Whittlesey, Stephanie and J. Jefferson Reid
1982 Cholla Project Settlement Summary. In *Cholla Project Archaeology*, Vol. 1, Introduction and Special Studies, edited by J. Jefferson Reid, pp. 173-204. Cultural Resources Management Division, Arizona State Museum, Archaeological Series No. 161.

Williams, J. W. and T. L. Bedrossian
1977 Coastal Zone Geology Near Gualala, California. *California Geology* 30(2):27-34.

Wiswell, Ella Lury (translator)
1979 Around the World on the Kamchatka, 1817-1819 by V. M. Golovnin. The Hawaiian Historical Society and the University Press of Hawaii, Honolulu.

Wolf, Eric
1982 *Europe and the People Without History.* University of California Press, Berkeley.

Wrangell, F. P. Von
1969 Russia in California, 1833, Report of Governor Wrangel. Translation and editing of original 1833 report by James R. Gibson. *Pacific Northwest Quarterly* 60:205-215.

1974 Some Remarks on the Savages on the Northwest Coast of America. The Indians in Upper California. In *Ethnographic Observations on the Coast Miwok and Pomo by Contre-Admiral F. P. Von Wrangell and P. Kostromitinov of the Russian Colony Ross, 1839*, pp. 1-6. Translation and editing of original 1839 publication by Fred Stross and Robert Heizer. Archaeological Research Facility, University of California, Berkeley.